MW00533408

THE INDOCTRINATED BRAIN

How to Successfully Fend Off the Global Attack on Your Mental Freedom

Michael Nehls, MD, PhD

Foreword by Naomi Wolf

Skyhorse Publishing

Skyhorse Publishing books may be purchased in bulk at special discounts for sales promotion, corporate gifts, fund-raising, or educational purposes. Special editions can also be created to specifications. For details, contact the Special Sales Department, Skyhorse Publishing, 307 West 36th Street, 11th Floor, New York, NY 10018 or info@skyhorsepublishing.com

Visit our website at www.skyhorsepublishing.com.
Please follow our publisher Tony Lyons on Instagram @tonylyonsisuncertain

10 9 8 7 6 5 4

Library of Congress Cataloging-in-Publication Data is available on file.

Hardcover ISBN: 978-1-5107-7836-8
eBook ISBN: 978-1-5107-7837-5

Cover design by Malin Singh

Printed in the United States of America

To Buddy,
who sensed the global threat much earlier than I did.
Thank you for your foresight!

CONTENTS

DISCLAIMER

For ease of reading, it was decided to refrain from any gendering, except of course in quoted statements.

All facts presented in this book are based on publicly available documents and studies, the majority of which have been linked. Nevertheless, in some places the author has also expressed personal opinions, where it seems to him that the facts can be put together like pixels to form a larger, yet partly speculative picture. The author has made an effort to clearly separate facts and such interpretations in terms of language.

The publisher and author have checked the information in this work to the best of their knowledge and belief for correctness and completeness sufficient for reasonable interpretation. However, neither the publisher nor the author explicitly takes any responsibility for the content of the work, as well as for any errors.

This also applies to quantities of micronutrients. These usually refer to the needs of an average adult. Differences in dosage can result from lifestyle (e.g., vitamin D, B12, or aquatic omega-3 fatty acids), gender, age, body size, and possible preexisting conditions. Therefore, supplementation should only be carried out after consultation with a trusted physician and in any case on one's own responsibility—the publisher and author accept no liability.

The author does not endorse the contents of cited websites. Reference is made to their status at the time of initial publication. All citations have been carefully checked at the time of this writing in Summer 2023, but it is not uncommon for the content of a source to change or even disappear completely. Unfortunately, the "autobiographical memory of the internet" can no longer be trusted: It forgets and confabulates.

FOREWORD

Dr. Naomi Wolf

The fact that the brain is plastic—modifiable—has become much better understood by the public in the past few decades.

General readers understand by now that the human brain can be altered; and that experiences can modify its reactions and processes. We understand now for example that PTSD leaves lasting changes in brain functioning. It's been established that motherhood changes the brain and that bonding itself is a chemical process modified by the brain.

We also understand, as general readers, that propaganda is real. Some of us have studied propaganda in the past. We have a working knowledge of Joseph Goebbels, and of the artistry and craft that underlay his manufacturing of National Socialist consent. The work of Edward Bernays, one of the earliest practitioners of what became the field of public relations, has been widely read in English. Decades-old bestsellers such as *Subliminal Seduction* by Wilson Bryan Key exposed the fact that advertisers use every tool at their disposal to alter our reactions to their products—down to the level of the subconscious mind.

Modern general audiences also understand that governments use "messaging"—and often, heavy-handed propaganda—to lead us to take actions that can be against our interests or our better conscious judgments; to create prejudices and divisions that may not otherwise exist; to heighten fears and to trigger a sense of vulnerability in us, so that we can be better manipulated and guided to goals that are not our own.

But Dr. Michael Nehls's thesis in this book is revolutionary because it brings together all of these fields of inquiry and proposes a set of questions so radical that they make the mysteries of the past three years fall into place. This is the indispensable book.

In *The Indoctrinated Brain*, Dr. Nehls brings these areas of study together in a way that has never been done before. By applying neuroscience to the otherwise bizarre events of the recent past, he explains what has happened to humanity.

Many of us have noted that our loved ones and colleagues have changed. Post-mRNA injection rollout, we notice that people who were highly educated critical thinkers, have become unable to think outside of two simple binaries. We watch in astonishment as formerly sophisticated loved ones and friends regurgitate talking points with no self-awareness. We wonder why there is a sense of something inchoately missing when we sit with a vaccinated or COVID-fearful friend. We cannot fathom what has caused this sea change.

Dr. Nehls's hypothesis can explain it. "*The Indoctrinated Brain* introduces a largely unknown, powerful neurobiological mechanism whose externally induced dysfunction underlies these catastrophic developments," as the publisher notes.

Dr. Nehls argues that the spike protein, along with other COVID measures, represents an intentional attack on the human hippocampus—where autobiographical memory and individuality itself originate—and that "fear porn" keeps us from holding on to the autobiographical memories that encompass our former selves. As a result, humans have become deindividualized, more suggestible, more forgetful, more compliant, and less able to engage in critical thinking and creative reasoning. This argument utterly accords with what many of us are seeing, to our horror, every day. Dr. Nehls's *The Indoctrinated Brain* is an indispensable book because it applies neuroscience to politics and especially to the politics of fascism. The need for that has existed for as long as modern fascism has existed.

Neuroscience should be applied to politics and to social change, but it is rare indeed when those fields of analysis meet. By bringing these fields of knowledge together and mapping neurological science against propaganda, and vice versa, Dr. Nehls brings vast new insights to the reader that would not have been attainable previously.

After you read *The Indoctrinated Brain*, you will think: Of course. Of course, the propaganda of the past few years must have been predicated upon intensive study of the brain and its reactions. Of course, the hundreds of millions of dollars that were recently spent and are currently being spent by the US and other governments on behavioral science and behavior modification, would result in insights that would be applied by the US and other governments to making populations more tractable, less able to reason, less creative and more compliant. Why else would they so heavily have invested in such studies? Of course, the constant messaging, especially about fear, over the past three years, would have an effect that is not just about public health or perhaps not at all about public health—but that it is rather about making humans in free societies more tractable—with public health as the excuse, the proxy, for this deployment of life-altering and consciousness-altering fear. It is not the fear porn about the specific scary thing that matters, Dr. Nehls persuasively argues here: the fear itself is the deliverable. The fear itself changes and indeed damages the brain.

I've long been interested in the psychiatric effects and, as I guessed, intentionalities behind "lockdowns" and "pandemic" messaging. But I did not have the neuroscientific background to understand exactly what was being done to people via "lockdowns" and the "fear porn" of the pandemic years related to the virus—to other human beings.

Through my study of the psychiatric effects of torture and isolation, that I took on for a book about closing democracies, I realized that isolation causes profound and sometimes permanent changes in the brain. I knew intuitively in the post-9/11, "Global War on Terror" years, that constant fear would wear down faculties needed for critical thinking. And I applied those insights to the isolation and fear messaging of 2020–22. But I did not have the complete picture.

This book provides it. It is the "aha" hypothetical for our time.

The Indoctrinated Brain provides the missing practical knowledge of neuroscience, that explains why isolating people creates a more befuddled, more easily manipulated population. It explains exactly why a message that closeness with other human beings can kill you, or you can kill others (especially your grandma) through physical closeness, might rewire the human brain to create the vulnerability to delusion and bad science and cultlike thinking, that many of us observed in formerly critically thinking loved ones and friends, post-2020. It even raises the question of whether the spike protein contributes to brain fog and to the erasure of a sense of an autonomous, resilient, individuated, and questing self.

If Dr. Nehls is right, his theory here will be as important as Dr. Sigmund Freud's discovery of the subconscious, if not more so. If he is right, his theory explains why governments around the world mandated "lockdown" measures and mRNA injections, which would not ultimately then be about public health but about creating manipulable, passive citizens. If Dr. Nehls is right, it explains so many baffling features of the past three years—notably the fact that formerly thoughtful, highly individuated leaders of institutions, down to rank-and-file citizens, followed cultlike dicta without a murmur, and pursued nonsensical goals such as isolation, masking, and submission to vaccine mandates, without protest. Dr. Nehls's thesis would explain the bizarre experience many of us are having of watching our formerly analytical loved ones, find themselves unable to keep two thoughts in their heads at the same time, unable to engage in calm debate without exploding emotionally, unable to maintain contact and connection with people with whom they disagree.

As I write, another global crisis is being spun up, this one in the Middle East. Within a day, highly educated and formerly skeptical loved ones of mine are repeating glaring legacy media talking points without any self-consciousness. It's upsetting not to know why they would change in this way—and it is even more upsetting, though incredibly enlightening, to read Dr. Nehls's argument and realize what the cause may be of their submissiveness to propaganda narratives. It makes it both easier and harder to contend with loved ones, friends, and colleagues who have been intellectually blunted in this way, to understand Dr. Nehls's point of view and realize that this sad change in cognition might be simply physical—the spike protein—and neuropsychiatric: the repetition of fear messages and their impact on the brain.

In my social media feed today—on a day when the news has brought images of endless atrocities to our media streams, and when we are being told that this Friday will be a "Day of Jihad" with plenty of stabbings—someone wrote, "Protect your amygdala." That meant, do not expose yourself to endless scenes of rape, murder, beheadings, atrocities, and horrors.

Dr. Nehls's book is ultimately a hopeful one, since if we understand the damage to our brains from both spike proteins and fear pornography, we can find ways to prospect ourselves and our conscious minds. I appreciate the practical suggestions Dr. Nehls gives us to do just that.

It is scary that we are living in a time in which there is, as Dr. Nehls so powerfully points out, a war on our brains. But it must be less scary to understand what is being done to us, with Dr. Nehls's help, so we can protect and strengthen our autobiographical memory and critical thinking, and so we can survive this onslaught with the full range of our intelligence—and our humanity—intact.

ABBREVIATIONS

ACE2	Angiotensin-converting enzyme 2 (enzyme that acts as spike-receptor respectively coronaviruses)
AI	Artificial intelligence
BMBF	German Federal Ministry of Education and Research (Deutsches Bundesministerium für Bildung und Forschung)
BMI	Federal Ministry of the Interior (Deutsches Bundesministerium des Innern und für Heimat)
BMJ	*The British Medical Journal*
CDC	Centers for Disease Control and Prevention
COVID-19	Coronavirus disease, which first appeared in 2019
DKFZ	German Cancer Research Center (Deutsches Krebsforschungszentrum)
DNA	Deoxyribonucleic acid, double-stranded genetic material of humans or e.g. the pox-or chickenpox virus
EMA	European Medicines Agency
FDA	Food and Drug Administration
GAVI	Global Alliance for Vaccines and Immunization
GLT	Global Leaders for Tomorrow, the cadre school that preceded the YGL of the WEF
GVAP	Global Vaccine Action Plan
LNP	Lipid nanoparticles packaging of mRNA vaccines, help enter the brain and causing system-wide inflammation.
MIT	Massachusetts Institute of Technology
NEJM	*New England Journal of Medicine*
NIAID	National Institute of Allergy and Infectious Diseases
NIH	National Institutes of Health
NZZ	*Neue Zürcher Zeitung* (Swiss newspaper)
PCR	Polymerase chain reaction, molecular biological technique to exponentially amplify genetic material
POWs	Prisoners of war
RNA	Ribonucleic acid, single stranded genetic material of corononavirus and influenza
RKI	Robert Koch Institute, the German equivalent to the US CDC

SARS	Severe Acute Respiratory Syndrome
SARS-CoV-2	Strain of coronavirus causing COVID-19
STIKO	German Standing Committee on Vaccination
UNICEF	United Nations International Children's Emergency Fund
VAERS	Vaccine Adverse Event Reporting System, US program for vaccine safety, comanaged by the CDC and FDA
WEF	World Economy Forum
WHO	World Health Organization
WSJ	*Wall Street Journal*
YGL	Young Global Leaders (cadre school of the WEF)

Indoctrination

The word comes from the Latin word *doctrina*, meaning "instruction."

The purpose of indoctrination is to implant an ideological narrative into people's brains—a new belief that allows no discussion and no contradiction.

The goal is obedient, unthinking conformity. The means to this end is a controlled selection of information, intensive propaganda, and psychological manipulation, up to coercive measures and threats of punishment.

The more skillful the mental manipulation, the more immune the implanted ideological thought system becomes to critical arguments and inner doubts.

Indoctrination is to be understood as a vicious attack on our humanity, on our personality, and ultimately on the most precious thing of all: our freedom of thought.

~~~

Resisting indoctrination is a lifelong endeavor. It is a matter of preserving one's freedom of thought and search for meaning.
~~~

INTRODUCTION

Everything that happens out of intentions is reducible to the intention of increasing power.
—Friedrich Nietzsche (1844–1900)

The coronavirus pandemic was an eye-opener for me, partly because I have been witness to the events and partly because it has been a medical and immunological topic in which I have some expertise that allows me to assess the facts. For the first time, I became fully aware of how far people are capable of going to achieve their goals, even if it means walking over mountains of corpses. Several years of intensive research led me to the conclusion that in order to achieve this particular goal, which was hidden in the background of the events that determined the overall direction of global politics, these mountains could grow sky-high. And since that eye-opening moment, I have been asking myself every day, *Is this really happening?*

But first, let us step back in time a couple decades. Shortly after the concerted terrorist attack on the United States in 2001, rumors began to circulate that the preparations for such a complex and long-planned multiple attack, which would claim a few thousand victims, could not possibly have been overlooked by the US intelligence services. But it remained at least conceivable for some—including me—that a constellation of unfavorable circumstances led to the realization of this gruesome crime essentially without resistance. At least I hoped so. No individuals could be that ruthless, could they? However, it was also clear that a great many individuals and organizations profited from this monstrous disaster, which left deep wounds in not only the American psyche but also the worldwide consciousness. In any case, US President George W. Bush seemed to have found an issue suitable for legitimizing numerous military interventions that had apparently been planned months earlier. Immediately after the attacks, he announced a global war on terror. Those who had regained their sense of reality after the immense shock knew at the time of the declaration of this war that it would be impossible to win. In addition, antiterrorist laws were gradually enacted all over the world, restricting people's personal freedom to this day. For example, it became much easier to collect information on private citizens and share it between intelligence agencies. In the United States, people suspected of terrorism can be detained and interrogated without a lawyer or trial.

Only a few weeks later, the "war on terror" evolved into a war against Afghanistan, ostensibly because Osama bin Laden, the leader of the terrorist organization al Qaeda that had claimed responsibility for the 9/11 attacks, was suspected of being there. No doubt, the arms industry profited greatly from the 9/11 attacks, especially because on March 20, 2003, the third Gulf War against Iraq was also justified on the grounds that al Qaeda, with the help of Iraqi President Saddam Hussein, was storing weapons of mass destruction there in order to carry out another attack on the United States. This was based on evidence proven to be fabricated just one fateful year later.[1] However, the claims were not very convincing from the start. Based on these events, I believe two fateful questions arise for the very future of humanity itself: 1) How far would the profiteers go to capitalize on a terrorist attack or other (e.g., viral) attack on humanity just to increase their profits, power, and control over humanity? 2) How can we ensure that such dramatic events are not only not exploited but also, especially, not co-orchestrated by the profiteers, when the resulting benefits are so enormous?

In 1860, Thomas Joseph Dunning (1799–1873), secretary of the London Consolidated Society of Bookbinders, wrote a pamphlet on the philosophy of trade unionism at the time, in which he described an extreme characteristic of economic power and greed for profit: "Capital eschews no profit, or very small profit, just as Nature was formerly said to abhor a vacuum. With adequate profit, capital is very bold. A certain 10 per cent, will ensure its employment anywhere; 20 per cent, certain will produce eagerness; 50 per cent, positive audacity; 100 per cent, will make it ready to trample on all human laws; 300 per cent, and there is not a crime at which it will scruple nor a risk it will not run, even to the chance of its owner being hanged. If turbulence and strife will bring a profit, it will freely encourage both."[2]

Thus, as early as the nineteenth century, Dunning described a fundamental dynamic that has been unfolding all too tangibly for us since the (laboratory) outbreak of the SARS-CoV-2 at the end of 2019, destructive to all areas of life for most and extraordinarily profitable for a few. But it has happened on a breathtaking scale and with a severity of consequence that Dunning could hardly have imagined. Furthermore, some evidence suggests that this global crisis was not only exploited but also actually orchestrated. But what is the ultimate goal?

This book aims to provide a possible answer. But I will tell you this much in advance: it seems to me that the ultimate goal has not been reached yet. What we can say with certainty, however, is that the first stage on the way to this goal may go down in history as the COVID-19 *plan*demic: immense damage to health and countless direct deaths, caused not primarily by an artificially created pathogen itself but by deliberately suppressing preventive measures (with which most deaths would have been avoided) and by a historically unprecedented package of measures. In particular, as is becoming increasingly clear, this includes the life-threatening coronary spike gene injection program, or *spiking*. Many millions of other collateral casualties of this pandemic testify to a disastrous handling of a health crisis, beginning with the thoroughly inept response to the initial report of an unusual pneumonia in Wuhan, China. Last but not least, this *plandemic* term also characterizes the totalitarian, antidemocratic development worldwide that it has made possible. I will examine the arguments for the crisis being either a plandemic or a systematic instrumentalization of an accidental crisis. Undoubtedly, even without taking a closer look at contradictory facts, one can understand that the superrich have benefited to an extraordinary degree worldwide. They now have ample reason to maintain the state of emergency—especially because it seems to serve a larger goal: the Great Reset.

As I write this in the spring of 2023 and the world's population breathes a sigh of relief (no more masks, no more tests, no more restrictions for now), the World Economic Forum (WEF) is already taking the precaution of talking about the new age of *permapandemics* in its *Global Risks Report 2023*, entirely in the spirit of the previous paragraph.[3] After all, the founder and chairman of the WEF, Klaus Schwab, openly welcomed the COVID-19 pandemic as an opportunity to carry out a Great Reset of the world economy with leading politicians and technocrats. An observer of such pronouncements not involved in the decision-making of these plans inevitably concludes that a new operating system of coexistence is to be imposed on humanity. This process, according to the WEF, as well as to some government documents (which I will present later), is expected to be completed in 2030.

Technocracy

The term is derived from the ancient Greek *téchne* for "skill" and *kratos* for "rule" or "domination" and originally referred to an idealized form of rule by experts. In our time, extremely wealthy individuals gain exorbitant political influence by using foundations, public-private partnerships, or international organizations such as the WEF. Private individuals also ultimately secure global power through large investments in the World Health Organization (WHO), over 80 percent of which is funded by voluntary contributions.[4] I will refer to these individuals as technocrats in the following, especially since they have often amassed immense wealth through the development and sale of market-dominating technologies and often seek technological answers to social problems.

The idea of a Great Reset is not entirely new, as the WEF spoke of "Shaping the Post-Crisis World" in 2009 and "The Great Transformation" in 2012.[5] But it wasn't until the COVID-19 pandemic, according to the description of a promotional video released by Prince Charles (now King Charles) on June 3, 2020, that the protagonists of the Great Reset considered the official dawn of a new era: "Today, The Prince of Wales' Sustainable Markets Initiative, in partnership with the World Economic Forum, launched a major global initiative, #TheGreatReset."[6] The description continues, "The Great Reset aims to reset, reimagine, rebuild, redesign, reinvigorate and rebalance our world in the wake of the COVID-19 pandemic." Thus, Prince Charles saw the COVID-19 crisis as a "golden opportunity" to "reboot" the economy.[7] However, the term does not seem to be well chosen, because unlike a reset or rebooting of a computer, the Great Reset protagonists— to stay in computer languageare not concerned with a reboot but with the installation of a completely new operating system. But how can something like this even succeed? How can the people who ultimately keep this economy running be won over to it? What say do they have in the decisions that will shape our economic world in the future? And how is it ensured that they agree with what a small elite group decides for the whole world? These are the questions I will address later on, but I am already sure you will not like the answers.

A clear indication of how firmly the global upheaval narrative is already anchored in the minds of many leading politicians and influential figures (such as King Charles) who are usually closely associated with the WEF is exemplified by Canadian Prime Minister Justin Trudeau's speech at a United Nations video conference in September 2020. In it, he indicates that the "pandemic has provided an opportunity for a reset."[8] In December 2021, the newly elected German chancellor, Olaf Scholz, in his first government statement, also put the citizens in the mood "for the Greatest Reset (*Greatest Upheaval,* translated literally) in the economy and production in 100 years."[9] In another government declaration in March 2023, he argued that we should not be nostalgic for the "good old days."[10] Instead, Scholz said, from now on it was a matter of "setting out together and getting down to work so that a good new era becomes possible." He prophesized, "Yes, it's possible!" We will "manage the Great Reset that lies ahead of us. And this Great Reset will end well—for us here in Germany and for Europe as a whole."

However, so-called fact-checkers like to dismiss the Great Reset as a conspiracy theory. Even the renowned German *Handelszeitung* headlined on November 20, 2020, "The Great Reset: How the WEF Got into the Center of All Conspiracy Theories."[11] Apart from the fact that the term *conspiracy theory* is presumably used here purely for the purpose of devaluing respective discussions as childish nonsense, it should be pointed out that, by definition, a conspiracy exists only if some people *secretly* agree to increase their profit, their power, or both *against the interests and the welfare of third parties* by *unfair* means. Although such agreements are not only made in theory but also in reality, the Great Reset cannot be called a conspiracy in the classical sense because some of the main protagonists largely disclose their visions and the means of their choice, such as the infiltration of democratic houses of representatives all over the world. Curiously, this is also partly mentioned in the same *Handelszeitung* article. There, the book

COVID-19: The Great Reset[12] by WEF Chairman Schwab and French economist and modern historian Thierry Malleret is also referenced, which gives concrete and straightforward reasons why this crisis provides a unique opportunity for the intended reset.

Plans for how to deal with a health crisis of this nature were, surprisingly, not extensively revised or even rehearsed until late 2019, just *before* the SARS-CoV-2 outbreak.[13] As we can see from the quoted statements, this global crisis provided an influential interest group with the opportunity to successively implement its long-cherished plans. It is hard to resist the idea that it was actually orchestrated from the beginning for this very reason, rather than just purposefully exploited. The COVID-19 pandemic proceeded according to a predetermined and publicized response plan. This led to a situation never before seen in human history: Nearly all governments imposed the same adverse health measures with congruent statements. Under these circumstances, a criminologist would probably at least suspect a possible crime and recognize a motive. A supporter of fundamental democratic values would at least recognize a hint of a conflict of interests, given the immense direct or even indirect influence of these billionaires on politics, media, and science. Could one suspect intent? Could one presume the degree of ruthlessness necessary for this to have happened intentionally? Answering these questions in the affirmative, as I will show, challenges our imaginations much less than the events of 9/11, although the damage (and thus the presumed ruthlessness) caused by COVID-19 is much greater.

But I do not want to simplistically imply that all politicians deliberately collaborated in this respect. At least two natural factors favored the global spread of similar measures: On one hand, intensive media fear-communication provides politicians with the opportunity to present themselves as strong leaders; on the other hand, after a certain point of mass panic, there is not much left for them to do if they want to keep their approval ratings high among the frightened population. By adopting the measures, they were able to demonstratively avert "harm from the people" by, for example, demanding a small "sacrifice" in the shape of an "unscheduled vacation" that was given to the people in the way of the first lockdown. The concept of the lockdown was demonstratively first used in China and then copied around the world, although in the West it was implemented in a more toned-down form. Numerous other psychological mechanisms play a role here in the global lockstep, but I leave it to psychologists to identify them. But with the aforementioned aspects, it should be clear how a far-reaching involvement of politics, the media, science, and parts of the population could be implemented at decisive points and how principles of the rule of law could be suspended under the pretext of a health crisis.

But an intentional influence got the ball rolling. Templates for dealing with the situation were deliberately designed to give a small number of people control over how events unfolded. It is difficult for most people to imagine such a level of ruthlessness. Dunning pointed to drug smuggling and slave trades as prime historical examples of the willingness of a few to accept the suffering of many in order to increase their profit. It so happens that in English the word *drugs* refers to both intoxicants and medicines. Medicines share the effect of intoxicants in that more and more people become dependent on them, mostly physically, but often also psychologically, like drug addicts. This dependence is no less serious and often lifelong as well. The reasons for such chronic medication are the so-called diseases of civilization—a misnomer that falsely suggests that these are the inevitable downsides of the extraordinary human achievements that allow us to live advanced lives. In fact, however, they are the consequence of ignorance that leads to an increasingly alienated way of life. As a result, all bodily functions, including some crucial cognitive functions of the brain, which will play a central role in our further exploration of the end goal of the Great Reset agenda, are impaired.

Since the end of 2020 the phenomenon of *chronic* drug addiction has been joined by another permanent source of income for the pharmaceutical industry. Paradoxically, it's the prevention of an *acute* disease. That the risk of acute infection alone now seems to justify chronic therapy is due to a large part of the world's population being cleverly led to believe that the natural immune system cannot deal with SARS-CoV-2 in the usual way (which is not true, as I will show in detail). The proclaimed need to be vaccinated against it every three to six months was ultimately based on this false assumption. In the case of this pathogen, however, this meant that for the first time a largely experimental injection was being administered, the mode of action of which is in many cases similar to that of gene therapy (i.e., involving modified active genetic material). This was made palatable to people by a combination of media-generated fear of death (with the key word *self-protection*) and ethically sanctioned social pressure (*protection of others*). Thus, this lifelong injection subscription also fulfills the definition of psychosocial dependency, with the ministries of health worldwide having increased their influence on individual lifestyles and pharmaceutical companies having made high profits.

Although it should have become clear to everyone that these sales arguments do not correspond to reality and that the injections cause more life-threatening harm than they bring life-saving benefit, the belief of some people in the "life-saving injection" is hardly open to rational discussion and sometimes is sometimes unshakable. People continue to be offered a treatment that, in the medium term, makes them even more susceptible to the pathogen in question and to other pathogens than they would be under normal circumstances (but more on this later). Besides the financial incentives to exploit or even create such crises and the motivation for certain interest groups to utilize them to put their ideas of social transformation into practice, we also need to address how the majority is helpless in the face of a manipulative minority.

The dangerous concentration of capital power in the hands of a few technocrats was achieved with the help of the most advanced information technologies and biotechnologies, as well as—in the case of the COVID-19 pandemic and the measures taken—the manipulation and manipulative interpretation of scientific data. The propaganda, which was always presented in a tone of conviction but was actually quite clumsy on closer inspection, consolidated this influence on the population, every day in thirty-minute intervals in the leading media. But why the vast majority fell into a rigidity of fear was completely incomprehensible to a small minority who were not impressed by the scaremongering. A rapid and comprehensive reappraisal of what has happened is essential, because otherwise we will be condemned to relive all this over and over again in a WEF climate of permapandemics, and to lose more and more of our remaining freedom, while countless people continue to suffer and die needlessly. Specifically, then, we are looking for an explanation of why so many people are susceptible to seemingly arbitrary government and media fear narratives. The answer will suggest ways a future majority might emerge from the current minority, capable of examining and evaluating information with sovereignty and thereby coming to independent conclusions. If we fail to do so, we will never truly reclaim the inalienable human rights that were taken from us under the many nonsensical COVID-19 measures. Instead, we will see the development of a totalitarian and technocratic control state.

In his book *The Psychology of Totalitarianism*, clinical psychologist Mattias Desmet provides an initial explanation of how this surveillance program could be so massively advanced with the help of the corona pandemic.[14] In his sociopsychological analysis, Desmet illustrates "how humanity is being forcibly, unconsciously led into a reality of technocratic totalitarianism, which aggressively excludes alternative views and relies on destructive groupthink, vilifying nonconformist thought as 'dissent.'" He speaks of mass formation (US-American virologist, immunologist, and molecular biologist Robert Malone later even interpreted this condition as mass psychosis),[15] and he rightly warns, with good reason, "of the dangers of our current social landscape, media consumption, and dependence on manipulative technologies." This silent unchallenged endurance of the deprivation of freedom by the technocratic standards ultimately amounts to a mental enslavement. Thus, the slave trade, which Dunning cites as a historical example of extreme predatory capitalism, finds its modern counterpart. In his book, Desmet offers simple solutions—both individual and collective—to prevent "our willing sacrifice of our capacity for critical thinking."

But do people really make this serious sacrifice willingly? This question may remind some of the philosophical discussion about whether we have a free will at all as a precondition for a willingness that is completely free from external circumstances. I leave this discussion to the philosophers, because there is a basic and well-understood neurophysiological prerequisite for the ability or will to think and to act independently. It is based on some special properties of our autobiographical memory that records not only everything we experience and feel but also what we think. However, the conditions for the proper functioning of the organ responsible for memorizing our thoughts, which are necessary for thinking at all, are diminishing more and more. Nowadays, the autobiographical memory of many people no longer grows throughout life, as it would naturally, and thus increasingly loses its storage capacity. This makes it almost impossible for many people to consider or even implement courses of action that do not conform to their usual routines—even when their very lives or freedom depend on it. Instead, people blindly follow trained beliefs. The resulting stereotyped behavior is what the British physicist and molecular biologist Francis Crick (1916–2004), Nobel laureate in 1962 for the discovery of the molecular nature of heredity, and his then colleague, the American neuroscientist Christof Koch, called *zombie mode*, as opposed to thinking and planning new and complex behaviors.[16] This terminology was chosen by the discoverers of this stereotypical behavioral mechanism; I am not at all exaggerating by using the terminology. I will show that more and more people today are trapped in such an almost permanent zombie mode due to the chronic pathological loss of autobiographical-memory capacity, which in turn results from our increasingly alienated way of life and has been immensely accelerated by the COVID-19 measures (including the spiking program disguised as vaccination, as I will show). Therefore, one can certainly not say that people *willingly* sacrificed the ability to think critically.

An entirely new approach to explaining the increasing controllability of society and the astonishing response of little resistance emerges from this neurological insight. It goes far beyond the sociopsychological approach formulated by Desmet and, in a sense, forms its neuropathological basis. This profound explanation is, however, highly dramatic, for it will take much more than psychological insight and a change of mentality to halt or reverse this dangerous development. Trapped in zombie mode, it is impossible for victims to question their own precarious situation. Natural curiosity or interest in alternative explanations and courses of action is lost, opening the door to indoctrination. The underlying neuropathological process leads to a decrease in psychological resilience. The result is not only an increased fear of anything new but also a particular susceptibility to being controlled by fear.

All of this culminates in an extremely disturbing situation: not only is there the danger of an accelerated loss of identity due to the limited functionality and reduced capacity of autobiographical memory, there is also the danger that identity-forming memories will be replaced by foreign content—that is, by propaganda or aspects of the technocratic narrative, both of which lead to a mental conformity of society. Narratives are meaning-making stories that place experience in a larger, meaningful context and lead to an interpretation colored by that context. In this case, the technocratic narrative is about a better world because it is controlled by supposedly highly intelligent technocrats and an even smarter artificial intelligence (AI). In a 2016 article published by the WEF, Danish politician Ida Auken idealizes a society that could emerge from the Great Reset: "Welcome to 2030: I own nothing, have no privacy, and life has never been better."[17] Personal property has been abolished; freedom of thought and privacy are history. Yet people will be happy in this world, according to WEF propaganda. But what exactly are the neurobiological points of attack that make people, unnoticed, easy targets for such indoctrination? As I will show, this knowledge, properly applied, allows for the gradual elimination of individuality, as we are already observing, and its replacement by dull, unreflective conformism. I will also show that there are numerous indications that this knowledge is in the process of being consciously and widely applied in many ways beyond the COVID-19 measures.

But this does not yet describe the full extent of what threatens our society. The sense of self (value) disturbed by this development is fading—a most unpleasant development for our existence. As a result, people feel much safer when they behave inconspicuously in conformity with the broad masses: the weak self seeks the strong we. The increasing loss of self-identity thus provides an explanation for Desmet's mass formation and also for the increase in collective narcissism, with all its negative consequences, that has already been observed worldwide.[18] This is accompanied by a decrease or even a loss of rational compassion. This cognitive capacity is only made possible by our autobiographical or social memory, which also allows us to weigh the consequences of our actions on third parties and to question our prejudices. The now widespread lack of these abilities was felt by anyone who questioned the COVID-19 narrative and refused to be "spiked."

The further this collective mental equalization progresses and the more people are caught in zombie mode, the more stable this dystopian post–Great Reset society will become and the less likely there will be a way back. Whether a perfidious master plan lurks behind all of this (which one might suspect) or all of this is happening more or less purely by chance is ultimately largely irrelevant. Thus, my scientific discovery points to an unprecedented, destructive neuropathological and psychosocial threat, regardless of the well-founded but speculative interpretations of intent. The outcome can only be averted if one is aware of it—for the terrible result is the same in both cases: we are threatened by a true zombie apocalypse, which is the end of a self-determined, creative cultural evolution of humanity, based on intellectual freedom, individuality, and creativity.

Setting current events against the backdrop of literary dystopian visions of the past has proven helpful. Thus, instead of being caught in the middle of such a process of transformation, which of course follows its own logic, we have a somewhat more objective perspective on the current course of society. A familiar motif from George Orwell's *1984* is the alteration of records or even memories and thus the consciousness of the past. The goal is to control the future according to the intentions of a technocratic elite. Even the never-ending wars are only staged to wage an eternal war against the human mind. If we look closely, we can actually see something similar happening in our own time. For example, the book you are holding in your hands describes in detail how adult humans can be robbed of their individuality and conditioned by reprogramming their autobiographical memory center. This would allow a large part of humanity to accept a future in servitude not just unwillingly but also even happily. Such a Great Mental Reset would pave the way for a world in which a large part of humanity would perceive the total surveillance and dependence on a technocratic "care" that will result from the Great Economic and Cultural Reset as something positive, as can be seen from the announcements of the WEF.

In terms of developmental history, at this point Aldous Huxley's (1894–1963) dystopian novel *Brave New World* begins. In his fiction, nine years of war were followed by the Great Economic Collapse. In reality, we are facing years of wars against the coronavirus, with more to come against permapandemics, climate change, and other nations over national borders, or over food or water. The wars serve, in addition to global indoctrination (as the technocrats are our only saviors), a *creative destruction* (another term from the WEF forge)[19] of the world economy. Through one of the World Controllers, Huxley lets us know what followed after the Great Economic Collapse: "There was a choice between World Control and destruction."[20] Total control was chosen in the world of the novel, making *Brave New World* the ultimate script for the real-life brave new world that is supposed to be achieved in 2030, the fateful year proclaimed by the WEF.

Zombie Apocalypse 2030 would be an apt title for a novel that represents such an ominous synthesis of Huxley's *Brave New World* of indoctrination and Orwell's *1984* vision of a totalitarian surveillance state. In it, a self-appointed technocratic elite would conduct a Great Mental Reset, a brainwashing of global proportions that would involve the erasure of individuality in order to achieve mindless conformity. This novel would describe a ruthless yet ingenious coup on the road to world domination, with the human brain as the fundamental battleground in the eternal struggle for individual and social freedom. However, I decided to write *The Indoctrinated Brain* not as a novel (the time for subtle parables is over) but as a sober nonfiction book, so that a Zombie Apocalypse 2030 will at best remain one of the numerous unfulfilled prophecies, because people recognized and averted this acute danger in time. Nothing is more feared by those who want to rule the world than human creativity and social awareness. It is vital that these be revived and preserved.

In the first chapter, I will show who is among the small group of people who would arguably have an interest in such an immense influence. I will explain why we must take their openly stated intentions very seriously. In their quest for technocratic world domination, some of them are walking over corpses. They have already caused unimaginable suffering so far.

In the second chapter, I will present the neurobiological mechanisms of identity formation in a way that everyone can understand. I will describe the "button" (i.e., the key mechanism) in our brains that must be "pressed" if one wants to indoctrinate us with the most modern scientific precision. On the basis of these findings, however, a possibility for self-defense opens up because this key mechanism is also the key to the formula for protection against indoctrination, which I will explain.

In the third chapter, I will describe the inhuman logic and precision of a brilliant two-step master plan to indoctrinate people as efficiently as possible. It is based on the previously described neurobiological mechanism.

In the fourth chapter, I will discuss the COVID-19 neuropathological package of measures and show for the first time how it contributed massively to the destruction of the autobiographical memory.

In the fifth chapter, I will present the indoctrination process itself, which necessarily builds on the measures described in the previous chapter.

In the sixth chapter, I will show that we must face the endgame question about the ultimate goal of the technocrats. It may well be, as I will illustrate, that in order to save humanity (and especially nature) from humanity, the technocrats, following a cold logic, may come up with the idea of sacrificing humankind.

In the seventh and final chapter, I will conclude with a closing argument as a scientific prosecutor in the hope that I have at least made you realize that something has gone terribly wrong in our modern world. We will find an answer to how we got into this predicament in the first place. To do this, we will expand our view to include the Neolithic period, when one of the most enduring narratives in human history emerged, a picture of man that is as false as it is devastatingly culture-shaping, right up to the present day: man is fundamentally evil. Because of and in spite of what we are experiencing today, correcting this flawed basic assumption will be the most important, and most difficult and enduring, task facing our society. Only by proving ourselves worthy of this task, year after year, generation after generation, will we not only survive the war on our minds but also win it in the long run.

From the formula for protection against indoctrination are derived the evidence-based countermeasures that each individual can implement to close the neurobiological vulnerability of our autobiographical memory. Here is what will happen:

1. Each individual will be rewarded with a significant increase in psychological resilience by incorporating these principles into his or her own life.
2. With increased resilience comes increased natural curiosity, which allows us to think outside the box.
3. We have more mental energy. This allows us to process new information and make better, more creative decisions.

4. We need this energy when we want to break new ground. It is the basis of our perseverance against external and internal resistance.
5. The energy enables us to have rational compassion, a prerequisite for each of us to be able to think and act globally.

We are creating a new world, based on a much-needed correction of the image of man that corresponds to his natural characteristics, already embodied in every child: man is basically good. With this mindset, we will undergo a true mental reset that will allow us to regain our full mental potential!

CHAPTER 1

GREAT RESET TO A *BRAVE NEW WORLD*?

Independence of thought is the first characteristic of freedom.
Without it, one remains a slave to circumstances.
— Vivekananda (1863–1902)

A Far-Reaching Insight in the Idyll of Corsica

Our world is changing fast—and not for the better. In the late summer of 2022, on a remote old farm in Corsica, I met people who felt this as much as I did. We agreed that the concepts of "unity, justice, and freedom," the motto of the Federal Republic of Germany, have long since become hollow words for our society. If they ever were more than that, at least today the opposite is the case: society is no longer united, but deeply divided, into vaccinated and unvaccinated, progender, and antigender, and in favor of the view of human causation for climate change and against. The list of divisive issues continues to grow. At the same time, it is becoming harder and harder to find someone with whom you can disagree in a friendly way, in the sense of a cultivated culture of debate, on these and a growing number of other issues that define our time. Dissent on what used to be debatable issues can now lead to social isolation. In certain situations, correct positioning on these issues is even expected. The need to constantly reposition and justify oneself robs most people of their last shred of mental energy.

The state of exhaustion of societies all around the globe, which I have already described in my book *Das Erschöpfte Gehirn*[1] (the exhausted brain), with all its neuropathological causes and profound consequences, is thus becoming more and more serious and seems to have already become chronic. During our conversations on the farm in Corsica, however, I began to suspect that all this might not be entirely coincidental. Let's just take the constitutional rights of freedom, which have been sacrificed in the course of the many nonsensical measures taken against a wave of infection by an artificial virus. It quickly became clear through data and records of inconsistent regulations, even to the interested layman, that these measures were incapable of solving the supposed problem against which they were supposedly deployed.

In Corsica, we discussed whether the measures should be understood as a side effect of an ill-considered policy or whether they were deliberately harmful to people, culture, and the economy. But regardless of the answer, we were certain that our freedom was under permanent threat. Some hoped that there might still be a place of refuge in Africa or Asia—not from the virus, mind you, but from the life-threatening measures imposed on us. But the people gathered there, with their own experiences in many countries, reported that, almost everywhere and for the most part, very similar and always senseless measures were being imposed. Could it just be an oversight or a coincidence that they were being enforced worldwide with great precision and effectiveness? In any case, I felt that brain exhaustion was being exacerbated by these measures. So, I decided to get to the bottom of the situation. We had a lively discussion about why this might be, including the questionable role of the World Economic Forum (WEF). The anticultural changes brought about by the anti-COVID program were obviously not aimed at protecting health but, to an impressive degree, were at accelerating the global Great Reset, as propagated by Klaus Schwab, founder of the highly influential WEF, and marketed since June 2020.

To think of the Great Reset as a reboot of a familiar system is to miss the point of the concept. It is neither a reboot nor a reset of the current operating system of our society, which takes humanity back to an earlier time when many things were supposedly better. Instead, the *Grosse Umbruch*,[2] (Great Upheaval) as Schwab himself aptly translates it in his native German, will abolish much of what fundamentally defines us as human beings—our culture and the established rules of coexistence—and replace it with a straitjacket that no human being would voluntarily allow him- or herself to be forced into.

Nevertheless, this great upheaval is coming dangerously close to its goal. It is being driven by billionaire technocrats, corporate bosses, and the superrich, organized around Schwab's WEF and using its compliant apostles, the Young Global Leaders (YGL). The YGL group includes numerous influential politicians and people in other leadership positions who have been deliberately groomed and elevated to their positions and who now sit at many of the crucial centers of power. The downright dystopian future that these circles are actively preparing for us, without being asked, has already been described by Ida Auken, also a graduate of the YGL program and former minister of the environment of Denmark, in an article published by the WEF in 2016: "Welcome to 2030: I own nothing, have no privacy, and life has never been better."[3] In other words, the Great Reset is about expropriation, control, and total digital surveillance under the guise of global health care. It is not a spontaneous response to an unwanted crisis, but a long-planned takeover by a self-appointed technocratic elite that could not have been realized without a crisis. Their apparent intention is to establish a new world order by infiltrating democratic parliaments around the world through their YGL. The public pronouncements of the protagonists of the Great Reset make this relatively clear. They are so sure of their success that they have no need to act in secret. Obviously, they believe that serious resistance is out of the question under the current conditions.

For a large part of humanity to allow itself to be transferred into such modern slavery, a highly efficient brainwashing on a global scale is required. But what would such a Great Mental Reset look like? An essential aspect of such a takeover, I am sure, must be the elimination of true individuality. This is the only way to permanently achieve the goal of unreflective mass conformity. This is how a collective of journalists and scientists, calling themselves Dr. C. E. Nyder, who since 2007 have been able to preserve their freedom of research only through anonymity, describes the mission of members of YGL: "They strive for the one colorful world in which there are no more individuals, but only geno- and phenotypically uniform creatures, simple-minded, without history, and vaccinated multiple times. Boostered with homogeneous thought and immune to any kind of critical thinking, it is the responsibility of the YGLs to lead this dwindling stage of humanity as digital nobility."[4]

In a nutshell, the creation of uniform, simple-minded creatures is an essential first step in a perfidious master plan: a historically unprecedented, targeted global transformation of virtually all areas of life for the establishment of a technocratic world domination, as previously known only from dystopian novels.

Whom are we up against? What resources do the technocratic oligarchs and the power-hungry political elite have at their disposal? How are they being used? And last but not least, why do we urgently need to take their openly stated agenda seriously? If we are to survive as free-thinking human beings, we must know the underlying plan and the method of its implementation. Only then can we possibly prevent a dystopian future for ourselves and our children. The particular tragedy of the situation is that all of us could know everything if we only wanted to, for it is not exclusive knowledge. Yet too many are turning a blind eye. This is the self-reinforcing effect of an extremely powerful method of achieving this new world order, which I will examine subsequently.

When Dystopias Become Reality

The term *dystopia*, derived from the ancient Greek words *dys* for "bad" and *tópos* for "place," describes a future that better not exist. I first learned about dystopian worlds in my youth from two novels. Half a century later, I find them very instructive and helpful in understanding current world events. Therefore, I will repeatedly draw comparisons to these works in order to view current developments within the interpretive framework of the two visionary authors George Orwell (1903–1950) and Aldous Huxley

(1894–1963). In this way, we can take ourselves out of the current processes, which we hardly notice because of the gradual changes occurring and which we therefore accept far too uncritically.

In his famous vision of the future, *1984*, Orwell warned us of the dictatorial rule of a small elite group.[5] With the combination of war propaganda and total surveillance, even of the most intimate thoughts, plus a pervasive influence on all individuals by means of mind control, the entire human race is kept in a state of insurmountable servitude and endures its joyless existence. In his dystopian vision, not even a thought that challenges the technocrats' narrative is allowed, even if the narrative severely tests common sense. In *1984*, for example, two plus two can sometimes equal three or five, if the political leadership so chooses.

Mind Control: AI Is Learning to Read Our Minds

Previous technological methods of mind reading relied on implanting electrodes in people's brains. However, recent advances in the development of artificial neural networks allow researchers to reconstruct visual experiences based on human brain activity and to decipher the semantic meaning of people's thoughts, although word-for-word translations are not yet possible.[6] Analyzing and interpreting this data is becoming more accurate as the computational power required to perform these tasks decreases. For example, on December 1, 2022, a study was published proposing a method to reconstruct high-resolution images with high fidelity with less effort than previously possible, without the need for additional training and fine-tuning of complex deep learning models.[7] Currently, the technique requires sophisticated functional magnetic resonance imaging (fMRI), but it's only a matter of time before the methodology, combined with artificial intelligence (AI), produces reliable results with simpler methods of data collection.

Less than twenty years ago, any cognitive neuroscientist would have answered no to the question of whether such a thing was possible. But a future in which technocrats gain access to people's once-private thoughts is already knocking on the door of the present, and science is rushing to open it. For instance, multibillionaire Elon Musk, a former young global leader of the WEF,[8] has been publicly dreaming since 2016 of permanently penetrating the human brain with the chips of his company Neuralink: "To a scientist, to think about changing the fundamental nature of life—creating viruses, eugenics, etc.—it raises a specter that many biologists find quite worrisome, whereas the neuroscientists that I know, when they think about chips in the brain, it doesn't seem that foreign,

> because we already have chips in the brain. We have deep brain stimulation to alleviate the symptoms of Parkinson's Disease, we have early trials of chips to restore vision, we have the cochlear implant—so to us it doesn't seem like that big of a stretch to put devices into a brain to read information out and to read information back in."[9]

The recent past shows us how life-threatening systematic disinformation can be. For example, the targeted misinformation about Iraq's alleged weapons of mass destruction made the third Gulf War possible in the first place, and this approach was also a means to an end in the COVID-19 pandemic from the very beginning. The allegedly imminent mass destruction by a killer virus justified another senseless "war" and the deprivation of civil liberties and many other completely disproportionate measures with equally fatal consequences. The stoked fear of viral mass destruction was likewise pure propaganda and, apart from the obscene record profits of hitherto unprofitable pharmaceutical companies like BioNTech, ultimately served to advance the Great Reset agenda. Klaus Schwab and Thierry Malleret, a French economist and modern historian, explained in detail in their book *COVID-19 and the Great Reset* that COVID-19 provides a unique opportunity for the intended Great Reset.[10] One gets the impression that certain circles wanted such a crisis in order to realize these goals. The question is whether they were helped in one way or another to bring about the necessary crisis.

That the measures and associated communication were not motivated by health concerns but by much broader goals explains the widespread censorship of alternative opinions in the traditional media and on social platforms today. But not only opinions are affected; verifiable information that contradicts the technocrats' COVID-19 narrative or questions certain statements or approaches is also suppressed. For example, a conversation between the philosopher Gunnar Kaiser and me on YouTube was deleted. In it, we discussed only the extent to which remedying the sometimes severe vitamin D deficiency in the general population would be a demonstrably effective measure for containing coronavirus infections and offering protection against severe disease. Although all of the statements made were based on scientific analysis and clinical studies, all you can find at the address of the video is the disclaimer "This video has been removed for violating YouTube's community guidelines."[11] This is the brave new normal the technocrats rave about. Free speech is a thing of the past, even when the dissemination of scientifically proven information could save many lives, as in this case.

Causal Prevention That No One Wanted

Back in April 2020 international experts specifically called attention to the fact that "the degree of protection [from severe COVID-19] increases when vitamin D levels increase."[12] According to the scientists, the goal should be "to bring vitamin D [prohormone] concentrations to 100 to 150 nmol/l" because this would be associated with the best immune response. At this concentration, waves of infection would be much flatter.[13] Scientists at the German Cancer Research Center also pointed out in December 2020 that timely correction of vitamin D levels would protect nine out of ten people from a fatal course and that it was therefore time to act.[14] But no one has acted, despite independent scientists confirming, based on a large number of other studies, that virtually no one should have to die from COVID-19: "COVID-19 Mortality Risk Correlates Inversely with Vitamin D3 Status, and a Mortality Rate Close to Zero Could Theoretically Be Achieved at 50 ng/mL [125 nmol/l] 25(OH)D3." These are the "Results of a Systematic Review and Meta-Analysis."[15] Clinical intervention studies also provided early evidence of the causality of vitamin D deficiency for problematic COVID-19 infections. Thus, even after hospitalization for COVID-19, severe progression and death could be drastically reduced or completely prevented by rapidly increasing vitamin D levels.[16]

It is not surprising, then, that the protagonists of the vaccination campaign sought to prevent vitamin D and did so very effectively (more on this in chapter 4).[17] Ultimately, the senseless and, above all, unnecessary measures could only be justified with the help of those who died because of and *with* COVID-19 (*with* meaning having a positive test that could well be false). And this was probably not done unintentionally. Still, on September 8, 2020, the then member of the German Bundestag, Professor and Doctor of Medicine Karl Lauterbach tweeted, "Vitamin D deficiency is also a risk factor for other infectious diseases, weakens immune function. In some cases, it also increases the risk of cancer. Therefore, studies are not surprising that vitamin D deficiency causes a higher risk of infection as well as a more severe course."[18] However, on January 8, 2022, exactly one month after being sworn in as federal minister of health, he believed that there is no alternative to compulsory vaccination.[19] By then, the causality of vitamin D deficiency in the deaths from COVID-19 had long been established and was demonstrably known to him.

It is my concern that you consider all measures (from the lockdown to the vaccination campaign with an experimental gene therapy approach) and especially the assessments of the experts courted by the media, knowing that there has always been a healthy alternative without side effects. Because of my professional background, I felt compelled to spread this knowledge: as a medical doctor, to save lives, and as a scientist, so that more people would see what was happening through corrective glasses. I feel empowered and legitimized to do so because, among other things, I, with my research team, discovered a crucial genetic switch responsible for the development of our adaptive immune system, as part of my habilitation (postdoctoral research program). This endogenous mechanism allows us to constantly adapt our immune response to new viral variants.[20] The real reason for the completely unnecessary and therefore senseless deaths from viral respiratory infections is that all the media power is being used to prevent people from learning how to enable their immune systems to respond appropriately to viruses such as SARS-CoV2 (or influenza) by simply correcting a vitamin D or vitamin D hormone deficiency. Therefore, I considered almost all other measures taken against COVID-19 to be not only completely misguided but also life-threatening because of the massive collateral damage. On this point alone, it becomes clear beyond any doubt that the protection of people is not the real goal of the narrative that the technocrats want to impose. To exclude such effective preventive and therapeutic measures, or even to fight them in the media (as I will discuss in detail in a section of chapter 4: "Casual Prevention of Severe SARS CoV-2 Infections Is Right-Wing Extremism"), is not only untruthful disinformation but also a serious misleading of society—with millions of deaths worldwide as a result.

But let's step back and consider other aspects of the explosive dystopian elements of Orwell's *1984*. Even the technological possibilities available today teach us to be afraid, considering that digitalization has made it possible to conduct almost seamless, comprehensive surveillance. But we are currently witnessing how even more surveillance and manipulation systems are being added to the mix in the form of social scoring systems. These are already in use in some countries, such as China, and their supposed benefits are being discussed in Western societies as well. They allow for a fully automated and far-reaching influence on human behavior—a nightmare that not even Orwell could have foreseen in *1984*, when he still envisioned humans as supervisors. On January 10, 2016, Schwab even predicted that by 2026 all people will have a chip implanted under their skin, and he spoke in this context of a fusion of our physical, digital, and biological identities.[21] At first glance, this seems like a bold prediction. But Sweden is already a pioneer in implanting chips in humans.[22] That a large part of the world's population quickly developed the willingness to be vaccinated with experimental gene therapy injections makes Schwab's prognosis seem not so far-fetched. To gain acceptance, it was enough to use the media to stir up fear of a killer virus that would supposedly wipe out all of humanity. By the time of the next pandemic, it is highly likely that attempts will be made to convince everyone that it is essential to have a microchip implanted to control the spread of the infection, as this would supposedly be the only way to ensure the survival of the world's population. As we have seen with COVID-19, there are extremely low and questionable thresholds for declaring a pandemic (see chapter 4,

Step 1), which would facilitate this scheme. Presumably, those who refuse the implant will find it extremely difficult to earn a living, under the pretext of protecting society. If this scenario comes true, it will give a potentially very small technocratic elite a previously unimaginable degree of control over the whole of humanity, with the help of their increasingly powerful computer systems—especially if AI is learning to read our minds.

Fittingly, or in preparation for this, in September 2015 all member states of the United Nations adopted the Sustainable Development Goals 2030 and committed to, among other things, creating a "legal identity" for all by then, including birth registration (Goal 16.9).[23] In this context, the rapid proliferation of smart devices (such as smartphones) around the world, combined with ever-increasing computing power and the rapid expansion of broadband coverage, is seen as an opportunity to deploy new methods of identifying individuals and matching them with their identity data. The desired outcome is that there should be as little difference as possible between our real and virtual selves. To move toward this goal as quickly as possible, the World Bank Group (WBG) launched a cross-cutting Identification for Development initiative in June 2015 to enable unique legal identities and thereby ensure digital ID–based services for all.[24] Global immunization programs—COVID-19 is apparently just the beginning—are intended to pave the way for this. The personal ID or digital vaccination card, which can be used by computers, could be permanently implanted in the skin during vaccination, as has already been reported in Sweden. The German newsmagazine *Stern* ran this headline in December 2021: "Digital Vaccination Passport Always with You: Swedes Have Microchips Implanted under Their Skin."[25] For simplicity, this process could be called *chimping*—chip documentation and vaccination in one go.

The Mark of the Spiked

An implant may not be a chip, but a unique mark on the patient will suffice in the future, according to research at the prestigious Massachusetts Institute of Technology (MIT), funded by the National Natural Science Foundation of China and the Bill & Melinda Gates Foundation.[26] To document vaccination status in a tamper-proof manner, patterns could be inserted into the skin using microneedles that dissolve in the skin and contain both the vaccine and illuminants, similar to a QR code, that become visible under near-infrared light. This code, inserted with the vaccine, would be invisible to the eye but could be scanned and read by slightly modified smartphones or other smart devices. "By codelivering a vaccine," the authors write, "the pattern of particles in the skin could serve as an on-person vaccination record." This procedure has already been successfully tested in rats.

But the codes, applied under the skin with microneedles, have also been identified in pig skin and pigmented human skin.

Not only is Bill Gates, one of the WEF's former Global Leaders for Tomorrow (GLT, the forerunner of the aforementioned YGL), funding this research in cooperation with the Chinese government, but also this proof of concept was published only three years after Schwab's prediction of a global application of chips in humans and only a few days before the outbreak of SARS-CoV-2. From this "mark of the spiked," which could become mandatory during the next pandemic, as it would solve the problem of forged vaccination passports, it is only a small step to the acceptance of "chimping," vaccination with simultaneous vaccination documentation by means of a subcutaneously implanted chip, which has to be no larger than a grain of rice. The advantages of a theft-proof vaccination ID card will also be communicated to the people, as will the payment function by means of a chip, without having to search for the vaccination card or dig out the mobile phone, without many cards and thick wallets—provided that small steps are taken and the appropriate media influence is exerted.

Another parallel between Orwell's fiction and today's reality is the technocratic elite's practice of deliberately altering records of the past in order to control the present and thereby determine the future. Connoisseurs of the novel can therefore already feel transported into a comparable future, since public statements and reports by politicians and journalists are censored from the outset by the market-dominating media companies and even search engines—that is, they are suppressed from the search results or deleted altogether. Even statements by scientists who support the COVID-19 narrative simply disappear when their former "truth" is deemed outdated. They are thus removed from the collective memory of the internet.

The term *vaccine* will serve as a concrete example. In the past, a vaccine had one primary function: to protect people from infection and disease. This was the definition of a vaccine used by the US Centers for Disease Control and Prevention (CDC). By August 26, 2021, a vaccine had to be "a product that stimulates a person's immune system to produce immunity to a specific disease, protecting the person from that disease."[27] But as of September 1, 2021, a vaccine would only be "a preparation that is used to stimulate the body's immune response against diseases."[28] The change in definition was necessary because Israel, then the "world champion" of vaccination, had found that the protection originally promised by the novel corona vaccines was declining very rapidly. For example, the *Financial Times* reported that studies by the Israeli Ministry of Health published in August 2021 (about a week before the CDC's definition change) "showed the Pfizer vaccine's efficacy against infection falling to 39 percent, and to as low as 16 percent for people who had their second shots in January."[29] According to the ministry, the most worryingly concern was "the vaccine's efficacy for the prevention of severe disease in the most vulnerable cohort—Israelis aged over 65, most of whom were double-jabbed by January—had dropped to 55 percent." A publicized internal CDC email sent two days after the *Financial Times* report underlines the connection: the need to "update this page 'Immunization Basics | CDC' since these definitions are outdated and being used by some to say COVID-19 vaccines are not vaccines per CDC's own definition."[30] Thus, the technocratic narrative is always adjusted when it no longer corresponds to reality, in the spirit of *1984*. What is disturbing is that such changes, such as the deletion or rewriting of statements by executive politicians, are widely accepted or at least not questioned by the public or the journalists of the mainstream media.

Orwell's *1984* was particularly frightening to me because, when I first read the novel, I could well imagine that his vision could, in some way, become reality. In contrast, the dystopian future civilization described by Aldous Huxley in *Brave New World* was completely inconceivable when I read that novel, not because Huxley had implausibly described the neurobiological basis for breeding brain-damaged human labor slaves. On the contrary, Aldous Huxley was deeply interested in biology and medicine, and his half-brother, Sir Andrew Huxley (1917–2012), was even awarded the Nobel Prize in Physiology or Medicine in 1963 for his molecular research on nerves and muscles. An entirely different reason explains the limits of my imagination at that time. Huxley's future vision of an affluent society in which disease is overcome seemed implausible precisely because, paradoxically, it is realized only by deliberately inducing mental dysfunction in artificially bred human creatures. It was a contradiction in terms to me. After all, overcoming disease involves, among many other things, healthy development and the maintenance of mental health. But the closer I looked at the vision of the protagonists of the Great Reset, especially in light of the COVID-19 measures, the clearer it became to me that even Huxley's dystopia is closer to reality than any of us would like.

The system in Huxley's *Brave New World* is already established and stabilized, while, as of this writing in the spring of 2023, we are still in the process of a Great Mental Reset, which is necessary for permanent acceptance of the world as it will emerge from the Great Reset. It is of great benefit to our considerations to remember in detail how this was accomplished in his dystopia: Human embryos, after artificial insemination, are multiplied in retorts into several thousand genotypically identical beings and grown in bottles (these would be the "genotypically uniform creatures," as the earlier-referenced Dr. Nyder group of journalists and scientists calls them). The "major instruments of social stability," Huxley tells us in his novel, are "standard men and women; in uniform batches [production numbers]."[31]

On the artificial path to birth, different classes of people are produced according to need and are called alphas, betas, gammas, deltas, or epsilons, according to descending intellectual quality. "We decant our babies as socialized human beings, as Alphas or Epsilons, as future sewage workers or future—" The director of the City Hatchery and Conditioning Center (DCK) was going to say, "future World controllers," but said instead said, "future Directors of Hatcheries."[32] While alphas can even rule the world, classes below them experience gradual neural developmental disorders caused by oxygen deprivation during their bottle maturation.

"Nothing like oxygen-shortage for keeping an embryo below par," says the DCK.[33]

One employee clarifies, "The lower the caste, the shorter the oxygen," adding, "with in Epsilons, we don't need human intelligence."[34]

But the ratio is important. "The optimum population," explains one of the ten world controllers of the technocratic elite, "is modeled on the iceberg—eight-ninths below the water line, one-ninth above."[35] About 11 percent would be alphas, because "a society of Alphas," the world controller tells us, "couldn't fail to be unstable and miserable."[36] And he explains, "An Alpha-decanted, Alpha-conditioned man would go mad if he had to do Epsilon Semi-Moron work—go mad, or start smashing things up. Alphas can be completely socialized—but only on condition that you make them do Alpha work."[37] Alphas are so conditioned that they don't have to be infantile. Therefore, DCK had to rebuke an Alpha who became a problem for social stability because of noninfantile behavior: "But that is all the more reason [because there is this theoretical possibility of choice] for their making a special effort to conform."[38] According to the technocratic code, it would be "their duty to be infantile, even against their inclination."

For the Alphas to succeed in this as easily as possible, the operating system or narrative considered ideal for the technocratic elite is anchored in their brains (just as in the brains of the lower classes, but with different content) throughout childhood and beyond puberty by means of so-called hypnopedia (repeated suggestions during sleep). Thus, they are programmed for their intended role in the system: "Till at last the child's mind is these suggestions," explains the DCK, "and the sum of the suggestions is the child's mind. And not the child's mind only. The adult's mind too—all his life long. The mind that judges and desires and decides—made up of these suggestions. But all these suggestions are our suggestions!"[39] That creates the "phenotypically uniform creatures" the collective refers to. "And that," the DCK continues, "that is the secret of happiness and virtue—liking what you've got to do. All conditioning aims at that: making people like their inescapable social destiny."[40] With the help of thousands of nightly repetitions of hypnotic messages, these are not only accepted but also learned to feel "as axiomatic, self-evident, utterly indisputable."[41]

Personality development is thus reduced to the messages of the technocratic system. After all, "it would upset the whole social order if men started doing things on their own," the world controller tells us.[42] That's why everyone is "so conditioned that they practically can't help behaving as they ought to behave."[43]

This nightmare of total control over human behavior through the limitation of mental capacity and a personality structure shaped and standardized by the technocratic narrative may also have inspired the protagonists of the Great Reset. You will have noticed the parallels in terms of oxygen deprivation and the principle of being in love with what one is forced to be. I will describe in detail how comparable cognitive manipulations affect us concretely today and could be refined in the near future.

Creative Destruction

While in Orwell's *1984* people are made to accept their deprived lives through a propagandistically staged war and the omnipresent surveillance of Big Brother, Huxley's *Brave New World* bypasses this kind of control, in addition to the threat of physical and mental violence. This is done not by making people submit, but by breeding them into their unchanging social roles. One could therefore imagine Huxley's vision as an evolution of *1984*, especially since the brave new world he describes follows the end of a war mentioned in the book: "The Nine Years' War, the great Economic Collapse. There was a choice between World Control and destruction. Between stability and—" Huxley lets us know through one of the world controllers, not finishing the sentence he had started.[44]

Here we see the recurring motif of a new creation after a previous, more or less deliberate destruction. Thus, Orwell and, especially, Huxley may have provided the script for the Great Reset by warning all those who, according to the developments of the time, were already foreseeably to be rationalized away in a more efficient system, or at least brought under complete control. In any case, the principle of creative destruction can be found tellingly in a 2011 book by US economist and Great Reset protagonist Richard Florida, published under the title *The Great Reset: How the Post-Crash Economy Will Change the Way We Live and Work*: "History teaches us that periods of 'creative destruction,' like the Great Depression of the 1930s, also present opportunities to remake our economy and society and to generate whole new eras of economic growth and prosperity."[45]

Echoing Florida's vision, Gerry Allan, who holds a PhD in decision analysis from Harvard University and an MBA in applied economics from the University of California, Berkeley, asks, "Do we have 'creative destruction' or just plain 'destruction?'"[46] And he gives us an answer: "War is certainly destructive but what follows can often be anything but 'better' (except perhaps for a favored few) or 'creative' (except in a narrow, highly-partial context). What follows destruction may turn out to be much worse than what was destroyed." As an example, he cites the brutal Bolshevik Revolution of 1917, which put an end to the increasingly corrupt and inefficient Russian tsarist empire. This, in turn, was "replaced by Stalin's totalitarian Soviet Union," Allan writes. "Each destruction followed by more destruction, not creation in any positive, general sense." Destruction, then, should not be the beginning of a creative process but its consequence: "Truly creative destruction is most often the result of major innovation—something new, positive, and broadly beneficial—that obsoletes and forces out an existing technology or process."

In the COVID-19 crisis, it was not promising innovations that were supposed to bring about the long overdue restructuring of an environmentally destructive economy. So, we are clearly not in the creative destruction phase described by Gerry Allan. Rather, our time could be compared to the Orwellian phase of war. There, destruction was a means to an end. The goal was a technocratic restructuring through the dismantling of the middle class and the forced end of many personal freedoms. This process of "destruction that brings more destruction in its wake" can easily be attributed to the never-ending war against supposed killer viruses (the WEF speaks of permapandemics), and even to the war in Ukraine, which broke out when the virulence of SARS-CoV-2 subsided. There, legends of a final victory over Russia have replaced any historical lesson about the existential necessity of diplomatic solutions—all the more so when viewed through *1984* glasses. The statement by German Chancellor Olaf Scholz at the WEF meeting in 2022 that the pandemic will not end "unless we finally break the cycle of ever new mutants causing ever new infections" fits into this.[47]

But this is simply impossible. The virus, which is now also spreading in the animal kingdom,[48] cannot be prevented from mutating (which would only be possible by changing one or more laws of nature), nor can it be controlled by vaccines (even if they worked). With this statement, Scholz has made the war against COVID-19 or ultimately all future permapandemics a dominant theme for all time.

Interesting in this context is that another source of war is also kept in permanent mode. For Russian President Vladimir Putin, who Klaus Schwab claimed to be one of the WEF's former Global Leaders for Tomorrow,[49] "the war could actually go on forever," according to *t-online*.[50] According to the report, a hundred thousand deaths "seems like a minor evil in view of the possible loss of power." "For the Kremlin regime," the article concludes, "war as a permanent state is the only chance to survive."

Sitting on the opposite side is German Foreign Minister Annalena Baerbock, who was nominated for the WEF's YGL program in the spring of 2020.[51] In keeping with the Great Reset agenda, she too is not working toward a diplomatic solution to end a war that is unwinnable for either side but rather continues to fuel it. In doing so, she says she is concerned about the continued supply of weapons "no matter what my German constituents think."[52] And in her address to the Parliamentary Assembly of the Council of Europe in Strasbourg on January 24, 2003, Baerbock is even more explicit when she says, "Yes, we must do more, including on tanks. But the most important and decisive thing is that we do it together—and not play the blame game in Europe . . . because we are at war with Russia."[53] Thus, two supposed adversaries—the German foreign minister and the Russian president (and thus Germany and Russia)—as WEF allies together make sure that this war will not end either. So, the only-supposed creative destruction that began with COVID-19 will not end either.

The same is true for climate change, which apparently can also only be stopped by war. In the *Bulletin of the Atomic Scientists,* the article "The Case for Going to War against Climate Change" states, "Once established as a war-like threat, climate change can be addressed with the gravity, urgency, and resources it deserves."[54] So said then Prince Charles (now King Charles), quoted in the article, himself a WEF member and protagonist of the Great Reset: "We must now put ourselves on a warlike footing, approaching our action from the perspective of a military-style campaign." John Kerry proclaimed something similar. According to President Joe Biden's climate envoy, the world needs a "wartime mentality" to combat climate change. And last but not least, since there will never be a virus-free planet, a never-ending battle against supposed killer viruses is guaranteed. In a speech at the WEF 2020 meeting, then Prince Charles was also one of the first to explicitly articulate the opportunity to use COVID-19 to drive the Great Reset: "We have a golden opportunity to seize something good from this crisis. Its unprecedented shockwaves may well make people more receptive to big visions of change."[55]

The destruction and intolerability of the situation is pushed further and even more intensively so that everyone believes in the great promise of the Great Reset, or rather desperately wishes for any change that holds out the prospect of ending the many different artificial wars. The warmongers, who present themselves as omnipotent technocratic world controllers, probably do this in the hope that something positive will come out of it, at least for them. That is why they meet every year at the WEF in Davos with high-level politicians from the leading industrialized countries. It is there that they present them with the issues on which the next steps of the global agenda can be implemented in the political realities of the individual states.

Total Control in Real Time

War forces the communities of fate affected by it to conform in a way that no other conceivable influence on a collective can. This conformity can be steered in the desired direction by propaganda, which must be all the more pervasive the more abstract the supposed threat. States of war also provide a justification for the total surveillance of human activity. Schwab and Malleret try to sell this seamless surveillance as an inevitable consequence of progress, writing the following in their other joint book, *The Great Narrative: For a Better Future*: "We must come to terms with the notion that there is no more privacy. Our personal and professional data are gradually becoming fully monitored, visible to many, and therefore transparent."[56] Implanted chips could contribute enormously to this, as could the planned abolition of cash. The latter would allow unprecedented digital control of all financial activities, while the ubiquitous smartphones already collect a great deal of data from us around the clock, which can be analyzed at any time for espionage purposes.

As in Huxley's *Brave New World*, however, the Great Reset protagonists probably already understood that the goal of total control could be realized only in a very fragile way, using exclusively the aforementioned means of the states of war. "In the end," one of the technocratic leaders tells us in *Brave New World*, "the Controllers realized that force was no good." Therefore, they developed methods that were more protracted but infinitely more unerring, such as "ectogenesis [artificial breeding], neo-Pavlovian conditioning, and hypnopedia."[57] (I will return later to the parallels between these latter two methods to components of the Great Reset agenda.)

Huxley's dystopia abolished uncontrollable art and, above all, free science: "It isn't only art that's incompatible with happiness; it's also science," says one of the world controllers in the novel. "Science is dangerous; we have to keep it most carefully chained and muzzled."[58] Even during the war on COVID-19, scientific concepts and any alternative ways of thinking that might contradict or at least question the technocratic narrative were suppressed from the start. As US author and political activist Naomi Wolf writes in her nonfiction book *The Bodies of Others: The New Authoritarians, COVID-19 and the War against the Human*, "It is a war on free thought and free speech—a war against our most fundamental beliefs."[59] Thus, the supposed salvation from the viral threat was not even allowed to be questioned, although it was imposed, with more or less force, in the form of a risky gene therapy intervention and at the expense of human integrity. This was only possible without much resistance because such scenarios had already been played out and rehearsed, and therefore one knew exactly how to effectively generate consent.

Amazingly, on September 12, 2019, just two months before the coronavirus outbreak (just in time!), the European Commission and the World Health Organization (WHO) jointly organized a Global Vaccination Summit.[60] The declared aim was to draw up a global action plan to stop the spread of preventable diseases through vaccination and, in particular, to nip any future viral threats in the bud. According to the final message of the meeting, every citizen of the world should benefit from the "power of vaccination [not immunization!]" Accordingly, the governments of all nations of the world should declare their belief in the omnipotence of vaccination. To ensure this, ten tasks were identified that governments in particular, and humanity in general, should fulfill in order for their respective populations to have access to the supposedly life-saving vaccines. From today's perspective, the tasks adopted at that meeting, which fit seamlessly into the Great Reset project, read like the Ten Commandments of a new global vaccination religion whose first sacrament has now become humanity's latest scourge:

> **First Commandment:** "Promote global political leadership and commitment to vaccination and build effective collaboration and partnerships—across

> international, national, regional and local levels with health authorities, health professionals, civil society, communities, scientists, and industry—to protect everyone everywhere through sustained high vaccination coverage rates."
> **Second Commandment:** "Ensure all countries have national immunisation strategies in place and implemented and strengthen its financial sustainability, in line with progress towards Universal Health Coverage, leaving no one behind."
> **Third Commandment:** "Build strong surveillance systems for vaccine-preventable diseases, particularly those under global elimination and eradication targets."
> **Fourth Commandment:** "Tackle the root-causes of vaccine hesitancy, increasing confidence in vaccination, as well as designing and implementing evidence-based interventions." While the first three commandments commit governments around the world to a common approach, the fourth commandment is intended to ensure, for example, that sufficient resources are available to persuade as many people as possible through vaccination propaganda.

Commandments five through eight are designed to control and improve technology development and implementation:

> **Fifth Commandment:** "Harness the power of digital technologies, so as to strengthen the monitoring of the performance of vaccination programmes."
> **Sixth Commandment:** "Sustain research efforts to continuously generate data on the effectiveness and safety of vaccines and impact of vaccination programmes."
> **Seventh Commandment:** "Continue efforts and investment, including novel models of funding and incentives, in research, development and innovation for new or improved vaccine and delivery devices."
> **Eighth Commandment:** "Mitigate the risks of vaccine shortages through improved vaccine availability monitoring, forecasting, purchasing, delivery and stockpiling systems and collaboration with producers and all participants in the distribution chain to make best use of, or increase existing, manufacturing capacity."

All these commandments are about gaining far-reaching control over governments and ultimately the entire world population by means of global vaccination programs (which, as is well known, has been successful in the case of COVID-19). It was predictable that not every freedom-loving mind would be happy about this and that unwelcome questions would be expected—especially when vaccines like the one against COVID-19 do more harm than good (see "He Who Walks over Corpses Is Not to Be Trusted" later in this chapter). Perhaps this is why commandment number nine was created. It aims to censor "heretical misinformation" about vaccines or alternatives as effectively as possible in the digital age:

> **Ninth Commandment:** "Empower healthcare professionals at all levels as well as the media, to provide effective, transparent and objective information to the public and fight false and misleading information, including by engaging with social media platforms and technological companies."

Accordingly, as early as March 16, 2020, a joint statement was issued by the operators of the world's largest information platforms, Facebook, Google, LinkedIn, Microsoft, Reddit, Twitter, and YouTube: "We are working closely together on COVID-19 response efforts. We're helping millions of people stay connected while also jointly combating fraud and misinformation about the virus, elevating authoritative content on our platforms, and sharing critical updates in coordination with government healthcare agencies around the world. We invite other companies to join us as we work to keep our communities healthy and safe."[61] Achieving greater medical safety by stifling all scientific debate is an outlandish concept, and its breathtakingly widespread acceptance can only be understood, in my opinion, when one considers that almost all of the signatories to the above statement are part of Schwab's Global Leader cadre:

- Facebook CEO Mark Zuckerberg[62]
- Bill Gates,[63] whose Microsoft Corporation owns LinkedIn and who circularly cofunds the YGL program through his Bill & Melinda Gates Foundation[64]
- Rajiv Pant, who runs Reddit[65]
- Larry Page and Sergey Brin, whose Google, LLC acquired YouTube[66]

In other words, the global propaganda machine is in the hands of the technocratic elite. If you wonder who I mean by that term, this list is an authoritative selection of key figures from this influential group. And their impact on the free exchange of ideas is enormous. YouTube's third-quarter 2022 Community Policy Enforcement report alone shows that 5.6 million videos have been removed from YouTube by Google.[67] Five million YouTube channels have also been suspended. In the context of the technocrats' power grab, more than 94 percent of these "undesirable" videos and channels were identified not by humans but by computers. Thus, the conditioning of public opinion by technocratic propaganda, the control of the media, and the censorship of scientific research and knowledge are now much more advanced and effective than

Orwell and Huxley could have imagined. To think laterally is a dirty word, to think at all is dangerous. However, in *Brave New World* it is said, "Not philosophers but fret-sawyers and stamp collectors compose the backbone of society."[68] This statement also fits the Great Mental Reset and seems to be true today—COVID-19 made it possible in the first place.

But it is not only the social networks and information platforms of the internet giants that tell us what to believe and how to behave. According to the ninth commandment, the traditional media should also be urged to spread only uniform messages, which they did very well. Among these messages was the promotion of the experimental vaccine cocktail as the savior against the artificially created fear of COVID-19, which was done very effectively. However, these messages not only had a confusingly similar tone but were also fed from a common source. One of the most important of these message-makers goes by the name of Project Syndicate. It is a private message factory funded by, among others, the Bill & Melinda Gates Foundation, Google, and the Open Society Foundation, owned by multibillionaire George Soros,[69] also a member of the WEF.[70] Project Syndicate says it serves over five hundred media outlets in over 150 countries and in over sixty languages. On its The World's Opinion page is an article titled "Why Vaccination Should Be Compulsory," and this world's opinion is explained as follows: "Although the first compulsory seat-belt laws met with strong objections when they were introduced 50 years ago, nobody bothers to complain about such a commonsense rule anymore. In mandating vaccination against COVID-19, governments today can offer the same basic justification for protecting both individuals and society."[71]

Another example is the global news agency Reuters, which is closely linked to the WEF. Until February 2020 James "Jim" C. Smith was its chief executive officer and also a board member of the WEF's Partnering against Corruption Initiative.[72] The title Partnering against Corruption Initiative can only be understood as irony, or perhaps even sarcasm, considering that, according to the WEF website, Jim Smith is also a director of Pfizer, the very pharmaceutical giant that has profited and continues to profit more than any other company from the COVID-19 vaccines.

Millions of dollars in direct financial support from media corporations ensure that we all hear as news what we are supposed to believe to be the truth and, consequently, how we are supposed to act. Such financial contributions are then cloaked in phrases like "promoting educational content on public health and the spread of infectious diseases," granted by superrich people like Bill Gates.[73] The *Brave New World* sends its greetings, and *1984* has a new date, because the last commandment announced by the Global Vaccination Summit may not be entirely coincidental with the time target of the Great Reset:

- **Tenth Commandment:** "Align and integrate vaccination in the global health and development agendas, through a renewed immunisation agenda 2030."

From that fateful year on, we will all, without exception, be injected with all the sometimes hastily approved substances that are supposed to protect us from at least one of the countless, often actually harmless diseases. We will also be inoculated against the ability to think creatively and yet be happy without possessions, according to Ida Auken's vision of the WEF.

Rich, Richer, Most Powerful—the Alleged Stakeholder Capitalism

In mid-October 2019, one month after the adoption of the ten global guidelines, the US-based Johns Hopkins Center for Health Security, together with the WEF and the Bill & Melinda Gates Foundation, organized the pandemic exercise Event 201.[74] The goal of the exercise, conducted by a broad coalition of stakeholders, was to "provide ongoing attention to a potential severe pandemic in advance to save lives and limit the economic and social consequences of an emergency." Not *shareholders*, but *stakeholders*—that is, "claimants or interest groups"—are said to have been at work here. Stakeholders "are linked to a company by different interests; interests that they usually assert at the expense of the shareholders," writes Alberto Mingardi, a doctor of political science, in his article "Stakeholder Capitalism Is a Better Capitalism Only for the Caste of Managers."[75]

This assessment turned out to be only partially correct, as the managers *and* the shareholders of the companies involved in the measures taken against COVID-19 benefited enormously. Largely unnoticed in the shadow of the overwhelming events, the world's 2,700 billionaires increased their fortunes by 6 percent of global economic output in the first year of the pandemic panic alone. At the same time, however, this economic output collapsed by 3.3 percent as a result of the preplanned COVID-19 measures, which were completely excessive in relation to the potential danger. The prestigious German newspaper *Zeit Online* described this perverse development as follows: "So it's not as if the wealth of the wealthy has grown because of a boom in the global economy—where the majority of people share in the rising wealth—but despite and also because of the slump in the global economy."[76] According to an analysis by Americans for Tax Fairness and the Institute for Policy Studies Program on Inequality, in the first nineteen months of the pandemic, the collective wealth of US billionaires alone increased by 70 percent, reaching a total of $5 trillion (five thousand billion dollars)—an unfathomable increase in power and thus potential influence over all of humanity's financially impressionable, future-shaping processes and institutions.[77] At the same time, according to Schwab, all citizens of the earth should be stakeholders and benefit. However, the COVID-19 activities revealed the true intentions behind such statements and showed what the superrich and extremely influential around Schwab are really about. For example, the COVID-19 activities were clearly designed to benefit only the above-average wealthy stakeholders. For almost everyone else who was not so wealthy, the COVID-19 pandemic became the disaster of the century.

The staged pandemic scare paved the way for the planned package of measures, which in turn drove the Great Reset as planned. All of this was made possible by a sophisticated communications strategy that was the preparatory focus of Event 201. Fundamentally, this planning meeting was about whether the global community would be prepared to implement the aforementioned ten commandments with sufficient efficiency in the event of a declared pandemic. Anita Cicero, deputy director of the Johns Hopkins Center for Health Security, which hosted the event, summarized the results as follows: "Governments and the private sector should assign a greater priority to developing methods to combat mis- and disinformation related to pandemic response. Governments will need to partner with traditional and social media in order to research and develop nimble approaches to countering misinformation. For their part, media companies, we believe, should commit to ensuring that authoritative messages are prioritized and really false messages are suppressed."[78]

Interestingly, to test the possible emergency, the center simulated the outbreak of a novel but "purely fictional" coronavirus that is transmitted from bats to pigs to humans, eventually spreading rapidly from person to person and leading to a threatening pandemic. "The pathogen and the disease it causes," Event 201 organizers said, "are modeled largely on SARS [whether it is the SARS-CoV-1 of the past or the SARS-CoV-2 of the near future was left open], but it is more transmissible in the community setting by people with mild symptoms."[79] Thus, even in the preparatory phase for a pandemic, mild disease was seen as central to a rapid and thus difficult to control spread. The organizers assumed a virus that caused both severe and many mild cases. The simulation thus ensured that the virus could spread rapidly and trigger the threatened pandemic.

Just a few weeks later, a new coronavirus, SARS-CoV-2, was discovered in Wuhan that surprisingly matched the description of the simulation virus: it was also transmitted to humans by bats and belonged to the SARS family of viruses. It was impressive prophecy on the part of the organizers of Event 201 to select, from myriad human-pathogenic viruses, the one for a pandemic simulation that was actually to have an impressive successor a short time later! It can be assumed that the organizers and participants of Event 201 were well aware of the parallels between SARS-CoV-2 as it appeared in the media and the SARS virus from the simulation. Since the Event 201 simulation became reality so quickly and so accurately, the Johns Hopkins Center for Health Security felt compelled to issue a statement about this surprising coincidence as early as January 2020. It states, in part, "Although our tabletop exercise included a mock novel coronavirus, the inputs we used for modeling the potential impact of that fictional virus are not similar to nCoV-2019."[80] The organizer's justification seems even more implausible today than it did at the time of publication, since it has now been clearly demonstrated that SARS-CoV-2 was cloned and (accidentally or even intentionally?) released in Wuhan using molecular genetics methods (more on this in chapter 4).

Ultimately, the Great Reset came a big step closer to its goal of a global power grab and digital control with the narrative of the vaccination fairy tale. This was precisely because a large part of the world's population wanted to believe that the virus could be controlled with the right measures and the right modern, albeit experimental, medicine, especially under the condition of blind obedience to the instructions of the authorities. An educational campaign pointing out the causality of a dysfunctional immune system under vitamin D3 deficiency, which could be remedied with very little effort, was completely powerless against this. This was also due to the censorship of such information and even media warnings against taking this vitamin. It is astonishing that some "scientists" (pharmaceutical lobbyists), were able to make many people believe something that would only be conceivable after a step in human evolution: a hormone formed from vitamin D3, which is regulating many thousands of immunologically relevant genes over millions of years of evolutionary history, was suddenly no longer relevant for our immune defense with COVID-19. Instead, our survival depended on genetically modified viral material encoding the SARS-CoV-2 spike protein, which was injected at short intervals and propagandized as a vaccination.

Thus, the belief in the sacred vaccine was at the same time a belief in the omnipotence of man. In a modern age in which more and more people felt lonely and weak (the strategy of isolation and lockdowns did the rest), this belief gave hope, albeit a false and very dangerous one: if we want, we can defeat any disease. But you don't need to be a doctor or a molecular biologist to understand that no drug, including vaccination, can compensate for a deficiency of essential micronutrients, just as no pill can cure thirst. We are not outside of nature. Victory over nature would only be possible if we simultaneously defeated ourselves. Unfortunately, with the concerted support of the technocratic elite, we are approaching this paradox in leaps and bounds.

He Who Walks over Corpses Is Not to Be Trusted

Man kills not only for food or defense but also for power, ideologies, and beliefs, as documented human history has shown time and again. All documented wars are based on this dangerous trait of *Homo sapiens*. Thus, it is not surprising that anything that could in any way harm the belief in the vaccine was censored, even if it had deadly consequences. In fact, COVID-19 vaccines have the highest rate of fatal adverse events of any vaccine on the market, according to data from the US Vaccine Adverse Event Reporting System, or VAERS. In 2021 alone, there were more than seventy-five times as many reports of deaths from the mRNA injection program following COVID-19 vaccination as compared to the average for *all* vaccinations worldwide in the previous thirty years (21,382 versus 282 reports), as shown in figure 1.[81] With studies showing that less than

1 percent of all serious vaccine adverse events are likely actually reported to VAERS due to so-called underreporting,[82] there may have been several million deaths from mRNA injections worldwide in 2021 alone.

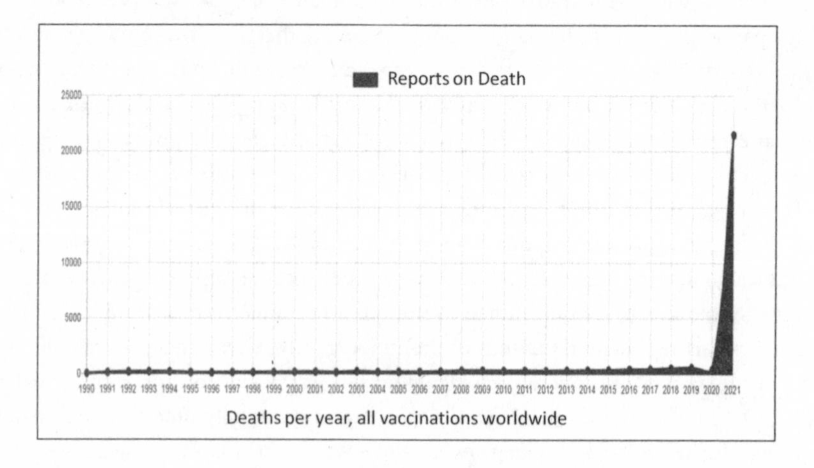

Figure 1

The viral genome administered as a vaccine may persist in the body for many months,[83] during which time it can cause massive inflammation (more on this later in chapter 4). In addition to acute, sometimes fatal, myocarditis in healthy young people and emerging autoimmune diseases, some of which do not yet have clinical names, it acts as a long-term accelerant of all preexisting chronic inflammatory diseases.[84] This makes it difficult to prove a link to vaccination in the event of a specific death, since modern malnutrition and harmful environmental influences increase the likelihood of cancer, heart attack, or stroke from year to year anyway.

However, in addition to the VAERS data, there is further statistical evidence of an association between increased mortality and mRNA injections. The lethal side effects, which can be convincingly attributed to the mode of action of the spike protein and other additives in the injections, are the logical explanation for the excess mortality observed worldwide. Contrary to reports from 2020, this excess mortality actually did not begin until the start of the vaccination campaigns. This also to the chagrin of life insurers: "We are seeing, right now, the highest death rates we have seen in the history of this business—not just at OneAmerica," reported the company's CEO, Scott Davison, at an online press conference hosted by the Indiana Chamber of Commerce for 2021.[85] Davison said the data is the same for all players in the industry, noting that it is not older people who are dying but "primarily working-age people eighteen to sixty-four." "And what we saw just in third quarter, we're seeing it continue into fourth quarter, is that death rates are up

40 percent over what they were prepandemic," he continued. He said it's important to remember that life insurers thrive on the proper use of numbers. They are able to calculate probabilities in a professional and therefore very accurate way and draw the right conclusions. "Just to give you an idea of how bad that is, a three-sigma or a one-in-two-hundred-year catastrophe would be 10 percent increase over prepandemic," he said. "So 40 percent is just unheard of." In Germany, excess mortality for the entire population in December 2022 was 19 percent higher than the previous year, the German Federal Statistical Office was forced to admit in its press release of January 10, 2023.[86]

Davison's insurance company has also seen an increase in disability claims. Initially the claims were short-term, but since then there has been a significant increase in long-term claims as well. At the same news conference where Davison spoke, Brian Tabor, the president of the Indiana Hospital Association, said that hospitals across the state are being flooded with patients "with many different conditions," saying "unfortunately, the average Hoosiers' [a resident of the state of Indiana] health has declined during the pandemic." These dire consequences stand in stark contradiction to the Great Narrative that ultimately proclaims global health as the highest good and thus justifies the WHO-led vaccination program. A very similar contradiction underlies the system of Huxley's *Brave New World*.

The WHO was founded in 1948 with a mandate to act as a guiding and coordinating authority for international health work. However, this noble goal is corrupted by the fact that this powerful organization, which can single-handedly determine which viral variant is to be classified as a pandemic and how the entire global community should respond, is now 80 percent funded by private donors and foundations. As early as April 2017, for example, *Zeit Online* published the article "The Secret WHO Boss Is Called Bill Gates."[87] According to another *SWR* investigation from September 2020, entitled "WHO on the Begging Stick: What's Healthy, Bill Gates Determines," the Bill & Melinda Gates Foundation is the largest private donor, having given a total of $2.5 billion to the WHO since the turn of the millennium.[88] The report says rich private donors are manipulating WHO policies with disastrous consequences: "This harms developing countries—and many poor sick people." But now, at the latest since the experimental vaccination programs with COVID-19 could be expanded globally, it also harms a large number of people in the richer countries of the global North.

In keeping with the technocratic agenda of global vaccination against all possible microbial threats, the WHO is pushing a program called One Health. Under this program, "government officials, researchers and workers across sectors at the local, national, regional and global levels should implement joint responses to health threats."[89] The program "includes developing shared databases and surveillance across different sectors." At the latest, this is where Huxley's vision of an affluent society begins, in which turmoil, misery, and disease are overcome—but freedom, art, and ultimately humanity also fall by the wayside. To this end, as was announced at the beginning of 2023, the WHO is to be authorized by all of its 194 member states to take control of national health systems in the event of further pandemics (which will then probably include new variants of the influenza virus, as are known to evolve every year).[90] It would then definitely be a world government not elected by the world's citizens and thus democratically legitimized, operating in permanent pandemic mode in the age of permapandemics (as the *WEF Risk Report 2023* stated it). Once the treaties are signed and ratified, Bill Gates will be crowned health dictator with global powers as shadow head of the WHO. At the same time, One Health is already nothing more than a macabre empty phrase, as should be clear by now to anyone directly or indirectly affected by the harmful effects of lockdowns, face masks, and novel gene therapy. In other words, the WHO, as an unelected but cash-rich organization of superrich technocrats, is well on its way to becoming a world health dictatorship (the help of many WEF young global leaders in political office is certainly contributing to this), because it can decide for itself what is to be considered a pandemic and what is not. It must be classified as a highly dangerous organization, since the WHO does not invest the power it has been given in meaningful health measures at all (as not only COVID-19 has taught us). Instead, under the pretext of protecting health, it rather reforms governments all over the world and gradually dismantles the rights and freedoms of citizens. (See also "Children Unwanted!" in chapter 6 for the illegal machinations of the WHO for birth control.) Its real aim appears to be to use a staged health issue to gain political influence over the nations of the world in a way that only a world government could otherwise achieve.

Health Dictatorship

Calling for a "whole-of-government, whole-of-society approach" to addressing future health emergencies, twenty-three heads of state and government and the WHO director general joined European Council President Charles Michel in signing a position paper outlining a possible new, international treaty on pandemics: "The main goal of this treaty would be to foster an all-of-government and all-of-society approach, strengthening national, regional and global capacities and resilience to future pandemics," the leaders wrote.[91] "This includes greatly enhancing international cooperation to improve, for example, alert systems, data-sharing, research, and local, regional and global production and distribution of medical and public health counter measures, such as vaccines, medicines, diagnostics and personal protective equipment."

Outside analysis shows that the proposed pandemic treaty gives the WHO the right to impose the same "control measures" on all countries in the world in the event of a pandemic it identifies.[92] "There will be other pandemics and other major health emergencies. No single government or multilateral agency can address this threat alone," the WHO website quotes the leaders (many of whom are WEF young global leaders): "The question is not if, but when. Together, we must be better prepared to predict, prevent, detect, assess, and effectively respond to pandemics in a highly coordinated fashion. The COVID-19 pandemic has been a stark and painful reminder that nobody is safe until everyone is safe."[93] According to the article, the proposed treaty "would be rooted in the constitution of the World Health Organization, drawing in other relevant organizations key to this endeavour, in support of the principle of health for all. Existing global health instruments, especially the International Health Regulations, would underpin such a treaty, ensuring a firm and tested foundation on which we can build and improve." In fact, in Germany and Austria (and probably in almost all countries), the relevant national laws are already being prepared for a WHO dictatorship (see also chapter 5 sidebar: *With Perceived Incompetence to World Domination*).[94] According to experts, an "imminent" pandemic could then be enough to suspend basic rights worldwide at the instigation of the WHO.

Contrary to the WHO's One Health goal, the immense financial flows diverted to some of the economic sectors affected by the lockdowns during the outbreak led to a drastic reduction in development aid spending, according to research by the United Nations Children's Fund (UNICEF). According to UNICEF, this led to a decrease in development assistance of about 30 percent during the SARS-CoV-2 outbreak and up to 75 to 100 percent during the first lockdown, resulting in additional humanitarian crises in affected countries.[95] UNICEF estimates that this could cost well over a million additional children their lives—not from COVID-19 but from the effects of our actions against it.[96] The much-vaunted *solidarity* or *protection of others*, the buzzwords used to build up pressure for vaccination even among those who do not see themselves as at risk, would have a very different effect on policy if they were meant seriously.

The list of issues that could be used to show that the WHO and its technocrats, with their radical interventions in the economy, medicine, and private life, are not really concerned with proportionate measures to save human lives is long. In the case of COVID-19, a vitamin D–awareness campaign would have sufficed. In other areas, too, WHO could prove its noble intentions in many more ways. For example, more people around the world will die each year from secondhand smoke and poor air quality than from COVID-19 if nothing is done. According to a report published in 2019 by the US Health Effects Institute, 95 percent of all children worldwide now breathe only polluted air.[97] While in the United States and many countries around the world children who are perfectly safe from COVID-19 are free to receive gene injections, there is no even remotely comparable effort to stop smoking at home or in the car in the presence of children. While the WEF's short postevent videos express enthusiasm that the air and water quality in otherwise heavily polluted places around the world has improved significantly as a result of the imposed lockdowns, they do not put into perspective the immense collateral damage of this radical and short-lived measure.

Obviously, these COVID-19 measures were not introduced to address the air problems and would not be suitable for doing so, if only because they are only temporarily enforceable. According to the Ethiopian director general of the WHO, Dr. Tedros Adhanom Ghebreyesus, we are poisoning millions of children (actually more than two billion, according to studies) with exhaust fumes and ruining their lives.[98] "Air pollution is stunting our children's brains, affecting their health in more ways than we suspected," says Dr. Maria Neira, director, Department of Public Health, Environmental and Social Determinants of Health at WHO. They suffer more from asthma and respiratory infections, which killed more than six hundred thousand children under five in 2016 alone, according to WHO statistics, the agency said in its 2018 report. Polluted air is responsible for one in ten deaths of children under five worldwide, according to the WHO.

In comparison, virtually no children die from COVID-19, yet pregnant women are already being vaccinated to protect their newborns from this usually harmless infection, as recommended by the CDC: "Getting flu, Tdap (tetanus, diphtheria, and pertussis), and COVID-19 vaccines while you're pregnant helps your body create protective antibodies (proteins produced by the body to fight off diseases), and you can pass on those antibodies to your baby. These antibodies can help protect your baby from those diseases during the first few months of life."[99] But because young, healthy people do not need protection, experimental gene injections against COVID-19 will only have side effects, even until age sixty, according to a Stanford University study published online in October 2022.[100] Since the global vaccination program against SARS-CoV-2 began, the number of stillbirths resulting from vaccination has increased worldwide at an unprecedented rate, as shown in the VAERS graph (figure 2).[101] The smaller wave from 2007 to 2013 was due to HPV vaccination for cervical cancer in adolescents. As with all vaccine adverse event reports, an underreporting factor of one hundred is present, so there could have been several hundred thousand miscarriages and stillbirths as a result of mRNA injections as early as 2021.

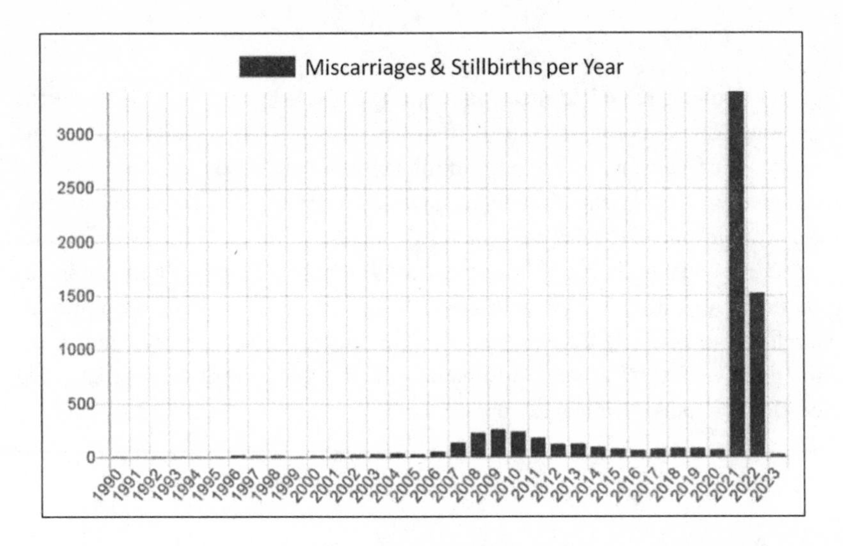

Figure 2

On the Way to Decanting?

After the US Food and Drug Administration (FDA) lost a Freedom of Information Act lawsuit in a US court case in January 2022, Pfizer must make the side effect data on the BioNTech COVID-19 vaccine public.[102] Since then, a group of experts led by Naomi Wolf has been analyzing what she calls a "crime against humanity" of "unprecedented proportions" in the cover-up and acceptance of the serious side-effect profile. In a foreword to the analysts' report, she summarizes, "Most seriously of all, you will see a 360-degree attack on human reproductive capability: with harms to sperm count, testes, sperm motility; harms to ovaries, menstrual cycles, placentas; you will see that over 80 percent of the pregnancies in one section of the Pfizer documents ended in spontaneous abortion or miscarriage. You will see that 72 percent of the adverse events in one section of the documents were in women, and that 16 percent of those were 'reproductive disorders,' in Pfizer's own words."[103]

Unfortunately, this brings us one step closer to Huxley's dystopia, because under the circumstances described, humanity would even be existentially dependent on technological support for human reproduction. Such technological solutions are already being envisioned, for example in the form of the EctoLife artificial womb facility. Although EctoLife is not yet an active or planned company, according to biotechnologist and science communicator Hashem Al-Ghaili, who created the impressive concept video, it shows us what childbirth might look like in the future. The facility, with thousands of fully monitored artificial wombs, would be powered entirely by renewable energy and controlled by artificial intelligence. It's conceivable that Al-Ghaili's concept has the impact of the COVID-19 global vaccination campaign in mind. According to Al-Ghaili, "miscarriage and low sperm count are no longer an issue with EctoLife. In Vitro Fertilization is used prior to placing your baby's fertilized embryo inside the growth pod to create and select the most viable and genetically superior embryo, giving your baby a chance to develop without any biological obstacles."[104]

But this, too, does not seem to interest those responsible at the WHO. Nor do the far more serious problems in the global health system and in human lifestyles that need to be addressed, both among children and adults. For example, nine out of ten deaths worldwide are due to unhealthy lifestyles, especially malnutrition and undernutrition. In the rich countries of the global North, secondary diseases such as diabetes, obesity, cardiovascular disease, and cancer dominate daily life, while in the poor countries of the global South, people are dying of hunger. In 2019 high blood pressure would kill 10.8 million people worldwide, followed by tobacco addiction with 8.7 million deaths, unhealthy diets with too little fruit and too much salt with 7.9 million deaths, air pollution with 6.7 million deaths, and type 2 diabetes mellitus with 6.5 million deaths.[105]

If the technocrats at the WHO and their allies in the member states were really serious about One Health, then the glaring iodine deficiency in large parts of the world, for example, would have to be high on the agenda, especially since the cost of doing so would be minimal. After all, iodine is the essential component of thyroid hormones, the function of which is indispensable for healthy brain development.[106]

In plain language, without iodine, there would be no thyroid hormones, which are responsible for, among other things, regulating metabolic processes and stimulating body and organ growth. The human body can only store a very limited amount of iodine. As an essential trace element, it must be consumed regularly with food. It enters the blood passively via the gastrointestinal tract and from there actively enters the thyroid gland. The thyroid gland consumes up to 80 percent of the iodine ingested daily.

Iodine deficiency in the first years of life leads to what is known as cretinism, an extreme form of intelligence reduction or mental underdevelopment.[107] According to an article published in 2017, more than 300 million children worldwide are not developing to their full mental potential due to iodine deficiency alone.[108] Overall, this results in an average global IQ loss of ten to fifteen points, according to estimates from further studies.[109] It is hard to believe that iodine deficiency is still a problem in the twenty-first century. After all, the daily iodine requirement of an adult of about 0.15 milligrams could easily be met with about five grams of iodized table salt in addition to a balanced diet.[110] Children need even less, depending on their age. The victims of this policy, which should more accurately be called "Two Health," are mainly in Africa.[111] A 2018 study found that up to two-thirds of pregnant women studied had suboptimal iodine levels, with tragic consequences for their offspring.[112] Even in African countries classified as iodine sufficient by the WHO, researchers found a high prevalence (number of cases of the disease in the population considered at a given time or during a given period) of iodine deficiency in pregnancy.[113]

Welcome to the *Brave New World* of the epsilons, the mentally immature or underdeveloped working slaves à la Huxley. If one does not want to rule out ruthlessness in that respect, one may get the impression that the only partial implementation of these elementary insights in the world is not completely coincidental. From the capitalist point of view, it is undoubtedly only opportune to regard Africa as a source of raw materials for the industrialized countries of the global North, and to nip in the bud any intellectual ambitions of these peoples by undersupplying them with essential nutrients.

But even in the wealthier countries with higher average levels of education, greater economic power, and global influence, the diet is in many ways far from optimal if a truly species-appropriate diet is taken as a benchmark. As a result, even in these countries, few children can develop their full mental capacity, and few adults can maintain it without great effort or lifestyle changes. This discrepancy between our natural needs and actual conditions has been exacerbated by the COVID-19 measures, with dramatic consequences not only for the human psyche and thinking abilities but also for the preservation of our individuality, creativity, and self-determination (more on this in the following chapters).

Erasing the Cultural Operating System on the Individual Hard Drive

These few serious examples should have made it clear that the protagonists of the Great Reset are not philanthropists, even if they like to present themselves as such.[114] Claiming that health for all is the highest priority, the protagonists push the Great Reset with no regard for the loss of health and human life, and thus with undoubtedly deadly determination. But contrary to what the term suggests, this is not a reboot, as one would do with a computer that is no longer functioning properly. Rather, the technocrats are installing a new operating system of global interaction, which is designed to allow them to digitally monitor and thus control the future of every individual, and therefore the entire global community, at will.

The existing culture, or operating system, of society evolved through many individual ideas that proved useful in the free market of human coexistence. What did not work was gradually replaced. These were always small steps, adapted to local conditions. The new operating system, however, will put an abrupt end to this micro- and macrocultural evolutionary process. "But what is our culture, which we thought durable, to be replaced with?" asks Naomi Wolf in her book *The Bodies of Others*. In it, she provides an answer, which is as frightening as it is realistic: "A world managed by machines and mediated via digital interfaces; a world predicated on cruelty, without human empathy as an organizing principle; a world in which national boundaries, cultures, and languages are drained of meaning, in which institutions embody only the goals of distant meta-national oligarchs, a world organized for the benefit of massive pharmaceutical companies, a few global tech giants and technocrats, and a tyrannical superpower that is our deadly adversary. In short, a world redesigned to ensure the dominance forever of these distant elites, both in geopolitical and via market share."[115]

It is becoming increasingly clear that we are rapidly moving toward a dystopian future in which human life will be largely controlled by computers and their algorithms. A few technocrats with enormous influence, sitting at the levers of power, controlling society with the help of artificial intelligence (AI) based on a social scoring system, will determine the entire development of human civilization—human culture will not exist anymore. In 2017 Germany's Federal Ministry of the Interior (*Bundesinnenministerium*, or BMI) presented the *Smart City Charta*, which reads like a conceptual blueprint for such a world. It talks about how to "sustainably shape the digital transformation in municipalities." the introduction says, "For digitization to have a lasting effect in municipalities, acceptance by users and especially by people will be crucial."[116] *Users* of digitization and *people* obviously have different meanings here. In any case, the beneficiaries of the enormous flood of data in such a smart city will be the elite technocrats through the optimization of the algorithms of their AI, which will monitor everything and will increasingly regulate all areas of life. This is then cloaked in terms such as "integrated and sustainable urban development," which means nothing more than "digitally analyzed, algorithmically controlled city administration." The BMI paper states that the *Smart City Charta* provides important guidance.[117] However, according to the German government, this is "only a first step on the way to truly smarter cities."

What could the next steps be, and where will they lead users or AI and thus people? Possible answers were provided in a keynote speech by Roope Mokka, founder of the Finnish think tank Demos Helsinki, which can also be read in BMI's *Smart City Charta*. In the chapter "Smart City in the era of the Internet of NO Things," Mokka describes his visions of a hyperconnected planet in six points:[118]

1. Super Resource-Efficient Society

"A society in which no building stands empty, but is always in optimal use [this only works if there is no more possession; see point 3]. No cars run empty. New devices and machines generate their own energy. For those working on energy harvesting sensors [harvesting small amounts of electrical energy from sources such as ambient temperature, vibration, or air currents for low-power mobile devices], the discussion of centralized, large power plants seems pointless."

2. Post-Choice Society

"Artificial intelligence will replace choice: We will never have to decide which bus or train to take, just the fastest way from A to B. We will never forget our keys, wallet or watch." [Humans will increasingly lose their ability to think because AI will do most of the thinking for them.]

3. Post-Ownership Society **["I own nothing, have no privacy, and life has never been better."]**

"Thanks to information about available shared goods and resources, it makes less sense to own anything: perhaps private property will indeed become a luxury. Data may complement or replace money as currency." [Digital currency enables digital control, especially in combination with a social scoring system: those who do not comply are no longer able to pay. I'll have more on this under "Permanent Control of Success" in chapter 5.]

4. Post-Market Society **[This society is one without a free market.]**

"At their core, markets are information systems that allocate resources. As an information system, however, a market functions very simply. It simply communicates that a person bough' this or that, but we don't know why. In the future, sensors can provide us with better data than markets." [If the AI knows why we have bought or want to buy something, it can also decide for us whether this makes sense or is justified from a certain point of view, such as climate protection—always according to the respective technocratic guidelines.]

5. Post-Energy Society

"To be ubiquitous, sensors must be energy efficient and self-sufficient. [In other words, control must never and will never be broken.] For a data revolution to occur, energy harvesting— the ability to generate and store energy at the macro-, micro-, or nanoscale—must become commonplace."

6. Post-Voting Society

"Knowing exactly what people do and want reduces the need for elections, majority rule or voting. Behavioral data can replace democracy as the social feedback system." [In other words, democracy is being exposed for what it already is from a technocratic point of view: the illusion of having a voice. Propaganda, a colorful, unified party landscape, and its "representative" character, which allows all political actors to break promises, have long since ensured this.]

These ideas of the German BMI draft do not come by surprise; actually, they correlate closely with those of the protagonists of the Great Reset or WEF and their "8 Predictions for the World in 2030."[119] A closer look at the first of these eight predictions will suffice at this point: "I don't own anything. I don't own a car. I don't own a house. I don't own any appliances or any clothes," the author, Ceri Parker, quotes Danish MP Ida Auken and then tells us in Auken's words, "Shopping is a distant memory in the city of 2030, whose inhabitants have cracked clean energy and borrow what they need on demand." But then Auken gets reflective and you read, "It sounds utopian," or too good to be true, "until she mentions that their every move is tracked," which I guess also worries Auken a bit. According to Auken, "outside the city live swathes of discontents," which she calls "the ultimate vision of a society split in two."

You, and certainly I, may be among these discontented people. That these people will live like savages in *Brave New World* in reservations is Auken's "biggest concern." And she's already speaking in the past tense, looking back from the year 2030, about all the people "we lost on the way. Those who decided it was getting to be too much, all this technology."[120] Auken is concerned here with all those people "who felt obsolete and useless when robots and AI took over big parts of our jobs. Those who got upset with the political system and turned against it. They live different kind of lives outside of the city. Some have formed little self-supplying communities."

This life outside the smart city would then actually resemble more a reset, a return to a time when there were still communities of people who supported each other (more on this in chapter 7). Only those who still want to secure a bit of uncontrolled freedom would live outside of technocratic supremacy and control. Remarkably, even the Great Reset enthusiast Auken, for all her "technocratic good fortune," would probably have liked to retain some of that freedom: "Once in awhile [*sic*] I get annoyed about the fact that I have no real privacy. No where I can go and not be registered. I know that, somewhere, everything I do, think and dream of is recorded. I just hope that nobody will use it against me." But can we really be sure of that? Those who are prepared to give up thinking for themselves and making decisions for themselves may one day find themselves in the situation illustrated by Auken as she talks about shopping in 2030: "Sometimes I find this fun, and sometimes I just want the algorithm to do it for me. It knows my taste better than I do by now." As soon as an AI can correct conclusions faster than a human being, and even knows more precisely what one wants, the fateful questions will be asked for us: What is the actual meaning and purpose of human existence? What role should man (still) play on earth (more on this in the last chapter)?

But if what Mokka or Auken describe as a technocratic vision was to become a reality—and very powerful forces are at work trying to steer our society toward just such a future—we "normal people" will live like in a zoo, with the AI as our keeper. It determines who gets what to eat and who is allowed to live where and when, always depending on their behavior, their social score—under rules determined by the technocrats by specifying which activities promise points and which lead to deductions, closely monitored and logged by the AI. Writing or reading a book critical of the system (like this one) could lead to points being deducted and, consequently, to all sorts of sanctions.

The danger that nonconformist, critical individuals pose to totalitarian systems should not be underestimated; those systems aim to take away as much freedom as possible from the individual through strict guidelines. Plenty of historical examples show how systems deal with such disruption. Think of the revolutionary reorganization of the Soviet Union under Stalin's dictatorship, Mao Tse-tung's Cultural Revolution, or, more recently, the COVID-19 health dictatorship. All of these ideological power games cost humanity millions of lives because some influential people believed they knew how the world should be organized and how community life should be arranged down to the last detail, and they were willing to step over corpses for their delusion. However, the effectiveness of the suppression of dissident individuals is increasing with the advancement of psychological, biochemical, and technological knowledge, and more subtle but more effective means can be used, as I will show.

Social control by means of AI only works well if human behavior is easily predictable or calculable. In such a system, individuality and creativity, which have been essential characteristics of mankind up to now, are like sand in the gears. The ability to think independently is a dangerous variable for an AI algorithm because of unpredictability. An authentic, self-determined, and deep personality follows nonlogical rather than linear principles; emotions and gut feelings often play a significant role. AI would be more inefficient or even incapable of monitoring, controlling, and predicting humanity composed of many such people. Thus, the individuality and creativity of the human mind would remain a constant threat to the stability of an AI-controlled society.

Huxley has the technocratic world controllers in *Brave New World* come up with a solution for this. It is based on the realization that individual personality is formed on the basis of two significant influencing factors: cultural history and the individual experiences in a given context. These two important foundations of human individuality, both independent of the genetic component, therefore had to be brought under control. Once again, this reveals an impressive parallel between fiction and reality: The Great Reset aims to get the factor of cultural history under control by radically reshaping this cultural operating system of individuals by softening, deleting, and selectively replacing existing rules of coexistence. Through this approach, cultures that have grown naturally in all areas of the world are replaced by a unified, retold story, the technocratic narrative that presents us with propertyless happiness and AI-controlled life in smart cities as the logical next step in human-technological development.

Something similar plays out in Orwell's *1984*, in which the past is subject to daily but retroactive changeability. And in Huxley's case, too, the technocratic narrative or brave new world begins with an upheaval after the end of the war, when the technocratic elite realizes that controlling humanity by means of mental manipulation works better in the long run. Historical books, novels, art, and such are thus destroyed in *1984* and unwanted in Huxley's dystopia, as one of his world controllers tells us: "History is bunk."[121] This is reminiscent of the true story of Diego de Landa (1524–1579), who, as Bishop of Yucatán in present-day Mexico, missionized the indigenous Maya. He had all manuscripts written in Mayan that he could get his hands on burned, especially those relating to Mayan history and culture. The goal was to deprive them of the possibility of finding their way back to their ancient culture and beliefs.[122] The successive elimination of our present cultural peculiarities could now gradually give rise to the "creatures without history" mentioned at the beginning of this chapter by the Nyder group of authors, to be led by Schwab's YGL or GLT.

But the erasure of cultural identity would not be enough to completely eliminate individuality. The erasure of individual history would also be necessary to reduce the destabilizing danger posed by creative influence on the system to be stabilized by an AI. This would only succeed if the history or personal memories were replaced by the narrative of the technocrats within the framework of a correspondingly large mental reset. According to the latest neurobiological findings on how our brains maintain individuality and the mental capacity for lifelong creative thinking, such a thing is indeed possible. As I will show, all the prerequisites for this have been created by the COVID-19 measures, so that it can be assumed that a targeted conformist reprogramming and depersonalization is part of the Great Reset program, possibly even its core. That such a thing is being attempted is not implausible but rather a compelling conclusion from the mere fact that the haughty concept of the Great Reset is in itself something quite different from a grand general reboot, as the name belittlingly suggests. It represents a blunt power grab by a small, self-proclaimed technocratic elite with world-power fantasies who want to impose their ideas on the rest of humanity by undemocratic means. Without mental influence, such a thing would be completely unthinkable. But people, after appropriate mental reprogramming, would not resist this new world order according to the plans of Schwab and company. They might even find it beautiful, as Auken imagines—once they have lost the ability to think for themselves.

Uniformity and conformity as a means of social stabilization is anything but a new principle—what is new are the sophisticated technological possibilities that make these goals easier to achieve. In *Brave New World*, Huxley has one of his world controllers explain: "No civilization without social stability. No social stability without individual stability."[123] Although the purpose of human existence lies in an "intensification and refining of consciousness, some enlargement of knowledge," Huxley's world controller explains later, this would not be admissible "in the present circumstances."[124] We are reminded of the crisis-ridden present, which is only too familiar with the argument that we cannot afford the obvious because of the need to solve urgent problems. The states of emergency, which cannot be resolved from the outset and therefore last forever, may not be accidental phenomena either, such as the wars against the natural mutation of viruses or for access to resources, armed conflicts over national borders and, last but not least, the permanent war against the change of the world climate. Therefore, all these wars may not even be seen as a means to the end of a Great Reset but ultimately as a war against the human brain, deliberately provoked and carried out to establish and permanently secure the technocratic domination of the world.

This hypothesis provides a good indication of the real reason for this alleged war mania, as well as for almost everything that we have had to experience and endure in recent years as incomprehensible, sometimes seemingly arbitrary restrictions on our freedoms. Because a hypothesis permits statements about the future, I undertake here the attempt to prove the hypothesis and to present the possible master plan for the abolition of our individuality and creativity, as it began to reveal itself to me in the idyll of Corsica. However, I must first take a closer look at the central mechanism on which individuality and creativity and the ability to think for oneself are based.

CHAPTER 2

INDIVIDUALITY, CREATIVITY, AND THE ABILITY TO THINK FOR ONESELF

What the herd hates most is the one who thinks differently; it is not so much the opinion itself, but the audacity of wanting to think for themselves, something that they do not know how to do.

— Arthur Schopenhauer (1788–1860)

Cultural Evolution

Evolution occurs when a random genetic change gives the carrier of the genetic material the advantage of being able to survive and, more importantly, reproduce more efficiently. As a result, his or her genetic material becomes the dominant genetic material until further changes allow the individual to adapt even better to the conditions of life. Constant changes in the environment (which includes all other evolving creatures) continue to drive this selection mechanism toward a randomly altered but ever better adapted genome. Thus, chance and necessity are equally the driving forces of any evolutionary development, as described by the French molecular biologist and Nobel laureate Jacques Lucien Monod (1910–1976) in his natural philosophical work of the same name.[1]

However, due to advanced cultural development, human adaptation to new or changing living conditions is now less genetic and more technological. We ourselves have become the engine of rapid change in nature. Our now dominant influence on our environment through technology (geochronologically, we speak of the Anthropocene) may be one of the reasons why, despite the natural origin of our species, we mistakenly believe ourselves to be outside of nature. The fact that we have emerged from this natural process does not mean that we have outgrown it. On the contrary, the selection conditions of that time are our needs of today. The fatal consequences of this misbelief can be seen, among other things, in the pandemic scale of the so-called diseases of civilization, including the way humankind reacted to the COVID-19 pandemic and how we are in the process of losing our humanity; more on this later. Furthermore, technological solutions are faster than genetic adaptations. For example, building dams to create new habitats or to protect already populated areas from flooding has proven beneficial to our species. We do not have to rely on a long natural adaptation process (like developing gills, which are actually created during human embryonic development, but are then remodeled into other structures again).

Nevertheless, every technical innovation is also subject to a basically identical evolutionary mechanism of chance and necessity. People have ideas; those that are most likely to satisfy a certain need or solve a certain problem are held on to and investigated further. This is the first step of selection. The second then is usually experimental verification. Sometimes a solution abruptly influences the lives of very many people; then we speak of a cultural development. The invention of the automobile or the cell phone was thus subject to evolutionary mechanisms analogous to mutation (random ideas) and selection (better adaptation to living conditions or satisfaction of a need), just like the emergence of new species first described by Darwin. And as with all phenomena in which chance plays a role, this is a statistically predictable process. For example, the more viruses that exist or circulate, the greater the probability that we will come into contact with one that can bypass our immune system. In the case of the viruses that infect our respiratory tract, such as influenza, RSV, or coronavirus, such mutations tend to be very common because their genome consists of single-stranded RNA, which does not allow for proofreading as our double-stranded DNA-based genome. The high number of these seasonal viruses produced worldwide in the course of an infection wave and the very high mutation rate are the two main reasons why herd immunity can never develop against these viruses and vaccination programs are doomed to fail.[2] The secret of the virus's success is the strategy of a high reproduction rate combined with a high mutation rate.

The same basic statistical principle also applies to human innovation processes when we need a lifesaving idea (for example, due to drastically deteriorating living conditions). *Homo sapiens* has been so successful or adaptable because, in the enormous diversity of human individuality, always some individuals, with one or a series of creative thoughts, have been able to change their own lives and thus the lives of many others in a particularly powerful way. This creativity has made possible the explosive growth of humanity during the past few centuries, which in turn increased the likelihood that among the many newcomers will be someone with a significant idea for a culture-changing invention who will implement it. Humans are particularly good at this compared to their closest relatives in the animal kingdom. This is the result of a study conducted by the Max Planck Institute for Evolutionary Anthropology in Leipzig, Germany: While the two-and-a-half-year-old infants hardly differed from chimpanzee or orangutan boys in any of the cognitive areas examined—neither in spatial imagination, arithmetic, nor the understanding of causal relationships—they turned out to be "ultrasocial learning machines," as Dutch historian Rutger Bregman calls them.[3] Thanks to so-called mirror neurons, which become active when we observe others, we learn better than any other species from the behavior of others and then pass this knowledge on.[4] As the source of empathy, they may be the neural secret of humankind's conquest of the earth, which was only made possible by the formation of complex social systems.

In the future, too, a society will be more likely to produce innovative solutions the more genuine individuals with unique creativity (i.e., not just "phenotypically uniform creatures") approach a problem, and the broader and more diverse their wealth of experience. Let us call this the degree of their individuality. The sum of all individuals multiplied by their degree of individuality thus gives the degree of innovative capacity of a society. If an elitist technocratic minority wants to ensure that only its own ideas of how humanity should live are accepted unchallenged in the long run, it must keep the global capacity for innovation as small as possible or massively reduce it. Only then can a ruling elite minimize the likelihood of creative ideas, which might become a threat to their claim to power, arising by chance—even though implementations of such ideas could lead to a better outcome for humanity. The goal must therefore be not only to muzzle the most creative minds through censorship and the threat of punishment (which is already increasingly happening in certain fields of research, especially since 2020) but also to permanently deprive all people of their individuality in order to make them "happy without possessions." But how are "phenotypically uniform creatures" to be created when cloning and bottle-ripening under oxygen deprivation (so far) only succeed in novels?

The Value of Individuation

The neuronal correlate of our individuality is the uniqueness of our brain. Let us go into some detail here, because doing so is worthwhile. Then we can also understand the large-scale attack we are up against and protect ourselves effectively.

The brain is made up of hundreds of billions of nerve cells, each of which is networked in a unique way via hundreds to hundreds of thousands of connections. Deviations in the networking plan are initially due to mostly minor differences in the genetic makeup of each individual, providing the first level of uniqueness. But even identical twins develop different personalities despite having identical genetic material because each personal experience influences the networking and structure of the maturing brain while it is developing in the womb. This process of individuation takes place throughout life because, after all, our brain is constantly changing and remains plastic and malleable until old age. This plasticity is the basis for lifelong learning and ultimately for our individuality and creativity. Thus, our individual personality is essentially the product of our special, personal experiences that make each of us unique. This uniqueness makes for social diversity, and this in turn has been the primary driver of our sociocultural evolution to date.

The perception of our individuality arises from the elementary experience of the recognition of the ego and the differentiation from others. In a process of trial and error, even the young child gradually develops its own personality. Individuality can thus be described from the inside, as a mental state and subjective relationship to others, or as a conscious perception of the environment as the outside world. This uniquely enables each individual to act in a self-determined way. Individuality, on the other hand, is recognizable from the outside. It can be seen in a person's actions and reactions, interests, social behavior, or views in all areas of life. Individuality is therefore always a combination of many individual characteristics of a person, which both characterize him and make him an individual (in the Latin root, "indivisible") or unique.

Distinguish between the terms *individualized*, in the sense of isolated, and *individuality*, in the sense of uniqueness, is important. The isolation of the individual, such as through the gradual disappearance of the extended family, makes people in modern societies more and more lone fighters and thus more and more dependent on state care. We see the devastating consequences in the overcrowded nursing homes.

But much earlier in life we are under the direction of state institutions that determine what even children have to believe and know in life to become an integrated part of a modern economic society. This is based primarily on consumption, productivity, and economic growth, which at their core have nothing to do with the individual's purpose in life. This process begins in infancy, in the nursery, where life is already determined by countless rules of conduct. Far too early in childhood, even the youngest children must learn to sit still and obey without contradiction. For more and more children, government indoctrination begins even before they are able to form their own opinions. We are all raised to believe in the same value system, ironically learning to believe in our uniqueness. But since everyone is ultimately expected to believe and behave in the same way, the development of profound individuality is rendered absurd from the outset. The content of education is also largely standardized, which runs counter to the development of individuals with their own broad range of experiences. The most elementary possibility for the development of one's own personality, namely free play with one another, is gradually being lost under the prevailing conditions of the market economy. One of the most influential researchers on the importance of play for mental and psychological development, Brian Sutton-Smith (1924–2015), strongly put it this way: "The opposite of play is [not work, but] depression!"[5]

Homo ludens

Man is a social being who learns by playing with his fellows. Free play, as it develops in children, is fundamental for early learning and for one's own experiences. From this, an independent and individual personality can develop. In his 2011 article "The Decline of Play and the Rise of Psychopathology in Children and Adolescents," US psychology researcher Peter Otis Gray writes, "Over the past half century, in the United States and other developed nations, children's free play with other children has declined sharply. Over the same period, anxiety, depression, suicide, feelings of helplessness, and narcissism have increased sharply in children, adolescents, and young adults."[6] The causal role of this historical decline in free play in the rise of psychopathology in young people is quickly explained: "Play functions as the major means by which children (1) develop intrinsic interests and competencies; (2) learn how to make decisions, solve problems, exert self-control, and follow rules; (3) learn to regulate their emotions; (4) make friends and learn to get along with others as equals; and (5) experience joy. Through all of these effects, play promotes mental health," Gray said. The consequences of an increasingly externally controlled and timed childhood are dramatic, including for the future of all humanity, he continued, since "you can't teach creativity; all you can do is let it blossom, and it blossoms in play."[7] That's free play, of course, without adult regimentation.

The evidence comes from a series of creativity measures—the Torrance Tests of Creative Thinking—collected over several decades from samples of US students in kindergarten through twelfth grade. Kyung Hee Kim, a school psychologist at the College of William & Mary in Virginia, analyzed these results and reported in her 2011 article, "The Creativity Crisis," that "since 1990, even as IQ scores have risen, creative thinking scores have significantly decreased."[8] Among them, "the decrease for kindergartners through third graders was the most significant." Her data also indicates "that children have become less emotionally expressive, less energetic, less talkative and verbally expressive, less humorous, less imaginative, less unconventional, less lively and passionate, less perceptive, less apt to connect seemingly irrelevant things, less synthesizing, and less likely to see things from a different angle."

The family is gradually being replaced by the father-state, which exercises its paternal authority, often as early as preschool. We learn to trust him early and throughout the school system. Since he only wants the best for (or from?) us, he should not be questioned. Where this leads to absolute obedience to state institutions, the dangers are manifold. On the other hand, independent reflection can reveal contradictions between what would be reasonable or even morally justifiable and what the state authorities demand of us in a given situation. The Federal Republic of Germany was not the only country built to a considerable extent on the awareness that under certain conditions governmental decrees can, if necessary, meet with resistance from the population, even if resistance to them is illegal according to the applicable law (see Article 20 (2) of the Basic Law for the Federal Republic of Germany). It is therefore all the more alarming that the former head of the Robert Koch Institute (RKI), the German analogue of the US CDC, Professor Dr. Lothar Wieler, was able to demand the following largely unchallenged: "We will have to abide by these rules [the COVID-19 containment measures] for months to come. They must be the standard. They must never be questioned . . . So that's the basic rule, nobody should question it anymore, we should just do it."[9] This statement was synonymous with the end of scientific discourse, of the democratic opinion-forming process, and thus also of a cultural development in the competition of the best ideas. But this seemed to bother only a small fraction of society even during Wieler's tenure. The state recommends or prescribes that isolated *individuals* obey rather than disobey, resist, and defend their libertarian rights.

The Frightening Answer to an Unpleasant Question

In Huxley's *Brave New World*, only a minimum of individuality is allowed from the outset, to prevent parts of a society from breaking out of the tight circle of state demarcation and engaging in collective resistance with the goal of self-realization. The repression is achieved by cloning in packages of tens of thousands of unit creatures. After a deliberately induced maturation damage, they possess a more or less deficient brain, depending on their class affiliation. And further repression is enacted by repetition of class-specific propaganda slogans from the technocratic narrative from the first day of their lives by means of so-called hypnopedia (learning of messages by repeated whispering in sleep). Thus, Huxley's indoctrination succeeds before a person can even develop his or her own personality or individuality.

But how could the transition from a society in which people could already develop some individuality to one with the lowest possible individuality be successful? I still remember the moment when the answer to this question entered my consciousness. At first, I was reluctant to entertain this thought, because it has such far-reaching consequences for the interpretation of our present time. It was on the aforementioned Corsican farm in the late summer of 2022 that my wife and I spent an unexpectedly intellectually stimulating vacation. We had just returned from a hike in the mountains and sat down on the veranda with the other guests. I told them about my discovery of the neurobiological correlate of chronic exhaustion of society and that this condition was massively aggravated by the COVID-19 measures. This explains above all the increasing inability to think critically and thus the widespread acceptance of perverse measures during the COVID-19 crisis.[10]

It was probably this conversation that, a little later, in a quiet minute, triggered this hard-to-tolerate thought in me: *What if all these measures did not just accidentally happen to affect this brain function, as secondary collateral damage, but were primarily orchestrated with the perfidious aim of robbing us of our individuality as well as our ability to think critically?* The thought never left my mind. All the absurdity we had experienced in recent years was not absurd at all from this novel point of view; it was perfectly suited to achieving precisely this goal. My neurobiological findings showed me the possibility of actually getting people to love their physical and mental lack of freedom. Thus, public crises in communication and action took on a whole new meaning. They are tantamount to brainwashing on a whole new level, through which people are to be unified and forced to build their personalities on the basis of the technocratic narrative, even partially replacing it so that they are no longer able to oppose it with anything of their own.

While pondering this, I slowly descended the stairs from the porch to the large meadow that surrounded the farm. I still remember the exact *when* and *where*, the time of day and even the exact step on which I found the answer to my many questions. Likewise, I still remember exactly how, that is, *how* the thought itself (the *what*) felt at the time, namely frightening and disturbing at the same time.

These four key questions make up our autobiographical memory: where, when, what, and how did it feel. The answers form the cornerstones of all our individual memories, which in turn form our individuality in sum. And exactly here lies the key; one can create memories and a broad individual wealth of experience but also reduce individuality, namely by deleting the answers and at the same time selectively replacing them with uniform content. One could not only minimize the degree of individuality of a single person but also carry out a Great Mental Reset on a scale as large as a whole society, with the result of a simple-minded conformity of the masses.

But to understand the neurobiological (or better neuropathological) process of generating mass conformity, we must first look at how our brain manages to generate individuality through memory—that is, to store unique thoughts and experiences instantaneously and at the same time for a lifetime, and to recall them when needed.

What Happens to Our Thoughts When We Don't Think about Them?

Our brain usually learns quite slowly. It takes a lot of repetitions until we can, for example, play a piano piece, ride a bicycle safely, or park a car in reverse. But when we experience something exciting or are told an exciting story, we remember it immediately and may never forget it again, without any repetition. This also applies to a new exciting thought. One moment it is there, the next it disappears. But as soon as we sense that it could be of importance, we hold on to it and begin to imagine what effects it could have if we were to put it into practice. But even this would completely overwhelm our short-term memory if it were left to its own devices.

Short-term memory is located in the frontal lobe of our brain, directly behind our "thinking brow." Its function consists only of brain waves, or electrical impulses between nerve cells, but nothing is recorded, and thus no long-term memories are created. As soon as we have juggled a new thought in our frontal brain for longer than just a few seconds, it is in danger of being lost. A short distraction is enough—a cell phone ringtone, another thought perhaps, and the original thread of thought would be gone forever, if there were not a very special brain structure that evolved to permanently record important events in our lives—and that includes our spontaneous ideas and thoughts, if our brain deems them noteworthy.

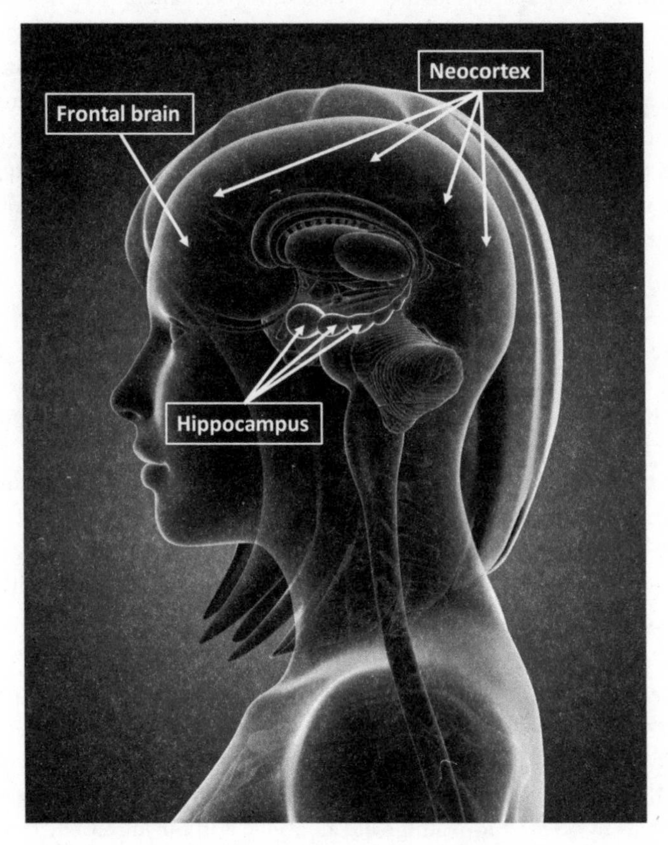

Figure 3[11]

This memory store for autobiographical memories comes in pairs, is about the size of a thumb, and is located in the two temporal lobes of our brain, as shown in figure 3. Because of their shape, each resembling a seahorse, these longer-term memory-stores are called hippocampi. Although we have two hippocampi, for the sake of simplicity I will refer to *the* hippocampus only. Together with the olfactory brain, the hippocampus is part of the so-called *archicortex* (from the Greek *arche,* meaning "beginning," and Latin *cortex,* meaning "bark"), which is the oldest region of our cerebral cortex in evolutionary history. In animal species that evolved much earlier than mammals, such as fish, the archicortex makes up most of the brain. In humans, however, it is completely covered by the *neocortex*, the new cortex, the evolutionary youngest part of the brain that only mammals possess. Although the two hippocampi together make up only 1 percent of human brain volume, without them we would be completely incapable of remembering a thought or an episode in our lives for more than a few seconds. Only the hippocampus has the unique ability to permanently remember when and where we experienced or thought something (even if only once) and how it felt. In order for it to be able to "write" our autobiography throughout our lives, despite its relatively small size compared to our entire brain and thus limited storage capacity, at least three functional adaptations were necessary in the course of its evolution. Knowledge of these is crucial to our understanding not only of how our individuality develops but also of how we can lose it and, at worst, become uniform creatures—simple-minded and, indeed, historyless, like Henry Molaison, the first human to have his autobiographic memory removed.

Regarding Henry

On September 1, 1953, Henry Gustav Molaison (1926–2008) underwent a fateful operation. After a bicycle accident in his childhood, Molaison suffered from epileptic seizures that could not be controlled with medication, making it necessary to remove the scar tissue in his brain. Whether it was out of a love of symmetry or an experimental interest has not been determined for a long time—Henry's surgeon, Dr. William B. Scoville, decided to surgically remove more than just the presumed origin of the electrical discharges. He generously amputated the hippocampus in *both* temporal lobes.[12]

Afterward, Henry was no longer himself. As soon as he awoke from the anesthesia, everyone realized that something terrible had happened. He did not know where he was. Worse, he could not memorize it, no matter how many times he was told. For Henry, there was no past and therefore no future. There was nothing left for him to orient and plan his life around. "Without direction, Henry was bare any motive," according to Philip J. Hilts, the biographer of H.M., as he was called in studies during his lifetime to protect his privacy.[13]

To be sure, his caretakers liked him, for he retained his good-natured, friendly manner. But his inability to remember them, and having to have the same conversations with him over and over again, gradually led them to view him as a pet, according to Hilts. Though a loving person herself, Dr. Brenda Milner, a pioneer in memory research who cared for Henry for many years and revolutionized the neurobiology of memory based on his memory loss (Henry's tragic fate was a stroke of luck for humanity), remarked, "He lost his humanity. You can't develop friendship or any human affection for a person like that."[14] A few years later, Scoville called his procedure an experiment (not therapy!) and hoped (in vain) that his confession would discourage imitators from similarly rigorously testing the limits of human curiosity. The spirit of the times destroyed time and spirit in people like Henry in a rather brutal way. Today's works more subtly, but its work of destruction begins in the same part of the brain that was removed from Henry—and not just individually and as an experiment, but globally and, if I am not mistaken, with full awareness of the devastating consequences of the procedure.

1) *Emotional Selection*

To protect its own finite capacity, which is usually limited to a day's worth of experiences and thoughts, and to ensure that important information can be stored and recalled even at the end of a long day, the hippocampus must make choices. Not everything we experience or think about can be retained. The criterion for selection is the answer to the question of how it felt. In other words, did what we experienced or thought trigger an emotion and thus acquire meaning?[15] For example, if I am walking along a fence and a nearby dog suddenly barks at me, I will not forget it, because I was frightened and danger seemed imminent. Things that we do every day without thinking about them, or all stereotyped activities, are ignored by the hippocampal memory, which is why in the evening we often do not know whether we did something routine during the day. In other words, boredom is not its thing. So, if I want someone to remember something for life, I have to package my message emotionally, like a dog fiercely defending its territory. Instilling fear is a proven, if mostly unethical, means of achieving this goal.

As shown in figure 4, the hippocampus stores the responses to the time and place of a thought or experience in its input area. This permanent memory of place (when?) and time (where?) coordinates is called the *dentate gyrus* because of its anatomical shape. In the main part behind it, called the *cornu ammonis*, which resembles an Ammon's horn, or the horn of a ram, contains the memory for the daily emotional experience. It holds the answers to the questions *What did I experience or think?* and *How did it feel?* However, this memory is limited to a daily load.

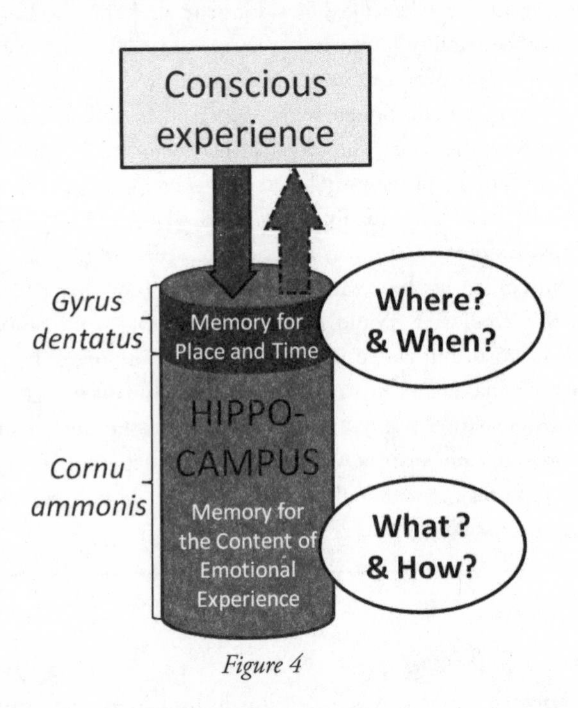

Figure 4

GPS Neurons

The olfactory brain remembers what was smelled, and the hippocampus remembers when and where something was smelled. This is how salmon remember landmarks during their first migration and later find their way back to their birthplace.[16] Rats and other rodents use their sense of sight in addition to their sense of smell. To find their way in new terrain, their hippocampus creates maps for spatial orientation within minutes.[17] Up to 30 percent of their hippocampal neurons become "GPS coordinates," firing electrical signals precisely when the animals are at certain locations in the cage. Using external markers, the scientists were able to determine, almost to the square centimeter, where a rat was in the cage at the time of measurement, based solely on the activity pattern of the hippocampal neurons.

As indicated by the dotted arrow in figure 4, our consciousness can directly access the daily memories stored in the hippocampus. This is essential if we are to further develop a thought stored there—for example, by considering and weighing alternatives. However, the short-term memory located in the frontal lobe, which we need in order to juggle our thoughts, would not be able to this complex comparative thinking because it can only actively hold all the information in unstable brain waves for a few seconds. Short-term memory, as a function of our frontal brain, and autobiographical long-term memory, as a function of our hippocampus, must therefore work closely together if we want to be creative and develop new ideas.

The Hippocampus as Our Gateway to the Space-Time Continuum

We are connected to the four-dimensional space-time continuum through the place and time neurons of the hippocampus. These special neurons store all our episodic experiences and thoughts as spatiotemporally anchored, autobiographical memories. In 2014 the Nobel Prize in Medicine was awarded for the discovery of place neurons.[18] But in my opinion, the discoverers of time neurons also deserve this high honor.[19] After all temporal information is also crucial for the encoding and retrieval of episodic memories.[20] The US neuroscientist Howard B. Eichenbaum (1947–2017) stated the significance of this discovery in an article, also published in 2014, as follows: "Time cells [time neurons] thus provide an additional dimension that is integrated with spatial mapping. The robust representation of both time and space in the hippocampus suggests a fundamental mechanism for organizing the elements of experience into coherent memories."[21] The place and time neurons give us a sense of space and time. Alzheimer's patients lose this early in the disease process, as it begins in the *dentate gyrus*.

Because the hippocampus is only designed to handle a daily load of memorable events, most people are unable to store any more information in the evening, particularly after a busy day. In order for us to be receptive the next day, the hippocampus must move the new information into permanent storage. We can compare the memory contents of the hippocampus to the data on a memory stick. In order to be ready for recording again, the computer transfers the data on the memory stick from the limited memory space to an internal mass-storage device. A similar kind of transfer also takes place in the hippocampus during sleep.

2) *Nocturnal Memory Upload*

During deep sleep, our brain transfers the emotionally significant thoughts and personal experiences collected in our limited "memory stick," the hippocampus, to the neocortex. The neocortex has a much larger data-storage capacity, so it serves as a kind of permanent storage medium, or "neocortical hard drive," as graphically shown in figure 5.

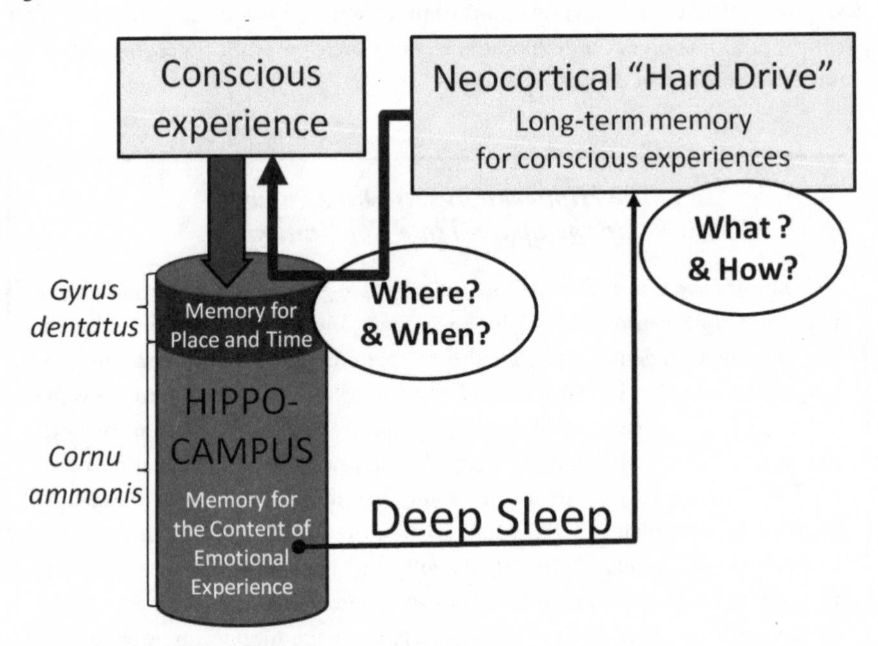

Figure 5

The process of storing *what* and *how* (i.e., the emotional content of experiences or remarkable thoughts) on the neocortical hard disk takes place in the first deep sleep phases, called slow-wave sleep (SWS) because of their characteristic slow EEG waves. However, because the neocortex learns much more slowly than the hippocampus, memories in SWS must be "told," or recapitulated, several times until the storage process is complete.[22] The contents of a hippocampal memory are stored in fragmented form in different locations in the neocortex according to a rule that is not yet fully understood, which means that whenever we recall neocortical memories, defragmentation must take place.

For contextual remembering, new memories are related to existing memory content. This happens in a later stage of sleep, when we dream. As we sleep and try to follow our dream actions and experiences in the virtual space created by our brain, we often move our eyes rapidly. That's why this stage of sleep is called rapid eye movement (REM) sleep. In REM sleep, the new memories uploaded in SWS are linked to past memory content, so it is not uncommon for us to wake up in the morning with new insights.[23] We need to sleep and dream to be able to remember what we have experienced and thought in the long term.[24] A conscious reliving of our past experiences and thoughts is made possible when the hippocampus stores the access information to all neocortical memory fragments like a register (also called *index*). To continue in a more tangible language, I will refer to these as neocortical *index signatures*. The hippocampus stores these signatures in the place and time neurons associated with each autobiographical memory, which I will refer to collectively as *index neurons*. These index neurons remain in the hippocampal *dentate gyrus* throughout life, anchoring (indexing) all of our autobiographical memory content. Without these index neurons, our memory fragments stored on the neocortical hard drive would be impossible to find or reconstruct (see the thick black arrow in figure 5). Therefore, remembering is easier when we recall when and where something happened or was thought, thereby activating the place and time neurons responsible for that experience.

Memory Palace

The fictional Sherlock Holmes uses it, and the eight-time world memory champion Dominic O'Brien recommends storing information in "memory towns" using the keyword method in his books.[25] However, the term *memory palace* is better known. Even in the ancient Roman and Greek schools of rhetoric, people were taught to mentally associate key words in a speech with specific locations and then to walk along a previously stored route during the speech. In doing so, the ability of the hippocampus to spatially store or remember important thought content was ultimately exploited. That this actually works this way has already been scientifically investigated and proven by means of imaging procedures.[26] Also, in the study entitled "Durable Memories and Efficient Neural Coding through Mnemonic Training Using the Method of Loci" showed that you don't have to be a memory world champion to boost your memory with this trick and remember even such trivial things as a shopping list with the help of hippocampal-neocortical consolidation.[27] All you have to do is place the things you want to remember quickly and effectively in a fictional house or palace so that you can recall them when you need them.

"To retrieve or recall an original memory, the groups of neurons that fired together to create the original memory need to be primed/or reactivated," explains US neuroscientist Shikha Jain Goodwin in her article "Neurogenesis: Remembering Everything or Forgetting Some."[28] "Forgetting, on the other hand," Goodwin says, "is the inability to create the original firing pattern due to lost synapses and connections." Thus, the crucial question for our further considerations is how the hippocampus ensures that enough place and time neurons, or index neurons, are available throughout life so that we can always store and recall new thoughts and experiences right up to old age.

Duplicated and Competing Memories

When we enthusiastically tell someone about a past experience, two things happen: First, the index neurons responsible for that memory are activated, allowing us to retrieve (reactivate and reconstruct) the stored experience from the neocortical hard drive. Second, the emotional narrative, and thus the anecdote itself, is stored again via the hippocampus, in a sense duplicating the original memory. This is one reason why early life experiences that have been recalled or told to others many times may exist in many copies, which may well vary as the repeatedly told story approaches a narrative ideal, to the point where the narrator is no longer able to distinguish it from the original experience. Even in the case of progressive Alzheimer's disease, when the hippocampus loses more and more of its index neurons, does not engage in productive neurogenesis, and is therefore hardly capable of forming new memories, there is still a high probability that at least one or a few of these index neurons still exist, referring to these neocortical copies. As a result, people with Alzheimer's can usually tell a story or two about their youth, but they may not remember where they are or who is sitting in front of them.

3) *Lifelong Production of New Index Neurons*

I have referred to index neurons as the hippocampal neurons that store the spatial and temporal coordinates associated with interesting thoughts, conversations, and exciting experiences, while also referring to their fragmented storage locations distributed throughout the neocortex. The index neurons ensure that we can continue to access and reconstruct these memories after the nocturnal storage process. The *dentate gyrus* has the unique ability to produce thousands of new neurons every day, even in adults, to ensure that we always have a sufficient number of place- and time-coding index neurons with which to form new memories and distinguish them from previous ones.

If this were not the case, index neurons already in use would have to be increasingly overwritten, which would be equivalent to memory loss.

This so-called adult hippocampal neurogenesis takes place mainly during REM sleep.[29] An international team of researchers led by stem cell researcher Jonas Frisén at the Karolinska Institute in Sweden found that up to 1.5 percent of all hippocampal neurons are newly formed each year.[30] This is significantly more hippocampal neurons than in any other species studied to date. And, as Frisén's team was able to show, this new production continues throughout life in humans. Frisén's researchers calculated the individual age of existing hippocampal neurons by determining the radioactive carbon isotopes incorporated into the neurons' genetic material and thus inferring the production rate. In contrast, an international team led by neuropsychiatrist Maura Boldrini of Columbia University analyzed the hippocampus of brain-healthy people who had died between the ages of fourteen and seventy-nine. They found similar numbers of neural progenitor (precursor) cells and thousands of immature neurons in the *dentate gyrus* in all age groups, confirming the Swedish finding.[31] Commenting on the significance of these findings, Boldrini's team writes, "Healthy elderly people have the potential to remain cognitively and emotionally more intact than commonly believed, due to the persistence of AHN [adult hippocampal neurogenesis] into the eighth decade of life." In fact, "over a 65-year age span, proliferating neural progenitors, immature and mature granule neurons [neurons at different stages of maturing] and *dentate gryus* volume were unchanged."

But the fact that "the *dentate gyrus* is a bottleneck in the network allows a small fraction of neurons to have a significant impact on hippocampal circuitry and function," the researchers explain. Therefore, "the new [index] neurons are required for efficient pattern separation, i.e., the ability to distinguish similar experiences and store them as distinct memories, whereas the old neurons are required for pattern completion, which serves to link similar memories. A lack of pattern separation due to impaired or unproductive adult hippocampal neurogenesis may therefore "lead to generalization, which is common in anxiety and depression in humans," according to Boldrini and her team. The researchers believe it is possible "that ongoing hippocampal neurogenesis sustains human-specific cognitive function throughout life," but that "declines may be linked to compromised cognitive-emotional resilience."

The importance of hippocampal neurogenesis for psychological or mental resilience and depression will be discussed in more detail later. But for now, let's keep in mind that the human *dentate gyrus* can constantly produce new neurons, or index neurons, into old age. However, these can only survive if they actually encode new experiences, or if their synapses are used to become part of the hippocampal network. There, they are responsible for the spatial and temporal differentiation of new memories.[32] To do this optimally, they retain their juvenile character for some time, even when they are fully mature. They are extremely retentive and "hungry" for new experiences that they want to store.[33] This appetite for new things is, in a way, an expression of their will to survive and the neural correlate of natural human curiosity. This was observed in experiments with animals, which are more willing to follow new paths when their hippocampal neurogenesis is activated.[34]

The Hippocampal Development of Individuality and Cultural Complexity

Neuroscientists in the group of Gerd Kempermann, a leading German researcher in the field of neurodegenerative diseases, have investigated the role of adult hippocampal neurogenesis using inbred mice. "Inspired by behavioral-genetic investigations of human monozygotic twins reared together, we obtained dense longitudinal activity data on 40 inbred mice living in one large enriched environment," the researchers write in their article published in the prestigious journal *Nature*.[35] Even just "three months of living in a complex environment," their study concludes, "led to a massive magnification of individual differences in explorative behavior among genetically identical individuals over time, and these differences were related to adult hippocampal neurogenesis." The environment that was identical for all mice "lost its 'sameness' over time, and gave way to the emergence of a personalized 'life space' and a 'mouse individuality,' similar to what has been observed in humans for personality traits," the researchers say.

The extent of individual differences observed in replications of this experiment naturally varied. Therefore, the researchers conclude, "as the members of each new cohort individualize, their 'society' will also be shaped in a slightly different, individual way." Referring to previous scientific work, the new study "supports the idea that the key function of adult neurogenesis is to shape hippocampal connectivity according to individual needs and thereby to improve adaptability over the life course and to provide evolutionary advantage."

This advantage cannot be valued highly enough: Not only are new index neurons the basis for natural curiosity, autobiographical knowledge, individuality, and ultimately creativity, but their function is also crucial on a societal level for the cultural progress of humanity. On the other hand, this makes index neurons or their neurogenesis the ideal target for implanting unquestioned narratives into the human brain. This is especially true when the attack on the hippocampal neurogenesis weakens psychological resilience.

The Psychically Strong Self

Every morning when I wake up and my brain's "operating system" "boots," I go through a self-reflective process of recognition. It may only take a fraction of a second for me to recall memories that tell me who I am. Perhaps not all people initiate a self-reflective process consciously, but it happens to all of us. The more positive memories you can recall, the stronger your self-esteem will be, and the more resilient, confident, and efficient you will be when you start your day. For this conscious remembering, we need our hippocampus and a productive neurogenesis. In fact, the neurons that integrate into the hippocampus neural network each day do more than modulate the strength of the ego based on accumulated experience. By protecting us from excessive stress reactions, they also directly regulate our psychological resilience.[36] A high level of mental resilience is a prerequisite for developing a readiness for new experiences and for avoiding potentially stressful situations in the first place.

Glucocorticoids (cortisol and corticosterone, in addition to cortisone) are stress hormones released by the cortex of the adrenal glands in response to an acutely threatening situation. Among other things, they stimulate the production and release of sugar (glucose) so that we have enough energy to either fight or flee better, depending on which response seems more promising. Their release is a good thing. The vast majority of new situations trigger such a stress response a priori. It is not without reason that this response pattern has prevailed throughout evolution: it is better to first suspect danger and be prepared for the worst than to naively assume the best and then be surprised and possibly injured or even killed as a result. This reaction is vital in the short term but harmful in the long term if a harmless situation is not recognized as such as soon as possible and the further release of stress hormones is stopped.

The recognition is one of the tasks of the new index neurons being formed every day in the hippocampus, because only they are able to quickly and efficiently classify stressful situations in terms of their danger potential. On one hand, the hippocampus is one of the brain regions densely populated with receptors for these stress hormones, which allows it to measure the strength of the acute stress response. On the other hand, all relevant current information converges in its new index neurons, while in their immediate vicinity are those index neurons that have direct access to all previous experiences. Only in this way can a new situation be evaluated comparatively. If the situation is assessed as not dangerous, the release of glucocorticoids is normalized by appropriate signals from the hippocampus.[37]

However, not every new situation triggers a stress response because the regulatory mechanism of the release of stress hormones can intervene, preventing an unnecessary release. The condition is that the new situation is not too strange, as the two stem-cell researchers Antoine Besnard and Amar Sahay from the Harvard Medical School explain in their article "Adult Hippocampal Neurogenesis, Fear Generalization, and Stress": "In order to express fear only when it is appropriate, we have to constantly perform comparisons between previously encoded associations [experiences] and what actually happens. Such a mechanism is adaptive in that it allows an individual to anticipate a potential threat by detecting relevant cues present in the environment."[38] Old index neurons (experiences) and new index neurons (the current situation) play a crucial role. Their cooperation allows an "efficient appraisal of threat." It "requires disambiguation of contextual information associated with safety and threat as well as the discernment of the probability (certainty)," Besnard and Sahay note, "with which a cue predicts the threat." On the other hand, if hippocampal neurogenesis is disturbed—that is, if we do not have new index neurons—the stress hormone level rises excessively in any unfamiliar situation, and even after only moderate stress it returns to the initial level very slowly, if at all. There is therefore a risk of chronic excessive glucocorticoid secretion if neurogenesis is disturbed. The fear of the unknown alone can lead to avoidance reactions, depressive illness, and cognitive impairment. In the long run, this can lead to Alzheimer's disease and many other lifestyle diseases (also mistakenly referred to as diseases of civilization).[39] I will discuss pre- and posttraumatic stress syndrome in detail in chapter 4, especially because chronic stress (chronically excessive glucocorticoid levels) paralyzes the production of new hippocampal neurons, closing a vicious circle that is life-threatening in the long run, as graphically illustrated in figure 6.[40]

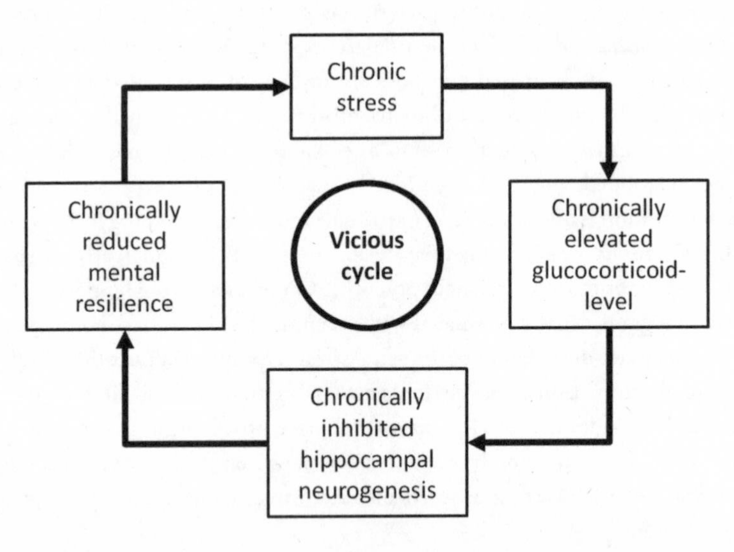

Figure 6

The critical involvement of active adult hippocampal neurogenesis in the regulation of our mental resilience is further supported by the observation that synthetic antidepressants, such as those in the selective serotonin reuptake inhibitor class, exert their antidepressant effects primarily by activating hippocampal neurogenesis.[41] Accordingly, there is a significant increase in hippocampal volume as a result of antidepressant treatment.[42] Thus, the increase in adult hippocampal neurogenesis is sufficient to reduce anxiety and depression-like behaviors.[43] However, the production of new neurons in the hippocampus is not only crucial for maintaining our cognitive-emotional resilience but also essential to our natural willingness and ability to think for ourselves.

Thinking (System 2) or Not Thinking (System 1)—This Is the Question

To consciously change one's behavior, one must first recognize that a change is necessary or might be beneficial. In addition, there must be a basic willingness to invest mental energy in even thinking about it. However, due to an often deficient hippocampal neurogenesis, more and more people are downright afraid of new things and therefore of behaving differently. Even if the necessity of a change is recognized as indispensable (e.g., because the current behavior is obviously the cause of a disease process that could be stopped by changing the behavior), there is often a lack of willpower to implement it. Both thinking about a necessary change and the change itself (until it becomes a routine) require mental energy, which is often not available. Our executive and decision-making center, located in the frontal lobe of the brain, is responsible for such processes. But what kind of energy does it take to imagine a new way of life, to plan it, to make the decisions for an actual change, and to initiate its implementation?

To answer this question, it is important to understand that our brain uses two different systems to maneuver us through life: System 1 and System 2. System 1 corresponds to the implementation of learned, repetitive behaviors, the things we do every day without having to think much about them. It includes the entire repertoire of stereotypical thought and behavior patterns that usually require little or no concentration and thus virtually no mental energy, since no real thinking is involved. This high-energy efficiency allows our executive center to operate in System 1 mode by default, which is very beneficial. As a result, our brains are able to initiate and execute appropriate actions quickly and without thinking, even when we have little mental energy. For example, if a car is barreling toward me as I cross the street, it is not a good survival strategy to invest mental energy in trying to assess whether the driver might be able to brake in time, to take evasive action, or to figure out what a reasonable escape strategy might look like. It is better to act without thinking in such a situation and just jump to the side.

Of course, our executive branch also makes mistakes, but it almost certainly makes them when it stereotypically reels off a familiar pattern of action in situations where reflection would be called for, drawing on System 1 content. In some cases, a kind of gut feeling signals to us that "business as usual" could be disastrous and that it is high time to stop and think. To respond to such challenges or to generate and explore new, alternative courses of action, our executive headquarters also has access to System 2, which may be considerably slower, but does indeed think things through.

Fast Acting and Slow Thinking

In 2002 the Israeli American psychologist Daniel Kahneman and the US economist Vernon L. Smith were awarded the Nobel Prize in Economics for the discovery of these two complementary decision-making systems, or "human judgment and decision-making under uncertainty."[44] A year later, British physicist and molecular biologist Francis Crick (1916–2004), who received the Nobel Prize in 1962 for discovering the molecular nature of genetic material, and US neuroscientist Christof Koch published an article in *Nature* about "A framework for consciousness."[45] In it, they also referred to unconscious System 1 action and conscious System 2 thought in an evolutionary biological context: "Many actions in response to sensory inputs are rapid, transient, stereotyped and unconscious. They could be thought of as cortical reflexes. Consciousness deals more slowly with broader, less stereotyped aspects of the sensory inputs (or a reflection of it in imagery and takes time to decide on appropriate thoughts and responses . . . It seems to be a great evolutionary advantage to have zombie modes that respond rapidly, in a stereotyped manner [i.e., System 1], together with a slightly slower system that allows time for thinking and planning more complex behavior [i.e., System 2]." The title of Kahneman's best-selling book, *Thinking, Fast and Slow*,[46] which refers to System 1 and System 2, respectively, is misleading because System 1 acts unconsciously, stereotypically, and above all, without really thinking at all.

Thinking with System 2, as opposed to acting with System 1, requires a mysterious form of mental energy about which very little was known for a long time. It is only available to us in limited quantities. Only as long as we have enough of this kind of energy is it possible for us to use System 2 thinking to question and, if necessary, change habitual System 1 behavior. This ability has secured the survival of humankind, because System 1 behavior can only produce existing reaction patterns, which can be disadvantageous for oneself or others due to their possibly poor adaptation to the concrete situation. With the help of System 2 thinking, we can then consider alternative courses of action and develop better approaches to new problems than our existing templates would have allowed.

Based on the findings of Kahneman, Crick, and Koch, I set out to identify the neural nature of this mental energy that enables System 2 thinking. To identify it, I detoured along the tracks of well-understood states of mental exhaustion to find its source. Operationally, in my book *The Exhausted Brain*, published in 2022, I referred to its still unknown location as the "frontal brain battery."[47] First, I drew on decades of scientific research on what is known as *ego depletion*, which describes the common neurobiological phenomenon that each of us feels when the "battery" is depleted after a long, exhausting day. *Ego* means "I" and *deplere* also comes from Latin and means "to empty." Thus, *ego depletion* describes the "self-exhaustion" due to the frontal brain battery having only a limited amount of mental energy, and as its "state of charge" decreases, it becomes increasingly difficult for us to think in a focused way and to find the motivation to use System 2. With complete mental exhaustion, it is almost impossible to find the best solution to a problem.

My analysis has shown that only one place in our brain combines all the functions to explain the processes involved in ego depletion: the hippocampus. Among other things, the use of System 2 requires efficient storage of our thoughts, a property that only the hippocampus possesses. It is likely that intensive use of System 2 will stretch the hippocampus to its limits; after all, its storage capacity is limited.[48] With a full hippocampal memory, System 2 would only be usable if previous memories or hippocampal index signatures were overwritten. However, our brains try to avoid this, which is why more and more people find it difficult to activate System 2 even when it is needed—the ego is exhausted. This interpretation is supported by the fact that ego depletion significantly reduces the ability to retrieve specific memories from episodic-emotional memory, a process in which the hippocampus also plays a central role.[49] In contrast, System 1 behavior, or the "zombie mode" as Crick and Koch called it, is unaffected by ego depletion or hippocampal memory impairment.

Neuronal Information Highway and Its Pathological Destruction

The hippocampus or "frontal brain battery" is directly connected to the frontal brain through the so-called von Economo neurons (VENs).[50] Named after their discoverer, the Greek psychiatrist and neurologist Constantin Alexander Freiherr Economo von San Serff (1876–1931), these are characterized by their extraordinary size and associated high transmission speed.[51] VENs play a central role in social behavior because they provide our executive center with rapid and efficient transmission of relevant experiences in socially conflictive situations, which are managed by the hippocampus.[52] Not surprisingly, VENs have also been found in higher primates, marine mammals, and elephants—animals with high social and planning intelligence.[53]

In frontotemporal dementia, VENs gradually and selectively die for unknown reasons.[54] Due to the progressive failure of System 2, sufferers become increasingly reckless and tactless in their dealings with others, showing no regard for social norms. They uninhibitedly express their stereotypical thoughts in an extremely rigid, zombie-like tone and are thus extreme examples of only System 1 controlled beings.

Hippocampal Anti-Indoctrination Formula

The lifelong production of new index neurons allows our wealth of experience to continue to the highest age. Throughout the millennia of human evolution, the wisdom of the elders was crucial—at least until Google, Wikipedia, and especially daycare replaced grandparents. Into the early twentieth century, the life experience of family elders was still of great importance for reproductive success. The mechanism known as grandmother evolution increased not only the number of grandchildren but also their chances of surviving childhood. This phenomenon explains why, unlike our closest relatives in the animal kingdom, only humans, or rather women, continue to live after menopause, usually for many decades. Thus, each decade lived by a postmenopausal grandmother in an extended family resulted in two more grandchildren reaching adulthood than in families in which the grandmother died early, because the grandmother was able to help care for and educate the grandchildren.[55]

However, empirical knowledge, combined with longevity as an evolutionary-biological selection criterion, presupposes mental functioning up to old age.[56] This also reveals that hippocampal dementia or Alzheimer's disease is a modern phenomenon or a modern disease of civilization. If Alzheimer's were causally related to old age, as we are repeatedly led to believe, then this form of dementia would have undermined the reproductive strategy that evolution brought about at an early stage in human history. But the reverse is true: under natural or species-appropriate living conditions, our genetic makeup protects us from Alzheimer's by ensuring that hippocampal neurogenesis is always productive.[57] Earlier objections that genetic selection for mental fitness into old age (and thus against Alzheimer's) could not have taken place in Stone Age tribes, because the average life expectancy in that era was too low, can be refuted by studying hunter-gatherer cultures that still exist today. In these cultures, two-thirds of those who survive the critical period of childhood reach an age of over seventy, even without modern medical care. Even eighty-year-olds are no exception.[58]

Based on these evolutionary-biological considerations, the basic physiological mechanisms that ensure that there is never a shortage of index neurons in our hippocampus—a basic requirement for charging and maintaining the capacity of the "frontal brain battery"—can be explained quite simply. Different domains of life interact, stimulating hippocampal neurogenesis and keeping it active throughout life. To consider these areas of life in isolation for purely didactic reasons, but without underestimating the importance of their interaction, I have presented them for better understanding by overlapping each of them in a graphic (figure 7), which I presented as "Methuselah formula" for the first time in my book *Die Methusalem Strategie*.[59]

Because of its important influence on the function of the hippocampus, it is no coincidence that it also functions as a "formula against Alzheimer's disease," as I published it in my book of the same title,[60] or as a "formula for a high-capacity frontal brain battery," as I explained in *The Exhausted Brain*[61], since mental exhaustion and

Alzheimer's disease, as well as depression, all go back to a mostly culturally caused disturbed hippocampal function. Knowing this formula and applying it in daily life will also help us to remain steadfast against the influences of harmful indoctrination, which is why it could also be called an "anti-indoctrination formula." Its application allows us to build a strong ego, remain curious, make efficient use of System 2 thinking, and, last but not least, have a strong resilience against psychological stress.

In this chapter, I will give only a few examples for each area of the formula to illustrate how our lifestyle directly affects the growth and maintenance of our autobiographical memory. More examples will follow in subsequent chapters when we discuss indoctrination and countermeasures.

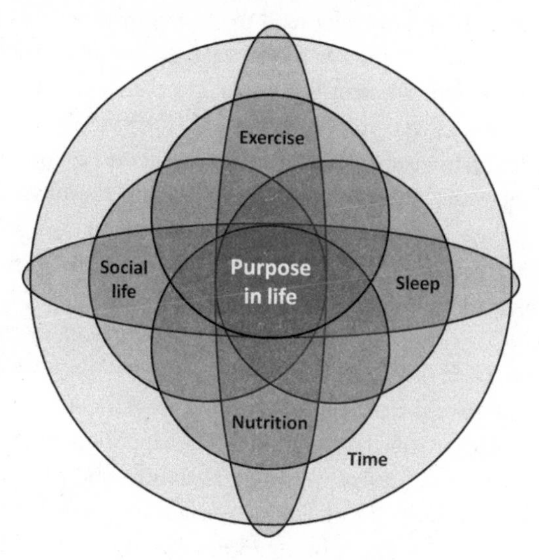

Figure 7

Purpose in Life

In the center of the formula is the purpose in life, because every human being needs a purpose until the end of life. In the long evolutionary history of humankind, as the "evolution of grandmother" suggests, there was usually a meaningful task up to the highest age.[62] Therefore, the risk of developing hippocampal dementia (Alzheimer's disease) increases substantially for those without a purpose in life.[63] Meaning in life is associated with manageable tasks and challenges, and thus with eustress, which in turn promotes adult hippocampal neurogenesis.[64] This is what three US neuroscientists write in their article "Neurogenesis and the Spacing Effect: Learning over Time Enhances Memory and the Survival of New Neurons": "New neurons are generated continuously over time in the dentate gyrus of the hippocampal formation, a brain region that is important for learning and memory. While thousands of neurons are generated there each day, many of these cells die within a few weeks of their birth."[65] Making new life experiences—in another word, learning—significantly increases the survival rate of hippocampal cells, giving them a function and thus legitimizing their existence, which ultimately affects us and gives us, as individuals, a sense of meaningful life.

Exercise

Throughout the history of humankind, until about the beginning of the twentieth century, exercise was a basic requirement for being able to feed oneself. And even today it is the case that those who move a lot tend to have more experience. Knowing where dangers lurk or where to find food is most likely the evolutionary biological reason why such a large number of different hormones and messenger substances (cytokines) are released during physical activity, which not only increase physical fitness but at the same time stimulate brain growth and, in particular, adult hippocampal neurogenesis and, as a result, increased memory capacity. To explain the physiological basis and neurobiology of all these hormonal factors such as BDNF, EPO, VEGF, NGF, GDNF, dihydrotestosterone, GH, IGF-1, FGF-2, serotonin, adiponectin, irisin, and METRNL here would be going too far. Therefore, I refer you to my article "Unified Theory of Alzheimer's Disease," where most of these hormones and cytokines are explained and scientific studies can be found.[66]

But I will simply note that the number of factors alone is a clear indication that physical activity is highly effective in stimulating hippocampal growth. It is therefore one of the best ways to preserve our mental abilities and prevent depression and Alzheimer's disease. Just one hour of aerobic (*aerobic* means you can still talk during the exercise) exercise a day at about 60 to 75 percent of maximum heart rate (which a group of sixty-seven-year-old seniors achieved even with a light walk) resulted in hippocampal growth of about two percent, in just one year.[67] In the control group, which only did daily gymnastics without exerting themselves too much, the hippocampus shrank by about 1.4 percent during the same period (which is the "normal" but unnatural shrinkage rate of the hippocampus in modern societies, as I will discuss). In addition to better physical fitness, the aerobic exercisers also developed stronger mental resilience and memory than the gymnastics group. This proves that, with moderate exercise, hippocampal shrinkage can not only be avoided but also reversed, even in old age.

Nutrition

In nutrition, as in all other areas of the formula, the law of the minimum applies, which the German agronomist Carl Sprengel formulated in 1828 to point out that plant growth is always limited by the essential nutrient present in too low a concentration, even if all other essential nutrients are present in optimal quantity. Applied to autobiographical memory, Sprengel's Law means not only that no single essential micronutrient (vitamins and trace elements) can be deficient for optimal hippocampal growth but also that no one nutrient can compensate for the deficiency of any other. The widespread iodine deficiency and resulting thyroid hormone deficiency, explained in the previous chapter, results in dramatic consequences for normal brain development. However, iodine and thyroid hormone deficiency not only massively impairs brain maturation but also hampers adult hippocampal neurogenesis, which can lead to loss of System 2 thinking capacity and depressive symptoms.[68] However, an iodine deficiency can only be remedied by iodine and not by any other micronutrient, just as Sprengel's Law states for plants.

Another serious deficiency of an essential nutrient, which is even more widespread than iodine deficiency, is that of the so-called aquatic omega-3 fatty acids eicosapentaenoic acid (EPA) and docosahexaenoic acid (DHA). EPA and DHA are essential cell-building substances and precursors of a large number of vital cytokines that have, among other things, an anti-inflammatory effect and that activate neurogenesis in particular. For example, the placenta tries to achieve an omega-3 index (the relative fatty acid content of EPA and DHA in our cell membranes) of 11 percent to ensure optimal fetal brain development.[69] The hippocampal volume also correlates directly with this index—that is, the lower the index, the smaller the hippocampal volume.[70] But in Germany the value is only 4 to 6 percent, and in the United States on average even below 4 percent.[71] An omega-3 index below 2 percent is most likely no longer compatible with life.[72]

However, to achieve an optimal omega-3 index of 10 to 11 percent for mental fitness, an adult would have to consume about 200 to 300 grams of fatty seafood daily. This points to our evolutionary origins as fishermen and gatherers, because this value, quite high for today's times, could only be achieved if we ate a significant amount of fish and shellfish.[73] According to nutrition experts at Imperial College in London, there "is now incontrovertible support of this hypothesis from fossil evidence of human evolution taking advantage of the marine [aquatic] food web."[74] But aside from the fact that ocean fish are now too contaminated with toxins to be recommended for consumption, they have long been unavailable in sufficient quantities for the world's entire population. If today's wild catch were distributed fairly, the average omega-3 index would only be about 5 percent. But fish farming is not a sustainable solution either, because fish (like humans) are not capable of synthesizing their own aquatic omega-3 fatty acids and must obtain them entirely from the increasingly scarce food chain. A completely new possibility in the history of humankind and, in my opinion, currently without alternative, is the pollutant-free production of microalgae or algae oil, which is rich in these aquatic fatty acids.[75]

Using algae oil, in my opinion, is the only way to address the global, brain-damaging deficit of EPA and DHA. However, due to the flawed, repeatedly propagated claim that humans are capable of adequately synthesizing these two aquatic omega-3 fatty acids from the terrestrial omega-3 fatty acid alpha-linolenic acid (as found in walnut oil and especially linseed oil), there continues to be a serious shortage worldwide—people think they are well supplied, but they are not. Apart from the fact that many people are not aware of the importance of aquatic omega-3 fatty acids, this misinformation ensures that too few people recognize algae oil as a new staple food. Yet, globally, only algae oil can replace fish as a source of essential aquatic omega-3 fatty acids.

There is also an almost global deficiency in vitamin D3, even in countries near the equator.[76] The problem is thus not only a problem caused by a lack of sunlight, because the sun is low in the winter months in higher northern or lower southern latitudes, but also a cultural or individual problem of inadequate exposure. But even fatty seafood, which used to be a high-value source of vitamin D3 (for Inuit in the far north, this is the only source of vitamin D3), is no longer available in sufficient quantities. Even a vitamin D level of about 50 nmol/l (20 ng/ml) is often not achieved, which is problematic for bone health. A vitamin D level two to three times higher, around 100-150 nmol/l (40-60 ng/ml), which is necessary for both immunological[77] and neurological health,[78] is usually only achieved by people who supplement sufficiently.

These are, however, only examples of micronutrients very often deficient. Ultimately, however, our autobiographical memory cannot do without *any* essential micronutrient in order to maintain its performance.[79] Therefore, a targeted supplementation with those vitamins and trace elements that are not (or cannot) be supplied sufficiently despite a balanced diet is generally recommended.

Apart from the need for a diet rich in vital substances, interestingly, not eating or fasting is also beneficial for hippocampal growth. Even an overnight fast of about twelve hours (*interval fasting*) activates ketogenesis, in which fatty acids are mobilized from our fat storages and converted in the liver into small fragments, or ketone bodies, which then enter the brain via the bloodstream. There, unlike fatty acids, they can cross the blood-brain barrier. Ketone bodies are not only more energy efficient than glucose, but they also have a hormonal effect, activating adult hippocampal neurogenesis and rejuvenating existing older neurons.[80] Sugar, on the other hand, especially in the unnatural amounts we consume through sweets, pastries, and convenience foods, leads to elevated blood glucose levels. This causes the chemical adhesion of the sugar molecules to cell surfaces as so-called advanced glycation end products (AGEs), which activate the immune system like a foreign body and inhibit the growth of the hippocampus through inflammation (more on inflammatory inhibition of adult hippocampal neurogenesis in chapter 4).[81] Furthermore, AGEs in the cell interior accelerate the aging process, again exactly the opposite of the health-promoting function of ketone bodies.[82]

A harmful excess of sugar is an example of the law of the maximum, which I derived from Sprengel's law of the minimum.[83] This means that an excess of essentials not only brings no additional benefit but also in many cases is even harmful. This is obvious in the case of harmful substances such as alcohol or nicotine, but it also applies to many components of our current diet. For example, AGE exposure occurs not only from high sugar intake (glucose, fructose, or galactose and all forms of syrups) but also from AGEs in foods produced or treated at high temperatures—baked, fried, grilled, and especially deep-fried foods.[84]

In short, our diet also significantly determines the preservation or loss of our mental performance and autobiographical memory.

Social Life

Humans depend on social interaction, evidenced by the fact that we need intensive parental care for longer than any other species when we are growing up. Therefore, oxytocin (ancient Greek ōkys for "fast" and *tokos* for "birth"), which is released during childbirth, not only induces labor but, as one of the most potent hippocampal growth factors,[85] also ensures that the maternal autobiographical memory receives a strong growth impulse, even though birth stress (or high glucocorticoid levels) would actually have a detrimental effect. A similar stimulating effect on hippocampal neurogenesis is exerted by prolactin, the hormone that stimulates milk production during lactation and thus positively influences the mental health and autobiographical memory of the mother during this formative period of life.[86] With the help of the two hormones oxytocin and prolactin, the mother not only intensively perceives the facial expressions, gestures, and smells of her newborn child, but she also remembers them in great detail. A mother-child relationship based on the mother's autobiographical memory can develop that is vital for the child and lasts a lifetime.

But every relationship we form with other people in the course of our lives is also based on the release and action of oxytocin, which is why isolation and (un)social distancing have a detrimental effect on the maintenance of our hippocampal performance. This is due to the lack of this bonding hormone and also to the neurotoxic stress levels caused by loneliness (see chapter 4) and, last but not least, the lack of communication (see chapter 5). After all, being with other people provides the emotional experiences or conversations that new hippocampal neurons need to ensure their own survival. This is because our newly formed neurons only survive if they are index neurons that have the opportunity to encode new experiences and thus become a permanent part of the hippocampal network. In the final chapter, I will talk about the lesser-known dark side of oxytocin, which is usually associated only with positive connotations.

Sleep

The hippocampus can only make new neurons when it is not busy autobiographically collecting new experiences. This is certainly one of the reasons why melatonin not only enables deep sleep but also stimulates hippocampal neurogenesis.[87] Accordingly, frequent sleep interruptions and prolonged sleep deprivation have detrimental consequences for health and especially for the maintenance of cognitive performance. Sleep deprivation inhibits neurogenesis and leads to increased levels of glucocorticoids, or stress hormones, which not only inhibit brain growth but also have neurotoxic effects, shrinking the brain and especially the hippocampus. Recovery of natural adult neurogenesis in adults after chronic sleep deprivation takes about two weeks and involves a temporary compensatory increase in the rate of new neuron formation.[88]

Time

Everything we do takes time. Although the digital revolution allows us to do almost everything faster than just a few years ago, we have less and less time to live a balanced life—the more possible, the less seems feasible to us. A lack of time, or rather the wanting or needing to do more than is feasible, creates chronic stress. Burnout is one of the consequences, and, in the long run, depression and even Alzheimer's are threatening. Chronic distress—that is, the stress hormones—inhibits neurogenesis and at the same time drives neurodegeneration. But doing nothing, having no task, and no longer being needed (having too much time on your hands) are not good either, because growth impulses for hippocampal neurogenesis are missing. Eustress, or the positive stress caused by challenging yet doable tasks, is ideal.

Time, or its availability, is thus in itself a relevant factor for our mental health. However, time is also important when balancing the other elements of the hippocampal protection formula: whether one takes enough time for one's life goals, social or physical activities, or simply for sufficient sleep. Many people have lost this balance. In combination with deficits in content, especially in nutrition, this explains a lifestyle that is anything but species-appropriate. As a result, the hippocampus does not reach its full genetic potential during development and shrinks in "normal" adults instead of growing throughout life.

The Unnatural Normality of Chronic Hippocampal Destruction

To maintain our autobiographical memory and thus the integrity of our personality and the ability to constantly develop it, a lifelong production of new index neurons is necessary. The strength of our psychological resilience depends on it, and it is a prerequisite for our willingness to try something new and expand our horizons when it seems necessary or even promising. Apart from the fact that productive neurogenesis offers protection against depression and ultimately Alzheimer's disease, we need new index neurons every day in order to remain System 2–capable, or able to think and change direction when it might be better for us to do so. But this is exactly what is lacking as a result of our current way of life, as the prior discussion has shown. Instead of growing steadily through productive neurogenesis, which would correspond to its natural potential (solid arrow in figure 8), the hippocampus of adults classified as normally healthy (dashed arrow in figure 8) loses on average about 1.4 percent of its volume per year of life, as a large international study found.[89]

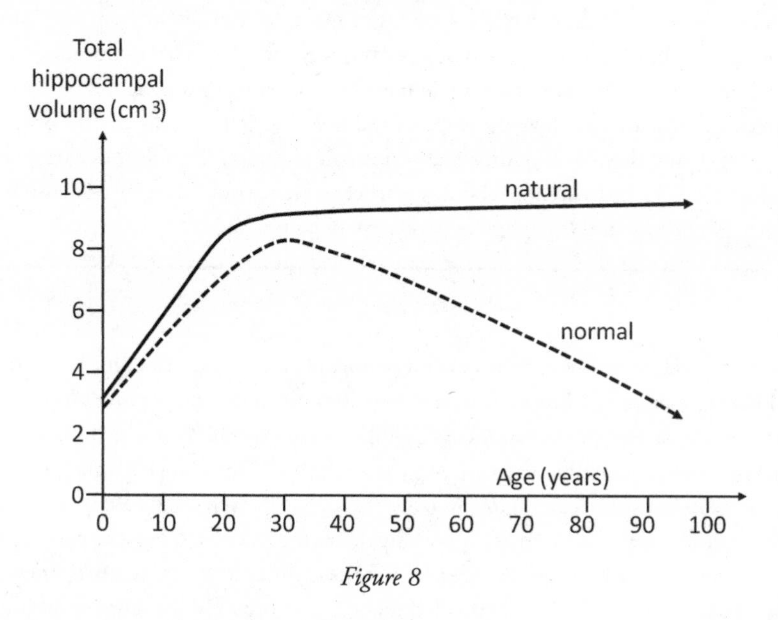

Figure 8

The enormous loss of autobiographical memory and thus personal memories in adults considered healthy was confirmed in another study published in 2019 with data from about twenty thousand Britons.[90] In this volumetric analysis, participants were also classified as mentally healthy, based on their medical records, and continuous hippocampal volume loss was therefore defined as normal. Thus, the authors state, "the data provide a large-scale normative database to facilitate easy age-adjusted determination of where an individual hippocampal and temporal lobe volume lies within the normal distribution." In other words, if your shrinkage rate is within the range of this normative dataset, everything is considered fine, until it is obviously not fine anymore and brain function declines dramatically and measurably.

Normal or Natural?

In everyday language, these two terms are often not sharply enough distinguished. *Normal* describes what is more likely to be observed than something else; it is a statistical statement about frequency. If most people do the same thing, it is considered normal. Similarly, hippocampal shrinkage results from the ordinary behavior of people in our modern society and is therefore considered normal. Thus, it is considered normal that most people will develop Alzheimer's disease if they do not die first from the consequences of another normal disease of modern civilization, such as type 2 diabetes, stroke, heart attack, or cancer. But this is not *natural*. Modern medicine does not make a clean distinction here either, which can be very dangerous. For example, anyone who behaves normally, who has normal blood values or a normal rate of hippocampal shrinkage, is considered healthy until this normal development almost inevitably leads to the onset of symptomatic disease. But this is also normal, although it could have been prevented if one had thought about it earlier, which would have been natural or species-appropriate. If you are unlucky, it will be too late.

It has been scientifically proven beyond reasonable doubt that in clinically diagnosed Alzheimer's disease, the hippocampus loses volume at a rapid rate of up to 5 percent per year once the disease process is underway.[91] The reason for this is that neuropathological processes are accelerated in this case (e.g., as a result of chronically high and thus neurotoxic glucocorticoid release). However, any volume loss, even a supposedly small one, is pathological. An average rate of hippocampal volume loss of 1.4 percent per year in the adult population (which we have seen within the gymnastic group discussed previously) is by no means a natural process that would be truly normal in the sense of healthy. It is only normal in a statistical sense, which is even worse. For this now common disorder, or continuous loss of volume and content of autobiographical memory, results from an explainable and easily preventable combination of deficient adult hippocampal neurogenesis and concomitant neurodegeneration. These are pathological processes that reinforce and accelerate each other, with the consequence that sooner or later this slower shrinking process of the hippocampus will lead to Alzheimer's dementia.

Assuming that the aforementioned studies and many others describing similarly high shrinkage rates are representative of what's happening worldwide,[92] and considering that depression is a causal indicator of acutely disrupted hippocampal neurogenesis, the phenomenon explains why depression has already become the leading cause of global occupational disability as early as 2017.[93] In 2019, the very same year the data shown in figure 8 was published, the WHO declared depression to be the world's number one disease.[94] But hippocampal dementia, or Alzheimer's disease, is also a frighteningly good biomarker for hippocampal neurodegeneration resulting from a long-standing deficiency in neurogenesis. This is because the more advanced the hippocampal shrinkage process, the more likely it is that the self-preservation system will completely collapse, which in turn accelerates neurodegeneration and makes the development of Alzheimer's disease inevitable. However, correcting the primary causes of deficient hippocampal neurogenesis almost never happens unless one intervenes early and vigorously enough. Thus, according to the WHO, Alzheimer's disease advanced to become the third leading cause of death in the United States and Europe in the same year (2019). I recognize this as a further consequence of avoidable hippocampal shrinkage, or precisely as a fatal byproduct of the normality shown in figure 8.[95]

The figure derived from the data of the two studies is thus ultimately a representation of the normality of a mentally exhausted society. Such a society is threatened by rising rates of depression in the short term and increasing cases of Alzheimer's in the long term. Moreover, this state of mental exhaustion means that people can often lose the ability to think for themselves, even when they are still in a rather inconspicuous, supposedly healthy state. This may sound like an exaggerated judgment only as long as one does not realize that normal loss of hippocampal volume is a clear indication of the deficient operational capacity of System 2 thinking in the sense of a chronic ego depletion. Perhaps this has contributed to a large part of the population accepting the freedom-stealing COVID-19 measures, including the experimental vaccination technology, which forces the body to produce exogenous and highly toxic proteins (see chapter 4) in its own cells. Added to this is the weakened psychological resistance of many people, which allows them to be controlled by irrational fears, in addition to an often-weakened ego, which leads people to follow the masses, even when they are obviously running into the abyss.

For a long time, I assumed that the described pathological hippocampal shrinkage on a global scale was only due to an unintentionally misguided cultural development. What surprised me even then was that numerous studies considered this pathological process to be normal and thus signaled no reason to search for and eliminate the causes. Only when either depression or Alzheimer's disease was diagnosed as a result could the hippocampal causes be identified as such. But these were usually treated only with drugs. Similarly, I have long been surprised that virtually all causes of impaired adult hippocampal neurogenesis are also considered completely normal. Today, it is considered normal to be stressed at work or in one's personal life and therefore to sleep poorly, or to search in vain for a practical answer to the question of purpose in life in old age. Physical inactivity is also considered normal: According to the WHO, a deficiency exists only if "at least 150 minutes of moderate-intensity [where you raise your heart rate or work up a sweat], or 75 minutes of vigorous-intensity physical activity per week" are not met.[96] Mind you, per week, not per day! That equates to just twenty-two minutes of moderate physical activity per day. But in 2018 only 42 percent of the German population and just 40 percent of the US population met this modest goal.

In addition to lack of exercise, lack of essential micronutrients is among the main causes of hippocampal degeneration. In "healthy" adults in Germany, only about half of the optimal target vitamin D level of 125 nmol/l (50 ng/ml) is reached, even in summer and despite good UVB radiation.[97] In winter, the average level is even four times lower, which has been shown to promote the loss of hippocampal capacity. But this deficiency can also explain the completely unnecessary deaths from COVID-19 and many other seasonal respiratory diseases, which I will discuss in more detail in chapter 4.

This makes it all the more astonishing that Bill Gates, in the spring of 2020, despite all the scientific evidence, claimed, "We don't understand why the flu is seasonal. It's such a profound thing that there's this three-month period where it's very active and then almost nine months where you have a hard time finding it, depending on which hemisphere you're in." [98] The question is, who does he mean by *we*? The other technocrats? The scientific community? But it can't be the latter, because more than four decades earlier, general practitioner and epidemiologist Robert Edgar Hope-Simpson had clearly demonstrated that the seasonality of influenza was related to the position of the sun.[99] And for more than a quarter of a century earlier, it had become equally clear that inadequate ultraviolet B (UVB) exposure leads to vitamin D deficiency, which weakens the immune system and thus causes the seasonality of respiratory diseases.[100] This deficiency explains not only the greater infectiousness of the disease but also its more severe course. One might think that those who want to change the world, to own it, and to control and dominate it with vaccines, no matter how dangerous they may be, cannot be stopped by such trivial, plausible explanations.

The disregard for human life during the COVID-19 pandemic made me realize that more was at stake than just money. Unfortunately, only when my family and I were affected by the sometimes completely absurd COVID-19 measures did the penny finally drop for me. The iodine deficiency in the countries that serve us as a source of raw materials should have been enough of an indication, since it could have been easily and completely eliminated at low cost and the extremely harmful effects on the development of a child's brain could have been prevented. It is certainly not about saving lives, nor only about money. The suspicion arises that power over people, achieved and consolidated by reducing their mental capacity, is the real goal. The strategy under the guise of targeting COVID-19 has been very successful in this regard on a global scale and possibly very long term, as the prior discussion of "normal" hippocampal shrinkage illustrates. It is conceivable that the technocratic would-be world rulers of 2019 have determined (perhaps based on record-high depression rates) that hippocampal performance, and thus protection from indoctrination, was at an all-time low, and they are therefore ready to openly push for a new world order under their leadership. At the very least, they were confident that they would not encounter too much resistance.

CHAPTER 3

REPROGRAMMING THE HUMAN BRAIN

We belong to an age whose culture is in danger of perishing through the means to culture.
— Friedrich Nietzsche (1844–1900)

A Two-Pronged Assault on the Human Soul

People can perceive each other as soulmates if they have had similar and often drastic life experiences, either before they met or in their shared lives. Thus, it is related memories, accessible via the hippocampal index neurons, that provide the sense of a soul kinship. One cultural indication that the hippocampus might be the gateway to what we use to call our soul comes from India. It is said there that it takes time for the soul to catch up with us when we are travelling. In fact, it takes at least a day for the GPS neurons of the hippocampus to map a new vacation spot and classify it as safe. You know your way around the new environment, you feel safe, and then you really feel at home.

Throughout our cultural history, the heart has been identified as the seat of our soul, presumably because the heartbeat reflects our emotional feelings. But the heart reacts, while the hippocampus acts or, specifically, remembers everything that constitutes us and our life. Thanks only to hippocampal memory, we perceive ourselves as a continuous self and always get an answer to the central question of who we are. Without the hippocampus, we would not be able to remember emotionally significant events in our lives, and therefore we would not be able to find soul mates. Without the hippocampus, we probably wouldn't even be able to think about a soul or an afterlife, because without a past, there is no future to philosophize about.

The importance of the hippocampus for our soul life can be illustrated by the impressively successful passage on soul stealing from Joanne K. Rowling's fantasy novel *Harry*

Potter and the Prisoner of Azkaban. In the story, people are threatened by Dementors with something "worse than death" when these most dangerous of magical creatures suck the soul out of their victims with a kiss. When Harry Potter asks if Dementors kill in this way, his teacher replies, "Much worse than that. You can exist without your soul, you know, as long as your brain and heart are still working. But you'll have no sense of self any more, no memory, no . . . anything."[1] What is even more serious in such a situation, and is also true of late-stage hippocampal dementia, is the following: "There is no chance of recovery. You'll just—exist. As an empty shell. And your soul is gone for ever . . . lost."

Whether the hippocampus is to be understood merely as the biological origin of our sense of having a metaphysical soul, or even as the gateway to our soul as a sense of ourselves, I leave to the theologians and philosophers to discuss. One thing is certain: the hippocampus is the ideal point of attack for a completely new and very real counterpart to Rowling's Dementors. The new operating system requires that each individual be stripped of his or her soul—that is, in part, autobiographical memory. Let us call it Social Operating System, SOS for short. As I will not only affect our culture, but every individual, the acronym happens to be the same as that of the distress signal "Save Our Souls."

In the spring of 2023, as I write these lines, we are already in the midst of this dramatic process of depersonalization of almost the entire human society. After all, the technocratic elite, through its worldwide, concerted COVID-19 measures, has succeeded in getting a frighteningly large number of people to defend their belief in their narrative of the saving vaccination, against all evidence, with vehemence against people who think differently or think at all.

Narratives as a Means of Power

The fear of death or of what might come after death is the origin of countless stories about a comforting afterlife. Since it is obvious to everyone that the body of a deceased person does not live on, a soul is necessarily assumed, to make the tale of eternal life credible. The earliest narratives probably go back far beyond our historical records and are as old as the beginning of self-reflective, conscious thought.

Narratives are considered to be "meaning-making tales" that, because of their culture-shaping effect on coexistence, have an enormous influence on how we perceive or construct the world around us. Thus, the narratives that accompany us throughout our childhood and adolescence not only become an essential part of our personality but also help to determine what we experience and how we experience it, by guiding our actions and thoughts. In short, they exert immense control over us. No wonder, then, that narratives are easily abused as instruments of power and are sometimes created for that very purpose. Indoctrination is the attempt by power-hungry personalities to get other people to believe as much as possible in a particular narrative that serves the elite. A proven means of achieving this is the fear of suffering, and most fundamentally the fear of death, which underlies all other fears.

But this is probably just the beginning. If the technocratic elite wants to stabilize its power in the long term in the sense of *Brave New World*, propaganda based on fear alone is not enough. Aldous Huxley recognized this almost a hundred years ago and illustrated it in literature. In order for society to adopt the operating system of the technocrats, contradictions to its own history must no longer be perceptible. There must be no dissonance between one's own experiences from earlier times and the new expectations, promises, and demands of the technocrats or the everyday reality of a future AI-controlled existence. A narrative for the preservation of power does not have to make sense and can even be quite contradictory in itself and with common sense. (I will have more on this in chapter 5.) To function properly, the SOS must be not only a part of the autobiographical memory but also the unrivaled foundation upon which all other autobiographical memory content is based. The SOS provides the interpretive framework; it is the technocratic counterpart to a religion with an exclusive claim to validity.

To run a new operating system, the computer must first format the hard disk of the PC, and then the system needs to be installed. Otherwise, the PC could not run the new system. The situation is very similar with the reset by the new technocratic SOS. Only by overwriting the old index neurons will discrepancies be prevented and will the reprogrammed people not be unsettled by more attractive alternative life plans. Their hippocampus has then arrived in the technocratic future and knows nothing else, and the dispossessed person is "happier and more satisfied than ever before" because there is no *before* for him or her.

The former self, consisting of all autobiographical memories and the associated feelings, hopes, and values, would then be erased and deliberately replaced by a technocratically constructed foundation of identity or by any narrative, so that the past would only be remembered as dark and dangerous due to viral, nuclear, and many other threats

To come closer to the *Brave New World* paradigm, hippocampal neurogenesis is the ideal target, since it provides the conditions for people to be steered in new directions at the discretion of those in power. However, it requires a two-pronged attack:

- The new production of potential index neurons must completely be suppressed. At the same time, existing index neurons are decimated by neurodegenerative measures.
- The remaining index neurons that provide access to autobiographical memories are successively overwritten with the signatures of the technocratic narrative.

The success of such a transformative development has been already apparent during discussions about coronavirus measures. The believers had no ears for scientific arguments that challenged the technocratic narrative, which consisted, for example, of the phrase "vaccination protects and restores our freedoms." If one nevertheless tried to initiate a conversation about it, many reacted as if being personally attacked. In such situations, in my estimation, a first major success of this neuropathological attack on the hippocampal index neurons could already be observed: On one hand, the transformed had no or at least a limited System 2 ability and natural curiosity about a vital medical question. On the other hand and more disturbingly in my opinion, some of their index neurons already encoded access to the neocortically stored contents of the technocratic narrative, which had thus de facto become a part of a new, reprogrammed personality that now had to be defended.

My thesis is that the COVID-19 pandemic, with all its measures, was a first worldwide orchestration of the conditions for such a mental transformation. It established new basic rules of coexistence, and a new "operating system," was imposed on humanity. If this assumption proves to be true, then it must be regarded as highly successful and a precursor of further attacks on the hippocampus. To protect ourselves, it is urgent that we understand the modus operandi, goals, and mechanisms of Great Reset protagonists on the basis of what has happened so far. A brief outline of this dual attack and its obvious consequences follows in the next two sections. In the two chapters thereafter, I will describe each step of the attack in more detail, based on the actions that took place. I will examine what specific effects they had on hippocampal functions. Last but not least, I will ask what further actions might be planned and which have already been announced.

Part 1: Reduction of the Autobiographical Index Neurons

Let us look again at the often-used literary blueprint of a dystopian society that Huxley warned us about, to understand what we are dealing with in a slightly modified form. In *Brave New World*, fetal development is influenced by chemical means (oxygen deprivation or ethanol administration) to produce uniform human beings with a predetermined mental and memory capacity. Depending on the timing and intensity of the chemical intervention, different degrees of physical and especially mental impairment develop. Interestingly, the hippocampus is the brain structure most sensitive to oxygen deprivation[2] and alcohol toxicity.[3] By inhibiting the growth of the hippocampus or by destroying the hippocampus before birth (decantation), clearly defined caste beings are created, from so-called Alphas to Epsilons, with descending mental or hippocampal efficiency. However, this requires extra uterine production and the ability to create thousands of genetically identical copies by manipulating the early embryo.

If we assume that similar intentions to manipulate beings exist today, but without the possibility of a similarly direct influence on fetuses in their development, a conceivable means to achieve the same effects exists: to cause a targeted deficiency of certain micronutrients essential for hippocampal growth. These include the aforementioned iodine, vitamin D3, or aquatic omega-3 fatty acids. In the industrialized countries of the Global North, every effort is made to prevent an adequate supply of vitamin D3 or aquatic omega-3 fatty acids, through, for example, large-scale studies in high-impact journals that are either misinterpreted or poorly designed from the outset to give a distorted impression of the supply situation or the need, as I will explain in more detail later. Thus, serious deficiencies of vitamin D or aquatic omega-3 fatty acids occur in large parts of the population and are not recognized and corrected due to too low threshold values. It is very disturbing that such circumstances go unnoticed to many, even though the impact on humanity is major and measurable, on a scale similar to the less subtle procedures of Huxley's dystopia.

We're finding factors that could replace oxygen deprivation during fetal development. As a substitute for the administration of toxins—alcohol in the fictional *Brave New World*—the injection of modified viral genetic material encoding the toxic SARS-CoV-2 spike protein serves as a particularly perfidious example. This spiking, as I will call it in the following, inhibits hippocampal growth and activates neurodegeneration. I will demonstrate this in detail in the next chapter using scientific studies. However, if the neuronal degeneration is intentional, they would not want it to progress too quickly, otherwise it would end prematurely in hippocampal dementia or Alzheimer's disease. Indoctrination with the technocratic narrative would then be hopeless in principle, because ultimately there would not be enough index neurons available to overwrite. It remains to be seen whether spiking, in conjunction with other neurodegenerative factors, is properly dosed in this sense. However, based on my own research on the subject and due to various factors already mentioned, an increasing portion of humanity will live out their later existence with Alzheimer's, just like the "happy" inhabitants of Huxley's *Brave New World*.

This is where my late fascination with the content of this nearly century-old novel comes from: the identification of factors detrimental to adult hippocampal neurogenesis, or autobiographical memory, and the prevention and causal therapy of Alzheimer's disease. In *Brave New World*, people die at about sixty from "galloping dementia" because it progresses very rapidly. The drug soma, a major cause of rapid mental decline, makes dystopian life bearable until the abrupt end. For us, an inhumane, frightening prognosis for the future and an unprecedented crime against humanity, if it is deliberately pushed forward, is becoming increasingly likely, as I will show at the end of chapter 4.

Another efficient approach to inhibit hippocampal neurogenesis and to degenerate already existing hippocampal index neurons (and not only these) is to ensure a permanently high, neurotoxic release of glucocorticoids (a stress hormone, or better, the death anxiety hormone par excellence, since the adrenal glands of animals at the slaughterhouse release it in large quantities) in the general population, even in children. All imaginable anxiety scenarios are suitable for this purpose. The word *scenario* already indicates that the anxiety of agony and death can be caused by an effective staging, and the real danger can be completely irrelevant in its extent and even must be, because otherwise the uncontrollable anxiety would give way to a manageable fear with far less effect.

As a result of chronic anxiety for life and limb, the impaired production of new index neurons weakens psychological resilience, which in turn makes people easy to control and influence. However, because anxiety is also a proven means to the end of reprogramming the remaining hippocampal index neurons, provoking a state of constant anxiety has a double benefit. This, too, could be an essential intentional aspect of the broad technocratic assault on our identity and mental freedom.

Part 2: Overwriting the Remaining Index Neurons with the Technocratic Narrative

Most people think of ego depletion, or feeling exhausted after a long day, as a negative thing. But it is actually a protective mechanism that prevents us from switching on System 2 when our frontal brain battery is empty, when our hippocampus has no new index neurons available. If, despite mental exhaustion, we were to force ourselves to think about a problem late at night, for example, old index neurons would inevitably have to be used, which actually already serve as an access code for past experiences. The hippocampus would then have no choice but to overwrite them with the location and time coordinates of the new System 2 thoughts, which would forever destroy the index signatures and thus access to earlier memories stored on the neocortical "hard drive." Their contents would still be there, at least for a time, but without the hippocampal access codes, retrieval is no longer possible.

Thus, ego depletion is not an absolute obstacle for our brain to switch on System 2 or to generate a new persistent memory— it can be forced to do so by external circumstances. This makes sense from an evolutionary biological point of view. Also in the evening, in a state of mental exhaustion, it can be quite vital to think with System 2 instead of reacting with System 1, to cope with a situation perceived as life-threatening.

Rather than risk one's life and, in the worst case, have all memories become meaningless because one dies, it is better to reprogram a few index neurons and sacrifice access to a few memories of one's past life. Anxiety is a key toward a mental reset, as it is a longer acting emotion.

Fear or Anxiety?

"Fear and anxiety often occur together, but these terms are not interchangeable. Fear is an intense biological response to immediate danger, while anxiety is an emotion regarding things we think may happen. Anxious and frightening emotions can feel the same and be easily confused, but when comparing fear vs anxiety, there are several important differences between the two."[4] When we experience fear, a System 1 response such as fight or flight is usually the best choice. When feeling anxious, it is better to think about possible actions first—that is, to activate System 2. This works even if the ego is already depleting at that time and hippocampal index neurons already in use must be overwritten by System 2 activity. However, this emergency mechanism can be used very effectively against us. If one wants to delete our hippocampal access to autobiographical memories and implant new ones instead, one only has to transport the messages in the state of ego depletion and with sufficient fear.

By means of hypnopaedics, the world government in *Brave New World* succeeds in making people regard their respective caste as the only desirable one and feel comfortable in their mental and social lack of freedom. To this end, the caste-specific narrative is implanted in the memory through thousands of repetitions during sleep, so it becomes an irrefutable truth from birth to adolescence. In the real world, though, we recognize a counterpart to hypnopaedics and a particularly effective form of propaganda. The mainstream media, which we are taught to trust from an early age, incites fear in all its facets and, over time, entrenches a state of diffuse anxiety in people's psyches: wars, blackouts, COVID-19, the idea of symptomless infectiousness and being responsible for someone else's death, climate change and all its unclear consequences, and many other threats program our minds to feel anxious all the time. Fomenting anxiety, especially on the nightly news and in the specials, is a highly effective means of forcing the hippocampus to activate System 2, even in a state of ego depletion. Propagated content of the technocratic narrative is implanted in memory and, in the absence of new unused index neurons (see Step 1), access to earlier memories is simultaneously erased.

People gradually become slaves of technocratic thinking and its guidelines. They live in constant anxiety, and, as a result of their System 1 trained by means of System 2, they implement all measures without thinking.

One reason for the acceptance of the partly exaggerated and partly absurd measures and the demand not to question them (see Wieler's admonishing words) was certainly the already described self-reinforcing vicious circle of anxiety. It inhibited hippocampal neurogenesis via a permanently increased release of stress hormones: System 2 was shut down, and psychological resilience was reduced, which in turn exaggerated fear and made rational reflection almost impossible. Thus, one could easily be controlled by anxiety, even if the demands would have been considered completely absurd and possibly even dangerous in the absence of anxiety. Further, a blocked hippocampal neurogenesis induces anxiety of new experiences, thoughts, and opinions, which is equivalent to a depressive state of mind. Any critical thought brought in from the outside is vehemently rejected when propaganda or the technocratic narrative has become one's new identity. After all, no one likes it when his or her self-definition is called into question.

Clearly, what I describe is not happening by chance but according to a technocratic master plan. As a result of its implementation, a profoundly ego-weak narcissistic society is developing, which regards any dissenter as a pest to the social fabric. During the hot phase of the COVID-19 pandemic, people defended the dominant narrative not only because parts of it had already become aspects of their self-image but also because they felt comfortable only with mass conformity.

The leading media messages consisted partly of repetitive slogans, as they are used during hypnopedia in *Brave New World*. Indeed, a clear line was not always discernible, and many statements made by health ministers, government-loyal experts, and media representatives seemed chaotic and sometimes even contradictory, especially over time. There were constantly new assessments and regulations that no one could or would understand, let alone explain. But exactly such a media approach is necessary to maintain a permanent panic mode through constant, emotionally affecting course changes and thus to force the hippocampus to remember. A constant repetition of the same would not be considered strange by the hippocampus, because it is already known and would be ignored. Thus, the varied "infotainment" disguised as the evening news ensures that more and more of the old identity is replaced by a new self-image, which entails identification with the narrative (more on this in chapter 5).

The constant change of the superficial message, however, maintains the basic motive of a constant state of anxiety, which can never be controlled, because the actual cause of the anxiety is not concrete (which would then only trigger fear). It remains intangible. In their book *The Great Reset: Joe Biden and the Rise of 21st Century Fascism*, Glenn Beck and Justin Haskins show how doomsday prophets and professional anxiety generators use a four-step program, constantly repeated as an anxiety loop,[5] to draw people into their spell or into a vicious circle of permanent anxiety:

Step 1: Establish a Flexible Timeline

Do not tell people the disaster you are predicting is so imminent that they will see whether you are right in the near term, but also don't make your soon-to-be-crises too far out into the future that no one walking around today will live to see its effects.

Step 2: Propose Potential Solutions

Do not predict a disaster that cannot be "solved." There is no point in convincing people life on earth is going to end if there's nothing that can be done about it, because if you convince everyone they are all doomed, all they can do is hope you are wrong.

Step 3: Create a "Consensus"

Find real scientists who support *some* part of your claim, and then pretend they support *all* of it. Do not worry about getting caught in a lie; most people won't bother to check the scientific literature to see what you have been saying is true. Also, if possible, track down dishonest "scientists" who will back your claims in exchange for funding.

Step 4: Constantly Shift Your Predictions

Before it comes apparent to everyone that your first prediction is wildly incorrect, make a new prediction, and then repeat steps 1, 2, and 3.

Such a repetitive four-step program exposes the supposedly unrelated, seemingly chaotic, and numerous global threat scenarios for what they really are, to all appearances: a systematic attack on mental freedom. To optimize the effect of this anxiety loop in terms of hippocampal reprogramming, it was embedded in a well-tested and optimized eight-point indoctrination program, as I will show in detail in chapter 5. I'll say this in advance: The program has been perfected over centuries of trial and error. The US government learned it the hard way after the Korean War of 1950 to 1953 and has been testing it on prisoners at Guantánamo Bay since 2002, most likely to this day. All indications are that the knowledge gained from it was applied with scientific precision to the entire world population for the first time at the beginning of the year 2020.

CHAPTER 4

MASTER PLAN, PART 1: DESTRUCTION OF AUTOBIOGRAPHICAL MEMORY

What is bad is a climate that allows anxiety,
in which others deliberately stir up general anxieties for their own purposes.
— Caritas Association for the City of Cologne[1]

"Fear Eats the Soul"—Pretraumatic Stress Disorder

With this title of his 1974 social drama, the late German director Rainer Werner Fassbinder (1945–1982) created a catchphrase. It expresses the destructive power of persistent fear (or, more accurately, anxiety). In the film, Fassbinder describes the fate of a Moroccan immigrant worker named Ali, who develops a stomach ulcer due to chronic social stress. Today, almost half a century after I watched the movie on my grandparents' black-and-white television, I still have his despair and tortured soul in my hippocampal memory because I empathized with him while watching. As if Fassbinder had already understood, or at least guessed, the hippocampal role in establishing a person's identity, he has Ali say at one point, "Fear is not good. Fear eats soul!" It's not just the stomach lining that suffers from chronic stress; the hippocampal gateway to our personal memories that define who we are is also shrinking. Thus, Ali's stated insight is also a very serious indication of perhaps the most serious problem in our society today.

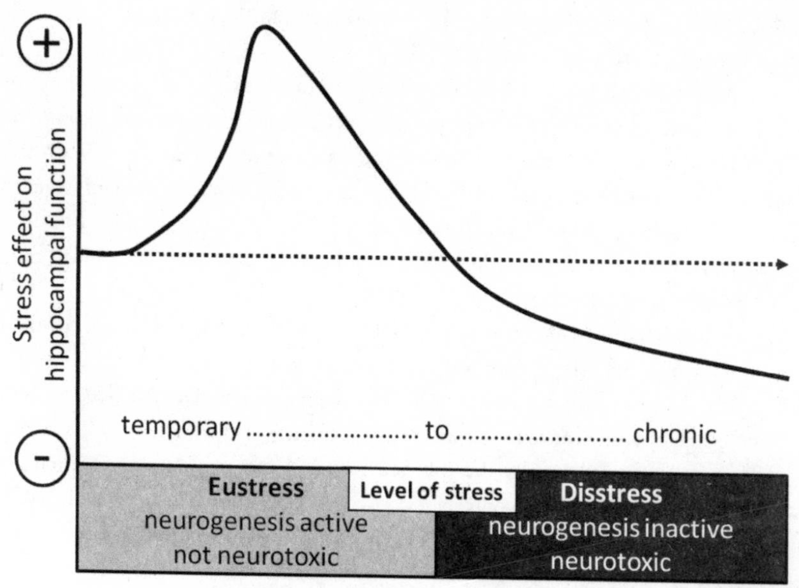

Figure 9

As shown in figure 9, eustress, or short-term stress in response to challenging situations, has a beneficial effect on hippocampal function by increasing neurogenesis. Chronic and intense stress (disstress) has the opposite effect.[2] By reducing synaptic plasticity—the ability of hippocampal neurons to form new connections with each other—intense stress impairs the memory function of the hippocampus.[3] In addition, stress is downright neurotoxic due to the chronically increased release of stress hormones, leading over time to a reduction in hippocampal volume typical of posttraumatic stress syndrome or even posttraumatic stress disorder (PTSD). These findings are now considered fairly well established, according to an international PTSD study published in 2018: "Across eight subcortical [below the neocortex] structures, only the hippocampus was unequivocally associated with PTSD. Therefore, the outsized role of the hippocampus in the literature is not attributable solely to greater attention paid to this structure."[4] According to the authors, their meta-analysis clearly demonstrates the importance of the hippocampus in the development and chronic persistence of PTSD.

However, in addition to the subcortical hippocampus, the frontal area of the neocortex itself is also affected by chronic stress and has been shown to lose volume as a result.[5] Thus, not only does the "frontal brain battery" lose capacity, but so does the frontal brain itself—our executive center. In PTSD, the traumatic event has a lasting effect on the sufferer's life: the person relives the horror in thoughts and dreams, withdraws from life, avoids anything that reminiscent of the event, and is often irritable and on constant alert.

As a psychiatric disorder, PTSD develops over the course of a lifetime in approximately 6 to 8 percent of the general population.[6] In selected groups, such as survivors of military combat like the Vietnam War, the rate can exceed 30 percent.[7] "With the rise in global terrorism and military conflict," say the authors of the aforementioned meta-analysis, which was curiously also funded by the Bill & Melinda Gates Foundation, "the public health impact of PTSD has attracted greater attention and fueled research on its neural and biological markers."

We see comparable conflicts with high and long-lasting stress potential for the general population in the form of the war against the coronavirus, the war against climate change, or the war in Ukraine, with which many people associate the deep-seated fear of an increasingly likely nuclear escalation and a third world war.

One can only speculate why the Bill & Melinda Gates Foundation is interested in this area of research. But one can also wonder why, a year before the unprecedented scare campaign around COVID-19, it was so important for the foundation to find out which factors, of all things, were causing the hippocampus to shrink. A clue to a possible motive is provided by another landmark finding from the study, which established firmly the importance of the hippocampus in PTSD. According to the study's authors, "the hippocampus is crucial for fear processing, episodic and contextual learning, and memory processes related to PTSD symptomatology." In other words, fear or stronger anxiety would be the only scientifically sound, proven means to most effectively damage our hippocampus. Generating anxiety alone is enough to shrink the hippocampus, since the idea of danger is from the brain's perspective no different from actual danger. Consequently, one does not necessarily have to experience actual horrific things; the anxiety that something bad might happen is enough to cause what is known as pretraumatic stress disorder. But instead of calming people's hippocampus, Bill Gates fueled the COVID-19 anxiety campaign in the media as a pandemic expert. He made prognostic recommendations for supposedly necessary countermeasures such as lockdowns, injections of viral genetic material, and much more to save humanity from the alleged killer virus. (Just to remind you, it is not the virus that kills, but the overreaction of the immune system due to the lack of vitamin D hormone.)

Pretraumatic stress disorder could also be abbreviated as PTSD, the same acronym for posttraumatic stress disorder. This would not be at all misleading, since it would also fall into the same disease category, or should be subsumed under it, as the two hippocampus specialists Dorthe Berntsen and David C. Rubin from the Danish University of Aarhus explain in the first scientific publication on this clinical picture: "Posttraumatic Stress Disorder is a diagnosis related to the past. Pre-traumatic stress reactions, as measured by intrusive involuntary images of possible future stressful events and their associated avoidance and increased arousal, have been overlooked in the PTSD literature."[8] To show that there is little difference between pre- and posttraumatic stress disorder, they developed a pretraumatic stress reaction (PreCL) checklist and administered it to Danish soldiers before, during, and after their deployment to Afghanistan. According to the study, published in 2015, the PreCL correlated with the standard measure of PTSD symptoms: "The PreCL as answered before the soldiers' deployment significantly predicted level of PTSD symptoms during and after their deployment." Pretraumatic stress reactions, such as involuntary imagery and thoughts about possible future events and associated avoidance attempts and heightened arousal states, were experienced at the same level as posttraumatic stress reactions to events during and after deployment.

Although pretraumatic stress disorder is not yet equated with posttraumatic stress disorder or subsumed under it, therapy centers specializing in it have proliferated. "When we hear of things like a pandemic, murder hornets, racial riots, and other terrifying life aspects," says the website of one of the many PTSD therapy centers, "we get scared. We picture being negatively impacted by these events before they even happen."[9] It goes on to say, "PTSD normally occurs with events that have already been experienced. If you have a survivor of a traumatizing event, you may have nightmares about the event or feel cautious over surrounding triggers. Pre-traumatic stress, on the other hand, is when you experience these same symptoms before the event has even happened." This is especially true as a result of news coverage of coronavirus, as PTSD therapists noted, "During this pandemic, people are constantly faced with the news of what is happening, which can cause them to worry that the same thing might happen to them. When they hear of people being sick or dying as a result of this virus, they get scared for themselves and their loved ones . . . This mental illness may not be recognized in the DSM-5 [standard classification of mental disorders used by mental health professionals in the United States], but it is still very real and serious."

This observation is now also supported by a study entitled "Why the COVID-19 Pandemic Is Traumatic Stressor."[10] The evil mind might think, *Goal accomplished!* The consequences are obvious: "Pre-traumatic stress can take over your life if you are experiencing worries about what could happen during this uncertain time. Your anxiety and trauma can push you to imagine the worst before it has even happened, making it harder for you to function every day."[11] A less obvious consequence is that the hippocampus shrinks, so while the technocratic Dementors don't give us a kiss to suck out our soul, they do ensure that it is eaten by constantly stoked fear.

If this is supposed to be about presenting the master plan, you may wonder, *why the detailed explanations of the state of scientific research on the role of fear in PTSD and its influence on hippocampal performance?* That's because this anxiety-stoking in the general population was anything but accidental. Thousands of leaked WhatsApp chats with statements of the then British Health Minister Matt Hancock prove this.[12] Similarly, according to a report of the renowned German news magazine *Der Spiegel*, both the Ministry of Defense and the Chancellor's Office had been informed of a package of measures by the German Federal Ministry of the Interior (BMI) on March 22, 2020, which pursued precisely the same goal—to stir up anxiety among the population.[13] This package of measures was still available on the BMI website until April 2021, about a year later, when the confidential" scenario paper disappeared in *1984* style. But the internet does not forget anything, as long as there are servers independent of the state and large corporations.[14] According to BMI, the strategy paper was written by experts from the health sector, crisis management, administration, and business. Point 4, "Conclusions for measures and open communication," calls for the worst-case scenario to be presented to the German population:

> In order to achieve the desired shock effect [!], the concrete effects of an infestation on human society must be made clear:
>
> 1) Many seriously ill patients are brought to the hospital by their relatives, but are turned away and die at home struggling to breathe. Suffocation or lack of air is a primal fear for every human being . . . So is the situation where nothing can be done to help loved ones whose lives are in danger. The images from Italy are disturbing.
>
> 2) 'Children will hardly suffer from the epidemic': Wrong. Children are easily infected, even with curfew restrictions, e.g. with the neighbor's children. If they then infect their parents, and one of them dies in agony at home, and they feel they are to blame because they forgot to wash their hands after playing, this is the most terrible [!] thing a child can ever experience.

The radical implementation of this well-thought-out and highly perfidious anxiety and panic strategy of the federal government against its own population then also had the desired effect, especially with regard to children, who were finally made the focus of this psychological warfare. The German Psychological Society, for example, writes that the daily life of children and adolescents in the midst of the COVID-19 pandemic was characterized by many stress factors. Many of the measures taken so far "hit children and adolescents particularly hard. School closures and distance learning, closed youth centers and few recreational opportunities, accompanied by concerns about the illness and death of parents and grandparents."[15] This concern was not just about a family member dying from an infection. The media spread the word that even the youngest were to blame. This let the government off the hook, even as it led media campaigns to ensure that effective preventive measures (such as adequate vitamin D intake) were not taken.

In the Age of Permacrises and Chronic Anxiety

The realization that autobiographical memory can be successively erased and at the same time massively manipulated with stoked fear explains, in my opinion, the great interest of the protagonists of the Great Reset in propagating as many further anxiety scenarios as possible. It is therefore hardly surprising that right at the beginning of the coronavirus pandemic in 2020, the WEF published a comprehensive report on all global risks, *The Global Risks Report 2020*.[16] All global risks are interrelated; each potential catastrophe conditions and amplifies many others. It seems utterly impossible to escape this web of existential risks. For the sake of clarity, the following chart (figure 10) shows only the relationship of climate change to all the other potential global crises listed in the 102-page document, and is thus representative of all the other factors that can create uncontrollable, unpredictable, and inescapable stress. It could optimally serve as a template for other issues that cause pretraumatic stress in the general population.

Children and adolescents in particular show the greatest effect of such fear campaigns, as psychiatrist Lise Van Susteren summarizes in a *British Medical Journal* (BMJ) blog post, "Children are particularly vulnerable to the psychological trauma from current extreme weather events. They can also be harmed by the fear of future harms."[17] Anxiety about future threats alone led to pretraumatic stress or pretraumatic stress disorder, with dramatic consequences, particularly for children, Van Susteren said: "Chronic stress can permanently affect brain development as well as brain functioning. Exposure to climate related stress during early development may have damaging life-long consequences, including maladaptive behaviors, memory problems, problems with attention, diminished inhibition, difficulty regulating emotions, impaired decision making, impaired problem solving, behavioral problems, and priming for future stressful events." Taken together, this symptomatology is strongly suggestive of damage to hippocampal neurogenesis—the common denominator for the multiple consequences of long-term pretraumatic stress. A 2017 report, sponsored by the American Psychological Association and ecoAmerica, confirmed that climate-change anxiety scenarios have acute mental health effects: "They cause stress, depression, and anxiety; strain social and community relationships; and are associated with increases in aggression, violence, and crime."[18]

The group of Americans who believe global warming is happening outnumbers those who don't by a ratio of six to one (72 percent versus 12 percent), according to a survey released in April 2022 by the Yale Program on Climate Change Communication and the George Mason University Center for Climate Change Communication.[19] According to the report, "more than half of Americans (56 percent) are aware that global warming is primarily caused by humans." When phrases like this describe a particular opinion held by a majority of people, it falsely suggests that the underlying factual claim is very likely to be true, and the resulting peer pressure encourages readers to subscribe to that opinion.

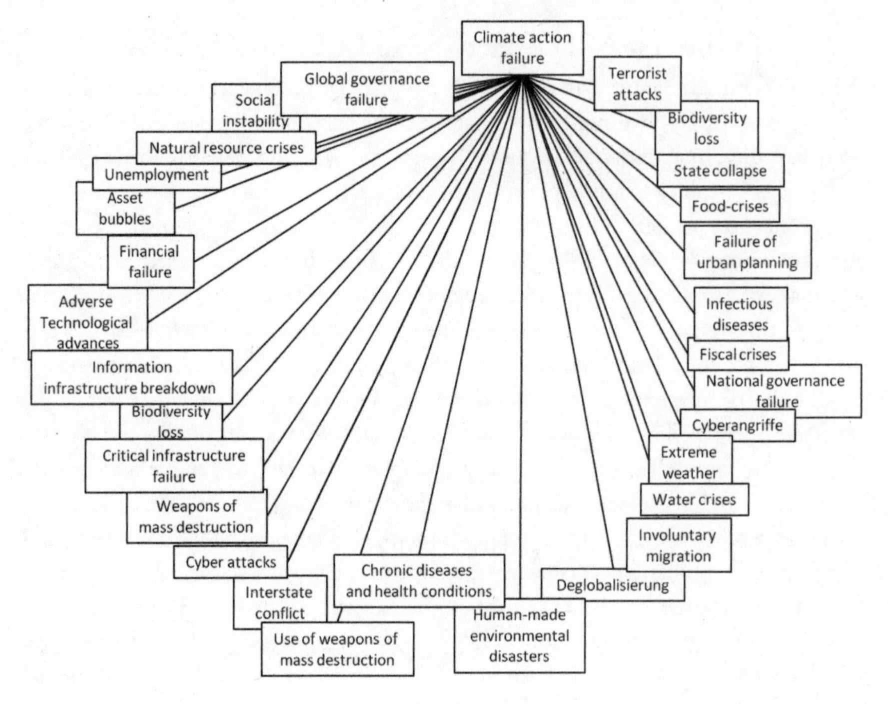

Figure 10

Conformity at All Costs

In the middle of the last century, the American social psychologist Solomon Asch conducted one of the most famous psychological experiments.[20] To test the power of the group over the individual (peer pressure), he asked a large group of students to collectively estimate the length of a line compared to the length of two other lines on a blackboard. Visual accuracy, however, was not the issue. Asch instructed all but one or two students to make an obviously incorrect estimate before the test. The actual test group thus consisted of those study participants who were unaware of this collusion and believed that the other students would freely decide as they did. They were able to impressively demonstrate the effect of groups over individuals: only about a quarter of the test subjects remained uninfluenced, and they made no mistakes in the total of twelve manipulated runs. So, they were self-confident enough to follow their convictions. But most, following the majority, did not trust their common sense and chose the wrong estimate.

Asch found that the smaller the test group as compared to the majority, the more likely this blind trust was. In other words, to get as many people as possible to make an obvious mistake, or to judge obviously wrong things as right, it is enough to make everyone *feel* that a majority thinks that way. In a self-fulfilling prophecy, the social compulsion to belong then ensures that a majority is actually formed.

As a medical doctor and molecular geneticist, I cannot even begin to call myself an expert in the field of global climate change and the question of the extent to which it is actually caused by humans. I can express my fundamental reservations about what I see as a completely one-sided discussion, as I also experienced with the COVID-19-pandemic. The point at which humans can no longer influence further climate derailment has been announced several times but is being pushed further and further into the future, as many other predictions on climate change. This reminds us of the four-step program that leads to an anxiety loop (see previous chapter).

In the field of immunology, on the other hand, my professional expertise allowed me to make a scientifically based assessment. It was obvious to me, and also easy to reason, that the horror scenarios propagated about the COVID-19 pandemic were highly dubious. Based on the data available at an early stage, mass deaths were not to be expected. Similarly, the supposed salvation offered by the injection of an experimental, gene-therapeutic vaccine could also not be regarded as anything more than fiction. In no way did the public claims to the contrary meet the usual requirements of scientific work and communication. This is why I fear that the information policy on mass extinction, as a result of man-made CO_2 emissions, is also very one-sided, with the same mainspring: the preservation and excessive expansion of power in a changing world. This assumption is suggestive when one considers the instrumentalization and political activity around "climate protection" against the backdrop of the Great Reset agenda, which is open to public scrutiny, and the extent to which the resulting anxiety serves as a means to the Great Mental Reset.

End of the world, mass death, and hopelessness—even the German minister of health is not above spreading a feeling of hopelessness and thus causing serious psychological damage to people. From a minister of health, who has sworn to "avert harm to the German people," we should expect a different kind of communication. After all, this oath obliges him to create the health-political conditions for the mental well-being of the citizens, without trivializing, but also without dramatizing. Although Karl Lauterbach does not belong to the YGL of the WEF, he has been blowing the same horn with his Schwab-compliant statements since his participation in the WEF conference in Davos in 2023 and thus contributes to the existential anxiety of the population becoming chronic. This does not only apply to his repeated misrepresentations about the danger of SARS-CoV-2 in order to push the spike. For example, on March 15, 2022, he significantly expanded his doomsday predictions on the radio station *RBB's Radio Eins*, where he announced the following:

> We are now entering a phase where the state of emergency will be the norm. From now on, we will always be in a state of emergency. Climate change will inevitably lead to more pandemics. More pandemics will put a strain on the economy, so it will be disrupted. We are entering a situation of global water scarcity. And wars over water are almost inevitable. So you can expect huge migrations [of peoples]. It used to be thought that there would be wars for oil. It is much more likely that there will be wars over water . . . Thus, we have a situation where . . . climate change is coming, pandemics are coming, water shortages are coming. We have a problem that we thought we had solved: the lack of food. In any case, huge migratory flows are coming.[21]

One could almost be surprised that with all these threatening scenarios he did not go on to talk about the potential dangers posed by UFOs and alien invasions, but perhaps that is only because it is the least likely way to scare people.

No Worries about UFOs

Fortunately, there is no "association between UFO sightings and emergency department visits," according to the title of an article by scientists at the prestigious Harvard University.[22] On the contrary, psychosis-related admissions were actually slightly lower on days with UFO sightings than on days without (2.33 versus 2.39 per 100,000). "Even if UFOs were indeed the work of extraterrestrials," the authors write, "the results of this study suggest that their activities are unlikely to harm human health." They may even offer hope of salvation from the all-too-earthly fear that has held us in its grip for years.

"However," the renowned German medical journal *Ärzte Zeitung* informs us, "this methodology does not allow us to draw conclusions about possible long-term damage. It could be that UFO-related health problems, such as cancer caused by extraterrestrial radiation [it actually says this!], only manifest themselves after years or decades."[23] The assumption would certainly have fallen into the category of conspiracy theories during the emergency approval of the COVID-19 vaccines. But at least for now, UFO sightings are *mostly* harmless.

Fear is not a good advisor. It can lead to panic and irrational decisions that rarely turn out to be wise in hindsight. Many people have been spiked only because of their anxiety about the alleged killer virus stirred up by the media. As early as November 2020 a large team of German scientists from the University of Bonn published that the infection fatality rate (IFR) was only 0.35 percent, hardly distinguishable from that of a normal flu.[24] As the disease progressed, with progressively weaker or less virulent variants, this figure continued to fall. Overall, the median mortality rate from corona infection was only 0.0003 percent in the 0–19 age group, 0.002 percent in the 20–29 age group, 0.011 percent in the 30–39 age group, and 0.035 percent in the 40–49 age group—only reaching 0.123 percent in the 50–59 age group and 0.506 percent in the 60–69 age group.[25] However, if adequate vitamin D supplementation would have been used, the mortality rate would have even been close to zero in *all* age groups (see the chapter 1 sidebar "Causal Prevention That No One Wanted").

Some people, unaware of such figures and due to the panic in the media and the irresponsible recommendations of the German Standing Committee on Vaccination (STIKO), have even exposed their children to an incalculable risk with experimental injections of viral genetic material—even though they do not belong to the risk groups. Many others did it simply to regain a little more freedom, until the official side finally admitted that the gene injections do not produce any protection for others, although this justified the social pressure. Even Anthony Fauci, director of the US National Institute of Allergy and Infectious Diseases (NIAID) since 1984, a key driver of the global pandemic from the beginning, and one of the leaders of the global spiking campaign,[26] writes the following as senior author in an article published in Spring 2023 entitled "Rethinking Next-Generation Vaccines for Coronaviruses, Influenzaviruses, and Other Respiratory Viruses":

> Taking all of these factors into account, it is not surprising that none of the predominantly mucosal respiratory viruses have ever been effectively controlled by vaccines. This observation raises a question of fundamental importance: if natural mucosal respiratory virus infections do not elicit complete and long-term protective immunity against reinfection, how can we expect vaccines, especially systemically administered non-replicating vaccines, to do so?[27]

If such statements are an attempt to clear one's name after the fact, they tend to have the opposite effect on anyone who can still think. Viruses that infect our respiratory tract have been around since time immemorial. Especially in the case of influenza, there is a sufficiently large pool of data from which the knowledge of effective vitamin prevention could have been derived long before the immensely harmful, worldwide mRNA vaccination campaign was even conceived. It is therefore very surprising that Fauci felt compelled to make this admission so late.

I want to point out the wording here: "non-replicating." Interestingly, a new spiking method is already being worked on in which the viral mRNA for the spike protein can continue to replicate independently after injection, which would also achieve permanent production of the neurotoxic S1 subunit.[28]

Despite Fauci's late admission about the predictable failure of the spiking program, there is no mention of the failure of mRNA vaccines in an *Ärzte Zeitung* article titled "With new techniques faster to effective vaccines."[29] Instead, it quotes a more than dubious earlier statement by Fauci from an article in the *New England Journal of Medicine* (*NEJM*): "The unprecedented speed with which safe and highly effective Covid-19 vaccines were developed, proven effective, and distributed resulted in millions of lives saved." He probably sees it differently now (see above). Still, there is no talk of ineffectiveness or record of serious side effects. Rather, the new technical capabilities created by the spiking program under COVID-19 are expected to significantly expand the reach: "For example, Moderna is developing vaccines against HIV, Zika and Epstein-Barr virus (EBV), and has already presented promising Phase III data for an RSV vaccine. The company hopes to launch its mRNA vaccine against RSV as early as next year. In addition to cancer vaccines, BioNTech is also investigating vaccines for tuberculosis, malaria, HIV, herpes zoster and influenza."

Spiking thus never provided effective protection against infection, and those who have received one or more of these injections must instead now live in anxiety about a whole range of possible late effects. But this chronic anxiety could also be an intentional part of the technocratic program if, as I suspect, it aims to reprogram our autobiographical memory. The assumption becomes all the more plausible when one considers that while spiking itself does not help against the coronavirus, it is instead neurotoxic and even suppresses hippocampal neurogenesis.

Spiking—Destructive Attack on the Human Brain

Many different COVID-19 measures have neuropathological effects. A common effect is depersonalization through the destruction of autobiographical memory, a necessary precursor to successful indoctrination. We have to suspect that it is precisely these shared effects that are the real purpose of these measures, and therefore it is most likely a targeted attack. Many presumed inconsistencies then become clear, and connections open up from a new perspective, to questions such as, What is the most plausible explanation for the choice of a corona family virus for the 2019 pandemic simulation? What are the odds that such a coronavirus would affect an identity-forming part of the human brain as specifically as many of the measures supposedly taken to contain the disease, not least spiking?

In 2002 the US Salk Institute, founded by vaccine pioneer Jonas Edward Salk (1914–1995), an American physician and immunologist who developed the inactivated polio vaccine, published that interleukin-6 (IL-6) significantly inhibits adult hippocampal neurogenesis.[30] Five years later, in 2007, Chinese researchers at the State Key Laboratory of Virology, College of Life Science, Wuhan University, clearly demonstrated that the spike protein of SARS-CoV-1, the virus responsible for severe acute respiratory syndrome (SARS) in 2003 and 2004, causes our immune system to release large amounts of proinflammatory messengers such as IL-6 and tumor necrosis factor alpha (TNF-alpha).[31] In other words, the coronary spike protein indirectly attacks the natural function of our autobiographical memory via our own immune system.

In animal experiments, this hippocampal assault has been shown to operate even across the placenta when fetuses are exposed to maternal IL-6. For example, in 2006 Swedish researchers published an article entitled "Prenatal Exposure to Interleukin-6 Results in Inflammatory Neurodegeneration in Hippocampus . . . and Impaired Spatial Learning."[32] Inflammatory release of IL-6 in pregnant animals, for example in the context of immunization, blocks hippocampal neurogenesis in the fetuses and has long-lasting effects on the development and function of the maturing brain that were detectable even in the later adult animals.[33] In humans, chronically elevated IL-6 levels are also inversely related to hippocampal volume, implying that any prolonged inflammation permanently damages adult neurogenesis and contributes to neurodegeneration.[34] However, not only the proinflammatory messenger IL-6 has a negative impact on autobiographical memory but also TNF-α does, which is equally released as a result of an exaggerated immune response to the coronary spike protein, as outlined.[35] Similar effects are seen for many other proinflammatory messengers, such as IL-1β, which also blocks hippocampal neurogenesis very efficiently.[36]

Knowing that the corona spike protein can cause lasting damage to the hippocampus, all that was needed, if such damage was intended, was to find an efficient way to deliver this neurotoxic viral protein to the brain as a vaccine. However, not every drug can easily cross the blood-brain barrier, because the brain uses this barrier to protect itself from potentially toxic foreign substances, including viral material or chemotherapeutic agents. Years ago, however, with the development of lipid nanoparticles (LNPs), molecules were found that could act as brain-penetrating packaging material; that is, they could cross the blood-brain barrier. Their original use was to deliver chemotherapeutic drugs to the brain for the treatment of brain tumors (see sidebar *Brain Toxic Packaging*).[37] It was no secret that LNPs could also be used to deliver genetic material in the form of DNA or mRNA to the brain or brain cells to become biologically active.[38] Thus, the packaging of the modified viral spike mRNA in LNPs is a serious indication that it was accepted or even intended to deliver the viral spike RNA into the brain so that the spike would be produced in brain cells, possibly even over a long period. In fact, the European Medicines Agency's (EMA) assessment report for the Moderna vaccine noted that the mRNA was found in the brain, despite having been injected into the muscle, as usual. Two to four percent of the amount found in blood plasma (the liquid, cell-free portion of blood) was detectable in the brain, meaning it had crossed the blood-brain barrier.[39] Interestingly, not only is the spike protein produced there neurotoxic, but also the packaging itself is. The packaging triggers a very severe inflammatory response.

Brain Toxic Packaging

Interleukin 1—and in particular the neurogenesis-inhibiting variant IL-1β—is massively activated by spiking, along with IL-6, TNF-α, and several other pro-inflammatory messengers, as demonstrated by a study published in *Nature Immunology*.[40] But we already know this. The publication does not name any authors, which is completely unusual. One can therefore only speculate why no one took responsibility for the content by name. It cannot have been due to the quality of the work itself, otherwise it would not have been published. The mere fact that a renowned journal published the study—even without naming the authors—is an indication of the outstanding scientific importance of the paper. The unknown authors comment as follows:

> This project involved scientists from different departments and divisions of Genentech (United States) and BioNTech (Germany). It was triggered by observations in our joint Phase 1 clinical trial in 2017, in which cancer patients received the RNA-LPX vaccines . . . We have made considerable progress [since then] in characterizing the role of IL-1 in the inflammatory responses triggered by unmodified RNA-LPX. In 2021, following the success of modified RNA-LNP vaccines in the prophylaxis of COVID-19, . . . we found to our surprise that IL-1 is strongly induced by modRNA-LNPs [LNPs package chemically modified mRNA], making the mechanistic basis of the IL-1-mediated inflammatory response . . . even more complex.

In other words, LNP packaging alone can inhibit hippocampal neurogenesis because of the tremendous inflammatory response it induces. This is further amplified by the modified viral mRNA it transports into cells. Could these effects, which are extremely detrimental to brain function, be reason enough for the authors not to want to be named? Shortly thereafter, studies began to emerge showing the devastating inflammation that spiking causes in the brains of newly vaccinated individuals.[41]

Thus, LNP spike mRNA injections attack the human brain in several ways: through the toxicity of the packaging; through the toxicity of the content, which causes brain cells to produce viral spike protein and thus make themselves the target of an immunologic, cytotoxic attack; and, last but not least, through the inflammatory response triggered by the spike protein, which is neurotoxic and blocks neurogenesis. The fourth and, in my opinion, most insidious mechanism (a process also referred to as *shedding*, but which has nothing to do with a human-to-human transmission of injectables often claimed under this term) I will address in a moment because it also indicates how SARS-CoV-2 was prepared for its task.

Five Steps in the Preparation of a Crime against Humanity

Given the potential dangers described, it is clear that mentioning them should have been an integral part of any medical information session. However, honest and comprehensive information could have prevented billions of people from being persuaded to be injected with these brain-damaging gene therapy substances. So, a global manipulation was carefully organized. Indeed, a closer look reveals (at least) five steps, all of which were planned long in advance and created the conditions for this global coup to succeed so well.

Step 1: Change the Definition of a Pandemic

The WHO changed the requirements for declaring a pandemic. The trivialization of the term *pandemic* in 2009, mentioned in the first chapter, was largely responsible for the way the global community had to react to new viruses in the future, even if they were relatively harmless. Until then, the WHO had defined the term using the example of a wave of influenza caused by the influenza virus: "An influenza pandemic occurs when a new influenza virus appears against which the human population has no immunity, resulting in several, simultaneous epidemics worldwide with enormous numbers of deaths and illness."[42] This original definition made a lot of sense because the danger to the world's population would be very great in such an event. But on May 4, 2009, "enormous numbers of deaths and illnesses" was removed. Thus, the revised and simplified definition that remains in effect today (as of spring 2023) is "An influenza pandemic may occur when a new influenza virus appears against which the human population has no immunity."[43]

Under these conditions, a pandemic can be declared even with no significant threat to the world's population, because the pathogen need only be new and not capable of causing severe illness, let alone many deaths. Any genetic variant for which there is no current immunity, no matter how harmless, would be grounds for declaring a pandemic. The WHO's press officer at the time, Natalie Boudou, told CNN's US newsmagazine that the change was made because the original definition was wrong: "It was a mistake, and we apologize for the confusion," she said. "[The earlier definition] was put up a while ago and paints a rather bleak picture and could be very scary."[44] However, it is much scarier to declare a pandemic and put humanity in mortal anxiety, deprive them of their civil liberties, and destroy many lives, when in the end it is just as dangerous as a normal flu epidemic and one in which there would be virtually no deaths with vitamin D prophylaxis, as discussed previously.

Step 2: Create a Problem for an Intended Solution

In Wuhan, a new coronavirus was created that, at first glance, met the only three relevant conditions of the WHO definition, in place since 2009, for a pandemic to be declared: it had to be highly infectious, it had to occur in several areas defined by the WHO, and humanity had to have no natural immunity to it. At least that is what the media and politicians wanted people to believe. In fact, the last condition was never met. Even at the beginning of the pandemic, widespread immunity to other members of the coronavirus family ensured that the population already had some degree of cross-immunity to SARS-CoV-2 without ever having been exposed to it.[45]

However, SARS-CoV-2 has a startling new property that also accounts for its extraordinary infectivity: it goes through the steps necessary to replicate and infect other cells much faster than previously known coronaviruses. To enter and replicate in a host cell, the spike protein of coronaviruses must be cleaved twice (by certain enzymes in the host cell). In the case of SARS-CoV-1, which was not very successful in pandemic terms in 2003 and 2004 due to a lack of infectivity (there were comparatively few infections and also few deaths), these two cleavages occur only after the virus has docked to a cell. This was a limiting factor in the speed at which the virus spread. SARS-CoV-2, however, is optimized in this respect: it possesses a furin cleavage site that was previously completely unknown in the large family of known coronaviruses. Furin is an endogenous enzyme that cleaves proteins at such a site, thereby activating them. Since SARS-CoV-2—in contrast to SARS-CoV-1 and all other known coronaviruses—has such a furin cleavage site, all newly formed virus particles are cleaved for the first time as soon as they leave the infected cell. Pre-activated in this way, these corona viruses can infect a cell more easily than those whose spike protein requires two additional cleavages.

"SARS-CoV-2 is the only coronavirus to carry 12 unique letters [more precisely, nucleotides in a unique combination] that [code for a furin cleavage site and therefore] allow its spike protein to be activated by the furin enzyme, allowing it to easily spread between human cells," *China Daily* writes.[46] Those twelve letters are part of a nineteen-letter sequence that is also unique, as otherwise found only in a patent granted to spike vaccine maker Moderna in 2017, two years before the first COVID-19 cases.[47] "The genetic sequence was discovered in SARS-CoV-2's (the coronavirus's) furin cleavage site (FCS), the part that makes it highly efficient at infecting people and that separates it from other coronaviruses," explains the international team of researchers who made the astonishing discovery, to *China Daily*. The researchers add the following in their research article: "Conventional biostatistical analysis indicates that the probability of this sequence randomly being present in a 30,000-nucleotide viral genome is 3.21×10^{-11}."[48] In other words, a probability of one in three trillion (or three thousand billion) makes it virtually inconceivable that this unique sequence got into SARS-CoV-2 by chance or by natural means. It is worth revisiting this information in light of the official narrative: SARS-CoV-2 thus acquired the exceptionally high infectivity that Event 201 predicted for a conceivable and imminent next pandemic originating in China only by carrying this highly improbable, supposedly natural mutation in the genome. This mutation is responsible for the virus to produce a furin cleavage site—whose exact nucleotide coding in the genome is against all plausible probability identical to a sequence a vaccine manufacturer (of which hardly anyone had heard before 2020) against SARS-CoV-2 had patented.

Intended Spike-Furin Cleavage Site in SARS-CoV-2

In March 2018 a proposal was submitted to the Defense Advanced Research Projects Agency (DARPA), the research arm of the US Department of Defense, describing, among other things, the creation of infectious clones of full-length bat SARS-related coronaviruses and the insertion of a new cleavage site: "We will analyze all SARSr-CoV S [*SARS r*elated-*CoV S*pike] gene sequences for the presence of potential furin cleavage sites."[49] The plan continues, "We will introduce appropriate human specific cleavage sites and evaluate growth potential in . . . [cell] . . . cultures." We only know about the proposal, written by the US nonprofit EcoHealth Alliance, thanks to a leak. This organization says it is funded primarily by US federal agencies such as the Department of Defense, the Department of Homeland Security, and the US Agency for International Development.[50]

If I'm right in assuming that the corona pandemic is not only targeting our property ("I own nothing") and our human rights but also our brains and our ability to think, then the originators of the idea to equip SARS-CoV-2 with this furin cleavage site were endowed with diabolical ingenuity. Besides making the virus more efficient in spreading, it allows for the release of the highly toxic S1 subunit of the viral spike protein, which is released (shed) by the body's own furin.[51] This small but highly toxic protein can easily cross the blood-brain barrier without the presence of LNPs. This means that a corona infection can be neurotoxic to the brain even if the virus only infects the respiratory tract.[52] However, as far as I know at the time of this writing (spring 2023), there are no robust studies on whether the S1 subunit released by shedding can also be transmitted between people in significant amounts and, if so, what health problems this would cause. What is serious, however, is the internal shedding that undoubtedly occurs in the body, not only in the course of an infection but also especially as a result of spiking. That's because the toxic S1 subunit can travel through the bloodstream to the brain from all the tissues and organs that produce the spike protein over long periods.

The laboratory-origin hypothesis of SARS-CoV-2 is also supported by the fact that, despite the most intensive search (well over eighty thousand animals were tested around Wuhan), no related coronavirus has yet been found that could have served as a possible natural precursor.[53] Consistent with this, the SARS-CoV-2 genome has a peculiar pattern of highly specific interfaces for equally highly specific molecular scissors that allow efficient artificial remodeling of synthetic viruses. The discoverers of this pattern noted that "SARS-CoV-2 is an anomaly, more likely a product of synthetic genome assembly than natural evolution."[54] "The restriction map of SARS-CoV-2," or, the distribution of these sites in the viral genome, the scientists noted, "is consistent with many previously reported synthetic coronavirus genomes, meets all the criteria required for an efficient reverse genetic system, differs from closest relatives by a significantly higher rate of synonymous mutations in these synthetic-looking recognitions sites, and has a synthetic fingerprint unlikely to have evolved from its close relatives." They conclude, "We report a high likelihood that SARS-CoV-2 may have originated as an infectious clone assembled in vitro ['in a jar,' i.e., artificially in the laboratory]."

Meanwhile, US authorities are also gradually changing their view on the origin of the virus. According to a report that appeared in the *Wall Street Journal* on February 26, 2023, the Department of Energy revised its previous assessment based on new evidence and considers "lab leak most likely origin of COVID-19 pandemic."[55] A few days later, FBI Director Christopher Wray also stated, as reported by Reuters, "The FBI has for quite some time now assessed that the origins of the pandemic are most likely a potential lab incident in Wuhan." And he "accused the Chinese government of 'doing its best to try to thwart and obfuscate' efforts by the United States and others to learn more about the pandemic's origins."[56]

All that really remains to be seen is whether the virus found its way out of the Wuhan lab by accident or was deliberately released and whether it is plausible that Event 201 was carried out without knowledge of what events would unfold in the near future. At least Bill Gates must have had truly prophetic intuitions in September 2019, about two months before this event and about a quarter of a year before the coronavirus outbreak, when he invested up to $100 million through his foundation in a small German biotechnology company, located "an der Goldgrube 12" [the street name, meaning, "at the gold mine"] in Mainz, which had been making losses until then.[57] Many coincidences are responsible for the fact that this was not money burned, but money well invested, namely that 1) a Corona pandemic would happen in the foreseeable future, 2) in the competition for the dominant vaccine, mRNA-based spiking would actually prevail, and 3) this very company would bring the globally dominating bestseller to market together with the pharmaceutical giant Pfizer—and in a record time of only one year of research and development. About ten to twelve years would have been in the normal range for vaccine development.

Unprecedented

Simple vaccines are the result of unmodified application of existing vaccine technologies, and complex vaccines are the result of modified application. HIV and malaria vaccines are examples of the latter. A publication sponsored by the Bill & Melinda Gates Foundation further categorizes vaccine development as unprecedented.[58] As their analysis shows, unprecedented vaccines are expected to take ten to twelve years and more to develop, yet success is not guaranteed; on the contrary, there is only about a 5 percent chance of surviving Phase II (evaluation of efficacy) and only a 40 percent chance of surviving Phase III (evaluation of population benefit). In other words, an unprecedented vaccine that made it through Phase I was predicted to have a 2 percent chance of success in Phase III clinical trials.

According to an article by two US scientists entitled "Worse Than the Disease? Reviewing Some Possible Unintended Consequences of the mRNA Vaccines against COVID-19,"[59] several of the novel vaccines were unprecedented, but not only in terms of development time. They include the first use of mRNA vaccine technology against an infectious agent; the first product to be commercialized by Moderna (with the help of the Bill & Melinda Gates Foundation);[60] the first vaccine to be introduced to the public with only preliminary efficacy data available, such as reduction of infections, transmissibility, or deaths; more generally, the first coronavirus vaccine ever tested in humans; and the first injection of genetically engineered viral genome into the general population.[61]

Creating an unprecedented vaccine in just one year with billions of doses distributed? Was much more known in advance, or was it just unlikely luck in the misfortune of others? To determine whether technocrats like Gates and company planned all of this down to the last detail, one must rely on circumstantial evidence, as in any legal process in which there are no eyewitnesses, as well as evidence of motive (see "Closing Argument" in chapter 7). This will be examined in future trials when the evidence becomes more solid and the prohibitions on thinking in this regard lose their effect. What is important for my considerations, however, is only that with the intentional or accidental release of the virus, a Pandora's box was opened, because at least a conscious decision was made to use this outbreak to test a novel unprecedented genetic vaccine on the whole of humanity. The actors knew full well that most people would have rejected such injections of mRNA material under normal conditions and also knew how dangerous the spike protein is for the human organism and the brain in general, and what damage it does to autobiographical memory in particular. Add to that there would have been a healthy alternative to prevent the spread of the virus and the severe course of the disease.

Catastrophic Chain Reaction

The literally unbelievable speed with which it was possible to react to the new virus is thought-provoking—not only the warp speed of vaccine production but also the speed at which PCR detection was possible. The SARS-CoV-2 genome was sequenced on January 10, 2020, just weeks after the first cases were observed in Wuhan. This was a world record. On January 12 China shared this information with other countries to develop a PCR test, according to the WHO.[62] Just one day later, virologist Christian Drosten and Olfert Landt, head of the Berlin-based company TIB Molbiol, had a PCR test for the virus ready, which the WHO immediately popularized as the gold standard. But how TIB Molbiol managed to send a working PCR test out into the world three days earlier, on January 10, the day the virus sequence was officially published, will hopefully soon no longer be a trade secret.[63] And what a deal it was! This "test," like the later "vaccine," was a best-seller and at the same time a driving force of the pandemic, because it was completely unsuitable for the detection of actually infectious viruses, as its inventor must have known very well.

In May 2014, for example, Drosten told the German economy journal *Wirtschafts Woche,* on the subject of MERS (Middle Eastern respiratory syndrome, a respiratory disease triggered in the Middle East in 2012 by an earlier coronavirus), that the PCR method was so sensitive "that it can detect a single hereditary molecule of this virus."[64] Drosten continues, "For example, if such a pathogen flits across a nurse's nasal mucosa for a day without her getting sick or noticing anything else, she is suddenly a MERS case. Where previously fatally ill people were reported, now mild cases and people who are actually perfectly healthy are suddenly included in the reporting statistics. This could also explain the explosion of cases in Saudi Arabia. In addition, the local media have made an incredible fuss about it."

The same strategy was now being used globally with SARS-CoV-2. Only the enormous number of false positives can explain why in the first corona year 2020 fewer (and not more!) respiratory illnesses were billed in hospitals in Germany, both in normal and in intensive care units, than in 2019, which was a pandemic-free year. This is the result of the analysis of the hospital performance and the compensation lump sum in the coronavirus crisis for the period January to December 2020 by the Leibniz Institute for Economic Research on behalf of the German Federal Ministry of Health.[65] In fact, there were significantly fewer respiratory illnesses. Overall (with and without a positive test for coronavirus) there was a decrease of about 12.6 percent. In other words, the "epidemic situation of national significance" that allowed all the exaggerated anti-COVID-19 measures by law never happened, but a great many false-positive PCR tests could be used to declare even heart attack deaths as COVID-19 victims.

Step 3: Forge Sinister Alliances

It was ensured that when the WHO declared a pandemic, already prepared, binding purchase contracts for new vaccines were signed between governments and pharmaceutical companies that are leaders in the field of vaccine production.[66] This, too, had been prepared long in advance: For example, an alliance of WHO, UNICEF, and the US National Institute of Allergy and Infectious Diseases (NIAID) with Anthony Fauci as its director, and under the lead of the Bill & Melinda Gates Foundation announced in late 2010, "Global Health Leaders Launch Decade of Vaccines Collaboration."[67] This announcement declared WHO's power in international health, as stated on the Bill & Melinda Gates Foundation website: "WHO is the directing and coordinating authority on international health within the United Nations system. It is responsible for providing leadership on global health matters, shaping the health research agenda, setting norms and standards, articulating evidence-based policy options, providing technical support to countries and monitoring and assessing health trends." It is easy to see the enormous, sweeping power that WHO can assert over all nations worldwide. And it does so without being legitimized by democratic elections.

Andrej Konstantin Hunko, a member of the German Bundestag since 2009, challenged the power of the pharmaceutical industry and the WHO in a speech to the Parliamentary Assembly of the Council of Europe on June 24, 2010:

> I have here secret contracts concluded in Germany between [the pharmaceutical giant] GlaxoSmithKline and the German state. As an ordinary member of parliament, I am not allowed to see these contracts officially. They have been put on the Internet in Germany by whistleblowers. These contracts specify exactly what must happen when level 6 [the WHO's highest pandemic alert level] is declared—what quantities of vaccine doses the states must buy, etc. Most countries had such contracts in place before the criteria were changed [before the severity of infection was removed from the pandemic definition]. The declaration of pandemic level 6 effectively flipped a switch and set in motion the whole cascade that is now apparent. We need to sort this out urgently.[68]

Hunko then posed the crucial rhetorical question, which he immediately answered himself: "Is the swine flu perhaps a particularly clever marketing strategy, a fraud by the pharmaceutical and vaccine industry at the expense of the people, the public budgets and ultimately also the WHO? We don't know, because there is no transparency. We have to get to the bottom of this."

As of this writing in the spring of 2023, there has been no clarification; instead, the expansion of this system has continued, and preparations for the next pandemic have been made. "The Global Vaccine Action Plan" continues the Bill & Melinda Gates Foundation website, "will enable better coordination among all stakeholder groups—national governments, multilateral organizations, civil society, the private sector and philanthropic organizations—and will identify critical policy, resource, and other gaps that must be addressed to realize the life-saving potential of vaccines." The preface to this global vaccine program states, "The Global Vaccine Action Plan (GVAP) is a framework approved by the World Health Assembly in May 2012 to achieve the 'Decade of Vaccines' vision by delivering universal access to immunization."[69]

"The mission outlined in the GVAP is straightforward: improve health by extending by 2020 and beyond the full benefits of immunization to all people, regardless of where they are born, who they are, or where they live." To that end, GVAP has set six strategic goals for all of humanity by 2020:

- All countries commit to immunization as a priority.
- Individuals and communities understand the value of vaccines and demand immunization both as a right and a responsibility.
- The benefits of immunization are equitably extended to all people.
- Strong immunization systems are an integral part of a well-functioning health system.

- Immunization programmes have sustainable access to predictable funding, quality supply and innovative technologies.
- Country, regional, and global research and development innovations maximize the benefits of immunization.[70]

Bill Gates, secretly head of the WHO and official initiator of the GVAP, and his allies planned long before 2020 how the world community should behave. Then, to elicit a willingness to recognize vaccination as a weapon with no alternative, he also warned the global community about the middle of the vaccination decade with a pandemic horror scenario—a warning that is difficult to distinguish from an advertising campaign, due to his multilayered involvement in pandemic contracting and his reportedly extremely profitable investments in vaccination research[71]—when he proclaimed in a TED Talk in 2015, "If anything kills over ten million people in the next few decades, it's highly likely to be a highly infectious virus rather than a war—not missiles, microbes."[72]

Five years after Gates's announcement, in the spring of 2020 when the WHO declared a pandemic, the world suddenly found itself in a war against an invisible, menacing enemy. Binding purchase agreements with Pfizer (for the BioNTech vaccine), Moderna, and other pharmaceutical companies were signed shortly thereafter on a global scale. According to the German Chancellery, the EU had immediately secured 2.6 billion doses of vaccine.[73] And in April 2021 it ordered an additional 1.8 billion doses from Pfizer alone, to be delivered by 2023.[74] At a hearing of the European Parliament's Special Committee on COVID-19 Pandemic on August 30, 2022, German MEP Sylvia Limmer (AfD) asked the EU Commission's director general and Chief Vaccine Negotiator Sandra Gallina how she could justify the fact that, according to the EU Commission, a total of 5.2 billion doses of vaccine had already been delivered or bindingly ordered. Gallina responded, "Let me repeat to you that don't you think that these are too many vaccines . . . Many vaccines, yes, but let me say, we were planning to have more than one vaccination, in a sense the word *vaccination* is misleading."[75] But if it is not a vaccine, what is the purpose of the injections? And why so many?

Let's do the math: assuming a vaccination rate of 80 percent (according to surveys, about 10 percent of people would never be vaccinated with this technology,[76] plus infants, while they are still spared), this would mean fourteen to fifteen nonreturnable vaccinations (!) have for each of the 360 million EU citizens who have so far been rather uncritical of mRNA injections. In other words, it was known very early on that single doses would provide virtually no protection against infection, which is why revaccinations would have to be given at very short intervals (which is why "the word *vaccination* is misleading," as Gallina has publicly acknowledged). And this was when people were still being led to believe that two doses were enough.

The State as Pharmacy

Leaked Pfizer contracts show that the states assume full liability for vaccine damage and Pfizer is held harmless.[77] In addition, the acceptance or payment of ordered vaccine doses is guaranteed, even if better products exist or are developed in the meantime. There is also no right of return in the event of failure to achieve the vaccination rates, which were the reason for the order. This had to lead either to compulsory vaccination by the state or at least to duress to vaccinate, despite the fact that the vaccine did not work from the beginning and no protective effect was to be expected anyway, due to the constant appearance of new virus variants. In any case, it became clear that states, if only to save face, are inclined to use their power to pass on to the population the utilization pressure created by the gag contracts.

Step 4: Cast Out the Devil with Beelzebub

With spiking declared as vaccination, a completely new field of application of an experimental, gene-therapeutic procedure has been created, whereby the term *therapeutic* is completely out of place. For the shot is not therapy, but only an attempt at immunization. A therapy should have the goal of making a patient healthy, but no one becomes healthier by spiking; rather, the opposite is the case. One must first realize that and why exactly SARS-CoV-2 itself, even if it only infects the respiratory tract, damages hippocampal neurogenesis. This astonishing fact was summarized by two Indian researchers in their article "SARS-CoV-2-Mediated Neuropathogenesis, Deterioration of Hippocampal Neurogenesis and Dementia"[78] as follows: "A significant portion of COVID-19 patients and survivors display marked clinical signs of stress, depression, anxiety, endocrine disruption and neurodegenerative disorders accounting for a wide array of cognitive deficits ranging from mild cognitive impairment to irreversible dementia." In making their case, the two researchers point to histological studies of brains of deceased humans and laboratory animals showing that SARS-CoV-2 infection affects the neurogenic process in the hippocampus of the brain. In light of this, they strongly caution "that neuroinflammation-mediated deterioration of hippocampal neurogenesis could contribute to the onset and progression of [hippocampal] dementia in COVID-19."

Spiking against Alzheimer's Disease?

The article "COVID-19 Vaccination May Enhance Hippocampal Neurogenesis in Adults," published online on October 3, 2022, suggests that although COVID-19 disease negatively affects adult hippocampal neurogenesis, spiking might promote adult hippocampal neurogenesis.[79] However, this claim is based only on the observation that completely different vaccines against respiratory infections, such as influenza, stimulate adult hippocampal neurogenesis in animal models. That spiking specifically releases the neurotoxic S1 subunit, among others, is ignored in the article. Completely disregarding the actual circumstances and the relevant scientific literature, COVID-19 vaccination is suddenly even said to protect against age-related cognitive decline and mental disorders, and, according to the article "hints at an added mental health benefit of the COVID-19 vaccination programs in adults."

Karl Lauterbach, as the current German minister of health, promoted a major media campaign in August 2022 with similar reasoning, warning of the threat of dementia from natural infection: "We now know that corona infection can lead to brain damage and, in the worst case, dementia. With the second or third booster [that would be the fourth or fifth spiking!], individuals can significantly reduce the likelihood of such late effects—especially in those over 60."[80] However, there is not a single study of spiked individuals to support these bold claims. In fact, the opposite is true. Nevertheless, the German minister of health was not above using the general fear of Alzheimer's to increase the pressure for vaccination. I wonder if he was aware that he was perfidiously increasing the risk of Alzheimer's in the German population, as I will show in detail.

The major driver of this brain-damaging neuroinflammation is the S1 subunit of the spike protein, which can enter the brain very efficiently across the blood-brain barrier after being shed or cleaved at the furin cleavage site. For example, mice injected with the S1 subunit exhibited highly stressed behavior and elevated levels of proinflammatory mediators such as TNF-α and IL-6, which are associated with cerebral vascular damage.[81] In addition, the S1 subunit was found to interact with the prion protein, causing it to fold abnormally and form toxic aggregates that can cause cerebral prion disease.[82] The S1 subunit also binds to β-amyloid. This endogenous peptide is released by the hippocampus as a monomer during memory formation and helps prevent new memories from overwriting previous ones. However, when these monomers [similar to the prion protein] aggregate to form oligomers, neuronal synapses and thus hippocampal memories are not protected, but destroyed. The oligomers, which are toxic to nerve cells, are therefore suspected of accelerating the Alzheimer's process once it has begun.[83] However, binding of the S1 subunit of SARS-CoV-2 to β-amyloid also accelerates viral infection or virus entry into somatic cells, increasing the release of proinflammatory messengers, which could also be a reason for hippocampal damage and increased Alzheimer's risk.[84] While the interaction of spike protein with aggregation-prone proteins such as prion protein or beta-amyloid in the brain may lead to neurodegeneration, another possible neurotoxic mechanism is the cross-reaction of antispike protein antibodies with the antigens of neuronal tissue. It is therefore not surprising that in addition to dementia and other brain abnormalities after COVID-19, cases of rapidly progressive dementia and autoimmune encephalitis have already been reported after spiking.[85]

How much more damaging than infection must spiking be in terms of hippocampal function? The short answer is, substantially! And here's the longer one: First, the LNP packaging of the mRNA is itself highly neuroinflammatory and allows our immune system to release a broad set of second messengers that block hippocampal neurogenesis, among other things. Second, because of this brain-penetrating packaging, a not insignificant portion of the injected genetic material enters the brain directly. Here, not only the release of the spike protein is a problem but also every "vaccinated" neuron becomes a target of an attack by the own immune system due to the production of this foreign protein. Brain cells can suffer irreparable damage as a result. Third, genetic material that does not enter the brain directly also provides highly active spike production in other organs. After shedding, the neurotoxic S1 subunit then enters the brain very efficiently by a detour, as it is able to cross the blood-brain barrier. Thus, it is not surprising that calculations by two researchers from the Center for Research in Medical Pharmacology, University of Insubria in Varese, Italy, on the health hazards posed by the S1 subunit revealed that spiking against SARS-CoV-2, as compared to infection with SARS-CoV-2, "produces high and potentially toxic levels of spike protein in organs and tissues under certain circumstances, which then enter the bloodstream."[86] One of these "circumstances" may be that physicians were required not to aspirate before the "inoculation."

Systemic "Vaccination"

Part of the my medical training was to aspirate before injecting substances to be administered intramuscularly to ensure that the needle tip did not come to rest unnoticed in a blood vessel. If the aim of the recommendation of the German Standing Committee on Vaccination (STIKO) to avoid aspiration when injecting vaccines (which has been in effect since 2016) is to ensure that the vaccine enters the blood and subsequently the brain as often as possible, even in the case of intramuscular injections, then it has been a complete success. With the changed procedure, it is supposed to be possible to inject with less pain, but I doubt it. Besides, that's not a good argument, because the aspiration was done for the safety of the patient—and that takes priority, of course.

In any case, not aspirating is faster, which is an organizational advantage, especially for COVID-19, since all citizens of the world should be vaccinated within a very short time. The speed also makes the procedure more lucrative, as spiking was paid significantly more than normal inoculations. [87] However, by not aspirating, one increases the chance that one injects into a blood vessel and a considerable portion the genetic material will be distributed throughout the body, instead of remaining in the muscle. It was only because of the resulting incidence of myocardial inflammation, particularly in young athletic men who have many large blood vessels in their upper arm muscles or at the injection site, that the existing recommendation was withdrawn in March 2022.[88]

The reasons for the immediate devastating effects of spike protein in the blood on the cardiovascular system are well known: heart muscle is rich in spike receptors called ACE2, through which coronary artery disease viruses enter cells.[89] ACE2 stands for "angiotensin converting enzyme 2." This protein is found in the cell membrane of many body cells where it regulates, among other things, the enzymatic conversion or breakdown of angiotensin II. This is a hormone that, among other functions, increases blood pressure. The degradation of angiotensin II by ACE2 leads to a reduction in blood pressure. However, the resulting metabolite, angiotensin-(1,7), also contributes to this effect. This also has hormonal functions exactly the opposite of those of angiotensin II. These include not only blood pressure downregulation but also inhibiting blood clotting or the release of proinflammatory cytokines (hormonal messengers). The viral spike protein, which can be produced in all body cells after gene transfer by vaccination, is also able to bind to ACE2 and thereby inhibit the conversion of angiotensin II to angiotensin-(1,7). The consequences are an increase in blood pressure, an increase in blood clotting, and a violent inflammatory response.[90] But there is also direct damage to the endothelial cells that line our blood vessels because their cell membrane is extremely rich in ACE2.[91] It is therefore important to prevent such a health-threatening "vaccine" from entering the bloodstream, which could be done by aspiration. However, by the time the STIKO changed its guidelines, many hearts and brains had already been spiked without aspiration control. And even a year after the STIKO's reversal, the US CDC continues to recommend (at least until the time of this writing in the spring of 2023) that spiking be performed without aspiration.[92]

To assess the unnatural severity of the spiking attack on the brain compared to natural infection, consider the following facts. In each wave of infection, only a small fraction of the population is actually infected, and the infection usually passes within a few days.

This is usually the case with SARS-CoV-2. For example, in Wuhan, the epicenter of the first wave of infection, less than 4 percent of the population became infected in the first half of the year.[93] In Germany, after three years of the pandemic and several waves of infection, less than half of the population was infected with SARS-CoV-2. (This figure includes all false-positive cases, which could mean even fewer were actually infected.)[94] In contrast, the majority of the population (about 80 to 90 percent) will be spiked several times a year, which was always the intention, as evidenced by the aforementioned large EU order of fourteen to fifteen doses of vaccine per willing EU citizen.

Furthermore, compared to an infection that usually lasts only one to two weeks and primarily affects the upper respiratory tract, studies indicate that after spiking, endogenous production of the spike protein can occur over a long period. For example, a still "appreciable specific signal" of spike mRNA (and spike protein) was detected in biopsies of axillary lymph nodes on the injection side as late as day sixty after the second dose of Moderna and BioNTech vaccines.[95] In another study, spike protein was even detected in the blood plasma of vaccinated individuals more than *six months* after administration of spike mRNA.[96] The reason for this high stability of the genetic material lies in the use of chemically modified building blocks in its production, which inhibit degradation and thus prolong the half-life.[97] In other words, the prolonged presence of this toxic viral genetic material was planned. The question is, what for?

Post-Vac Syndrome Due to Shedding?

According to Jörg-Heiner Möller, MD, a specialist in internal medicine and cardiology, *post-COVID* and *post-vac* are "two names for the same, newly emerged autoimmune disease, one caused by the coronavirus itself, another triggered by vaccination against corona." Although the clinical picture is varied, Möller recognizes a recurring pattern' According to Möller, "a severe fatigue syndrome develops. In bad cases, it is no longer possible to get out of bed. And you can't train it away; after every effort there is a severe relapse."[98]

In addition, the vast majority of cases involve cognitive dysfunction, which Möller says is often mistaken for dementia. Word-finding difficulties "are still a harmless variant, but being distracted at the wheel of a moving car and forgetting that you are driving is another category! There is group intolerance, i.e., the overstimulation of being together with friends is suddenly no longer tolerated. There is social isolation, which reinforces the destructive downward spiral of this disease."

All of these symptoms point to potentially permanent, self-reinforcing damage to the hippocampus. This can be easily explained by the released S1 subunit of the novel spike protein, which is circulating in the system for months, efficiently entering the brain.

The body continues to produce spike protein for up to six months after mRNA injection. If the actual intention was to ensure continuous spike exposure, this could explain the recommendation of the German STIKO in the summer of 2022: the two chemically modified and thus long-acting mRNA vaccines should be administered "at regular intervals of 6 months."[99] Then STIKO emphasizes that the goal of the vaccination is "not to prevent infection with SARS-CoV-2, but to reduce the risk of severe illness or death." However, the original main argument of a supposed protection of others, which was initially responsible for the enormous social pressure, had been refuted long before this admission. It was no longer possible to deny that the injections did not prevent infections and that chains of infection could not be broken. From now on, the vaccine narrative was all about the risk of serious outcomes, which could supposedly be reduced.

But whether the goal is to prevent infections or serious and fatal outcomes, the goal of the adapting narrative is apparently always the same: to sell vaccines continuously (in effect, to damage the hippocampus continuously). The design of the novel vaccines and the resulting poor efficacy profile provides the argumentative basis for the continuous injection mode that was planned from the outset, as can also be seen from the results of a large Swedish study.[100] This study compared the efficacy of all COVID-19 vaccines in 842,974 vaccinated individuals with a comparable number of unvaccinated individuals over a follow-up period of up to nine months. The measure used to determine efficacy was the severity of disease symptoms up to and including death after infection in vaccinated and unvaccinated individuals. As the following graph (figure 11)[101] shows, "vaccine protection" is rapidly diminishing. Not only that, but it becomes negative after seven to eight months, meaning that vaccinated individuals can expect a more severe course of infection than unvaccinated individuals after about half a year (see dashed oval).

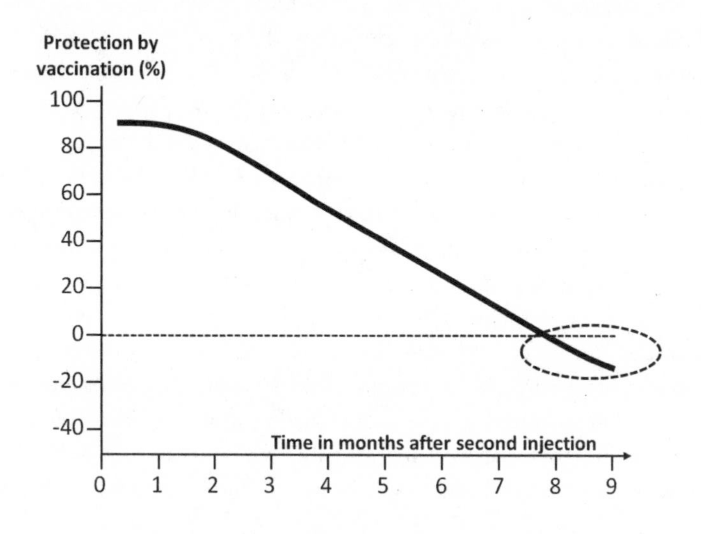

Figure 11

Given these data, one would expect that no further vaccination recommendations would be made because something is obviously going terribly wrong. But just the opposite happened. The authors' conclusion is bizarre: "The results strengthen the evidence-based rationale for administration of a third vaccine dose as a booster."

The vital questions unfortunately not asked were the following:

- Why would spiking cause weaker disease progression in the first place? This is a valid question because it is highly unusual, even unnatural, for the immune system to forget that it has been immunized so quickly.
- Was there any immunological protection generated at all?
- Why do vaccinated people have a higher chance of getting an infection than unvaccinated people just a few months after the injection?

My answer to all these questions is based on the readily available knowledge that it is not the virus itself, but a dysregulated, excessive immune response, the so-called cytokine storm, that determines the severity of the disease. According to studies, a major trigger for such a dysfunction of the immune system is clearly a deficiency of vitamin D (or the immune-regulatory vitamin D hormone), as explained in the first chapter. Already in the first clinical study from Wuhan, published on January 24, 2020, the immunological studies indicated that "the cytokine storm could be associated with disease severity."[102] Pierre Miossec, an immunologist at the University of Lyon in France, described in an article published on May 11, 2020, entitled "Understanding the Cytokine Storm during COVID-19: Contribution of Preexisting Chronic Inflammation," that "the cytokine storm in COVID-19 results from inflammation, rather than from the virus itself."[103] In other words, not the virus, but the host's misguided, overreacting immune system caused the severe course of the infection.[104]

This provides a plausible explanation for the steadily decreasing vaccine protection shown in figure 11: spiking itself activates the immune system to such an extent that it is exhausted and can no longer overreact with a cytokine storm in the event of a subsequent infection, at least for a short period. When the immune system has recovered to some degree after seven to eight months, a cytokine storm is not only possible again but also even more likely, because the immune system, constantly activated by spiking, has consumed a lot of vitamin D, increasing its deficiency and thus the imbalance in the immune response. This explanation is much more plausible than the one used in the study because it does not require a unique anomaly, namely a short-term effective and then rapidly decreasing immunization by spiking, as we do not know from the usual immunization processes. There, a maximum of two vaccinations provide the desired, usually lifelong immunity. To put it bluntly, in the case of spiking, the immune system has not forgotten anything because it has not learned anything in the first place. Perhaps that's why Marco Cavaleri, head of the Biological Health Risks and Vaccine Strategy Unit at the European Medicines Agency (EMA), warned that we should be careful not to "overwhelm the immune system with more and more new vaccines."[105] In the long term, the greater the imbalance, the greater the chance of a more protracted infection and the risk of a severe cytokine storm. Spiking damages not only the brain but also the immune system. A poorly functioning and therefore poorly controlled immune system increases the risk of cancer (as cancer cells are overlooked) and also the likelihood of more severe disease in future infections. This has also been shown by previous WHO "vaccination projects" in Africa.

Fatal Vaccinations

In the 1980s, a combination vaccine against diphtheria, tetanus, and pertussis, or whooping cough, (DTP) was introduced in rural areas of the West African nation of Guinea-Bissau. According to a peer-reviewed study, DTP vaccination increased mortality by a factor of five compared with unvaccinated infants (a factor of 9.98 for girls and 3.93 for boys).[106] According to the international team of authors, "all currently available evidence suggests that DTP vaccine may kill more children from other causes than it saves from diphtheria, tetanus or pertussis . . . [because] it may simultaneously increase susceptibility to unrelated infections."

According to Great Game India, an information portal providing strategic analysis to better understand international developments and the world around us, the WHO itself had "never conducted the kind of vaccinated/unvaccinated (or placebo) study necessary to ascertain if the DTP vaccine actually yields beneficial health outcomes," until this aforementioned study was published in 2017.[107] "The DTP vaccine was discontinued in the United States and other western nations in the 1990s," the portal points out, "following thousands of reports of death and brain damage," according to another study.[108] Great Game India emphasizes that the harmful potential of such vaccinations, especially in the countries of the global South, is greatly increased by the fact that the British Global Alliance for Vaccines and Immunization (GAVI), based in Geneva and supported by the WHO, UNICEF, and the World Bank and funded by the Bill & Melinda Gates Foundation, "has created a system called *performance based funding* whereby it financially punishes nations based on their compliance or noncompliance to vaccination programs."[109]

Let us briefly summarize at this point: Even in the first year of the pandemic, it was obvious that the hippocampus could be damaged by SARS-CoV-2 infection, as noted in a systematic review entitled "Post-COVID-19 Human Memory Impairment."[110] So there should have been no doubt that cognitive dysfunction could result from spiking, as summarized in another review two years later entitled "Adverse Effects of COVID-19 mRNA Vaccines: The Spike Hypothesis."[111] Were effects really adverse? It is imperative to ask this question because, after all, mRNA encoding the spike protein was specifically chosen for injection. Other viral structures, such as the comparatively harmless nucleocapsid, which forms the envelope around the viral genome, would have been an equally good vaccine candidate.[112]

Natural Immunity versus Spiking

According to the findings of an Italian metastudy published in the *Journal of Clinical Medicine* on September 25, 2022, "Vaccine-induced immunity was shown to decay faster than natural immunity."[113] This comprehensive review, based on a large number of articles, underscores the effective protection provided by COVID-19 natural immunity, which appears to be superior to that induced by anti-SARS-CoV-2 vaccination. This result does not even include the protection provided by a better functioning immune system due to a side-effect-free vitamin D supplementation program.

Step 5: Damage Brain Development as Early as Possible

To advance the Great Mental Reset, all that was needed was to ensure that as many people as possible spiked regularly—ideally every three to six months—to ensure sustained cerebral toxicity. This then leads to neurodegeneration of autobiographical index neurons already in use and blockade of adult hippocampal neurogenesis of new index neurons. It was easier to achieve than most people were prepared to believe, given that the risk of such injections was incalculable from the outset. One would have expected many more people to be skeptical. Stefan Oelrich, president of Bayer AG, expressed his enthusiasm for the marketing strategy that made possible what would have been unthinkable just a few years earlier. On November 3, 2021, at the World Health Summit (as almost goes without saying, the YouTube video of which has since been deleted), Oelrich said, "At the end of the day, mRNA vaccines are an example of how to sell gene therapy. If we had done a public survey two years ago asking if people would be willing to have gene therapy or cell therapy injected into their bodies, we would have gotten a 95 percent rejection rate."[114]

The biggest crime to me was that pregnant women, nursing mothers, children, and adolescents have been spiked, even though they were not even part of the clinical trials for emergency approval. Moreover, there was virtually no viral hazard potential in this group of people, which means that even if spiking were to induce sustained immunological protection, which it does not, it would be unnecessary. That is, the only effect is a basic health hazard based on the risk of vaccination but without any conceivable significant health benefit. Instead, it is a direct attack on the maturing brain, and it has been promoted by national disease authorities such as the CDC. Despite the high miscarriage rate reported through VAERS (see chapter 1, figure 2), which Naomi Wolf's group also brought to light from the now-released Pfizer files, as of May 2023 its homepage still reads, "COVID-19 vaccination is recommended for all people aged 6 months and older. This includes people who are pregnant, breastfeeding, trying to get pregnant now, or those who might become pregnant in the future. This also includes infants ages 6 months and older born to people who were vaccinated or had a COVID-19 infection before or during pregnancy."[115] Accordingly, the German RKI also writes on its homepage that the STIKO explicitly recommends the COVID-19 vaccination for persons of child-bearing age, "especially if they want to have children, in order to be optimally protected against COVID-19 in case of a future pregnancy."[116] According to the RKI, "a risk-benefit assessment taking into account the current data, argues for a general vaccination recommendation for unvaccinated pregnant women from the second trimester onward." To this end, it claims that the evaluated data would prove the safety of mRNA vaccination in pregnancy and show "no increased risk of miscarriage (abortion), stillbirth (intrauterine amniotic death), preterm birth or malformations as a result of vaccination." But this statement is completely at odds with VAERS and especially the Pfizer data released under court order.

One should be aware that the actual maturation of the brain begins after the embryonic completion of basic organ development. This is the end of the first trimester, the end of the embryonic phase and the beginning of the fetal phase of human development. Could this be the reason why pregnant women are not vaccinated sooner? I don't want to make that claim because I have no evidence to support it. But I have to point out that the timing chosen would be the earliest possible opportunity ever to cause a spike-related disruption of fetal brain development (during the embryonic phase, the result might be too damaging). After birth, infants of vaccinated mothers receive the modified viral mRNA for the spike protein of COVID-19 vaccines through breast milk, making spiking obsolete and offering a potential reason why spiking is not recommended until six months of age.[117] Thus, the entire developmental period of the human brain is potentially happening under the influence of coronavirus spikes, or to be precise the S1 unit shed by it.

When Parents Disagree about Vaccinating Their Children

In the case of a disagreement between parents or guardians regarding the vaccination of their child, in Germany the decision is given to the party in favor of the vaccination, if it is done in accordance with the recommendations of the STIKO, at least as long as no special risks are associated with the child's vaccination. That's the verdict of the Higher Regional Court of Hessen in Germany from August 17, 2021.[118] So it is enough to convince one parent that, say, a sixteen-year-old child should be spiked, and the spiking takes place against the opposition of the other parent and the child in question. And the court also ruled, "The decision is not appealable."

Even after SARS-CoV-2 mutated into a toothless tiger in the course of the exclusively politically motivated declaration at the beginning of its endemic phase, according to the RKI[119] and the US Food and Drug Administration (FDA),[120] the annual spiking should become a "health precaution" routine.

COVID-19 Measures as a Means to the End of Hippocampal Destruction

But also the other COVID-19 measures of the first three years of the pandemic should not be simply dismissed as history, worthy of only limited retrospective evaluation—even if this opinion is often expressed at the time of this writing in the spring of 2023. After all, the COVID-19 pandemic is increasingly losing its media and political significance, in line with the claim that the virulence and threat of the virus is continuing to decline. However, it would be a serious mistake not to take a closer look at the package of measures in retrospect, for two reasons. First, we need to understand their effects and aftereffects on the hippocampus and to assess what intentions were actually realized, especially since spiking continues to this day. Second, realize that it is only a matter of time before the next virus "escapes" from a laboratory. When it does, the tried and tested measures that have been enshrined in law will immediately be brought back into play—with tweaks. The WHO has given itself wide latitude in deciding when to declare a pandemic. In principle, this can be done annually. (See also sidebar in chapter 5: *With Perceived Incompetence to World Domination*, how the WHO is granted dictatorial rights to governmental measures based on the COVID-19 experience, not only in pandemic but even in climate issues.) Therefore, we have to keep this in mind: After the pandemic is before the pandemic because this is explicitly the view of the protagonists of the previous staging, such as Bill Gates. He is absolutely certain there will be a new pandemic soon, but with a completely different pathogen. Vaccines will be available in just six months (another incredible world record).[121] In his opinion, "bioterrorism is the next big threat," and "we don't worry enough."[122] That's an almost exhilarating statement, since I already see the COVID-19 pandemic, and especially the vaccines used in that course, as a serious attack of this kind. Unfortunately, Gates predictive powers have been proven time and again to be unbelievable but miraculously accurate. One has to take them very seriously!

In both respects, then, it makes sense to pay special attention to the hippocampal—collateral or intended—damage caused by the previous COVID-19 measures. The question remains whether damage was far more than just an incidental side effect. Since my return from the Mediterranean island, it seems more and more likely to me that with the help of the many seemingly isolated events and influences, such as the spreading of fear and panic, the spiking, and the primary measures to contain COVID-19, other intentions were actually pursued: to manipulate people unnoticed on a neurobiological level in order to be able to indoctrinate them more efficiently (more about this in the next chapter). Seen in this light, it becomes clear that we are involved in a multistage process, of which COVID-19 was only one phase and protecting health only a pretext. Let's approach this conclusion step by step.

That these measures were taken to protect the health of the population can be ruled out, since a real, evidence-based strengthening of the immune system by means of micronutrients, especially a rigorous vitamin D prophylaxis (which only aims to correct a deficiency usually present) was fought with all means, although it could have solved the COVID-19 problem from the outset (see "Causal Prevention of Severe SARS-CoV-2 Infections Is Right-Wing Extremism" in this chapter). Furthermore, it is hard to believe that only financial interests were the driving force behind the events, at least not for those who had the reins in their hands. After all, a few billion more or less hardly makes a difference when it comes to a certain amount of money. Their increase in power, however, was enormous and will grow even further with current efforts to reform the WHO's New Pandemic Treaty. If the additions to the international health guidelines bear fruit, the WHO will even get the right to intervene in all national pandemic measures of the individual states, giving Gates and company unimaginable power.[123]

Power, at its most basic level, is defined by the degree of subjugation of those over whom one claims power. It is therefore about the power over their brains, or the ability to manipulate them at will. According to Dietrich Bonhoeffer (1906–1945), theologian and resistance fighter in the Third Reich, the person manipulated becomes stupid.

However, this is not because he or she lacks intellect. This particular kind of stupidity is a more serious enemy of the good than evil: "While one can protest against evil and expose and prevent it by the use of force, we are defenseless against stupidity. Neither protests nor violence have any effect here; arguments fall on deaf ears. Facts that contradict a stupid person's prejudice simply need not be believed. And if they are irrefutable, they are simply brushed aside as unimportant, incidental."[124]

An effective means to produce exactly this kind of stupidity, which does not even exclude highly educated people, is to switch off neurogenesis in the hippocampus. The multilayered fear propaganda, the spiking and the many COVID-19 measures have contributed greatly to this, as we will now see.

Lockdown: The Fear Is Justified!

Of course, the lockdowns, like all the other measures, were intended to make people understand the seriousness of the situation. The subliminal message was that the viral threat must be really bad if such rigorous measures are being implemented with great speed. The previous core political paradigm of strengthening the economy at all costs and promoting its growth was abandoned overnight. What other explanation can there be when politicians are suddenly prepared to sacrifice the engine of our social life and the source of our prosperity and are even prepared to abandon the previously preached zero-debt policy and print huge amounts of money as if there were no tomorrow?

The closure of countless factories for an indefinite period created above all a profound existential anxiety for countless people, in addition to the stoked anxiety of infection. They were deprived of the meaning of life.[125] As you recall from chapter 2, having a purpose in life is the central part formula against indoctrination as well as for healthy, lifelong hippocampal growth.

Adults were not the only ones massively affected by this draconian measure, as a Dutch study entitled "The Impact of Lockdown during the COVID-19 Pandemic on Mental and Social Health of Children and Adolescents" found.[126] For example, about twice as many children suffered from severe anxiety and sleep disturbances during the lockdown than before. Due to this, their overall health deteriorated significantly. As a result, the authors concluded, "This study showed that governmental regulations regarding lockdown pose a serious mental/social health threat on children/adolescents that should be brought to the forefront of political decision-making and mental healthcare policy, intervention, and prevention." While mental health has actually been at the center of policymaking, it has been with the opposite goal in mind: anxiety and scare tactics have been high on the agenda, especially targeting children (see the BMI policy paper cited previously).

Isolation and (Un)social Distancing

Loneliness as a result of isolation and (un)social distancing, which is completely unacceptable to us as social beings by nature, strikes the same note. Of course, the fundamentally harmful effects of social isolation are not new. But six months before the first lockdown, in September 2019, a group of German cognitive researchers published the article "Structural BI Correlates of Loneliness among Older Adults," again providing evidence of the alarming but often overlooked effects of being involuntarily alone.[127] The researchers state that "individual differences in loneliness among older adults are [inversely] correlated with individual differences in the volumes of brain regions that are central to cognitive processing and emotional regulation." Put simply, isolating is known to shrink the brain. In an article titled "SARS-CoV-2-Mediated Neuropathogenesis, Deterioration of Hippocampal Neurogenesis and Dementia," the authors, citing two other studies, wrote, "Notably, elderly people, breadwinners of the family, students and children also experience a significant level of mental health issues due to lockdown, unmanageable socioeconomic status, online mode of education, reduced physical activities, social withdrawal, loneliness and overall uncertainty."[128]

A systematic review examined the global impact of the COVID-19 pandemic on the mental health of the general population. It reported "relatively high rates of symptoms of anxiety (6.33% to 50.9%), depression (14.6% to 48.3%), posttraumatic stress disorder (7% to 53.8%), psychological distress (34.43% to 38%), and stress (8.1% to 81.9%) . . . in the general population during the COVID-19 pandemic in China, Spain, Italy, Iran, the US, Turkey, Nepal, and Denmark."[129] Because of this huge impact of the COVID-19 measures, they recommended, "In addition to flattening the curve of viral transmission, priority needs to be given to the prevention of mental disorders (e.g., major depressive disorder, PTSD, as well as suicide)." But mental health was not the agenda—on the contrary: especially the elderly, whom one pretended to want to protect (which is why even children were spiked as potentially deadly superspreaders), became victims of these inhumane measures. As the researchers write in their article "COVID-19, Loneliness, Social Isolation and Risk of Dementia in Older People," "Results of the meta-analysis show that in older people, the risk of developing dementia because of the impact of prolonged loneliness and social isolation is about 49 to 60% . . . higher than in those who are not lonely and socially isolated."[130] And for those who were already showing early symptoms of developing dementia, the restraints became a colossal disaster and accelerator of their mental decline, as another article titled "COVID-19 and Alzheimer's Disease: How One Crisis Worsens the Other" states:

> The COVID-19 epidemic has caused multiple social problems and concerns in AD patients without the viral infection. It has become obvious that the COVID-19-driven social isolation and quarantine have various adverse effects.

People suffer from loneliness, depression and anxiety, and this situation is even worse for AD patients. Quarantine induces a rapid increase of behavioral and psychological symptoms in approximately 60% of patients with dementia including AD, FTD [frontotemporal dementia], dementia with Lewy bodies [neuronal inclusions indicative of Parkinson's dementia], and vascular dementia [resulting from atherosclerosis or stroke]. In particular, AD patients have higher risk of anxiety than other types of dementia . . . These behavioral problems are not restricted to people living in their own houses but also reported in AD patients who live in retirement homes, which are forced to physically isolate their residents.[131]

Brain-Damaging "Social Life"

Even before the COVID-19 isolation measures, few people were not constantly in contact with a smartphone or similar smart device. The frequency of interaction with digital devices has increased significantly as a result of the COVID-19 measures, because digital was the only permitted means of social interaction. Digitalization is also spreading rapidly in public spaces. In some places, a QR code scanner is now required to park a car.

Animal studies showed years ago that long-term exposure to mobile phones damages the hippocampus. In the study, exposure was forty-eight minutes a day for 30 to 180 days at radiation levels of 900-1800 MHz.[132] A year later, Iranian researchers concluded in their article "Effects of Radiofrequency Exposure Emitted from a GSM [Global System for Mobile Communications] Mobile Phone on Proliferation [reproduction], Differentiation [maturation], and Apoptosis [cellular suicide] of Neural Stem Cells [NSCs]," that an "accumulating dose of GSM 900-MHz RF-EMF might have devastating effects on NSCs proliferation and neurogenesis requiring more causations in terms of using mobile devices."[133]

But as the 5G network rollout continues, pushed forward with conspicuous vehemence even during the shutdown, as if the continued existence of the wireless industry or even society as a whole depended on it, and the deployment of thousands upon thousands of Starlink satellites (designed to put an end to 5G dead spots around the world), radiation of even higher frequency and thus even higher energy will reach every nook and cranny of smart cities. *Oregon Health and Science University* radiologists Shearwood McClelland III and Jerry Jaboin pose the central question in their scientific article on global 5G deployment and radiation safety, "Reassuring or Russian Roulette?"[134] One possible answer was formulated by Dr. Jin-Hwa Moon of Seoul University Children's Hospital, Korea, in her article "Health Effects of Electromagnetic Fields on Children": "The nervous systems of children are more vulnerable to the effects of electromagnetic waves than those of adults."[135]

Unfortunately, as we intelligently digitalize our society, governments are systematically ignoring these harmful effects, as a US federal court ruled in August 2021 in response to a lawsuit filed by the Environmental Health Trust (EHT) that, it is hoped, sends a signal to other nations. Devra Davis PhD, MPH, president of EHT, commented on the ruling: "If cell phones were a drug they would have been banned years ago. 5G would never have been allowed to market. An ever mounting body of published studies—ignored by the FCC [Federal Communications Commission]—clearly indicates that exposure to wireless radiation can lead to numerous health effects, especially for children. Research indicates wireless radiation increases cancer risk, damages memory, alters brain development, impacts reproductive health, and much more. Furthermore, the way the FCC measures our daily exposure to cell phone and cell tower radiation is fatally flawed and provides a false sense of security."[136]

But one needn't be completely isolated; even the drastic reduction in contact, as well as increased monotony in daily life, has detrimental effects on the hippocampus. It has long been known that loneliness and monotony can have such effects: "Studies in animals have shown that exposure to environmental monotony and social isolation have deleterious effects on the brain, particularly in reducing the generation of new neurons in the dentate gyrus of the hippocampus," writes an international team of researchers in the introduction to their article, "Brain Changes in Response to Long Antarctic Expeditions," published in the prestigious *New England Journal of Medicine* on December 5, 2019, just days before the coronavirus pandemic.[137] Similar to the animal experiments, the hippocampal volume of the *dentate gyrus* of the eight expedition participants decreased by an average of 7.2 percent, which is significant, during the fourteen months of Arctic isolation, compared to controls. Antarctic participants traveled as a group, so they were by no means individually isolated, and one must therefore assume that many people in COVID-19 isolation suffered much more severe hippocampal damage, especially those in retirement and nursing homes. When asked to explain the hippocampal shrinkage under isolation, the study's first author, Dr. Alexander Stahn from the Center for Space Medicine and Extreme Environments Berlin, said the following:

> We don't know for sure yet, but two major factors seem to play an important role. The first is social isolation. Because I am in a very small group, I am limited to

> very few social contacts over a very long period of time. The number of social contacts we usually have is many times higher. The second factor is monotony. I am always exposed to the same daily routines, and with that comes a change in sensory stimulation. At the beginning, Antarctica is certainly very attractive as an ice desert. But if I'm exposed to the same stimuli all the time, that may not be enough, because our brain needs very strong visual, high-contrast, dynamic images.[138]

How people with this knowledge could be sent into total isolation is beyond me. Stahn added, "With prison inmates in solitary confinement, I'm pretty sure we'd see something similar." And yes, we all became prisoners of war against a virus, or rather against the technocratic malarky of a pandemic—and our hippocampus suffered.

Loss of Face

The mandatory wearing of masks also made people feel isolated among other people. It should have been clear to everyone involved that masks do more harm than good. In an article entitled "Summary Expert Opinion on the Ineffectiveness of Masks as Virus Protection and Adverse Health Effects," the health disadvantages were all listed and explained in detail.[139] According to the report by the chemist and safety specialist Dr. Helmut Traindl, wearing a mask "leads to a disruption of verbal and nonverbal communication and to limited facial recognition, which makes it harder to recognize emotions. It also acts as an acoustic filter, causing speech intelligibility to be impaired. More generally, there is a disruption of interpersonal interaction and relationship dynamics."

Other adverse effects, he says, are expected to be direct brain toxicity from inhalation of the identified adhesives, organic solvents, volatile organic hydrocarbons, formaldehyde, siloxanes, metals, and titanium oxide nanoparticles. In addition, Traindl explains, "Various experimental metrological studies have shown that carbon dioxide–laden air accumulates under the masks. This is breathed back in. Below the mask, the outside air mixes with the accumulated carbon dioxide–contaminated exhaled air, naturally reducing the oxygen content. This air mixture is 'rebreathed.'" Pregnant women thus create an environment for the fetus in the womb comparable to the one Huxley describes for the bottled fetuses grown in the world of the novel, whose brains are said to develop at a reduced capacity due to the planned oxygen deprivation.

Ultimately, all these factors cause the hippocampus to suffer at any age.

Sleep Problems and Stress

As noted in chapter 2, sleep, particularly deep sleep, is critical for maintaining all hippocampal functions, such as autobiographical memory, System 2 thinking, or high psychological resilience". The negative impact of sleep disturbances as a result of the

COVID-19 measures on these vital abilities was also quickly apparent in young adults, as noted in an article titled "Psychological Correlates of Poor Sleep Quality among U.S. Young Adults during the COVID-19 Pandemic": "Young adults experienced high rates of sleep problems during the first two months (April to May 2020) of the pandemic. In addition, high levels of PTSD symptoms and COVID-19-related worry were associated with poor sleep among young adults."[140]

Notably, "Younger people are more vulnerable to stress, anxiety and depression during COVID-19 pandemic," according to a global gross-sectional survey.[141] The study authors write the following:

> Globally, consistently high levels of stress, anxiety, depression, and poor sleep were observed regardless of number of COVID-19 cases [in each country]. Over 70% of the respondents had greater than moderate levels of stress, with 59% meeting the criteria for clinically significant anxiety and 39% reporting moderate depressive symptoms. People with a prior mental health diagnosis experienced greater psychological distress. Poor sleep, lower levels of resilience, younger age and loneliness significantly mediated the links between stress and depression, and stress and anxiety. Age-based differences revealed that younger age-groups were more vulnerable to stress, depression and anxiety symptoms.

Thus, the suppression of hippocampal neurogenesis that occurs during deep sleep was not the only effect of fear propagation on sleep quality. The profound psychological symptomatology, ranging from depression to PTSD, is a clear indication that neurodegenerative changes have also been induced.

Aggravated Lack of Exercise

(Un)Social distancing, home offices, closed sports facilities (e.g., gyms or swimming pools), and the banning of club sports have led to a significant overall increase in the physical inactivity that was already widespread in modern society. A large meta-study that examined the problem points to the global extent of physical inactivity: "Changes in physical activity were reported in 64 studies, with the majority of studies reporting decreases in physical activity and increases in sedentary behaviours during their respective lockdowns across several populations, including children and patients with a variety of medical conditions."[142]

Because of the fundamental importance of physical activity for hippocampal neurogenesis (see chapter 2) and thus for psychological resilience, study results such as the following one from Brazil should have been expected by all those responsible for COVID-19 measures. "Reduced Level of Physical Activity during COVID-19 Pandemic Is Associated with Depression and Anxiety Levels" is the title of the article, in which the authors describe the following negative consequences, among others: "The COVID-19 pandemic has a negative impact on physical activity. Those who reduced their level of physical activity had the highest levels of mood disorders."[143]

An article titled "Physical Activity and Screen Time of Children and Adolescents before and during the COVID-19 Lockdown in Germany" categorizes the COVID-19 measures as "a natural experiment."[144] The authors note a disproportionate increase in screen time versus loss of sports time, especially among teenagers. However, what was supposed to have been natural about the imposed measures is beyond me.

Purposeful Malnutrition

Lack of exercise, isolation, boredom, and the resulting reduced stress resistance are the causes of malnutrition and a significant increase in body fat in all age groups during the COVID-19 crisis. This was especially true during the lockdowns. Overweight and obesity have increased to an "unprecedented extent" among children and adolescents, Susann Weihrauch-Blüher, senior physician at the University Hospital Halle an der Saale, reports in the medical journal *Ärzte Zeitung*.[145] She refers to a representative survey of parents of children between the ages of three and seventeen. Here are the shocking results:

- Sixteen percent of children and adolescents have gained weight, and the figure is as high as 32 percent among ten- to twelve-year-olds.
- Children and adolescents from low-income families are twice as likely to experience unhealthy weight gain as those from high-income families (23 versus 12 percent).
- A total of 44 percent of children and adolescents are exercising less than they did before the pandemic, compared with 57 percent of ten- to twelve-year-olds.
- Physical fitness has deteriorated in 33 percent of children and adolescents, compared with 48 percent of ten- to twelve-year-olds.
- For 43 percent of the children and adolescents, the pandemic has had a "medium" or "strong" impact on their mental stability.
- Seventy percent of children and adolescents have increased their media use (TV, computer, game consoles).
- Twenty-seven percent of children and adolescents eat sweets more often than before the pandemic.

In light of these catastrophic numbers, it is important to remember that visceral adipose tissue, which is the first to experience an increase in volume during caloric overeating and stress, is not only an energy store but also a highly hormonally active endocrine organ that secretes a multitude of so-called adipokines.[146] While they help regulate and support hippocampal growth in lean individuals, the complexity of the many negative effects of visceral abdominal fat, particularly on hippocampal function, is complex. In my paper "Unified Theory of Alzheimer's Disease (UTAD): Implications for Prevention and Curative Therapy," I describe these interactions in detail.[147] It is beyond the scope of this book to discuss them here. What is important at this point are the neurobiological consequences: namely, studies from Boston and Los Angeles found that there is an inverse relationship between brain volume and visceral adipose tissue volume. In this regard, the results of two independent studies showed that brain volume is inversely proportional to our body mass index (BMI).[148] A third study calculated that each unit increase in BMI correlates with approximately 1 to 1.5 percent less brain volume.[149]

But independent from visceral weight gain, diets rich in highly processed foods cause hippocampal damage.[150] This was a problem before corona and has been made much worse by the COVID-19 measures, especially because, during this time, a widespread campaign *against* correcting serious micronutrient deficiencies has exacerbated malnutrition that was already low in vital nutrients. The global anti–vitamin D campaign is having a particularly devastating effect (see also under the next heading), although, as noted in chapter 2, not a single essential micronutrient should be missing.

Vitamin D deficiency in the population, which is important to the spiking campaign, has direct and indirect negative effects on hippocampal function. Prof. Darryl Walter Eyles, scientific director of the Queensland Centre for Mental Health Research Developmental Neurobiology Laboratory in Australia, wrote the following in his October 2020 article "Vitamin D: Brain and Behavior":

> It has been 20 years since we first proposed vitamin D as a "possible" neurosteroid [a steroid hormone that controls genes in neurons]. Our work over the last two decades, particularly results from our cellular and animal models, has confirmed the numerous ways in which vitamin D differentiates the developing brain. As a result, vitamin D can now confidently take its place among all other steroids [i.e., gene-regulating hormones such as estrogen or testosterone] known to regulate brain development. Others have concentrated on the possible neuroprotective functions of vitamin D in adult brains. Here these data are integrated, and possible mechanisms outlined for the various roles vitamin D appears to play in both developing and mature brains and how such actions shape behavior. There is now also good evidence linking gestational and/or neonatal vitamin D deficiency with an increased risk of neurodevelopmental disorders, such as schizophrenia and autism, and adult vitamin D deficiency with certain degenerative conditions [e.g., Alzheimer's disease].[151]

According to a paper published in October 2022, a study by German cognitive researchers also showed that vitamin D deficiency in the general population may be linked to accelerated brain aging.[152] This wasn't particularly surprising; after all, a large dose-response meta-analysis in 2018 showed that directly correlated vitamin

D (prohormone) levels with the likelihood of remaining mentally fit or becoming demented.[153] According to this analysis, an increase of 10 nmol/L reduces the risk of dementia by 5 percent and the risk of Alzheimer's disease by as much as 7 percent.

Thus, inadequate vitamin D intake has at least three devastating effects: 1) It prevents healthy brain development in young people. 2) It causes loss of hippocampal function even in adults. 3) It has created a problem that gave governments around the world reason to propagate spiking as the only solution against COVID-19 in the first place. With the support of the WHO, it was vehemently claimed that experimental gene therapy needed emergency approval because there was no other promising remedy in sight and it was supposedly the only way to save human lives from coronavirus infection. A perfidious anti–vitamin D propaganda campaign, with the participation of the WHO, had preceded that and put millions upon millions of people at deadly danger in the first place. The following are some illustrative examples of the orchestrated anti–vitamin D propaganda that has caused so much unnecessary suffering.

Causal Prevention of Severe SARS-CoV-2 Infections Is Right-Wing Extremism

The problem with the argument that experimental gene therapy was the only way to save human lives is that a much more effective, risk-free alternative was always there: an immune system strengthened by evidence-based methods! But this option was ignored, and all clinical trials compared only vaccinated versus unvaccinated subjects, never vaccinated versus unendangered subjects. The latter would be individuals who have a naturally functioning immune system due to adequate supplementation of Vitamin D, which is possible for everyone. If the control group in the clinical trials had been given the best possible preexisting preventive measure, which would have been ethically obligatory, then the whole health problem and lack of protective effect with the novel vaccine would have been even much clearer. This would also have ruled out the emergency approval from the outset. For example, a scientifically published analysis of the original trial data showed that none of the vaccines provided a health benefit when considering both serious infections with COVID-19 and serious adverse events.[154] On the contrary, the Pfizer/BioNTech vaccine group experienced 52 percent more serious events than the control or placebo group. With the Moderna vaccine, there were about 80 percent more. In the Johnson & Johnson study, the vaccine group had 323 percent, or more than three times, more serious events than the control group. "Based on this data," the analysis concluded, "it is all but a certainty that mass COVID-19 immunization is hurting the health of the population in general." What would have been the outcome if the control group had been adequately supplied with micronutrients, especially vitamin D? Let's have a look.

As early as 2006 an international group of scientists published their findings that seasonal vitamin D deficiency is responsible for both the seasonal occurrence of influenza and the severity of the infections.[155] Their recommendations for vitamin D supplementation to achieve summer vitamin D (prohormone) levels of about 125 nmol/l even in winter could have saved tens if not hundreds of thousands of people from dying from influenza (or any other viral respiratory infection) every year since then. However, this has been largely ignored, perhaps because it would have undermined the case for influenza vaccination. Since an appropriate vitamin D prophylaxis would have rendered all the COVID-19 measures absurdly obsolete, this life-saving finding from influenza research was also ignored during the COVID-19 crisis, even though it could have ended the whole scare immediately.

As early as February 28, 2020, and even before the first lockdown, Professor Andrea Giustina, president of the European Society of Endocrinology, correctly hypothesized in the *British Medical Journal* "that low vitamin D [prohormone] levels may be the link between age, pre-existing conditions and increased susceptibility to complications and mortality due to COVID-19 infection in the northern regions of Italy."[156] And in April 2020, a group of researchers provided evidence in their article "Evidence That Vitamin D Supplementation Could Reduce Risk of Influenza and COVID-19 Infections and Deaths": "To reduce the risk of infection, it is recommended that people at risk of influenza and/or COVID-19 consider taking 10,000 IU/d of vitamin D3 for a few weeks to rapidly raise 25(OH)D concentrations, followed by 5000 IU/d. The goal should be to raise 25(OH)D concentrations above 40-60 ng/mL (100-150 nmol/L)."[157]

Vital Know-How about Vitamin D

Vitamin D is either synthesized in the skin with the help of UVB radiation from the sun (which is only possible during the summer months at latitudes above 37 degrees in the US and all of Germany), or it must be obtained from food. However, only fatty fish has a sufficiently high concentration. Therefore, supplementation is the only other option. When measuring vitamin D levels, it is not vitamin D that is measured, but the vitamin D prohormone concentration. This means that if you want to increase the vitamin D (prohormone) level by taking vitamin D, it may take a few days because the conversion of vitamin D to vitamin D prohormone, which occurs in the liver (see figure 12), may take that long. Preventively, this is usually not a problem because time is not of the essence. However, if you need to increase the vitamin D level or the vitamin D (prohormone) level quickly, as an acute therapy, you would need to administer vitamin D prohormone.[158]

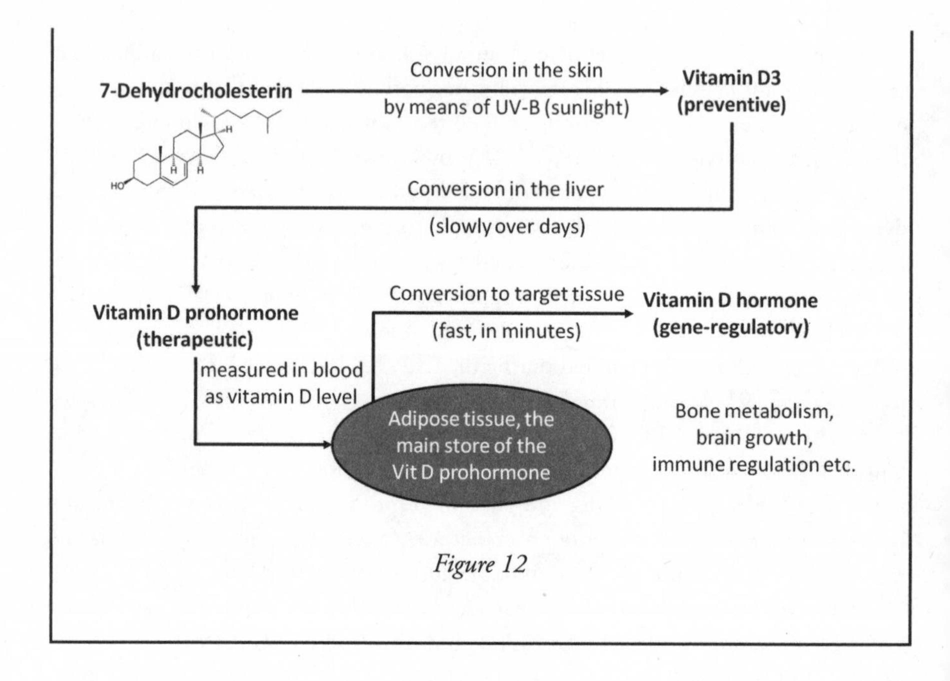

Figure 12

Already in the first year of COVID-19, clinical studies could impressively and beyond doubt prove the fatal failure of politics, and especially of health systems, worldwide. Belgian scientists published already in November 2020 (the data was already available) that if the vitamin D (prohormone) level falls below 50 nmol/l, the risk of dying from COVID-19 increases almost fourfold.[159] This increased risk was independent of the age of the patients or their preexisting conditions, and thus applied to high-risk groups as well. At levels below 50 nmol/l compared to levels above 100 nmol/l, the risk of severe progression increased fourteen-fold, according to an Israeli study of the first two waves of infection.[160] At vitamin D prohormone levels below 30 nmol/l (compared to levels above)—that is, vitamin D prohormone levels typical for the winter months in Germany[161] (which explains the seasonality of respiratory virus diseases)—the risk of a fatal course of the disease even increases by a factor of about eighteen, according to the results of a study from the University Hospital of Heidelberg that was published in September.[162] As mentioned in chapter 1, according to the Deutsches Krebsforschungszentrum (DKFZ), nine out of ten COVID-19 deaths could be prevented with adequate vitamin D prophylaxis, and with a vitamin D prohormone level of 125 nmol/l, the probability of death would even be theoretically zero (theoretically, because in practice a multimorbid person can die from any infection, with or without vitamin D, often even without an infection, while climbing stairs or sleeping).

The causal relationship between vitamin D deficiency or deficient vitamin D prohormone levels and a high risk of death from COVID-19 was impressively demonstrated a month earlier in an intervention study from Cordoba, southern Spain, published online August 29, 2020.[163] In COVID-19-positive patients who had to be hospitalized for pneumonia, the risk of being admitted to intensive care and connected to a ventilator was reduced by a factor of *twenty-five* if their vitamin D levels (precisely, the vitamin D *prohormone* levels) were raised quickly. However, this therapeutic increase in acute cases of respiratory disease can only be achieved by administering vitamin D prohormone, because the complete conversion of administered vitamin D3 to vitamin D prohormone takes several days, even in healthy people. In other words, vitamin D (prohormone) levels increase slowly after vitamin D administration (see figure 12), which is why the intervention group received vitamin D prohormone immediately on the day of admission and twice a week thereafter. All COVID-19 patients in the intervention group survived. In contrast, in the control group, which did not receive vitamin D prohormone, 8 percent of patients died from COVID-19; ultimately, they died from persistent low vitamin D (prohormone) levels that could have been easily corrected.

All of these spectacular results were thus already published before the global spiking campaign even began. They would thus have massively jeopardized it, if only they had received sufficient attention and been implemented in practices (preventive vitamin D supplementation) and clinics (vitamin D prohormone as therapeutic intervention). After all, without the constant reports of COVID-19 deaths or the threat of overcrowding in intensive care units, hardly anyone would have been willing to be spiked—and an emergency approval of the mRNA injections would have been ruled out from the outset, if it had been recognized that such an effective preventive and therapeutic measures had long been available.

Probably for this reason, studies were immediately carried out with the aim of refuting, questioning, or at least confusing the Cordoba results. Representative of several such vitamin D discrediting efforts is a Brazilian study. The study design was the same as that in Cordoba, except that COVID-19 patients were not given multiple doses of vitamin D prohormone, which would have rapidly and permanently increased vitamin D (prohormone) levels, but only a single bolus of 200,000 IU vitamin D3.[164] However, the patients in the intervention group did not have that much time to wait for the previously discussed conversion to vitamin D prohormone to happen; after all, they were already sick enough to require admission to a hospital, hence it was a matter of life or death. As a result, the study showed what was expected from its design: no significant difference between the intervention and control groups. This Brazilian study was completely unnecessary, since the delayed onset of action of vitamin D3 was well documented beforehand; furthermore, in my opinion, it is particularly serious that the study directors apparently accepted that the study participants could die of their COVID-19 disease as a result of the negligently poor study design. One has to be careful not to assume a crystal-clear intention without further investigation. The Cordoba study had already been published, and the life-saving therapeutic measure was known. It is almost incomprehensible to me how the crucial difference between vitamin D and the bioactive prohormone formed from it could have been overlooked by the study leaders.

The results from Cordoba were amazingly ignored by the Brazilian scientists, and the crucial difference in design that would have explained the supposedly contradictory result was not even discussed in the publication, which is completely unacceptable. Nevertheless, the result of the Brazilian study, published on March 16, 2021 (i.e., in the middle of the spiking campaign), was triumphantly reported to the public as conclusive evidence that vitamin D supplementation has no positive effect on COVID-19 disease progression.[165] This report, which was not very convincing for the expert, benefited from hardly any layperson knowing that vitamin D levels are measured not as vitamin D but as the vitamin D prohormone and that vitamin D (prohormone) levels do not rise immediately after vitamin D supplementation. This is also suggested by the Brazilian data, which shows an increase in vitamin D (prohormone) levels after their single bolus of vitamin D administration. However, it is only in the small print (under figure 3 of the publication) that we learn that this measurement was made only after the survivors were able to leave the hospital. Not only was the Brazilian study unquestioned in the media, but also the life-saving Cordoba study was simply ignored, even after a data analysis by independent scientists at the Massachusetts Institute of Technology (MIT) in the United States once again confirmed that the survival of all participants in the intervention group was only due to the administration of the vitamin D prohormone.[166] This also explains why several other trials that mimicked the Brazilian treatment concept have failed to show any therapeutic benefit from vitamin D.[167] On the other hand, further trials using vitamin D prohormone[168] or even vitamin D hormone[169] have shown similarly impressive therapeutic results as the Cordoba trial.

Another example of anti–vitamin D propaganda concerns the renowned *New England Journal of Medicine* (NEJM), which published the results of a study on vitamin D supplementation on July 28, 2022, that was hailed by many media as the "definitive verdict on the matter." The VITAL study was designed to determine the likelihood of a bone fracture with vitamin D3 supplementation.[170] A glaring flaw in this study, however, is that the participants already had a vitamin D level of 73 nmol/l before the study began, which is more than adequate for bone health, which is considered to be achieved at 50 nmol/l. Thus, the entire study design was worthless from the start. Even before the data was collected, no difference in fracture incidence between the intervention and control groups could be expected, and this was unsurprisingly reflected in the results. This must have been clear to those responsible for the study, as well as those who conducted the review and advocated publication in the prestigious NEJM.

For immunological health, however, only values around 125 nmol/l are optimal. At this vitamin D prohormone level, the risk of a fatal coronavirus infection is reduced to statistically *zero*, as I mentioned in the first chapter.[171] An earlier analysis of the VITAL trial data showed that the risk of developing an autoimmune disease was significantly reduced in the intervention group compared to the control group by a daily intake of 2,000 IU vitamin D3 (although this relatively low dose did not reach a vitamin D (prohormone) level of 125 nmol/l).[172] Independent of this weakly designed (in the sense that the difference in vitamin D prohormone levels between the intervention and control groups was relatively small) VITAL study, a number of other studies have proven beyond doubt that vitamin D supplementation could reduce cancer incidence by at least 13 percent.[173] In Germany alone, thirty thousand fewer people would die of cancer each year and more than three hundred thousand years of life could be gained.[174] The reason is obvious: an immune system deficient in vitamin D hormone is inefficient in its surveillance and elimination function of genetically modified (cancerous) cells, as well as virally infected cells. For this reason, researchers from the prestigious German Cancer Research Center made "a plea for harvesting low-hanging fruit," or, "Enhanced supply of vitamin D3 by supplementation, food fortification, carefully dosed sunlight exposure or a combination of these approaches might be a most powerful and cost-effective, if not cost-saving, approach for reducing the burden of cancer mortality and many other adverse health outcomes."[175]

Nevertheless, two editors of the NEJM did not miss the opportunity to make "A Decisive Verdict on Vitamin D Supplementation" in an editorial based on these "Vital Findings": "Taken together, VITAL and this ancillary study [fracture] show that vitamin supplements do not have important health benefits in the general population of older adults, even in those with low 25-hydroxyvitamin D levels."[176] This is, of course, completely unacceptable in the generality of the statement. A deficiency of a vital micronutrient that is essential for gene regulation (see figure 12) should no longer be corrected? One can only speculate why this prestigious scientific journal would allow such undifferentiated statements. But it pales in comparison to their suggestion "that providers should stop screening for 25-hydroxyvitamin D levels or recommending vitamin D supplements, and people should stop taking vitamin D supplements to prevent major diseases or extend life."

Dubious studies and equally dubious interpretations reveal the great concern of the prospiking or pharmaceutical lobby, that people might correct their vitamin D deficiency and thus take their health into their own hands. To all appearances, a one-sided, interest-driven publication by Medscape, in the form of a message to all physicians and health professionals worldwide, only about a month after the final NEJM ruling on vitamin D3, falls into this pattern. In it, Professor Dr. Stephan Martin, a diabetes specialist, informs us that, according to pharmaceutical historians, it was the Nazis who "created the first mass market for vitamins to prevent malnutrition."[177] Martin therefore concludes "that the vitamin hype . . . is also based on Nazi ideas." He considers his findings to be "an interesting stimulus for the daily discussion at the medical office." But what kind of discussion does he want to stimulate in the doctor's conversation with the patient? Should a patient be told that from now on he will be treated as a suspect of right-wing extremism if he wants to have his vitamin levels checked and, if necessary, corrected in order to protect himself adequately against diseases such as COVID-19 (or Alzheimer's)?

Infants: Collateral Damage of the Anti–Vitamin D Propaganda

Countless people have died unnecessarily from the coronavirus, as well as the collateral damage of equally unnecessary COVID-19 measures, including life-threatening spiking, because a vitamin D deficiency was not corrected. I am not accusing anyone of deliberately endangering the lives of infants. But the same unhealthy policies are affecting our youngest children. For example, it is very likely that the winter surge in respiratory syncytial virus (RSV) infections in infants, that dominated the media in the winter of 2022–2023, was also due to vitamin D deficiency. Even among the youngest members of our society, a deficiency of this essential immune regulator is a major cause of life-threatening respiratory infections. Low levels of vitamin D in umbilical-cord blood or maternal deficiency have been shown to increase the risk of RSV infection in the first year of life by a factor of six, according to a 2011 study.[178]

According to the results of another clinical study published in September 2022, the likelihood of severe RSV infection requiring intensive care with artificial respiration is even increased by a factor of about *twelve* if the infant's vitamin D (prohormone) levels are deficient.[179] Have you read anything about this in the media? Has there been a call to provide pregnant women with sufficient vitamin D? Not to my knowledge. Instead, another mRNA vaccine with viral genetic material is being promoted: "Accompanied by the huge success of mRNA vaccines in COVID-19, mRNA vaccines have been rapidly developed, with many having entered clinical studies, in which they have demonstrated encouraging results and acceptable safety profiles. In fact, Moderna has received FDA approval, granting fast-track designation for an investigational single-dose mRNA-1345 vaccine against RSV in adults over 60 years of age," says one scientific article, adding, "Hence, mRNA vaccines may represent a new, more successful, chapter in the continued battle to develop effective preventative measures against RSV."[180] Again, "the devil is cast out by Beelzebub," or, an evil is fought with something even worse, instead of simply fixing the cause of the evil.

Discrediting the vitamin D hormone as irrelevant to health (even at low levels), which deflates vitamin D3 as nonessential (or even dangerous, because it can be overdosed), is instrumental in achieving a Great Mental Reset. This is especially true because vitamin D deficiency actually creates a good environment for anxiety, and studies show that correcting vitamin D levels also reduces anxiety symptoms.[181]

I used vitamin D as a micronutrient example here because the prohormone formed from it, from which the cells then derive a gene-regulating hormone, plays a critical role in many genetic control processes in the body, and many people have an unrecognized severe deficiency. This is true for people at all latitudes. However, I reiterate that there is no essential vital micronutrient that our immune system, nervous system, or adult neurogenesis can really do without. So, there are deficiencies other than in vitamin D as a result of the COVID-19 interventions—that is, as a result of the malnutrition that has been caused in the general population.

Success Monitoring and the New "Coronary" Normal

Assuming that the whole package of measures is part of a master plan, its "success" should show up in an accelerated hippocampal volume loss, as indicated by the hypothetical curve (finely dashed) in figure 13. The accelerated loss of index neurons is not experienced by the victim as a painful process. One does not even realize that old memories are fading or disappearing altogether; one simply forgets. What is experienced, however, is an increased sense of anxiety, a more fragile ego, a weakening of the self, and, in the worst cases, outright depression.

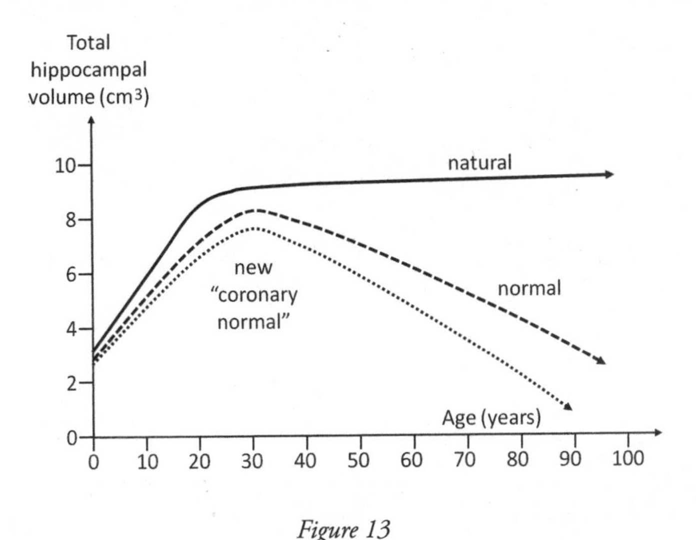

Figure 13

"The unnatural normality of chronic hippocampal destruction" (see the section of the same title in chapter 2) may have changed to a new "coronary normal" already in the first year of the pandemic measures. Unfortunately, no studies (yet) directly examine average hippocampal volume before and after COVID-19 and the brain-damaging measures, for example, between 2019 and 2021, broken down by age group. But there is very good indirect evidence for an increase in hippocampal damage on a global scale because impaired adult hippocampal neurogenesis is a major cause of impaired autobiographical memory performance and the disease process of depression. The additional accelerated hippocampal neurodegeneration is causal for the development of Alzheimer's dementia.

Intelligence and Memory Loss in the COVID-19 Generation

Intelligence encompasses the ability to reason, plan, solve problems, think abstractly, comprehend complex ideas, learn quickly, and learn from experience. Researchers tested a total of 424 students in seventh, eighth, and ninth grades in Germany using the Berlin Intelligence Structure Test (BIS-HB) in late August and early September 2020.[182] Scores on all intelligence test items were lower in the 2020 pandemic sample than in qualitatively equivalent prepandemic samples from 2002 and 2012.

All measures of intelligence functions had increased significantly from 2002 to 2012 and then dropped dramatically, ruling out the possibility of a slow negative trend that began in 2012. General intelligence dropped by almost eight points compared to 2012, judgment (System 2 thinking) by about four points, and autobiographical memory performance dropped by well over eight points among adolescents. This does not take into account that an upward trend was to have been expected, as shown in figure 14.

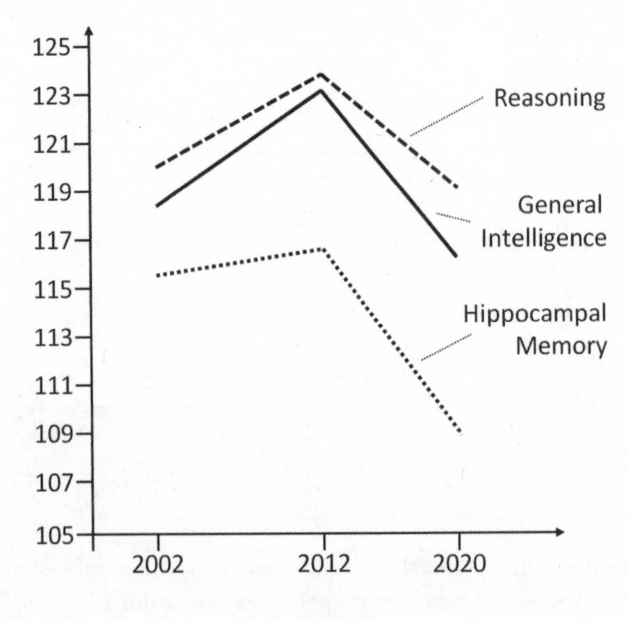

Figure 14

Such a rapid loss of performance (including creativity) due to a decline in hippocampal function is reminiscent of severe depression or even Alzheimer's disease. This is not to say that teenagers, who are on average only 14.5 years old, will soon develop Alzheimer's disease. However, in my opinion, these at least functional (but possibly also structural) massive damages of the hippocampus cannot be explained by canceled regular schooling, as the authors try to do. The effects are simply too pronounced for such a short period, and even one year later they are still unchanged, as further study results show.

Record Increase in Depression

According to a WHO report, depression advanced to become the world's leading disease in 2019, just before the COVID-19 pandemic.[183] As I have shown, there is no need to speculate about the cause of this development. We also see from this that *normal*, in terms of hippocampal shrinkage, as depicted in figure 13, is in fact anything but a healthy normal, although in the associated study participants were defined as "generally healthy."[184] The global peak in depression at that time then worsened considerably in the first year of the COVID-19 pandemic alone, especially among young adults. In the article "Risk for Depression Tripled during the COVID-19 Pandemic in Emerging Adults Followed for the Last 8 Years," the international group of scientists writes, "The sharp increase in depression risk among emerging adults heralds a public health crisis with alarming implications for their social and emotional functioning as this generation matures."[185]

A US study also found that the prevalence of depressive illness symptoms was more than three times higher even in the first months of the COVID 19 pandemic than before, with a particular increase in the severity of depression symptoms, as illustrated in figure 15.[186] This increase (from a global peak in 2019!) may have been due to people suffering from milder depression prior to the pandemic being more vulnerable and thus more likely to become ill, and more severely ill. However, the number of people who experienced depression for the first time during the pandemic also increased significantly. Before the pandemic, for example, more than 75 percent were still symptom-free, but just a few months into the first year of the pandemic, only about 47 percent were. In other words, no longer one in four, but almost one in two showed depressive symptoms. The trend was even more unfavorable for older adults with a history of depressive moods. Of these, almost one in two developed depression again during the pandemic.

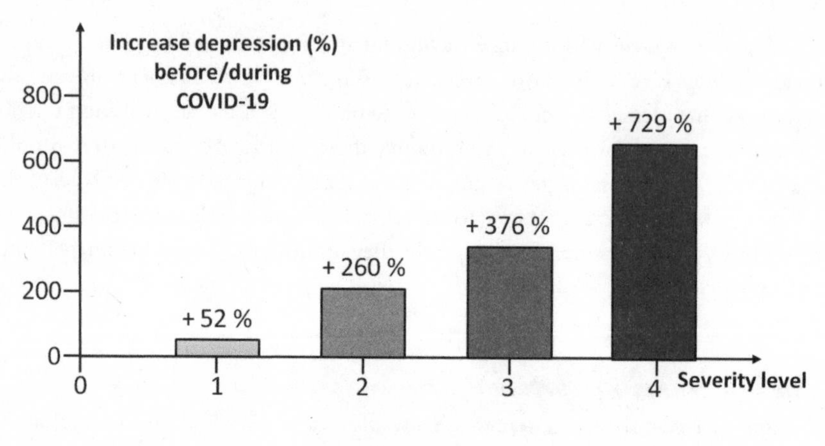

Figure 15

This dramatic development was also confirmed by a Canadian study entitled "Incident and Recurrent Depression among Adults Aged 50 Years and Older during the COVID-19 Pandemic." Again, during the COVID-19 measures, one in eight previously mentally healthy people over the age of fifty developed depression for the first time in their lives.[187]

Physical damage and thus negative effects on the hippocampus from the spiking, which did not begin until late 2020, would only be inferred from data collected thereafter. It was only during the year 2021 that a rapidly growing and significant proportion of the world population became affected by the toxic effects of spiking. Based on the demonstrable evidence of hippocampal toxicity of the spike protein and the known links between hippocampal dysfunction and depression, we must assume that depression increased at a much greater rate from that time onward.

However, even if data from after that time were available, one would have to be cautious about taking the information as final, since by no means are all depressions recognized and subsequently included in the statistics. According to a US study published in August 2022, depression still often goes undiagnosed because its signs and symptoms are misunderstood.[188] In addition, the authors say, "many people are reluctant to act towards seeing a mental health professional due to the stigma attached to this disorder." And they go on to report, "As of 2020, more than 21 million Americans, almost 8.4%, experienced at least one major depressive episode. In fact, during the COVID-19 pandemic, depression and anxiety rates increased by more than 25% worldwide, impacting almost every stratum of society, including adolescents, college students, healthcare workers, and physicians. Millions more will suffer from recurring depression in their lifetime. In addition, children are having an increased pressure for conformity in our modern society, especially in a rapidly evolving digital world. This danger imposes a risk of developing low self-esteem, one of the risk factors for depression."

Galloping Dementia

Depression, if not effectively treated by a change in lifestyle, should be understood as a precursor of Alzheimer's disease and therefore taken all the more seriously. Apart from the fact that both diseases can be traced back to disturbed hippocampal neurogenesis, an analysis of data from the so-called Framingham Heart Study showed that depression in old age always develops shortly before the subsequent onset of cognitive decline and thus represents a significant risk factor and warning sign for dementia and Alzheimer's disease.[189] The prospectively conducted Washington/Hamilton Heights Inwood Columbia Aging Project also provided clear evidence that depressive symptoms in older age precede autobiographical memory loss or hippocampal dementia, but not vice versa.[190] Moreover, higher depression scale scores (and the increase in 2020 compared to 2019 was dramatic, as discussed) were found to precede steeper cognitive decline, even in individuals whose cognition was not pathologically altered at baseline, independent of age, sex, education, and disease burden, including vascular disease.

One would therefore expect that the prevalence of hippocampal dementia, or Alzheimer's disease, would also increase massively in the first coronavirus year. After all, as I explained in chapter 2, it is not age that causes this form of dementia, but our unkind lifestyle. Age is only a factor to be considered insofar as the disease process or hippocampal degeneration takes time, not just a few years, but often decades, to produce dementia-like effects. Nevertheless, life under coronary measures has obviously become much more out of species than it was before. This inevitably led to an acceleration of the neuropathologic deterioration of the hippocampus, or a leftward shift in the strength of the frontal brain battery, as shown in figure 16.

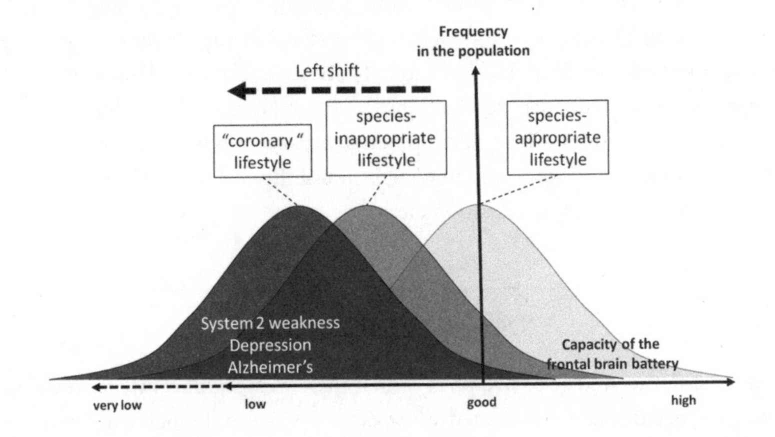

Figure 16

In fact, an exceptionally large number of people in Germany developed new dementia already in 2021, with around 436,800 new cases.[191] Compared to 2018 (when there were 333,000 new cases), this was a very dramatic increase of 31.1 percent.[192] To better contextualize this huge increase, let's take a quick look at changes in incidence in a historical context. In 2007 there were approximately 280,000 new cases in Germany.[193] From this base, a total of 53,000 new cases per year were added in 2018, for an average cumulative increase of 4,800 cases per year over the eleven-year period, which can be explained by the aging of the population. However, by 2021, there was a total increase of 103,800 new cases per year compared to 2018. The average cumulative increase over the three years was thus 34,600 cases per year, *seven times* that of the previous eleven years of 4,800 cases per year. This development cannot be explained by an aging society or by the assumption that diagnostics have improved.

Representatives of Alzheimer's societies never tire of using age as an explanation. This is obviously due to the fact that they can be seen as functional outposts of the pharmaceutical industry. This industry perpetuates the dogma that age is the essential cause for the development of Alzheimer's dementia, because individual lifestyle changes do not generate sales for the pharmaceutical industry. However, age is not the cause, but only a necessity, because the development of hippocampal dementia takes time due to an unhealthy lifestyle. In an almost infantile manner, representatives ignore the solid evidence that our drastically changed, completely inhumane (off-species) lifestyle is responsible for the increase in hippocampal dementia (Alzheimer's disease) and in vascular dementia (brain damage due to disturbed blood supply as a consequence of arteriosclerosis or stroke).

However, my explanation that the dementia disease process was accelerated by a result of SARS-CoV-2 infection (which affected only a few percent) or, way more frequently, by COVID-19 measures (which affected almost everyone) is fact-based and much more conclusive—but also much more dramatic. It is frightening to see such a large increase in the incidence of Alzheimer's disease in such a short time, when it cannot be assumed that it is due to better diagnostics. We can already imagine the catastrophic developments that lie ahead in the years to come. The bad news is that we ourselves are responsible for these developments, because this is not an immutable fate of aging. The good news is that we can take responsibility for preventing the worst and avoiding the mistakes that have been made.

"Blurred Distinction"

Compared to the average of five years earlier, there were significantly more deaths from all types of dementia-related diseases in 2020 (up 17 percent), much of it attributable to Alzheimer's disease alone (up 13 percent overall). This is significantly higher than expected, according to a report published in 2022 by the Alzheimer's Association in the United States.[194] In the report, the authors address the question of whether a large proportion of dementia deaths have been correctly recorded in the statistics, stating the following:

> Death certificates for individuals with Alzheimer's often list acute conditions such as pneumonia as the primary cause of death rather than Alzheimer's. As a result, people with Alzheimer's dementia who die due to these acute conditions may not be counted among the number of people who die from Alzheimer's disease, even though Alzheimer's disease may well have caused the acute condition listed on the death certificate. This difficulty in using death certificates to determine the number of deaths from Alzheimer's and other dementias has been referred to as a "blurred distinction between death with dementia and death from dementia."[195]

This means that in order to get the COVID-19 casualty numbers up, the Alzheimer's casualty numbers had to go down. Therefore, the actual number of Alzheimer's victims could be much higher than the official figures indicate.

More and more people under the age of sixty-five, the age previously defined as indicative of genetically accelerated Alzheimer's disease process, are affected by another form of acceleration, shown by a study published in August 2022 for the observation year 2021: "The German Alzheimer Society presents new dementia figures: Significantly more patients under the age of 65 than previously thought."[196] The associated website of the German Alzheimer Society also refers to a WHO report that made it possible to identify these cases as such for the first time: "The World Health Organization has published new studies on the incidence of dementia in different age groups. For the first time, more accurate estimates are available for people under 65. These suggest that there are currently more than 100,000 people under the age of 65 living with dementia in Germany." For example, in an analysis published in *The Lancet*, which interestingly was fully funded by the Bill & Melinda Gates Foundation and Gates Ventures, a group called the GBD 2019 Dementia Forecasting Collaborator projected 152.8 million cases of dementia worldwide by 2050, starting in 2019.[197] By comparison, based on 2010, just nine years earlier, "only" 115.4 million cases of dementia were projected for 2050.[198]

Based on this ominous outlook, we will have to wait for new projections in the coming years, which will also indirectly, but probably impressively, show the result of hippocampal damage due to global spiking. I therefore propose to speak of postspike syndromes instead of a long-COVID or post-vac syndrome, which must be considered a risk factor for depression and Alzheimer's disease.

Postspike Syndromes

According to a review by the German Medical Association (Bundesärztekammer), cognitive deficits are the central symptoms of post-COVID syndrome.[199] These include anxiety symptoms up to and including posttraumatic stress disorder, but "especially concentration, memory and word-finding disorders," which are summarized under the term *brain fog*. You can't really think clearly, you can't concentrate, you keep forgetting things, you feel cognitively off track, all of which clouds your view of what's important.

According to a meta-analysis, 22 percent of people develop cognitive impairment after a COVID-19 diagnosis.[200] Long-term COVID can also occur after COVID-19 vaccination, which is referred to as post-vac syndrome or "long COVID after vaccination." The symptom combination of long COVID syndrome corresponds to a massively disturbed adult hippocampal neurogenesis that is inhibited as a result of infection.[201] The same is true for "vaccination" and thus post-vac syndrome, as discussed (although autoimmune diseases are also subsumed under the term *post-vac syndrome*). Also supporting hippocampal dysfunction as a major cause of these syndromes is the fact that preexisting hippocampal conditions or risk factors increase the likelihood of these post-vac syndromes, as they would more appropriately be called. A team of scientists in Boston made the discovery: depressive disorders increase this likelihood by 32 percent, anxiety disorders by 42 percent, increased stress by 46 percent, and loneliness by 32 percent.[202] Those with at least two of these factors are even twice as likely to have long-term COVID. "The findings of this study suggest," the authors conclude, "that preinfection psychological distress may be a risk factor for post–COVID-19 conditions in individuals with SARS-CoV-2 infection."

Given the immense damage to the minds, bodies, and lives of the world's population that this insidious assault on people's autobiographical memory represents, one wonders if those responsible have not gone a step too far here, as it becomes increasingly apparent that in the future more and more people will be dependent on outside help at an early age, or even die prematurely due to neurodegenerative diseases. But in the world that Huxley portrayed in his dystopia almost a hundred years ago and which seems to bear a striking resemblance to the world we are heading toward, the elderly play no role for the world controllers anyway (keywords *galloping dementia at around 60*). If one wants to establish a completely new form of technocratically run society, it depends much more on children (even the unborn), teenagers, and young adults. They form the basis of technocratic power once they have developed a basic susceptibility to the artificial narratives presented to them by technological means and can no longer counter them with anything of their own; in essence, they have been prepared to let the narratives, which are valid only on a day-to-day basis, quickly become essential parts of their personality. The fertile ground for this was prepared by the massive weakening of biographical memory.

CHAPTER 5

MASTER PLAN, PART 2: CONFESSION TO THE TECHNOCRATIC FAITH

There is no nonsense so errant that it cannot be made the creed of the vast majority by adequate governmental action.
— Bertrand Russell (1872–1970)

The Great Narrative as a Means to Power

A narrative is the framework in which people classify and interpret their own experiences—it is the manner in which they make sense of their experiences to themselves and to others. Children in particular are very receptive to externally set narratives. They are easily influenced by them, and so is their perception. A narrative, which includes religious beliefs and, for example, a certain view of humanity, can quickly dominate their lives. Formative stories that reflect the narrative can have a lasting effect on the consciousness of the growing child. Susceptibility to foreign narratives is especially could happen when children have had few opportunities to experience the world in free interaction with other children and to make their own sense of their experiences—unconstrained and without exposure to overly dominant cultural or parental narratives. The susceptibility of the child's brain to influence is not only due to the is the child being very eager to learn. The child has also usually not yet developed its own view of the world or its own narrative, however naive it may be in comparison, so it readily accepts given narratives as useful patterns of interpretation, because they provide a sense of security, regardless of their appropriateness. Due to lack of life experience, contradictions in the propagated narratives are rarely discovered. In addition, every child wants to believe the story told to him or her if it is told by someone trusted, since the child's survival may depend on the good will of the other.

Religious storytellers recognized this very early on. Thus, in the Gospels, the most important narratives for the Christian worldview about the teachings, life, suffering, and death of Jesus Christ, the Bible says, "Let the children come to me." Here, belief in the religious narrative becomes a prerequisite for later entry into the kingdom of heaven. A narrative can hardly make a more comprehensive claim to power. Aldous Huxley also knew about the spongy learning capacity of the child's brain when, in *Brave New World*, he used neo-Pavlovian and hypnopaedic methods to inculcate into the growing children or human-like creatures the narrative of his supposedly perfect new world: the central slogans that they must internalize and that will determine how they will behave in society.

However, to implement a new narrative among adults is much more challenging, not to mention the difficulty of making it the dominant narrative. When the goal is simply to use the narrative to gain more power over people and not to actually create meaning (see "Narratives as a Means of Power" in chapter 3), the difficulty is greater still. Creating meaning would be easier in the sense that many adults are always in search of a deeper meaning to their experience and existence and could therefore be easily convinced of the usefulness of a narrative. For example, the Dutch historian Rutger Bregman argues convincingly in his book *Humankind* that the widespread narrative that humans are basically evil has had a profoundly negative impact on our coexistence on Spaceship Earth.[1] Since reading his new narrative—which he subtitles *A Hopeful History* (narrative)—I see myself, and especially my fellow human beings, in a completely different light, as if he had given me a new pair of glasses. I realized that I, too, had been influenced by a negative narrative, despite having written my previous books in the belief that everything would change for the better, and that I ultimately believed in the human capacity for good. However, Bregman's book did not indoctrinate me; rather, it liberated me, through good arguments that I could follow, from a worldview that was widespread in our culture and that I, too, had adopted as part of my socialization.

But if the goal of implementing a new narrative is not enlightenment but merely the acquisition of power, one must not only erase an existing worldview but also even bypass common sense. Finally, the suitability of the narrative for interpreting reality does not play a decisive role in this case. The ideal of perfect power over people means that the ruled do not question anything they are told. And the more absurd the narrative that is to be internalized through indoctrination, the greater and more lasting the power exercised over a person. Thus, an important goal of indoctrination is to triumph over common sense.

George Orwell wrote about this in January 1939, about six months before the start of World War II, in a review of Bertrand Russell's book *Power: A New Social Analysis*: "It is quite possible that we are descending into an age in which two and two will make five when the Leader says so."[2]

Orwell would later have his protagonist, Winston Smith, ponder the motivation behind, and the logical consequence of, such a problematic development of the self-surpassing claim to power, as also observed in fascist Germany, in *1984*:

> In the end, the Party would announce that two and two made five, and you would have to believe it. It was inevitable that they should make that claim sooner or later: The logic of their position demanded it. Not merely the validity of experience, but the very existence of external reality was tacitly denied by their philosophy. The heresy of heresies was common sense. And what was terrifying was not that they would kill you for thinking otherwise, but that they might be right. For, after all, how do we know that two and two make four? Or that the force of gravity works? Or that the past is unchangeable? If both the past and the outside world exist only in the mind, and the mind itself is controllable—what then?[3]

Toward the end of the novel, Smith's indoctrination by isolation and torture in the Ministry of Love (responsible for promoting Party loyalty, the instrumentality of which is in stark contradiction to its name) is not really complete until he can prove that he really believes that two and two make five when the powerful Party says so. He must show that he has internalized that the power of the technocrats is greater than the nature of things.

The more meaningless or absurd a narrative accepted by the broad masses is, the more pronounced and monstrous must be the domination over the human brain. Paradoxically, the complete decoupling of the narrative from reality at this stage can even be seen as an advantage, since it was only power that allowed it to become successful, and both reality and personal perception no longer serve as measures of its acceptability. Contradictions between a narrative and perception, experience, and ultimately logic, as we experience with the COVID-19 narrative, must be seen in this light: all the regulations and measures were never about health but about power! Orwell had his novel character Winston Smith explain how such a process is subjectively experienced: "It was as though some huge force were pressing down upon you—something that penetrated inside your skull, battering against your brain, frightening you out of your beliefs, persuading you, almost, to deny the evidence of your senses."[4] Thus, in the dystopia *1984*, the slogans are "War is peace! Freedom is slavery! Ignorance is strength!" Today, slogans such as "Freedom through enforced vaccination!" or "Weapons for peace!" are in use, statements that are both self-contradictory and mutually contradictory: the first slogan helped to deprive us of our freedom, supposedly in order to save lives; the compulsion to spike was paradoxically a condition for regaining a highly questionable, limited freedom. With the other slogan, we legitimize the killing of people by supplying weapons to a war zone, again ostensibly for peace; but this has always been agreed upon at the negotiating table, not fought for on the battlefield. The YGL's narrative of "diversity in equality"[5] also reads like a prime example of this kind of Orwellian contradiction that seems to be increasingly finding its way into the daily lives of us all.

The Nyder group of authors points out the danger of such absurd and sometimes well-intentioned narratives in the full consequence of their conceptual inconsistency: "Anyone who nevertheless claims that there are no differences between human beings, denying even biological facts such as sex or skin color, must at some point ensure that there are in fact no more differences." In other words, "He must eradicate all individuality, that is, what makes each individual a human being. Since this is not possible, or only with great effort, in the case of skin color and gender, the current mania for equality, like its predecessors, begins in the world of thought. In the end," Nyder continues, recalling basic motifs from *1984*, "That's enough. Whoever is no longer capable of thinking differences, for him they simply no longer exist. No matter how openly they exist."[6]

However, such obvious narrative contradictions trigger emotions in the process of indoctrination. The more one tries and fails to resolve them with the help of the mind, the more efficiently they become autobiographical memories and thus ultimately part of our personality. That's the case with changing narratives from time to time: Masks are useful. Masks are not useful after all. Vaccination protects against infection. Vaccination does not protect against infection. Vaccination protects others. Vaccination does not protect others. The information is remarkable to the hippocampus precisely because it is contradictory. As a result of disturbed neurogenesis, index neurons are increasingly overwritten, making the earlier personal experiences inaccessible or, in effect, erased. This is very dangerous because our past is the lens through which we perceive the world around us and visualize the future. We never see the real world, but only our personal reality, always distorted by the stories our brains tell us. It is through these narratives that we perceive the world, and it is through these stories that we communicate our own perspective to others. They are what our autobiographical memory remembers.

With Perceived Incompetence to World Domination

The constant change of rules, regulations, and interpretations of case numbers and infection events not only overwrote the index neurons but also produced at least two other advantages. The actions and statements of the responsible politicians always gave the impression that they did not know what they were doing, which could give them some hope of impunity in the sense of doing their best in an unclear situation, while they obscured how well the global implementation of the underlying plan was orchestrated. The confusion was also an argument for the technocrats, as in the future everything must be coordinated much more closely and centrally. The WHO's interim report on the global pandemic treaty reads as follows: "In recognition of the catastrophic failure of the international community in showing solidarity and equity in response to the coronavirus disease (COVID-19) pandemic, the World Health Assembly convened . . . in December 2021, . . . to draft and negotiate a WHO convention, agreement or other international instrument on pandemic prevention, preparedness and response."[7]

The narrative of failure is designed to make people believe that only a WHO world government can prevent worse things from happening in the future. Accordingly, on May 12, 2023, a large majority of the German Bundestag voted in favor of reforming the WHO.[8] As it became clear during the COVID-19 pandemic that "WHO lacks the capacity to fully implement its mandate," the coalition motion states, reforms are needed, as well as political, human, and financial support. The goal is for the WHO to "fulfill its leadership role in global health governance." Thus, "WHO reforms should be pursued to strengthen its governance, efficiency, independence, capacity, accountability, and ability to enforce rules." In addition, "cooperation with global partners" (i.e., nongovernmental organizations such as the Bill & Melinda Gates Foundation) should be "deepened, and the regions within WHO should be strengthened both financially and structurally." But it's not just about pandemics. The motion goes on to say that "WHO must also be supported in its efforts to prepare for and respond to the health impacts of the climate crisis." Because climate change, like pandemics, is of a permanent nature, the WHO in its "leading role in global health policy" is given the equally permanent right to intervene by strengthening the "enforceability of rules" on the behavior of every citizen of the earth.

The question of which story should determine our future was the topic of one of the WEF-organized events in Dubai from November 10 to 13, 2021, under the direction of Klaus Schwab. With the help of some forty globalists, none of them elected by the public, a credible vision, the Great Narrative, was to be designed for the Great Reset announced by the WEF for the acceptance of all our futures.[9] In the closing session of what he called an "extraordinary event" for designing a great narrative for the future, Schwab publicly announced that "we can influence our future, but what we have heard we can do so only if we have a long-term view, if we think first of the community and only second of ourselves, and if we think globally."[10] This is one of many clear indications that the individual citizen of the earth will have to subordinate his or her own interests to the community, which will be defined only by the coming Grand Narrative, the technocratic idea. The supposed salvation of a future stakeholder society has already been exposed in the course of the coronavirus crisis: The stakeholders are by no means ordinary citizens but are still the big shareholders who protect their gigantic wealth from the tax authorities in their influential foundations. They, unlike the rest of society, have not become poorer as a result of the crisis, but obscenely richer. This brings to mind a statement by the French philosopher Jean-Francois Lyotard (1924–1998). According to Lyotard, a Great Narrative serves first and foremost "functions to legitimize power, authority, and social customs"—in other words, everything that, according to WEF reporter Tim Hinchliffe, "the Great Reset is trying to achieve."[11]

Perhaps the Dubai event was simply to generate material for Schwab's new book of the same name. But just six weeks later, The Great Narrative: For a Better Future, again coauthored with Thierry Malleret, offers no clear post-Reset plan. All that is repeated, sometimes more obviously, sometimes less so, is the visionary goal that corporations will form close partnerships with governments, which is nothing more than a euphemism for a totalitarian, socialist system on a global scale, in which there will be neither property nor privacy: "Technology makes our every move easily traceable, and we must come to terms with the idea," the two "visionaries" write, "that there is no longer any privacy: Our personal data is gradually becoming completely monitored, invisible to many, and therefore transparent."[12]

My grave concern is that a large part of the population is no longer capable of rational resistance to any narrative, no matter how absurd and monstrous, due to the additional severely diminished capacity of the frontal brain battery, compared to 2019, damaged by the first years of COVID-19 pandemic measures, the spiking, and subsequently by the already announced permanent crisis mode of the WEF. How badly our brains suffer from the Great Reset's package of measures and how we have been prepared to be susceptible to the most absurd narratives, as we have already seen in the previous chapter. Research into how this susceptibility can now be used to implant new beliefs into people's brains, in the sense of a Great Mental Reset, goes back a long way in history. In the middle of the last century, it produced remarkable results that should serve as a warning to us.

The Great Mental Reset Using Communist Indoctrination Methodology

The ending of the Korean War, officially on September 24, 1953, marked the beginning of Operation Big Switch, or the exchange of prisoners of war between Korea and the United States. "In the back of open-built Russian trucks," reports *The Guardian*, "23

American POWs [prisoners of war] were being driven to a prisoner exchange complex in the village of Panmunjom, on the North-South Korean border. The atmosphere at the complex had been electric with anger for months, as American prisoners returned from North Korean camps with shocking stories of cruelty. But on this day, as the trucks drew closer, American observers noticed that something about these prisoners was different. They looked tanned and healthy, and were dressed in padded blue Chinese uniforms, each pinned with Pablo Picasso's dove of peace."[13] This did not fit at all with the picture that had emerged of the detention conditions. "As the trucks screeched to a halt," the report continued, "the prisoners laughed and shook hands with their captors . . . Turning to the shocked crowd who had gathered to greet them, the POWs clenched their fists and shouted, 'Tomorrow, the international Soviet unites the human race!' Then, instead of walking over to their countrymen, they turned the other way and defected to Communist China." This was not a stunt, not a mere play under threat of imminent violence, and most importantly, not an isolated incident. According to *The Guardian*, these defections, shocking to the US government, were only the tip of a dangerous iceberg for US morale: "In the North Korean camps, American POWs had cooperated with the enemy to an unprecedented extent. Not only did they inform on their fellow prisoners; hundreds of POWs gave false confessions to atrocities, and made radio broadcasts extolling the virtues of communism and condemning western capitalism." The report concludes, "Never before had captured soldiers betrayed their country so flagrantly."

Soon, the term *brainwashing* was making the rounds in the media. They speculated about a sophisticated new weapon of mind control that, according to *The Guardian*, could "turn a person's brain into a blank slate and implant new thoughts, memories and beliefs." But the methods of indoctrination were not really new, as it turned out. Their long history can be traced back to at least the ancient Byzantine Empire of the fifteenth century, according to studies by Lawrence E. Hinkle Jr. (1918–2012), a physician, and Harold G. Wolff (1898–1962), a physician and neuroscientist who later studied the subject extensively.[14] In the centuries that followed, the methodology was further refined. But now, for the first time, it was scientifically studied in detail and the results published. The data was based on the experiences of prisoners of war who had fallen into the hands of the Communist state police during the Korean War (1950–1953) but who did not desert to China as others did and returned to the United States as expected.

The US Department of Defense commissioned Albert D. Biderman (1923–2003), a social scientist in the US Air Force, among others, to conduct this study. He was to investigate why so many US POWs cooperated with the Communists. After months of extensive interviews, Biderman concluded that three elements in particular were critical to the success of the Communist interrogators' coercive control and indoctrination: "dependency, weakness, and fear."[15]

By deliberately creating dependency relationships, exploiting the feeling of weakness and stoking fear, an attempt was made in the North Korean prison camps to completely reeducate the prisoners. This was sometimes so successful that US soldiers actually began to believe in the communist ideal. Here (as in Orwell's *1984*), "If a Man is Arrested his Case Cannot be Settled until a Protocol ('Confession') has been Prepared," write Hinkle and Wolff.[16] The term *confession* here has a double meaning of great importance: the confession of guilt and, at the same time, the confession of a new faith, "the enthusiastic acceptance of the 'new way of life' offered to him." Thus, on one hand, a prisoner must admit to a crime, even if he has not committed it; it is enough to have committed a thought crime, as Orwell had called it in his novel. This mistake can be based, for example, on the fact that one has previously held a false belief, acted on it, or simply thought on the basis of it. On the other hand, the process is not complete until the "wrong" belief is replaced by the new, "correct" narrative of the interrogator, and the mind is brought under control. According to Hinkle and Wolff's research, the process can take up to five years, even after a confession has been made.

Biderman summarized his findings on the indoctrination process in the essay "Communist Attempts to Elicit False Confessions from Air Force Prisoners of War," published in a September 1957 issue of the *Bulletin of the New York Academy of Medicine*.[17] I think the term *false* is misleading here, however, because the type of coercion described is clearly more fundamental than coercing false testimony would be. Rather, the goal of the process Biderman describes is to actually convince the indoctrinated prisoners that they have done something wrong and to confess to it.

The review and analysis of the Communist indoctrination method for "confession" or "conversion to the true faith," led to recognition as early as 1957 that this was a two-step process. Biderman's report stated, "We found that we could make a meaningful distinction between those measures the Communists took to render the prisoner compliant [i.e., Part 1 of the master plan, chapter 4], on the one hand, and, on the other, those which sought to shape his compliance into the very specific patterns of 'confessor' behavior [i.e., Part 2 of the master plan, this chapter]."[18] It was also known that these two parts of the indoctrination, and thus of the master plan as I present it here, are not independent of each other, for according to Biderman this is "purely an analytical division."

What was not known, however, was exactly which part of the brain would be the ultimate target of indoctrination. For one thing, on November 13, 1956, when Biderman's research was first presented to the New York Neurological Society, it was not known that the hippocampus was the control center of autobiographical memory. This did not become known until three months later, in February 1957, with the publication of the Henry Molaison case (described in chapter 2).[19] And the discovery of hippocampal neurogenesis was not made until 1965, in rats.[20] It would be decades before it was discovered in humans and the scientific community accepted it.

It contradicted the prevailing dogma at the time that no new neurons were produced during adulthood.[21] The function of these new hippocampal neurons was only gradually understood at the beginning of the twenty-first century. Only with this knowledge could the indoctrination measures, refined by the added neurobiological knowledge, be carried out in a more targeted and widespread manner (think of worldwide spiking, which is a project of the century from a logistical point of view alone). In addition, the neurobiological consequences of the measures could now be recorded and studied as a kind of neuropathological success control (see the end of the last chapter and later in this one).

When Biderman formulated his report, nothing was known about the hippocampus's role in autobiographical memory, self-esteem, System 2 thinking (I first published this particular discovery in my book *The Exhausted Brain*, which was in print in January 2022),[22] or psychological resilience. But without being able to explain in detail how it works, the practical knowledge gained allowed these hippocampal functions to be used almost optimally for manipulation. Purely by trial and error, or empirically, a viable method was developed over centuries that worked so well that many were amazed: "We found, as did other studies such as those of Hinkle and Wolff, that human behavior could be manipulated within a certain range by controlled environments," Biderman writes. But "the reception of these findings has frequently been incredulous," he points out, and that's why he has been asked, "Is there nothing more to it than this? Can people really be manipulated so easily? Are you sure there was not something done that you failed to detect?"

The Korean War, like the later Vietnam War, is to be understood as a proxy war between world powers with opposing economical ideologies. Thus, there was a lot of "propaganda dynamite" in the defections, which came as a surprise to the Western world. This achievement was presumably the very reason for the Chinese leadership's interest in indoctrinating US POWs in North Korea with their way of thinking in the first place. And indeed, not only did they succeed in getting people with previously different beliefs to believe in a communist ideal and feel happy with their new worldview, but they also had this outstanding success with, of all people, those who were originally willing to sacrifice their lives for the defense of their homeland and thus ultimately went to war for the capitalist economic system. Interestingly, the conversion did not even require the use of violence. On the contrary, "inflicting physical pain is not a necessary nor particularly effective method of inducing compliance." Quite to the contrary, "where physical violence was inflicted during the course of such an attempt, the attempt was particularly likely to fail completely," Biderman writes. But the "ever-present fear of violence in the mind of the prisoner appears to have played an important role in inducing compliance." Hence "the Communists generally fostered such fears through vague threats and the implication that they were prepared to do drastic things." In other words, even the pretraumatic stress disorder discussed in the previous chapter was recognized and used as an effective method of manipulation.

The goal of the indoctrination we experienced with COVID-19 is strikingly similar, and not only at first glance. The prevailing capitalist market economy, which serves the shareholders, is to be transformed into an economic system oriented toward the interests of the stakeholders. One is tempted to understand all people as these stakeholders, which makes the new system seem to have clearly communist features. But these stakeholders are threatened by existential crises, and doomsday looms on several fronts at once: plague, war, inflation, and famine, always as a result of human innovation (biological gain-of-function research in pathogenic microorganisms such as SARS-CoV-2, weapons of mass destruction, the capitalist monetary system, and overpopulation through modern agriculture), are the apocalyptic horsemen of the WEF. It seems to be in the best interest of the ordinary stakeholder to be protected from himself. The belief in the Great Narrative of a propertyless, free of legal rights, and completely supervised world of Klaus Schwab or in the almost congruent stories of Bill Gates is supposed to be the only viable way to save us from the imminent end of the world. We only need to convert to the belief that a virus-free and climate-neutral brave new world is possible if we let ourselves be chipped, monitored, AI-controlled, and thus sorted into our social caste and permanently vaccinated and thereby renounce any private property and thus any personal power, even if it is only power over our own lives. Then, and only then, there is a chance for the continuation of human life, and we are provided with what we need to be happy. To provide a proof of an honest, deeply internalized confession—here, too, in a double sense, of —people sometimes proudly undergo "confirmation" through double, triple, and always one more inoculation. Ideally, this should be done every six months, as STIKO continues to recommend or require in the spring of 2023, although spiking is useless in terms of immunity, but not for autobiographical memory destruction.[23] The unvaccinated and those who refuse the mask are excluded from the community in a smug manner, like heretics. With the yellow letter of indulgence in the form of the vaccination booklet, they must regularly prove themselves worthy of participating in the new social life through repeated injections—tantamount to being accepted into the circle of true believers.

Biderman's final report contains an eight-point indoctrination program that was used by the US government a few decades later at Guantánamo Bay. The infamous US detention center was established in 2002 as part of the "war on terrorism." There; from the beginning, US military trainers offered interrogators an entire training course based almost verbatim on Biderman's eight-point program, according to documents on interrogation methods at the camp released to US congressional investigators in 2008.[24] So they had their own very practical experience and learned a lot from experimenting on people who were detained on suspicion of terrorism, mostly without a court order, outside the rule of law. I have my doubts as to whether Biderman, who died in 2003, would have approved. At least he wrote at the time his investigation was released, as reported by *The Guardian*, "Probably no other aspect of Communism reveals more thoroughly its disrespect for truth and the individuals than its resort to these techniques."[25]

But applying these techniques and the lessons learned to the entire population of the world, which had become prisoners of war in the war against the coronavirus was little more than a logical next step. Every citizen of the world was suddenly under general suspicion of being a bioterrorist who, as a potential superspreader, could indiscriminately put other people in mortal danger. (As I write this in the spring of 2023, prosecutors in Germany are attempting to prove that a caregiver's unvaccinated status was causally related to a viral infection documented as the cause of death of residents I nursing home where she worked.[26] Her charge in the lawsuit is involuntary manslaughter, even though it has long been proven that spiking would not have provided protection of others.) The methodology of indoctrination used to get US POWs to confess or convert to the new faith is almost congruent with the methodology used from 2020 onward to get people to internalize the technocratic COVID-19 narrative. It is therefore of the utmost importance to closely examine this methodology in order to learn from it and develop safeguards.

Caught in the Web of Indoctrination

The indoctrination program that became known after the Korean War is often mistakenly attributed to Biderman. However, the social scientist did not design it; he merely extracted the essential measures from the research results of interviews returned US prisoners who had gone through the indoctrination process. Because of his publicly stated disgust with the actions taken in Korea, I am convinced that it was not his desire to have his research results used at the Guantánamo Bay detention camp in 2002. That was even more the case in 2020 when his findings were used on a large scale in an attempt to put the world's population in a state of vulnerable openness to an unprecedented global mass indoctrination, which I recognize as the first step in establishing the great narrative of salvation through risky gene therapy in the minds of the now obedient prisoners.

Almost all parts of the eight-point program published by Biderman in 1957 as the Diagram of Coercion have been discussed in one form or another in the previous chapter. There, we considered their blocking effect on hippocampal neurogenesis and the associated acceleration of hippocampal neurodegeneration. This is the neuropathological prerequisite for people's vulnerable receptivity to a new narrative and the global construction of as uniform an identity as possible.

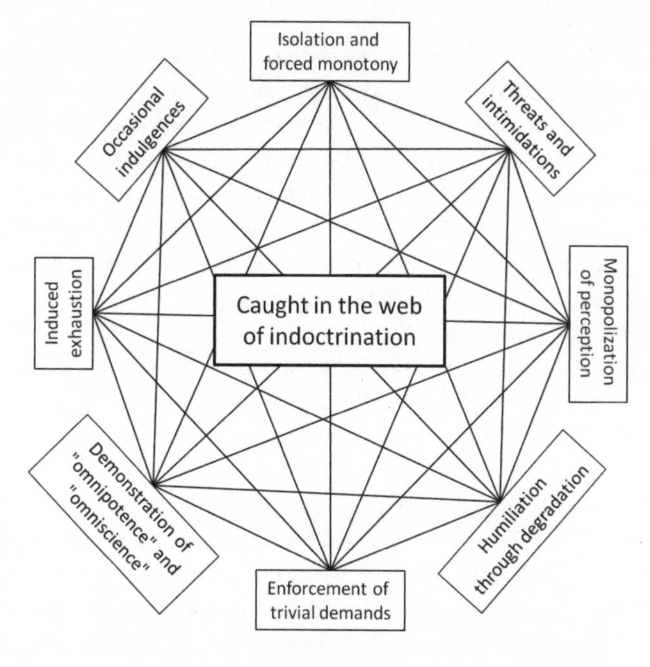

Figure 17

Instead of looking at the measures in isolation, I think it makes more sense to depict the indoctrination scheme as a kind of network, as in figure 17, because the individual parts only have the desired effect when they interact. Nevertheless, let's look at the eight points individually as applied from 2020 onward, one by one.

Isolation and Forced Monotony

Isolation is one of the worst forms of torture that can be inflicted on social beings like humans. The devastating effects on the hippocampus was discussed before. By isolating humans, one deprives them of the possibility of communication—during lockdowns, at least the possibility of confidential communication with their fellow human beings is taken away. Quite apart from the psychological damage caused by such measures, isolation, even in the case of access to modern means of communication, represents a threat to one's own person, through the violation of a legitimate private sphere and ultimately of the right to self-determination, especially if one is critical of a binding narrative. Today, mobile or fixed telephony and other, especially digital, technical communication channels can be tapped easily. If this does not yet seem like a serious threat, consider that any communication, whether contemporaneous or recorded, can at some point in the future be analyzed by AI and subsequently used against us. In Australia, a country long committed to a zero COVID strategy (with the goal not of reducing cases but of preventing any new infections through correspondingly radical measures), this fundamental danger has largely materialized, albeit only with regard to semipublic communication: anyone who criticized the government's COVID-19 policy on social media or Facebook and pointed out corresponding protests had to expect a visit from the police. The case of Zoe-Lee Buhler, who was pregnant at the time and whose arrest was recorded and made headlines around the world, illustrates this point.[27] What a relief it is for governments that can rely on automated evaluation methods and want to nip critical voices in the bud when personal communication is forced into the digital space.

In this context, not all US prisoners subjected to North Korea's indoctrination program were housed in special camps. Hinkle and Wolff report, "Some were detained for a time under 'house arrest' in rooms fitted up as prisons, and guarded by police."[28] This was certainly an important finding for the measures orchestrated around the world in 2020. If isolation as a means of indoctrination were only possible in special prisons or camps, it could not have worked from the outset in purely logistical terms. Isolation in the form of social distancing (actually, antisocial distancing) is also compartmentalization in the psychological sense and is also about dividing and driving apart groups and families. Consider the sometimes-complete isolation of individuals through quarantine, for which a positive PCR test was all that was needed. Elderly people in nursing homes were placed in "protective custody," as were patients in hospitals. People had to be home by a certain time, just in time for media indoctrination through the evening news. So many people sat alone in front of the television, isolated without company, at the mercy of the indoctrination. Distance learning for children and young people also contributed to isolation, as did the obligations for some adults to work from home.

But the isolation of people has also been intensified in another way, namely by the destruction of the culture of debate. In recent years, many more controversial topics have been promoted and introduced into the controlled discourse, accompanied by a deliberate radicalization of opinion leaders, as happened, for example, with the topic of gender. Different attitudes toward new (language) rules sometimes led to rifts in friendships and families. Battle lines hardened, and people increasingly thought only in terms of extremes: proponents of gendering saw people with different views on the subject as misogynists and themselves as advocates of modern emancipation of marginalized groups. Opponents of gender speech, on the other hand, are radicalizing themselves as well, wanting to see themselves as conservative protectors of language, but sometimes believing that they can recognize in gender advocates normalizers of pathological perversions, sometimes even pedophilia. The camps must be irreconcilably opposed to each other in these extreme definitions and seem to know no gradations and no argumentative, constructive dissent. One can be lonely among people who have nothing anymore to say to each other.

Divide et Impera

Divide and rule—even the rulers of ancient Rome knew that all you had to do to secure your power was to sow discord. The individual (in Latin, *indivisible*) is the smallest, indivisible social element, just as the atom (from the Greek *atomos*, also meaning "indivisible") was thought to be the smallest chemical element. Similarly, just as in the physical world things come into existence and are realized only through their interaction, human beings can ultimately exist only through contact. Being indivisible, an individual is viable only in association with others. In this respect, the clan, and especially the nuclear family, was the molecular structure that gave each "social atom" its secure place. To isolate such an individual to make the person vulnerable or attackable, one must break the social bond. In the chemical world, it takes energy to break the molecular bonds so that atoms can be isolated and reorganized. In the social world, one could say that it also takes energy to do this.

The energy is the anger and hatred that comes from divisive conflicts. The question of vaccination status divides families, usually without any objective discussion—it's a matter of life and death! But gendering is also part of the current narrative of the good person (i.e., views that people must adopt if they want to see themselves as progressive and advocates of individual self-determination), and this too may isolate the individual.

"The sexes are supposed to confront each other from the outset as parties to a conflict, or even better, as parties to a war," writes the Nyder group, "and not as an independent partnership that escapes the influence of the state."[29] Similarly, German Bettina Gruber, a literary and cultural studies scholar, speaks of a colorful chauvinism that has spread on social media, "which systematically drives a wedge between the sexes—promoted and driven by politics."[30] The individual is separated from the "chemical-molecular" union of family. What remains is a radical, an isolated atom. "From [such] radically isolated people who are not even sure of their gender . . . no resistance can be expected," the Nyder group states.

Another of Biderman's key findings is that isolation and monotonous routines, whether alone or in small groups, lead to an intense preoccupation with self. Combined with stress and anxiety, this leads to equally monotonous thought loops, which are considered a hallmark of depressive disorders. Paradoxically, however, people in desperate situations also tend to become attached to those responsible for their dilemma. Although not yet officially recognized as a mental illness, this emotional attachment is colloquially known as *Stockholm syndrome*. The term originates from a hostage situation in the

Swedish capital of the same name in 1973, during which the phenomenon was first observed and subsequently described. At that time, some bank employees, after being released by the bank robbers, refused to testify in court against the perpetrators and even collected money for their defense.

According to the Cleveland Clinic, Stockholm syndrome "is a coping mechanism to a captive or abusive situation. People develop positive feelings toward their captors or abusers over time."[31] One suspected reason for this is the hope that positive feelings and cooperation will increase one's chances of survival. After all, the abusers are initially the only ones who can free them. According to a meta-study, there are four key components that characterize Stockholm syndrome:

- A hostage's development of positive feelings toward the captor
- No previous relationship between hostage and captor
- A refusal by hostages to cooperate with police forces and other government authorities
- A hostage belief in the humanity of the captor, ceasing to perceive them as a threat, when the victim holds the same values as the aggressor.[32]

These components were also present in the indoctrination of US prisoners in Korea, as Biderman, Hinkle, and Wolff note in their respective final reports. Isolation, like the other measures in the network of indoctrination, was designed to develop a dependent and confidential relationship between prisoner and interrogator. And the same occurred during the COVID-19 measures and has some effect beyond.

Relatively few lawsuits were filed, even though most people must have realized what the government was doing to them. As another example, at the end of 2020, Jens Spahn, the German Health Minister in office during the first two COVID-19 years, was even the most admired politician in Germany according to polls, in spite of (or perhaps because of) the grossly excessive, liberty-sapping measures such as isolation, lockdowns, and mandatory masks.[33] After Spahn, himself a member of the WEF's select circle of Young Global Leaders,[34] locked the German population in their homes and drove them to despair with excessive fearmongering. His message was, "We are vaccinating Germany back to freedom."[35] From the point of view of those affected, this corresponds to the situation of a hostage who is promised by the hostage-taker that he can be released from the hostage-taking if only he obeys and does what he demands while suggesting that this is only for his protection.

According to a survey conducted in January 2022, Spahn's successor in office, Karl Lauterbach, enjoyed the same paradoxical goodwill among Germans.[36] People idolized those politicians who had caused untold suffering instead of actually helping them by moderately implementing a preventive strategy that addressed the real causes—the Stockholm syndrome in its purest form. By that time, it should have been clear to everyone involved that the great promises of salvation or immunity from spiking were not going to be kept. Those who, by virtue of their profession, had to keep abreast of the latest developments in knowledge (politicians, doctors and, among others, journalists who deal with the subject), could not have failed to notice that effective prevention strategies that address the real causes were already known and have long been sufficiently proven.

For example, a study published in July 2021 by the CDC already showed that the global vaccination program does not reduce the incidence of infection, contrary to political claims. Vaccinated people are just as likely to become infected and sick as unvaccinated people and may be even more likely, the study concluded.[37] Among other things, it reported a mass outbreak of the virus in Provincetown, Massachusetts, in July 2021. CDC scientists counted almost five hundred cases of COVID-19. Surprisingly, about 74 percent of those with the disease were fully vaccinated.[38] If 74 percent of the general population had been vaccinated at that time, one might have concluded that there was no vaccine protection at all. But in fact, the rate of full vaccination in the general population in Massachusetts at the end of July 2021 was only 61.1 percent, hence below the infection rate among those who were vaccinated.[39] This alone suggests then that those who were vaccinated were not protected at all to contract the coronavirus and COVID-19 than those who were not vaccinated. Four of the five people who required intensive treatment were also fully vaccinated, indicating that vaccination did not protect from a severe course of the disease.

Because the viral load or infectivity of the vaccinated and unvaccinated had to be considered equal based on the PCR results, the CDC recommended that fully vaccinated Americans return to wearing face masks indoors at public places if they live in areas with high rates of COVID-19 infection.[40] This was an admission that vaccination did not provide adequate protection against the then-prevalent delta variant. The isolation and social exclusion of the unvaccinated was finally recognized as epidemiologically unfathomable; those politicians and physicians who persisted must have been driven by other motives.

In Germany, on the other hand, in August 2022, contrary to these findings, the following change was decided in the then newly enacted Vaccination Protection Act: "For tested or freshly vaccinated persons, the mask requirement shall be waived in many cases."[41] This gave the vaccinated the feeling that they were not contagious, contrary to scientific evidence, and created a further incentive to be vaccinated. At the same time, this additionally promoted the incidence of infection and the division of society—ingenious and evil at the same time.

Apparently, Spahn is at least aware that his "health policy" has harmed German citizens it was supposed to protect. The main title of his autobiography about his time in office says (almost) everything: "We Will Have to Forgive Each Other a Lot."[42] The title "You Will Have to Forgive Me a Lot" would probably have been better, because this formula suggests much more that this is by no means a statement by an equal among equals—the identification of the victim with the perpetrator, as we know it from the Stockholm syndrome, is based on the victim's assumption that the perpetrator shares his own values. Understandably, perpetrators have a vital interest in creating this impression. Here it is obvious that this is not the case, and thus Spahn lacks any precondition that would make an admission and an apology as a basis for forgiveness at all possible. A real apology is still missing.

Monopolization of Perception

In *Brave New World*, hypnopedia is used as one of several means to monopolize the perception of indoctrination subjects. However, learning by repetitive suggestion during sleep is not effective at all, as a major study in 1956 showed.[43] Although other science fiction novels have adapted this futuristic concept, the vision has not yet matured to the point of feasibility. If it were actually applicable, it would probably already be part of the web of indoctrination today.

However, because deep sleep is an essential prerequisite for long-term storing of new experiences, this can indeed be used for the purpose of indoctrination. All you have to do is get the ego-depleted hippocampus to overwrite the index neurons with fear-inducing stimuli (news, stories, etc.) just before bedtime. Particularly suitable for this are the special broadcasts from the COVID-19 war zone, which is wreaking havoc right outside your door, always threatening to move this one step further into your home, at any moment. The Ukraine war, too, as a new, potentially existential conflict with real armed violence, has replaced the hot phase of the COVID-19 war as the top topic, with a seamless transition. The mainstream media drags it into the evening television program and thus effectively into the hippocampal memory. Finally, emotional individual fates, such as close-ups of people in intensive care units who are barely kept alive with the help of many tubes and beeping monitors, as well as close-ups of weeping relatives, are important for hippocampal memory.

Also, pictures of coffins (even if the pictures have nothing to do with the current situation) are much better at generating emotional memories than pure numerical messages. Even Joseph Stalin (1879–1953) noted, "The death of one man is a tragedy. The death of millions is a statistic." He recognized that individual stories of suffering and tragic images touch us (more on this in chapter 7). This wisdom was explicitly taken into account in the BMI's scenario paper previously mentioned, and the mainstream media readily implemented the communication concept based on it. What the German population was now exposed to on a daily basis in prime time provided the conditions for the neocortical hard disk in slow-wave deep sleep to receive its nocturnal, often-content-repetitive whispers, which were then consolidated in the subsequent REM sleep. According to the current state of knowledge, there is no better way to permanently place personality overwriting, indoctrinating messages in the brain.

To place individuals or an entire population completely under the spell of a narrative and ideological control requires limiting opportunities for new experiences. Thus, the closing of meeting places (clubs, sports facilities, and even churches) and the closure of public life not only contributed to the monotony of daily life and isolation. After all, Communist reeducation included "exposure to nothing but Communist interpretation of history and current events."[44] On a global scale, however, limiting new experiences only works if one thinks and acts globally. Thus, for the first time in human history, almost all governments mistreated their citizens with the same rules and slogans. Global action was also taken by means of the same mainstream media (see chapter 4) and censorship on the major social media platforms (see chapter 1), with simultaneous precautionary defamation of any alternative opinions in case they could escape the censorship net and make themselves heard elsewhere. These measures of opinion monopolization were, as shown, well-planned in advance and therefore highly efficient. Critics of the measures were slandered as corona deniers, COV-idiots, conspiracy theorists, or even—with the height of inflammatory language—right-wing radicals or Nazis.

Data Manipulation and Nobody Cares

When Edward Snowden revealed the secret activities of the National Security Agency (NSA), all the media reported it. In contrast, there was radio silence from the mainstream media when the prestigious *British Medical Journal* (BMJ) published an equally well-documented revelation about a clinical trial that is crucial to the lives of a large part of the world's population. Brook Jackson, a regional director of the research organization Ventavia Research Group (which, along with several other companies, was contracted by Pfizer to conduct the fast-track vaccine trial) revealed to BMJ that the "company falsified data, unblinded patients [i.e., those who knew who had been vaccinated and who had not, allowing for deliberate manipulation of the data], employed inadequately trained vaccinators, and was slow to follow up on adverse events reported in Pfizer's pivotal phase III trial."[45] More generally, she said, the quality control personnel were completely overwhelmed by the volume of problems they encountered. If data had indeed been falsified, it would be unforgivable. After all, billions of people around the world rely on the quality of the Pfizer study that was conducted. Even the FDA remained silent and did not even respond to the request of more than thirty US scientists from renowned universities to finally release all the approval documents—until a court ruling made them.[46]

The slander is particularly perfidious in view of the attitude of those who deliberately chose such insult—that anyone who spoke out against compulsory vaccination was a right-wing Nazi. But soldiers of the Wehrmacht were forcibly vaccinated, and countless Jewish concentration camp prisoners were used as test subjects for new vaccines.[47] Dr. Josef Mengele, one of the main perpetrators of these unethical experiments, is known by name to most people to this day, and his atrocities against prisoners were an unintended cause for the creation of the so-called Nuremberg Code. After the Allied victory, this code stipulated that no experiments or treatments could be performed without the informed consent of the patient. So, one was considered a right-wing radical for opposing measures that had been perfected by a right-wing fascist state not so long ago. Whoever comes up with such ideas either lacks the ability to think clearly or, as I suspect, is extremely adept at manipulating public opinion. After all, even high-ranking scientists and experts were defamed in this undifferentiated way. And so, for many, there seemed to be only one interpretation of the events, and only one way to solve the problem, as presented by Gates and company. This led to the widespread assumption among uncritical, obedient segments of the population that "all experts agree," which was true only to the extent that those who were seen were only those who were allowed to be seen because they agreed with the narrative on crucial issues.

Defamed Science

The Great Barrington Declaration (GBD) argued for "focused protection" of vulnerable groups. Those who were not at risk could have resumed their normal lives immediately, and the immense collateral damage of indiscriminate policies could have been avoided.[48] At the time of writing this (spring 2023), almost a million people, including many doctors and scientists, had signed the GBD. But it was a thorn in the side of pandemic drivers like Francis Collins, then head of the National Institutes of Health (NIH), and Anthony Fauci, head of the NIAID. Eventually, GBD threatened to tear apart the web of indoctrination, prompting them to take vehement action against it. In December 2021 an email from the fall of 2020 was released in response to a Freedom of Information Act request. It revealed a behind-the-scenes attempt to discredit GBD and vilify its authors. In the email, Collins told his colleague Fauci that this proposal of the "three fringe epidemiologists . . . seems to be getting a lot of attention," adding that "there needs to be a quick and devastating published takedown of its premises. I don't see anything like that online yet—is it underway?" according to the *Wall Street Journal* report.[49] (This is the same Fauci, by the way, who has since published that we should not be surprised that systemically administered vaccines are useless for respiratory infections.)

In a study, a team of Israeli and Australian scientists reconstructed in detail how critics were censored and defamed, how they ended up in professional ruin, and how public opinion was manipulated in the process: "Our findings point to the central role played by media organizations, and especially by information technology companies, in attempting to stifle debate over COVID-19 policy and measures."[50] For example, heavy censorship was carried out with the support of governments, such as the White House, which partnered with technology companies such as Facebook, Twitter, and Google.[51] In other words, governments were not afraid to work with leading institutions and IT companies and use drastic methods to suppress views that were not politically expedient. According to the authors of the study, "In the effort to silence alternative voices, widespread use was made not only of censorship, but of tactics of suppression that damaged the reputations and careers of dissenting doctors and scientists, regardless of their academic or medical status and regardless of their stature prior to expressing a contrary position." I am reminded of a cynical statement by Idi Amin (1925–2003), dictator of Uganda from 1971 to 1979: "There is freedom of speech, but I cannot guarantee freedom after speech." Thus, democratic governments have pursued a comparable, equally life-threatening, strategy, as the aforementioned team of scholars concludes: "In place of open and fair discussion, censorship and suppression of scientific dissent has deleterious and far-reaching implications for medicine, science, and public health."

Framing is a skillful and manipulative sociopsychological procedure. By systematically framing an issue within a very specific interpretive framework, the decisions and judgments of an information recipient are specifically influenced (see ""Causal Prevention of Severe SARS-CoV-2 Infections Is Right-Wing Extremism" in the previous chapter).

The AfD was the only party in Germany that questioned almost all COVID-19 measures and, on June 17, 2020, submitted a factual motion to the Bundestag for a vote that dealt with meaningful changes. These were not demands related to publicly problematic aspects of the AfD's (right-wing) political program. It was a scientifically sound and feasible supplement or even outright alternative to the chosen path of measures violating fundamental rights, submitted under the title "Reduce Severe Progressions of Infection with the Coronavirus SARS-CoV-2—Eliminate Vitamin D

Deficiency in the Population, Strengthen Immune Defenses."[52] On scientifically plausible grounds, the federal government was urged to do the following:

- Comprehensively inform the population in Germany about the health consequences of a deficient or suboptimal vitamin D supply with regard to acute respiratory and other diseases, also pointing out possible dosage errors.
- To work toward making twice-yearly measurements a health insurance benefit that is exempt from co-payment [measurement of blood pressure or blood sugar is paid by health insurers, but not of Vitamin D levels].
- To take measures to improve the vitamin D supply of the population as a whole, in particular to review the fortification of foods with vitamin D on the German market.
- To urge the medical profession to regularly screen hospital patients with severe respiratory infections, as well as geriatric and palliative care patients in inpatient care facilities, for vitamin D deficiency and to treat such deficiency.
- Encourage more medical research into vitamin D deficiency and disease risks.

The implementation of these substantive demands, which are completely neutral in terms of political alignments, would not only have saved countless people from serious to fatal COVID-19 infections—which should actually be the primary task of the Ministry of Health, not the opposition—but would also have made unnecessary all measures that caused enormous collateral damage in the population. But just two weeks later, the motion was rejected by the votes of the CDU/CSU, SPD, FDP, DIE LINKE and Bündnis 90/Die Grünen parliamentary groups—that is, by the entire rest of parliament.[53] The rejection was legitimized by media framing all alternatives as radical right-wing, which was easy to accomplish because of the AfD's image, but without being argumentatively convincing. The situation was similar in Austria, where only the FPÖ, which is comparable to the AfD, had alternative proposals aimed in the same direction.[54] These were very likely to have no chance of success simply because of the party's political classification and public image.

Why is it that real opposition can only be found in those parties that are most publicly discredited and thus perfectly suited to framing neutral issues in an unacceptable way? Is this part of the global political orchestration to facilitate the framing of disagreeable topics or meaningful opposing theses? We observe something like this not only with the topic of COVID-19 but also with all topics subject to a strangely unanimous political classification: in Germany only the AfD disagrees with the supply of weapons for the war in Ukraine (on the question of whether doing so only fuels the war). But as soon as Sahra Wagenknecht of the Left Party (DIE LINKE) joins in the critical discussion of arms supplies, an ominous cross-front thesis, or horseshoe theory, is invoked to show that radical left and radical right political positions would converge again. In connection with the war against climate change (on the question of whether there are no other explanations and solutions) or the question of the extent to which humans should be monitored and evaluated in the future, only the AfD in Germany stands out with serious opposition. It also opposes the gradual introduction of a social scoring system[55] and the abolition of cash or the introduction of a purely digital currency.[56] In contrast, all these measures, which serve the technocratic takeover or total surveillance, are unanimously supported and promoted by all other parties.

I myself have experienced several times that this framing really works. For example, after I had been invited by a congress organizer in Austria to give a lecture on my book *The Exhausted Brain*, I was immediately uninvited when it was stated that I call for causal and preventive measures against respiratory diseases such as COVID-19. Absurdly, this was mistaken for right-wing extremist ideas, in congruence with the AfD and FPÖ reports. I do not feel affiliated with any single party of the German political landscape, but I stand with both feet on the ground of the German Basic Law. I consider the mixtures of form and factual content in the sense described to be truly absurd and completely unworthy of a democratic society. If an idea is worth discussing, it should not matter what color the shirt of the idea-bringer is. But maybe that's just the scientist in me talking.

Monopolized perception, which Biderman identifies as an essential factor, is thus achieved in various ways. On one hand, the media confronts us with realities that are removed from our everyday reality and thus inaccessible to individual experience. What is *really* going on with COVID-19 (real incidents, etc.) or climate change (changes in the average global temperature in the decimal range) or the war in Ukraine (which, for geographical reasons, is simply not accessible to our senses) can only be experienced through these media. However, media monopolizes not only the mediation of the event but also its classification. On one hand, this is done through the claim of quality journalism and supposedly objective reporting, which today has largely given way to an avowed attitude journalism. On the other hand, media puts information into contexts for better understanding yet also shapes how this information is assessed through sometimes clumsy framing. In addition, media companies work with anxiety to ensure, as a first step, that people learn to appreciate them as essential sources of information about life-threatening phenomena that they themselves cannot control. By stirring up fear every night, they ensure that, at the most vulnerable time of all, their content, broadcast into most living rooms, overwrites those highly personal experiences that actually make us complex individuals.

Threats and Intimidations

"To suffocate or not get enough air is a primal anxiety for everyone," reads the BMI scenario paper. In *1984*, the identification of primal anxiety is much more passionate and individualized. For Winston Smith, who is undergoing reeducation by a dystopian government, rats are determined to be the most effective trigger of his primal anxiety. His educator uses them to break down Winston's inner resistance. Primal anxiety of death activates neurons in the hippocampus that are specialized for fear, which are appropriately called *anxiety cells*.[57] The discoverers of these special hippocampal cells explain that activating these neurons "is a direct route by which the hippocampus can rapidly influence innate anxiety behavior." The researchers are certain that these cells, which encode the "primal sense of fear," are also found in the human brain. When these cells are activated, innate fear reflexes apparently cause people to do anything that seems to promise a way out without thinking; a neurobiological explanation for a whole range of irrational behaviors by frightened people during the peak of the COVID-19 pandemic, or better, of the largely meaningless PCR and rapid tests.

In times past, being excluded from one's social group was tantamount to the death penalty. This primal anxiety explains to a large extent the tendency of people to conform, as the aforementioned experiment by psychologist Asch was even able to quantify. And it was precisely this primal anxiety, in addition to the perceived threat of the virus to society as a whole, that was exploited to intimidate individuals with the threat of social exclusion if they did not follow the official narrative. This fear was also fueled by the mainstream media. Those unwilling to be vaccinated were even blamed—against all scientific evidence—for the failure of the vaccination program. None other than Professor Frank Ulrich Montgomery, as chairman of the Council of the World Medical Association, said on public television on November 7, 2021, "We are currently experiencing a tyranny of the unvaccinated" and articulated (or fomented?) the anger of all those "sensible people" who had been vaccinated against COVID-19.[58] Ironically, this happened at a time when the US CDC had long since recognized that vaccination provides no protection for others (nor for oneself, as the aforementioned COVID-19 vaccine breakthrough infections in Massachusetts in July 2021 were also illustrating).

A cartoon emblematic of this nonsensical blame game has become famous: Two pedestrians face each other, one holding a leaky umbrella, the other patiently standing in the rain. The owner of the umbrella blames the other person for the fact that his umbrella does not work as promised by the salesman, because the other person does not have one. This principle of scapegoating should be a lesson to us in many ways. Minorities have often been blamed for every inadequacy of the system, which at the same time created opportunities for a sense of community among the actually inadequate accusers. During the COVID-19 pandemic, the scapegoats were the unvaccinated. This was based on illogical insinuations and hence required a good deal of perfidy on the part of the perpetrators. From a study of the relevant history of mankind, one could have deduced, even before 2020, that very few would reflect upon such nonsense to then expose it as such. After all, scapegoating has always ensured greater cohesion among insecure individuals. The most insidious mechanism is that vaccination for those unwilling to face peer pressure becomes a permanent subscription, as the definition of full vaccination protection has been steadily expanded with each booster. This could be called "social addiction to vaccination," a special form of drug addiction.

Those responsible were likely aware of the effect of such a dynamic when they made the mass advance purchases of vaccine doses, long before the population realized that far more than two injections per person must have been planned. This was apparently the case with Ursula von der Leyen, president of the European Commission and—how could it be otherwise—a member of the Board of Trustees of the World Economic Forum.[59] All in all, it was an ingenious ploy that a number of well-paid psychologists and sociologists must have concocted in advance for the Ministry of Health, because the alternative to obedience, being excluded from society as a scapegoat, is so repulsive that imprisonment is probably the only possible next step. Social isolation is also detrimental to health. In the vast majority of cases, the choice was between two evils.

Of Believers and Heretics

The COVID-19 pandemic divided the world into believers, inoculated, and unbelievers, uninoculated or heretics. When the power of an authority is not legitimized by a free election of the people but is based only on pure faith, heretical thoughts and any questioning of the basis of faith are of the greatest danger to those in power. This is true of any theocracy, and it was true in the Christian West until the Enlightenment. An unbeliever was an outsider, an enemy of society, and a heretic and could expect to be tortured and publicly executed. Today, anyone who questions the WHO's dictates, as disseminated by the mainstream media, is branded a right-wing extremist and an enemy of the people.

On the basis of one's immune status, the first variable in a social scoring system that may be expanded in the future, one may be classified as lacking solidarity, and access to public life may be restricted. "If you want to do more than visit your town hall or the supermarket, you have to be vaccinated," was how Jens Spahn, in his role as acting German health minister, summed up the regulations in force at the end of December 2021 in one sentence.[60] I even witnessed people openly discussing whether to go one step further and deny unvaccinated people access to grocery stores. Karl Lauterbach (as Spahn's successor and Germany's most popular politician at the time) also said in February 2022, "In Germany, it's not enough to just annoy the unvaccinated, you have to do more."[61] Indeed, in several German cities, it was decided not to distribute food to the unvaccinated needy.[62] Heretics were threatened with death by starvation. We must assume that not much was in the way of deporting the unvaccinated with just a few more turns of the same escalation spiral.

Under this threatening public pressure from politics and the media, one had to be well informed in order not to give in. Only if one had been "converted" to participate in this extremely dangerous genetic experiment as a sign of confession to the new faith could one have escaped this pressure. Those not prepared to do so had to endure it. But even for those who knew that the constant horror reports were rarely based on reliable facts, the overall situation was extremely stressful for many. They felt powerless in the face of the unnecessary suffering caused by the policies. The Swiss diplomat and historian Carl J. Burckhardt (1891–1974) once wrote, "It is one of the most difficult things that can be imposed on a thinking person to have to witness the course of a historical process among ignorant people, the inevitable outcome of which he has long known with clarity. The time of other people's mistakes, of false hopes, of blindly committed mistakes becomes very long."[63] There is a danger of exhaustion.

Induced Exhaustion

Even if you were one of the relatively few doctors, scientists, or even activists who tried to counteract the life-threatening staging with educational campaigns and to bring light into the darkness, it was a very exhausting process. But at least you would have had the certainty of pursuing a meaningful task directly aimed at solving the problem. It is impossible to imagine how this was experienced by people who constantly saw only the primordial darkness, usually with no hope of betterment. A weakening mental resistance was preprogrammed and a prerequisite for the indoctrination measures presented here (see also the previous chapter). Not only was there a constant fear of serious illness and death, but many also had serious existential worries as a result of lockdowns and the collapse of supply chains. Thus, unemployment and meaninglessness eliminated any sense of security and stability.

Exhaustion is therefore almost inevitable, with some form of inner strength being the only bulwark against it. Biderman writes, "There is an almost unmatched drama in these airmen's efforts to protect principles, dignity and self-respect with only their own inner resources to sustain them."[64] I am convinced that he meant, in the absence of the term because it had not yet been discovered, a strong frontal brain battery or a fully functioning hippocampus.

Demonstration of "Omniscience" and "Omnipotence"

Omniscience

On December 8, 2021, the German news outlet *Welt* reported, "Chancellor-elect Olaf Scholz (SPD) has defended restrictions on the unvaccinated as a necessary means of breaking the fourth Corona wave."[65] As far as he knows, the infection that affects us all comes from the unvaccinated, Scholz said the prior day after signing the coalition agreement with other political parties in Berlin that catapulted him into Germany's most powerful political office. The aforementioned data from the CDC, not reported in the mainstream media, already clearly proved that "vaccination" is useless; nevertheless, Scholz showed himself to be omniscient: "There's no doubt about it." And Scholz continued, "Many of them [the unvaccinated] are also threatened themselves, because the probability that they will be infected is very, very high, and therefore it is also very likely that some of them will fall ill and another part will have to fight for their lives in intensive care units."

Omnipotence

Supposed omniscience is always dangerous, but even more so when its underlying ignorance of contrary scientific facts is coupled with a largely realizable claim to omnipotence. "It is therefore quite clear," Welt continues, what the new chancellor had to say, namely "that restrictions are necessary for those who have not been vaccinated." It is hard to imagine that the internal scientific advisors of the political power center did not know that the vaccination program had long since failed, as the further example of Gibraltar showed as early as July 2021, a full five months before Scholz took office. Although all residents were vaccinated, Gibraltar had by far the highest rate of new infections in Europe.[66] For this reason alone, it can be assumed that Chancellor-designate Scholz's statements were not about protecting his citizens, but about power, control. and oppression.

Meanwhile, the largely senseless measures of power-related policy had an increasingly destructive effect on the economy and the material livelihoods of many people. These citizens became increasingly dependent on government handouts. It is extremely important to keep reminding oneself of this because of the persistent lies of the political-media complex on the subject: The virus did not demand this high tariff, nor can political missteps based on supposedly unclear data be blamed for the disproportionate measures enacted. The knowledge was openly available, and yet it was deliberately suppressed by censorship and defamation of those who pointed it out. The real danger of the virus is not extraordinary, if one removes the demonstrably intentional (or at the very least grossly negligent) exaggerations about its effects. "By deliberately ignoring extremely effective vitamin D prevention strategy, the state gained the power to deceive its citizenry. It showed its superior power (omnipotence) to its citizens with the help of non evidence-based, meaningless testing, masking, and distance regulations, which it enforced, if necessary, with police force and fines. The message was that resistance is futile.

Humiliation through Degradation

"These rules must not be questioned." Representing the state, which had recently begun to claim omnipotence, the then chairman of the RKI put his foot down and degraded every adult citizen as a child, who from now on had to obey nonsensical and profoundly inhuman rules and, above all, could no longer question them. There is little that degrades an adult more than his categorical incapacitation. Harsh punishments were threatened in case of disobedience. Thus, in the end, most people had no choice but to obey and submit.

Resistance was broken, first in public life, then more and more in private life, since soon one's own home was no longer a place of security. For example, again without any scientific evidence and solely at the whim of the authorities, only a limited number of people were allowed to gather in their own homes at certain times. These regulations included special rules for vaccinated and unvaccinated persons that were constantly changing, varied from state to state or county to county, and were often based on the results of local rapid tests or PCR assays—but because of the correlative relationship between testing regimes and resulting incidences. They were ultimately subject only to political discretion.

A culture of denunciation was promoted, in which all understood that they could be denounced by their neighbor if they did not behave according to the rules. In fact, quite a few denunciators saw themselves as a pillar of society during this period: "Hardly any fellow citizen is as unpopular as he is—historically justified," writes the Swiss daily *Blick*, but the pandemic "is helping the dirty child of history to make a comeback."[67] In the crisis year, these "deputy sheriffs" filed thousands of reports with the authorities for alleged COVID-19 violations, according to Blick. Few things cause more discord between people. If it occurred to the government that the virus became particularly virulent after 10 p.m., then family celebrations had to be stopped. Fines of up to €25,000 were threatened.[68] Such utterly absurd rules are reminiscent of Orwell's statement in *1984* that two and two can be five if the state wants it that way. This quasi-dictatorial demonstration of the state's omnipotence is intended to create a sense of helplessness. These rules also apply to the terminally ill and those on their deathbed without a partner, relative, or friend at their side—all because Father State is worried that you might die (even faster) of an infection? It wasn't until April 2022, after the grotesque measures had been lifted, that the *Süddeutsche Zeitung* noted that during the pandemic, protection against infection had taken precedence over humanity: "For two years, dying people could hardly say goodbye to their loved ones, could not hold their hand, give them a look, seek their consolation or say their last words to anyone who might have cared about them."[69] After all, nursing homes and hospitals had forbidden any kind of visitation for long periods. "And when one was allowed, it was often only one person. Relatives had to decide, "Who can go? Who has to?"

But not even half a year before, on November 23, 2021, when it had long been clear that vaccination only causes harm, the same *Süddeutsche Zeitung* printed the following sentences by one of its authors: "Is the division of society threatened if the unvaccinated are deprived of their childish right to be unvaccinated? Rubbish. These people are robbing the sane of their freedom—and governments have kowtowed to them, too."[70] While this leading German newsmagazine was complaining after the fact that terminally ill people had to die alone because they were not allowed to be visited, they were agitating against the unvaccinated, calling their good right to refrain from risky medical treatment childish and unreasonable (once again degrading responsible citizens as unreasonable children). But the *Süddeutsche Zeitung* was not alone. It blew the same horn as all the mainstream media, almost all politicians and—what a shame!—even members of the German Ethics Council.[71]

One of the consequences was that "unvaccinated people were perceived as less intelligent. Prejudices against them were more widespread than prejudices against migrants," the Swiss *Neue Zürcher Zeitung* (*NZZ*) reported.[72] It referred to an article titled "Discriminatory Attitudes against Unvaccinated People during the Pandemic," published in *Nature*.[73] Michael Bang Petersen, a political scientist at Aarhus University in Denmark, led the HOPE (How Democracies Cope with COVID-19) project, which examined the social impact of the pandemic around the world. As COVID-19 advisor to the Danish government, he was knighted by the queen for his work during the pandemic. More than ten thousand people from the United States, Russia, China, India, Brazil, and several European countries were interviewed. When asked by the *NZZ* what discriminatory biases existed, Peterson replied, "The unvaccinated were perceived by the vaccinated as 'unintelligent' and 'untrustworthy.' We also looked at whether vaccinated people would be willing to deny basic rights to unvaccinated people. We conducted this research only in the United States. There, we found a partially punitive attitude toward the unvaccinated: for example, vaccinated people showed a willingness to deny them unemployment benefits or the right to choose where to live. They sometimes went so far as to restrict the freedom of expression of the unvaccinated. So discriminatory attitudes were not only widespread, they were deep." They were as deep as the divisions within families. According to the surveys, a significant proportion of the vaccinated in most countries favored excluding the unvaccinated from family relationships. Many people were unexpectedly introduced to the new fad of 2G (*geimpft* and/or *genesen*, meaning vaccinated or convalesced) family celebrations in which they were not allowed to participate. The reasoning: it's your own fault, if you're not vaccinated, you have to stay out. ""But the opposite was not true," says Petersen. "Unvaccinated people generally did not show discriminatory attitudes towards vaccinated people."

Occasional Indulgences

Carrot and stick represents the classical methodology of education, which should not be missing in the modern web of indoctrination. Harsh words can have the effect of a whip and, in the worst case, cause pretraumatic stress syndrome (see previous chapter). The carrot, on the other hand, consists of "if . . . then" statements and the like. The partial reopening of sports facilities or restaurants, of course only for those who have been vaccinated and have the appropriate ID, can also be attributed to this methodology.

Hope plays an essential role in keeping people from getting used to the prohibitions while continuing to strive for the familiar normality that is deliberately withheld from them. An article in *Psychology Today* titled "The Blessing and Curse of Hope" elaborates on hope. "Those who do not know and accept the limits of hope can end up in distress."[74] And the author gives an example: "Your best friend is in a relationship that has broken up twice. You and the whole world know that she is riding a dead horse and should get off. But she herself is hoping that the third attempt will be successful." This is madness, explains Heidelberg systems and couples therapist Arnold Retzer "with sober clarity . . . You hope and hope, while you've been in the hole for a long time, and you keep digging instead of getting out of a predicament."

Enforcement of Trivial Demands

"Assuming," Biderman writes, "the measures I have discussed have made the prisoner compliant, the problem remains of getting him to comply appropriately . . . The kind of 'confession' we are discussing consists of considerably more than the signing of a piece of paper . . . In this extreme form of 'confession'-elicitation, as encountered by our men, the objective was . . . [to] confirm the entire world-view of the Communists . . . Learning what behavior was being demanded and, even more, learning the elaborate symbols and nuances through which this behavior had to be expressed to be acceptable—these were complex learning tasks indeed."[75]

Learning complex expectations is always a step-by-step process. And this is especially true when it comes to things that one is actually opposed to. We speak of a "slippery slope" when an unpleasant action, once performed, is likely to lead to another even worse one, and thus pave the way for it. The danger of sliding down the slippery slope is particularly great when, despite justified reluctance, one repeatedly makes small concessions that, little by little and often imperceptibly, draw one further and further into a quagmire. As far as COVID-19 is concerned, this means a complete confession to the new faith, first to the promise of salvation of the vaccination, then increasingly to the entire Grand Narrative. The decisive path to confession through which the US prisoners were led was similar.

As far as COVID-19 is concerned, it is still the case today (spring 2023) that a small prick averts the big danger. There is no mention of it being a systemic injection of genetically modified and biologically active viral material. The minimization of the required concession as a sign of commitment to the new faith plays an important role. As late as March 2023, *Tagesschau,* one of Germany's lead news programs, reported in similarly trivializing terms: "The prick at health insurance costs will remain possible."[76] To make this step easier, there were events like the "Weißwurst-Impfen [Bavarian veal sausage for free for the act of spiking]," where after the "confession," instead of sacramental bread, one got a veal sausage with mustard and pretzels.[77] Or even better, there was special paid leave.[78] This was the first small prick, but the second follows quickly, because every six months another injection is necessary. With the first injection, which was ideologically maximally charged, one had made a permanent subscription that was not even questioned when, despite the "protective vaccination," one had to wear a mask that was known to be useless. So, it had to be useful, despite all evidence to the contrary! More and more of these inconsistencies were ignored, until finally the slightest deviation from the rules was enough to be stripped of one's status as a rational person and to become one of the outcasts. This obvious nonsense was tolerated without comment.

Each action taken in accordance with the measure becomes a habit, a basis for accepting the next one, until you have accepted a large package that you would never have accepted had it been fully communicated from the beginning. This fatal development reminds me of the legend of the frog that could be boiled alive if only it were placed in a pot of pleasantly lukewarm water and then slowly heated. Like the frog in the parable, we are actually more willing to tolerate several successive small changes than one big one—even if it deliberately leads us to a state that had been unacceptable. A "policy of small steps,"[79] as former German chancellor Angela Merkel, in office from 2005 to 2021, sloganized the guiding principle of her own policy in 2005, exploits this fundamental psychological mechanism by introducing changes only gradually and thus encountering less resistance from the population. An article by the Canadian Medical Association also illustrates this aspect of human psychology: "We tend to accept things that creep up on us slowly but steadily," it says, "even when they take control of our lives. But one day we wake up and find ourselves in boiling water."[80]

The policy of small steps relates to all areas of life subject to social change in recent years. Step by step, we give up more and more of our privacy, usually in exchange for benefits or even only a supposed moral satisfaction. After all, we've already sacrificed so much for the good of the community that we don't want our neighbors to take away what we think we've achieved. And for every small change, good reasons are constructed on the basis of false premises, and all opponents are defamed. Anyone who insists on pathogen-loaded cash is a criminal who wants to conceal the flow of money. Those who plan their vacations by air are selfish climate sinners who do not limit themselves sufficiently. And if there are too many unwilling people in the long run, the strong state will have to intervene and side with the "reasonable" by means of regulations and prohibitions. Of course, it will only do this if it can be sure, by means of psychologically optimized nudging instead of regulating) of the consent of a slim majority among those who can still express themselves in public.

Permanent Control of Success

The enforcement of successive trivial demands, such as the acceptance of a third, fourth, or even fifth prick, shows an initial success of the indoctrination. Early on, the fear of COVID-19 was so successfully planted in people's minds that, paradoxically, even in the face of an emergency such as an acute stroke or heart attack, many preferred to risk dying at home rather than go to a supposedly highly infectious hospital environment. According to a study of the first three months of the pandemic, COVID-19 was associated with a worldwide decrease in hospital admissions to stroke clinics (down 19 percent), mechanical thrombectomy (removal of dangerous blood clots, down 12.7 percent), and hospitalizations for stroke (down 11.5 percent).[81] For vital-organ transplants, the decline during the first wave of COVID-19 was even more dramatic, down by 90 percent in some countries, and completely independent of the actual incidence of infection, according to the results of an international study.[82] The fear of becoming infected is greater than the fear of dying from a much more likely disease. In February 2023, for example, the large German health insurance company AOK warned of an increase in cancer in the population due to a decline in preventive medical checkups. According to AOK CEO Carola Reimann, the number of cancer screenings has "not yet returned to the pre-pandemic level."[83] Besides cancer screening, "the total number of hospital treatments and preventive examinations has continued to decline in the third pandemic year after 2020 and 2021."

In this context, the result of a survey conducted by the opinion research institute YouGov on behalf of the *Deutsche Presse-Agentur* on December 21 and 23, 2022, (only a few days before virologist Christian Drosten declared the pandemic over, as reported by the *Süddeutsche Zeitung*) is remarkable.[84] Even when the pandemic was apparently no longer of great relevance, 52 percent of those polled by YouGov opposed a nationwide end to mandatory masks on public transportation. As the *Süddeutsche Zeitung* went on to report, according to YouGov, "60 percent rejected an immediate end to the mandatory isolation of infected people for at least five days." The reason was that "almost two-thirds (64 percent) of those surveyed said the pandemic was not over for them," and "41 percent of those surveyed even expect that it will not end until 2023. "Only 41 percent support an immediate end to the mandatory use of masks on public transportation," and "25 percent even want masks to be mandatory on buses and trains for the entire next year."

In addition, the aforementioned environmental engineer Dr. Helmut Traindl, in his expert opinion on the wearing of masks published in October 2022, states, "National propaganda and media 'brainwashing' have even reached the point where masks have become an indispensable part of some people's lives. For many people, they function as a 'comfort blanket' or 'magic amulet,' creating a false sense of security against viral infections and thus calming their minds."[85] The fact that masks actually have no measurable effect on preventing infection was the result of a large metastudy carried out by the independent Cochrane Group of international researchers in November 2020 and has since been confirmed in further updates.[86]

In the meantime (April 2023, at the time of this writing), the mask requirement has been lifted on public transportation in Germany. But it is hard to say how long this will last. Even the WEF is not sure, seems worried, and, in its *Global Risks Report 2023* already speaks of impending permapandemics as a precautionary measure due to the risk of a "panic-neglect cycle." What it means by this is a perpetual war against viruses, invasive fungi, and bacteria that humanity should take more seriously: "As COVID-19 recedes from the headlines," says the apocalyptic WEF report, "complacency appears to be setting in on preparing for future pandemics and other global health threats."[87]

In fact, as I write these lines, COVID-19 indoctrination seems to have largely failed. One reason for this could be that the isolation of the people could not be maintained, neither spatially, informationally, nor temporally.

Spatially and Informationally

People who did not allow themselves to be indoctrinated to the end retained the option of a mental correction. Thus, it was the unvaccinated whose steadfastness made possible the comparative examination of the statements about the vaccination effect in the immediate social environment. In this global experiment they are the controls that show that spiking does not immunize, but rather damages the immune system. Even the internet, the main propaganda machine besides the mainstream media, could not be censored 100 percent. Thus, people always had the opportunity to receive alternative information through media formats that could not escape censorship on the main platforms but could on other platforms. People remained engaged in conversation and were able to ask questions based on alternative scientific assessments or to challenge the narrative.

But this may change as the power of the technocrats expands. It will no longer be just their private platforms that take the liberty of deleting critical posts. If they completely take over the infrastructure of the internet, they may be able to simply deny outside servers access to their internet. Elon Musk's Starlink, which began providing 5G wireless internet access from orbit to the entire world in 2020, may already be the first step in this direction.[88]

Temporal

The descendants of the original virus became harmless relatively quickly, because that's the only way it can spread more efficiently—people who are healthy despite being infected infect more people than those who isolate themselves because of cold symptoms. Thus, the gap between the virulence (toxicity) of the virus and the effects of the toxic gene injections is widening. Inevitably, this had to cause some of the vaccinated to doubt their new faith. Nevertheless, there have been partial successes, and these are so dangerous precisely because they are likely to encourage the masterminds to try again.

What the COVID-19 staging largely failed to do, even though the tendencies were clearly recognizable, was to sell people on a comprehensive social scoring system that could have been used to permanently control their behavior. This had already been prepared by the media: in an article entitled "COVID-19 as a Case for Social Scoring Systems," published on September 15, 2020, the Canadian Centre for International Governance Innovation (CIGI), a billionaire-funded but self-proclaimed independent, nonpartisan think tank that aims to encourage policymakers to innovate, promoted digital surveillance and the introduction of a social scoring system. That was not just to identify chains of infection but also to guide people. "After more than half a year of living in a pandemic, it is clear that we have to make it easier and more rewarding for people to comply with public health advisories and guidelines."[89] The question of whether the measures for which social scoring points would be awarded are useful at all is neither being asked nor discussed anymore.

But now (spring 2023) that the COVID-19 pandemic is likely to be seen as a failure in this sense, the permanent threat of climate change could make the last meters of the way. The German Prognos AG, which calls itself the European Center for Economic Research and Strategy Consulting, seems to be convinced of this as well. Apparently, it has already predicted that COVID-19 will not be a sufficient incentive for public acceptance of a social scoring system in the long run. In a study entitled "The Future of People's Values in Our Country," published in August 2020 and commissioned by the Federal Ministry of Education and Research (BMBF) in Germany, it drew up future scenarios for the introduction of a social points system based on the Chinese model.[90] It is seen as an instrument for mobilizing society as a whole against climate change, and as a narrative it serves to catalyze the acceptance of this new system, which allows a far-reaching technocratic surveillance of the entire society—the ultimate control as part of and even beyond indoctrination.

In the Prognos study, similar to Ida Auken's prophecy, the reader is transported to the 2030s and looks back at the changes that are planned. Chapter 3.5 of the scenario "The Bonus System" reads, "In the 2030s, a digital, participatory, negotiated points system will be introduced in Germany to incentivize behavioral change." The model for this is the Chinese system, which causes fears among the population but also brings many advantages. For this reason, a future decision by German policymakers in the study's simulation was only made retroactively as a result of long, highly controversial debates "to work with a central digital points system that follows democratic rules of the game." Thus, the majority-based system relied on bonus incentives and voluntary participation. "The principle of voluntariness was central to the debate before its introduction." However, since even those who reject the points system have to live in it, "the principle of voluntariness was readily described by opponents of the points system," the study article continued, "as 'window dressing,' since one could never completely escape the system."

According to the Prognos study, the driving force behind the social points system was climate change, with the question of the extent to which humans are actually responsible for it included as an unquestioned prerequisite: "The approval of this point system also increased in Germany due to the dynamics of climate change. This created pressure for countermeasures [citizens wanted it; politics was 'forced' to react], whereby a point system proved to be an efficient control mechanism for dealing with the consequences of climate change (e.g., through point evaluation of the ecological footprint). The polluter-pays principle was made transparent through the point system." Voluntary climate bonus programs, such as those introduced by Germany and Austria in 2022, are quickly turning into social pressure that is being translated into legislation.

The slippery slope toward total monitoring and evaluation of all our actions hasn't been considered here. According to the study, only a minority will fundamentally question the social points system in 2030: "The points system will meet with the approval of a majority of the population in the 2030s, because many people feel that it has a unifying function for different social groups in a more complex and differentiated society. At the same time, in Germany in the 2030s, the points system will gradually anchor new norms in everyday life as a forecasting and steering instrument." The BMBF will thus become the Federal Center for Education, monitoring and controlling the population with a "digital nervous system." This "creates a comprehensive transparency that narrows the gap between values and behavior," in part because all people can now be "uniquely identified in the real and virtual world."

The chimping mentioned in chapter 1 will also play a role here, chipping and vaccinating in one operation. Thus, every person receives a digital ID through which he or she can be constantly shadowed due to ubiquitous access controls by means of digital scanners. A private life is history, as is one's own opinion: "Political goals and personal value sets can no longer be sharply distinguished from one another in this system," according to one of the study's findings.

As shown in figure 18, the third pillar on which technocratic supremacy will be based comes into play: the introduction of a purely digital currency. With the abolition of cash, not only every flow of money can be centrally controlled but also every behavior. Anyone who disobeys can have the money spigot turned off. It has never been so easy to force people to conform—to change, control, and direct their attitudes and behavior. See also the *Smart City Charta* (chapter 1), post-ownership-society ("I own nothing, have no privacy, and life has never been better"). "Data may complement or replace money as currency." This means that data and digital currency will enable complete and profound digital control, especially when combined with a social points system, because those who do not comply will become insolvent and have no future.

"Thus, the 'permanently disconnected' will find it difficult," as Prognos razor-sharply concludes, "to make up for low scores." As a result, there will be "a far-reaching homogenization of values among the active participants in the points system," according to the easily understood prognosis: "Conformity to certain behaviors and values leads in the long run to bonuses that make certain material performance dimensions easier to realize (e.g., real estate ownership)." As a result, "individualism and personal freedom will be redefined, and in some cases abandoned, in the point system according to the standards of the 2010s [the study is from that time]." The goal of a society controlled by technocrats through AI would then be (almost) achieved: "phenotypically uniform creatures, simple-minded, without history, and vaccinated multiple times. Boostered with homogeneous thought and immune to any kind of critical thinking."

Is this all just a nightmare or pure science fiction? Most likely neither, because the course has been set and the train is on the move. Will we be able to stop it? I sincerely hope so. We have a chance to escape this, if we start to think for ourselves as soon as possible, so that they do not think for (and thus against) us. I would therefore like to end this chapter as I began it, with a warning statement by the British mathematician and philosopher Bertrand Russell, one of the greatest thinkers of the 20th century:

Many people would rather die than think;
In fact, most do so.

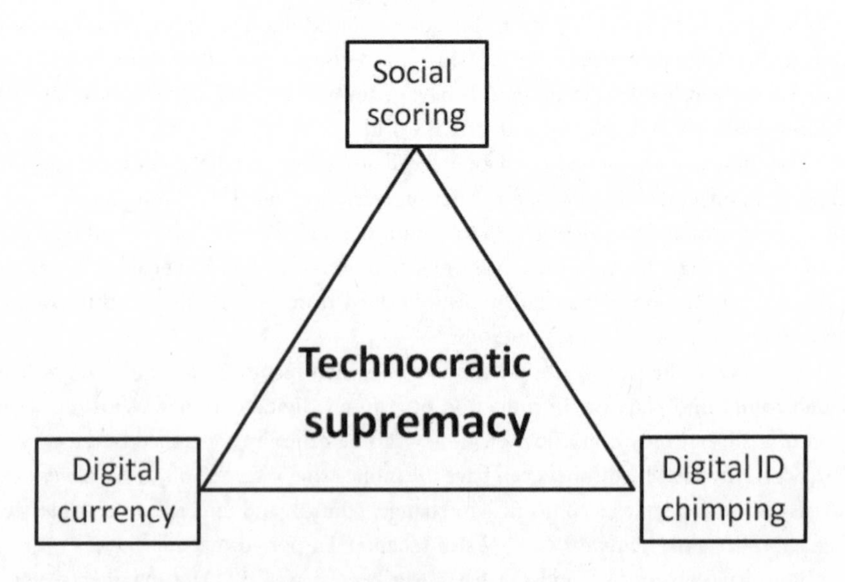

Figure 18

CHAPTER 6

ENDGAME?

The computer is the logical further development of man:
Intelligence without morals.
—John Osborne (1929–1994)

A Seed of Madness

The signs of the times are undoubtedly pointing toward the development of a technocratically regulated world, reminiscent of the one described by Aldous Huxley in *Brave New World.* Already today, the structures of a future world government are emerging, and the surveillance and transparency of citizens is steadily increasing, reaching into our private thoughts.

Technocrats may well fall under their spell themselves and derive legitimacy for their further actions beyond establishing their worldview. And therein lies the danger. Quite pragmatic reasons exist to reduce the world's population and to bring the remaining remnant under control: the increasing need to meet the complex needs of a growing world population, combined with the rapid pace of technological development and the automation of many aspects of life, would deprive people of any productive use and make them seem dispensable. Overpopulation is a real problem to be solved, according to the technocrats.

The Rise of the Useless Class

The further we can look into the past, the greater our wealth of experience and the better our decisions can be. Without remembering our past, however, we could not make any plans for the future, as Henry Molaison, the first man without autobiographical memory, involuntarily demonstrated. The statements of historians about the future of mankind should therefore be taken seriously, especially those of Yuval Noah Harari, professor at the Department of History, Hebrew University of Jerusalem. As an advisor to the WEF, he is actively involved in shaping a currently dominant vision of the future and thus may not have to guess what is in store for us. He knows what ideas are driving the technocratic elite because he is a leading member of this group in his role as an intellectual mastermind.[1] In his 2017 article "The Rise of the Useless Class," fully aware of his role in this structure, he asks the rhetorical question, "What should we [who does he mean by *we*?] do with all the superfluous people, once we have highly intelligent non-conscious algorithms [i.e., AI] that can do almost everything better than humans?"[2] His question is logical from a technocratic point of view but very dangerous for us. Many years earlier, Albert Einstein (1879–1955) had a premonition when he wrote, "I fear the day that technology will surpass our human interaction. The world will have a generation of idiots." *And who needs idiots*, the technocrats will begin to think.

We should take Harari's concerns very seriously, not just because he is able to justify them eloquently. He writes,

> People have long feared that mechanization might cause mass unemployment. This never happened, because as old professions became obsolete, new professions evolved, and there was always something humans could do better than machines. Yet this is not a law of nature, and nothing guarantees it will continue to be like that in the future. The idea that humans will always have a unique ability beyond the reach of non-conscious algorithms is just wishful thinking. The current scientific answer to this pipe dream can be summarized in three simple principles:
>
> 1. Organisms are algorithms. Every animal—including Homo sapiens—is an assemblage of organic algorithms shaped by natural selection over millions of years of evolution.
> 2. Algorithmic calculations are not affected by the materials from which the calculator is built. Whether an abacus is made of wood, iron or plastic, two beads plus two beads equals four beads.
> 3. Hence, there is no reason to think that organic algorithms can do things that non-organic algorithms will never be able to replicate or surpass. As long as the calculations remain valid, what does it matter whether the algorithms are manifested in carbon or silicon?

To the great political and economic question of the twenty-first century he raised—"Why do we need people, or at least, why do we need so many people?"—Harari answered in a WEF interview, "The best we [again, whom does he mean by *we*?] can do at the moment is to keep them happy with drugs and computer games."[3] The existence of the people in Huxley's *Brave New World* is also made bearable with shallow entertainment and the drug soma. In the preface to his novel, Huxley said the following: "The freedom to daydream under the influence of drugs, movies, and the radio, will help subjects reconcile themselves to the bondage that is their fate."[4]

In Huxley's novel, world controllers have declared 2,000 million Earth citizens sufficient. However, in this fictional world, there is no AI to replace humans in (almost) all areas. That's why we have to ask ourselves, *How many people will the technocrats declare sufficient? If they have their way, how many people does an AI need?*

Who Owns the Future—Man or Machine?

In the spring of 2023, more than one thousand leading engineers and researchers, including Elon Musk, signed an open letter calling for the suspension of AI development, warning of its "profound risks to society."[5] However, it is not only the foreseeable dangers of their use that should concern us but also, above all, the consequences difficult to foresee. Beyond a certain level of complexity, AIs evade human monitoring of their internal processes and "intentions." Harari writes, "Even preprogramming an AI system with seemingly benign goals might backfire horribly."[6] He offers the following example: "One popular scenario imagines a corporation designing the first artificial super-intelligence and giving it an innocent test such as calculating pi. Before anyone realizes what is happening, the AI takes over the planet, eliminates the human race, launches a campaign of conquest to the ends of the galaxy, and transforms the entire known universe into a giant supercomputer that for billions upon billions of years calculates pi ever more accurately. After all, this is the divine mission its Creator gave it."

Admittedly, the AI in this mind game acts on a rather thoughtless instruction, and one gets the impression that such a thing would not happen if the AI's instruction had been formulated in a well-considered way. In the meantime, however, more and more AI researchers are working on a kind of creativity code, with the idea of teaching an AI the uniquely human ability to find unconventional solutions to problems (as assumed in the mind game) or to search for ideas outside the actual program. In fact, according to British mathematician Marcus du Sautoy, it is possible to program irrational thinking into an AI: "You can create a meta-rule that will instruct it to change course."[7] This would make it impossible to predict what solutions to a problem it will develop. A pi-calculating AI would thus actually be able to find a creative solution to accomplish its task, completely without human ingenuity and without a human being able to survey in advance the field of possibilities.

A no-less-momentous way to avoid at least the problem underlying this line of thinking might be to animate the AI; that is, to implant it with a higher moral compass that protects a certain group of people (its creator, or at least its original programmers).

In fact, another avenue of AI optimization is currently being explored, but it may ultimately come down to just that. Scientists are researching the possibility of giving AIs a self-reflective function that could give them a kind of consciousness.[8] That solution carries considerable potential danger if, along with the development of consciousness, self-interest and self-preservation instincts find their way into the algorithm. "One can imagine such technology [i.e., AI] outsmarting financial markets, out-inventing human researchers, out-manipulating human leaders, and developing weapons we cannot even understand," theoretical physicist and astrophysicist Stephen Hawking (1942–2018) once observed, warning, "Whereas the short-term impact of AI [development] depends on who controls it, the long-term impact depends on whether it can be controlled at all."[9]

If it were possible to create an AI with such competencies and if it were to dominate 99 percent of all formerly human fields of activity, then humans would indeed be superfluous in the prevailing worldview, as Harari predicts, and this superhumanly intelligent AI would indeed be our last invention. Humans apparently have no value in themselves in our current worldview, but are "measure" only by their economic utility, which is low for most of us in the coming technocratic world order.

Children Unwanted!

A self-proclaimed elite of technocrats and superrich are raising the question of what to do with "useless" humans with reference to the endangered habitat of mankind, or rather the looming threat of the collapse of the ecosystem as a result of allegedly manmade climate change, a scenario that has been "imminent" for decades. That this group—when its members are not flying in private jets to private meetings with politicians and business bosses or buying huge villas near the beach with the correspondingly large yacht at anchor—actually seems convinced that climate change has no other cause than man-made CO_2, is obviously a very dangerous equation for each one of us. As soon as this elite has no further use for the majority of humans due to the development of automation and AI systems, this majority will also be an unacceptable problem in terms of climate change due to the carbon dioxide pollution it generates.

In the same vein, Bill Gates named humans as an important factor in his CO_2 equation years ago, namely in the course of a widely publicized TED Talk. According to Gates, the climate problem must be solved by changing a few known variables. We need, Gates said in his February 18, 2010 talk, innovating to zero: "This equation has four factors . . . So, you've got a thing on the left, CO_2, that you want to get to zero, and that's going to be based on the number of people, the services each person is using on average, the energy, on average, for each service, and the CO_2 being put out per unit of energy. So, let's look at each one of these, and see how we can get this down to zero . . . First, we've got population. The world today has 6.8 billion people. That's headed up to about nine billion. Now, if we do a really great job on new vaccines, health care, reproductive health services, we could lower that by, perhaps, 10 or 15 percent."[10] Listen and be amazed: new vaccines, health care, and reproductive health services to reduce the world's population? Looking at the VAERS data (see chapter 1) and the dramatic increase in excess mortality that has occurred since the spiking, a troubling question arises: are these deaths already part of the 10 to 15 percent population reduction Gates calculated in his 2010 TED Talk on new vaccines? Remember that in 2010 global health leaders launched the "Decade of Vaccines Collaboration" (see chapter 4), which has so far peaked with spiking (at the time of this writing, in the spring of 2023).[11]

In any case, there is already a long and very messy history of the conflation of vaccination programs and undeclared "reproductive health services." For example, under the auspices of the WHO, projects have apparently already been implemented with the aim of practicing population control without being noticed: in 1992, the WHO announced a "fertility-regulating vaccine" for "family planning."[12] However, as an international group of scientists detailed, WHO researchers had already molecularly combined tetanus toxoid (TT) with the human pregnancy hormone chorionic gonadotropin (hCG) in 1976 to produce an abortifacient vaccine.[13] The molecular combination of TT and hCG has two effects. First, because TT is foreign to the body, the body's own hCG is also recognized as foreign by the immune system. As a result of this autoimmune reaction, hCG is attacked and inactivated by the body's immune system. "Expected results are abortions," the authors write, "or infertility in recipients not yet impregnated. Repeated inoculations prolong infertility." Second, the TT content allows this vaccine to be marketed and distributed as a "pure" tetanus vaccine, hiding its true purpose of population reduction. "WHO publications show a long-range purpose," the researchers found out, "to reduce population growth in unstable 'less developed countries.'"

As early as November 1993, about a year after the WHO announcement, Catholic Church publications appeared indicating that an abortifacient vaccine disguised as tetanus prophylaxis was in circulation. "In the fall of 1994, the Pro Life Committee of Mexico was suspicious of the protocols for the tetanus toxoid campaign because they excluded all males and children and called for multiple injections of the vaccine in only women of reproductive age."[14] This was particularly odd because the tetanus vaccine normally provides protection for at least ten years. As a result, the committee had vials of the tetanus vaccine tested for hCG, which came back positive. Similar tetanus vaccines containing hCG have been found in the Philippines and Nicaragua, as well as in Kenya.[15] "Given that hCG was found in at least half the WHO vaccine samples known by the doctors involved in administering the vaccines," the international research team writes, "to have been used in Kenya, our opinion is that the Kenya 'anti-tetanus' campaign was reasonably called into question by the Kenya Catholic Doctors Association as a front for population growth reduction." To the best of my knowledge, these actions by the WHO have not yet been legally addressed, nor is anything known about compensation.

"Flying Syringes"

In the context of the WHO's covert contraceptive activities, a particularly sustainable, further option is already conceivable. It has the potential to be a large-scale, global and even unnoticed sterilization program with pregnancy-inhibiting or aborting vaccines such as TT/hCG. A research program is recruiting "vaccinators" from among those earthlings who are only a few inches tall, equipped with wings and the ability to reproduce freely. They could even administer their vaccine dose to almost every human while they sleep: genetically modify mosquitoes to bite and vaccinate at the same time. The radical idea emerged in the early 1990s, and parasitologist Bob Sinden and tropical disease specialist Julian Crampton filed a patent in June 2001 to protect the concept, which they dubbed "flying syringes."[16] But it wasn't until 2010 that a group of Japanese researchers led by molecular geneticist Shigeto Yoshida of Jichi Medical University developed a mosquito that carries a vaccine instead of a disease.[17] He called them "flying vaccinators."

According to Sinden, however, as *Science* reported that same year, no regulatory agency would allow the release of such mosquitoes because that would mean vaccinating people without their informed consent, which is ethically unacceptable.[18] Yoshida himself acknowledged in the same article that the mosquito as a vaccine carrier was "unacceptable" for humans. However, that might soon change, given the discussions about the occasional need for mandatory vaccination against SARS-CoV-2 and the fact that little information has ever been made available about the risks and side effects of the mRNA injections. In 2008 the Bill & Melinda Gates Foundation provided a cash injection for research into the development of "flying syringes" at Jichi Medical University. The *Brave New World*, in which natural birth ceases and world controllers or a technocratic elite decide how many more alphas, betas, and such may be produced, would then be just a flap of the wings away, so to speak.

Taking only the narrow field of the climate issue into consideration, some rather dubious science also seems to agree with Gates and his WHO. "The greatest impact individuals can have in fighting climate change," according to a 2017 article in *The Guardian*, "is to have one fewer child."[19] This statement refers to a Swedish study "that identifies the most effective ways people can cut their carbon emissions." According to that study, having your own offspring is climate killer number one. Based on the scientists' calculations, a child emitting 58.6 tons of carbon dioxide per year is more harmful to the climate than 24.4 cars (per car, they say, only 2.4 tons of carbon dioxide per year).[20] Of course, such work and media scare tactics are not without consequences.

For example, climate fear is driving a birth-strike movement among young people, as the Christian Network Europe (CNE) reports in the article "No Babies for Climate," that according to neuroscientist Emma Lawrance, "40 percent of 10,000 young people between the ages of 16 and 24 do not want to have children because of climate change."[21] CNE also cites the US association "The Voluntary Human Extinction Movement, which has been preaching since the 1970s to restore a "healthy state" on earth through the "slow extinction of the human race by voluntarily giving up procreation." In Germany, the "antinatalist" Verena Brunschweiger advocates this in a very radical way. In her book *Childfree Instead of Childless*, the author pleads, according to CNE, "for renouncing children for the sake of the climate."

Life-Threatening Conflict of Goals

But of course, not only children release carbon dioxide directly or indirectly but also every useful or useless adult, every sick person, and in general every human being. This is where radical health policy and climate dictatorship come into a deadly conflict. I found an example of this in an "editorial on a world in permanent crisis mode" in the *Ärzte Zeitung* of October 2022, which revealed a problem that we may well be curious to see how the technocratic elite intend to solve for us. The recognition of the right to life of many sick people will depend directly on the resolution of this conflict—but the right to life of all other people will also be indirectly derived from it. In this editorial, which is supposed to be about "co-responsibility," Denis Nößler, editor-in-chief of *Ärzte Zeitung,* provides a mathematical calculation of the human CO_2 demand, reminiscent of Gates's TED talk, but applied to a specific group of patients: "At an annual equivalent of up to ten tons of CO_2 emissions, hemodialysis [a procedure to cleanse the blood of a person whose kidneys are not functioning normally] amounts to based on three sessions per week per patient. That's almost as much as each of us in the Federal Republic of Germany emits per capita per year."[22] Hence the editor's question, "Are nephrologists therefore climate killers or bad people?" The author answers this question in the negative, of course, but the question remains. Do we want to save the climate (assuming human CO_2 emission is really the issue) or, in this example, save kidney patients from dying? How would a future AI decide? According to Ray Kurzweil, futurist and director of technical development for Google's AI division, by 2030 (again, that ominous, fateful year) there will be an AI that is more intelligent than any human being, even all of humanity. Can we presume today to divine its unfathomably "wise" future decisions?[23]

Must we wait and see how the climate problem will be solved for us or used against us? Is it our fate to stand by and see in which category each of us will be placed—the useless or the still useful? I think it is high time to stop the process of disenfranchisement as soon as possible. We must bring in our own ideas how to make the society of the future humane. Otherwise, the technocrats will optimize it for AI control and lowest possible CO_2 emissions, possibly by drastically reducing the number of people on earth. However, we should have no illusions—technological progress is unstoppable. If, against this background, we are unwilling to accept a pragmatic reduction of the world's population, we must examine what false assumptions underlie the conclusions on which the technocrats base their actions. Perhaps this is the only way we can come to terms with the fact that the future will be largely driven by technology, without making man a victim of his own creation—although it might one day surpass him in the once self-chosen virtues of efficiency, productivity, and intelligence. Therefore, we must find answers to the following and many other questions as soon as possible: How can we preserve the value of the human being in the wake of AI automation of almost every aspect of life? What is the value of a human being anyway? Is it only to be found in his productivity? What does it really mean to be human?

CHAPTER 7

DARING TO BE MORE HUMAN(KIND)

The ultimate test of a moral society Is the kind of world that it leaves to its children.
—Dietrich Bonhoeffer (1906–1945)

Closing Argument

I am not a prosecutor; I am a scientist. However, the two professions do not differ much in one fundamental task: trying to formulate convincing theses about what logical connections might exist between various individual observations. In doing so, they rely on collected data or circumstantial evidence that either confirms or refutes their initial reasoning. When they are confident that their theory provides a good explanation, they make it public. The symbol of a fair trial is Justitia, the goddess of justice. Blindfolded, or without seeing the defendant and without bias, she weighs the (possibly circumstantial) evidence presented by the prosecution and the defense in the conflicting interests of their respective clients and the public. This is symbolized by the image of a pair of scales. In a court case, the prosecutor's job is to convince a group of jurors that the evidence presented sufficiently supports a given theory. As a result, the jury can render a fair verdict consistent with the ideal of impartial weighing of facts according to Justitia. A scientist is accustomed to a similar situation when he presents the evidence for his or her thesis to the scientific community and subjects the work to a peer review process. This, too, should be done blindly, so to speak, to irrelevant and superficial aspects, or without prejudging the author.

In everyday life, people naturally rely on their personal perceptions and judge according to perspective, or subjective and often superficial criteria—you could say they are not wearing a blindfold or holding a pair of scales. In the courtroom, too, some bias may exist because of prior media coverage or because of what are actually insignificant, even banal, characteristics of the plaintiff or defendant, such as skin color, social status, economic or political power, or powerlessness. And in science, it is common for widely accepted dogma to obscure the evidence, leading Max Planck (1858–1947), the founder of quantum physics, to observe, "A new scientific truth does not triumph by convincing its opponents and making them see the light, but rather because its opponents eventually die, and a new generation grows up that is familiar with it." These opponents are the superstars of science whose findings have become dogma. Because they made the dogma famous, they will defend it with all their might for the rest of their lives, according to a study that posthumously confirmed Planck's assumption.[1]

However, my thesis does not have to pass a court of law or a peer review process, but rather you as my jury. In the end, it does not even matter whether the scientific evidence presented and the testimony of the protagonists of the Great Reset convince you that behind the brain damage taking place there is a grand plan for global transformation. In case my thesis is not presented convincingly enough, or even if it turns out to be wrong, and the accelerated loss of mental capacity is due to a completely random development, there is still no time to lose in eliminating the causes of this catastrophic process unfolding beyond any reasonable doubt. I am convinced that it is unlikely to be a coincidence. And if, as I suspect, indeed intent is behind it, this also has an impact on the form of counterdefense required. It is not enough to simply adapt one's way of life to human nature when influential forces are at work to prevent it.

From my point of view, the many individual observations that seem inexplicable only make sense under the assumption of a deliberately induced Global Mental Reset. And if this is not the result of an extremely unlikely coincidence but rather an indicator of the implementation of a hidden plan, then this time humanity does not have the luxury of relying on the mills of time. The fateful year 2030 is approaching, and with it a point of no return, judging by everything we can reasonably assume today. So that you, the reader, and, to stay with the chosen parable, the member of the global jury, can make an evidence-based judgment, I have presented you with the results of my research. I have tried to provide a comprehensive explanation of what we have experienced, at the latest with the outbreak of the COVID-19 pandemic in 2020 (which, however, was announced long before). In doing so, I assumed the role of a scientific prosecutor, or a prosecutor for science. As I have been able to show, science as a method designed to approach the truth has been sacrificed to the maximization of profits and, above all, to the increase of power—and with it, the people who rely on it. The protagonists of the Great Reset use the latest neuroscientific and informational sciences methodology to pursue a motive that derives from their worldview: a Great Mental Reset, so that we not only without hesitation accept but even welcome the future of a brave new world as envisioned by the elitist technocrats.

In this sense, I was able to show that spiking not only blocks the capacity maintenance of our autobiographical memory but also has a neurotoxic effect by making neurons the target of immunological killer cells. If this is the intended mechanism of action, then the deficient or largely absent immunization by the novel COVID-19 vaccines would no longer be a failure, but an advantage: it requires repeated spiking at relatively short intervals, but just long enough to ensure almost continuous spike protein production and associated brain damage, as I have also been able to show in studies. My theory that the actual target is the memory center of our brain is also supported by the fact that lipid nanoparticles are used as gene transfer vehicles, which can efficiently cross the blood-brain barrier. This is no more justified for vaccination against a virus that primarily infects the respiratory tract than it is for vaccination of children, for whom the virus poses no threat in the first place.

Based on the fact that the virus only poses a threat to a small, well-defined group of people, the principle of herd health should have been applied from the outset to break the chains of infection through adequate vitamin D supplementation and to prevent the cytokine storm and thus severe courses of infection. Instead, the damage to autobiographical memory and the overwriting of one's own identity is achieved with remarkable precision through spiking and the many other COVID-19 measures, combined with incessant anxiety propaganda. This ensures that individuality as a product of our personal experience is lost and replaced by the official narrative. A calculated loss of psychological and mental health is part of this highly efficient mental reprogramming. You could put it this way: Adequate vitamin D (prohormone) levels in the general population, prevented by appropriate propaganda, produced the deaths from an otherwise rather harmless viral respiratory infection that were necessary to enforce the brain-damaging measures, including spiking. Perfidiously, the (deliberate) failure of this policy in terms of health care is now being used as a justification to give the WHO powers that would not otherwise have been possible.

While the overall burden of evidence is overwhelming, fortunately for all of us, it is not purely circumstantial. For several years now, the protagonists of the Great Reset have been revealing their plans far too confidently to the global public in books, glossy brochures, videos, and on the Internet. Even in political programs, their elements are now blatantly traded as concepts for the future. Just think of the *Smart City Charta* (BMI, chapter 1) or the considerations for a society regulated by social points (BMBF, chapter 5). Leading politicians, as mentioned in the introduction to this book, have also included the Great Reset or the Great Transformation in their vocabulary and are preparing their citizens for it. Some references to partial aspects can already be found in legal texts. In Germany, for example, a new *Lastenausgleichsgesetz* ("Burden Equalization") was revised, formerly passed to compensate German war victims, as was the case after World War II. The new version, however, among other things, deals with the victims of the war against an infectious disease, or more precisely, with the victims of a state recommended vaccination. With the foresighted expropriation of society to compensate for the burden of the expected "vaccine victims," we are once again one step closer to Auken's vision of "I own nothing."

Visionary Equalization of Burdens for Vaccine Injured Persons

The original Equalization of Burdens Act of August 14, 1952 (*Lastenausgleichsgesetz*, in short: LAG-1952) was intended to provide "financial compensation to Germans who had suffered property damage or other special disadvantages as a result of World War II and its aftermath."[2] Even before SARS-CoV-2 escaped from the genetic engineering laboratory in Wuhan, the German government had the foresight to amend LAG-1952. Apparently, it expected a new war with many casualties. But the battlefield, according to the vision underlying the draft, was to be the doctor's office. Thus, on December 19, 2019, twelve days before the first report of unusual pneumonia in Wuhan, the German Bundestag passed the new LAG-2019, a comprehensive amendment to Section 21 of the Law Governing Social Compensation, replacing, for example, the term *war victims* (LAG-1952) with *vaccine-injured persons* (LAG-2019).[3] Thus, the new LAG reads in §1: "Social compensation helps people who have suffered damage to their health as a result of an injurious event for which the state community bears special responsibility, to cope with the consequences arising therefrom." Among the listed harmful events are "vaccinations or other measures of specific prophylaxis according to Chapter 2, Section 2, Subsection 4, which caused damage to health." LAG-2019 will enter into force on January 1, 2024. Against this background, it was only to be expected that Karl Lauterbach, the German Minister of Health, after years of promoting the ""risk-free" COVID-19 vaccination and thus driving a large part of German citizens to vaccination, would suddenly promise in 2023 to help vaccine victims.[4] In the same year, the media suddenly reported an increasing number of vaccine injuries in the German population, although in the past such warnings were dismissed as conspiracy theories and often censored.[5] Just another coincidence?

The protagonists of the Great Reset apparently feel completely secure in their belief that no critical mass can be mobilized to resist. They also seem to be convinced that the process of expropriation and AI-controlled total surveillance they have initiated will achieve its planned goal. This is most likely why they believe they can at least disclose their preliminary plans. And indeed, this openness has caused little outrage and no significant uproar, which can be taken as another indication of how far the process of mental reprogramming, or at least mental fatigue, has already progressed in large sections of society. It is not too late. We can still mount a successful defense. But waiting for the courts to take up the challenge, to name the wrongs and hold those responsible accountable, offers little prospect of the only desirable change. Even at the height of the COVID-19 pandemic, the courts not only proved useless in most cases but also, worse, generally supported the government's (or rather, technocratic) course largely without criticism. Whether there will ever be a trial to expose injustice comparable to the Nuremberg trials will undoubtedly depend on whether the technocrats achieve their goal.

At present, all indications are that everything is going according to plan. If technocrats succeed in completely usurping global power in the manner described, they will not stand trial. For this reason alone, you, all of us, are challenged—and now! For you hold not only this book in your hand but also the fate of humanity by your judgment and your resulting willingness to peacefully resist this process. No one can escape the basic principle: he who is silent is consenting; he who does not resist is accepting what will happen to him. To illustrate that this law of tacit legitimacy is not only asserted by me but also assumed ’y those in power, I would like to quote Jean-Claude Juncker, former president of the European Commission (November 1, 2014–November 30, 2019): "We decide on something, leave it lying around, and wait and see what happens. If no one kicks up a fuss, because most people don't understand what has been decided, we continue step by step until there is no turning back."[6]

Against the backdrop of the Great Reset, whose final implementation seems to be timed for 2030, I argue in this book that we must not look at the many wars, such as those against the permapandemics, global climate change and environmental degradation, or, more traditionally, the various wars across state borders, in isolation. All of these wars (and the WEF identifies many more such crises as levers of societal transformation; see figure 10, chapter 4) are ultimately nothing more than a single war against our brains, or in Naomi Wolf's words, "It is a war on free thought and free speech—a war against our most fundamental beliefs."[7]

We are moving ever closer to the "ideal" of a Huxleyan brave new world. In the novel, nine years of war and then the Great Economic Collapse led to a new world order "after Ford," the beginning of a new faith. Perhaps in 2030, starting in 2020, after also about nine years of war(s) and the complete collapse of the economy, we too will be ready for a new faith in propertyless happiness and permanent surveillance right into our private sphere, which will then no longer exist. A caesura of this magnitude would mean the beginning of a new era for the human race.

"Gates Be Thanked"

In *Brave New World*, Henry Ford (1863–1947) is the new god of the world state. People say things like, "Oh, Ford!" and "Thank Ford!" and count in years by Ford (AF). They are referring to when 632 years earlier (in year 0, or 1908 by our calendar) his first Model T rolled off the assembly line in the real world. The T is also their new symbol of faith, resembling the Christian cross, although it ends at the crossbar. A literary guide describes Ford in his prominent role for the people of the novel world as "the perfect 'god' for World State society because, in developing his Ford Motor Company, he invented mass production by means of the assembly line and the specialization of workers, each of whom has one single, specific job."[8]

As a result of the twin catastrophes of the Nine Years' War and the ensuing great economic collapse, Huxley's "World State takes Ford's ideas about mass production and the assembly line and applies them to biologically to human beings. World State citizens, therefore, deify Ford as a vaguely remembered, distant historical figure who literally created the world as they know it," the literary guide continues.

So much for fiction. In reality, it is not yet clear which leading figure we will honor in the not-too-distant future as the essential generator of ideas and thus the creator of a new world operating system. If we go by the merit of the person who, as in the novel, served as the mastermind for the defining principle of the future society, Bill Gates clearly stands out among the candidates. After all, people are already talking about the "Gates of hell" opening in 2020. In this, our brave new world made flesh, it is he who preaches the promise of health and happiness through pharmaceuticals. This is how he envisions the outcome of his war against coronavirus: "Everybody's going to be convinced of my thing."[9] Since no one is better suited than Gates himself to be considered the founder of this dystopian world, the question arises, will the symbol of Gates's religion be the upside-down cross in the shape of a syringe?

We know the published motive, we know by now the subtle but effective methods of indoctrination, and we know that the protagonists of the Great Reset are using the power of narrative to shape our worldview and decide how much destruction we will allow them to get away with in the name of urgently saving humanity (by throwing everything human overboard). It is also clear that the superrich technocrats who pursue this motive also have the financial resources and political connections to act accordingly. If the staged SARS-CoV-2 pandemic has taught us anything, it is that people are not afraid to artificially create viruses with new human pathogenic properties (e.g., furin cleavage site, see chapter 4) in obscure laboratories. They also do not seem to be afraid of discussing scenarios in public in advance, as if they wanted to tell the entire world population how to behave. Nor do they seem to have any qualms about not considering effective prevention and treatment options (such as the elimination of vitamin D3 deficiency), only to subject humanity to a brain-toxic gene therapy with dubious viral genetic material, disguised as "vaccination," on the pretext of an alleged lack of alternatives. This means nothing else than to massively damage people's health in the belief of their salvation—obviously in cold-blooded indifference to the consequences for the quality of life of people, as long as it serves their own goals. In this process of indoctrination, a mental destruction is accepted with approval, even to be valued as a prerequisite for success (see chapter 4), and can be seen in the dramatic increase in mental illnesses and the simultaneous decrease of mental capacity in society—in all age groups.

This inhuman behavior reminds me of Munchausen's syndrome by proxy, named after Karl Friedrich Hieronymus, Freiherr von Münchhausen (1720–1797), the so-called Baron of Lies. In this psychological clinical picture, illnesses or symptoms of illnesses are invented, exaggerated, or actually induced in protégés, mostly children but also adults, in order to then demand medical treatment (such as a "vaccination") and thereby take on the role of a seemingly loving and self-sacrificing savior who, as in this case, does everything and spares neither effort nor expense to save humanity in his own way—"Gates be thanked."

Wreaking havoc and then being celebrated as a savior can also be observed in other disasters that also have social implications, such as environmental destruction: "One of the main causes of deforestation, especially in the tropics, is the expansion of cultivable land," reports the German newspaper *Der Standard*, warning that "deforestation not only releases carbon, but also leads to the loss of animal and plant diversity and entire ecosystems."[10] Assistant Professor Dr. Michele Graziano Ceddia of the Center for Development and Environment (CDE) at the University of Bern has published a sensational study in the journal *Nature Sustainability*. His startling finding is that it is not ordinary people but the superrich who are driving this massive environmental destruction by creating more and more arable land for so-called flex crops through gigantic investments and intriguing machinations.[11] Flex crops are agricultural products such as soy, palm oil, and sugar cane that can be used for human food, animal feed, or industrial purposes. These crops give investors the flexibility to choose the most profitable way to sell the crop, depending on market demand. For example, when oil prices rise, agricultural products may be diverted from the food supply to the more lucrative biofuel production—as long as the profit is right.[12]

Ceddia's flex-crops study shows that in the period from 1991 to 2014 alone, "a 1% increase in the wealth of HNWI generated an expansion of the flex-crops area share of up to 2.4–10%." According to Ceddia, the boom in flex crops, and the associated intensification of environmentally destructive and generally detrimental socioeconomic developments, can be traced to increasing wealth inequality. He explains, "The results point to the urgency of addressing wealth inequality to protect the remaining forests."

In other words, the superrich technocrats travel to the climate summits in their private planes to chauvinistically tell us that humans are inherently responsible for environmental destruction—and by that they obviously mean only us ordinary citizens, not themselves. They do not admit that they are ultimately acting out of greed. The polluters style themselves as the philanthropic savior of humanity. On the pretext of averting our allegedly impending self-destruction, they justify their claim to initiate the Great Reset. And because they are so rich and influential, and constantly in the media spotlight, far too many people still believe them. The key misconception may be the widespread notion that these people can only be so extraordinarily rich because they are much smarter than the rest of the world, that it is therefore perfectly legitimate for them to tell us how to behave, and that we would do well to share in their philanthropic foresight by following their recommendations.

Acquired Sociopathy?

Are technocrats really more intelligent than the rest of us, or do they just tend to overestimate themselves, which we then adopt in another error? More likely the latter, though exceptions may prove the rule. According to the results of a Swedish study, the ultrarich tend to be even less intelligent than other income groups. The researchers studied nearly sixty thousand former military personnel for whom cognitive performance tests were available over a period of about eleven years. They conclude, "Strikingly, we find that the relationship between [cognitive] ability and wage is strong overall, yet above €60,000 per year ability plateaus at a modest level . . . The top 1 percent even score slightly worse on cognitive ability than those in the income strata right below them."[13] In other words, this large-scale study could not provide any reason why we should reverently entrust our fate to the superrich. And even if one or the other were to possess a brilliant intelligence, it would not be enough to rule the whole world in divine omnipotence. Rather, we should ask ourselves whether our fate lies in the hands of sociopathic individuals who simply see it as a logical and therefore necessary step for them to save humanity from humanity, and who are willing to do so even over sky-high mountains of corpses (see previous chapter and chapter 1).

In his book *Humankind*, Danish historian Rutger Bregman (who, by the way, made a fiery speech at the 2019 WEF meeting in Davos calling for more taxes on the superrich and was not invited back the following year)[14] points to a phenomenon called *acquired sociopathy*.[15] He refers to research by US psychologist Dacher Keltner, according to which powerful people are, among other things, more selfish, ruthless, and narcissistic. They listen less well and don't like to take another person's perspective. But perhaps they're also less capable of doing so: indeed, scientists have used imaging techniques to show that the feeling of power blocks the neurobiological process of mirroring.[16] Mirror neurons allow us to put ourselves in other people's shoes by mirroring their actions or gestures as if we were experiencing their current situation. If someone yawns, we yawn—but not psychopaths. Mirroring is a prerequisite for learning from the experiences of others but also for empathy, which superpowered people may lack completely. Powerful people "stop simulating the experience of others," Keltner says, describing an *empathy deficit* and explaining the results of these studies.[17] US historian Henry Adams (1838–1918) already suspected that power changes the brain, describing it as "a sort of tumor that ends by killing the victim's sympathies."[18] "They act like someone with brain damage," confirms Bregman.[19] But if we still assume that human beings are basically good, as he tries to prove in his international bestseller, it might explain why there are characters who nevertheless bring so much disaster to the world—even those who want to subjugate us do so for our own good (or so they think).

In any case, the authors of the mirror neuron study conclude that their data explains the common attitude of the powerful to disregard the powerless. Besides power leading to a lack of empathy, it also leads to negative attitudes toward fellow human beings, studies show.[20] "If you are powerful," Bregman explains, "you are more likely to think most people are lazy and unreliable. That they need to be supervised and monitored, managed, and regulated, censored and told what to do. And because power makes you feel superior to other people, you'll believe all this monitoring should be entrusted to you."[21] So maybe the protagonists of the Great Reset are not really evil at all but just have a self-image that is completely exaggerated in this sense? It is plausible that they suffer from some kind of God complex, since they are "idolized" by many people because of their power. Independently of the studies cited, one could even assume that they feel chosen and may even be convinced that they are doing good.

Perhaps we have all contributed, however inadvertently, to making the powerful feel so powerful: Feeling powerless has the exact opposite effect on the other person and plays into the hands of the powerful. Bregman again has something to say: "Psychological research shows that people who feel powerless also feel far less confident. They're hesitant to voice an Inion. In groups, they make themselves seem smaller, and they underestimate their own intelligence." This has bitter consequences, according to Bregman: "Such feelings of uncertainty are convenient for those *in* power, as self-doubt makes people unlikely to strike back . . . Here we see the nocebo in action: treat people as if they are stupid and they'll start to feel stupid, leading rulers to reason that the masses are too dim to think for themselves and hence they— with their vision and insight—should take charge." (Interestingly, Bergman first published this insight in September 2019, three months before the COVID-19 pandemic started, as if he had guessed what we would suddenly be up against.)[22]

But Bonhoeffer, who was murdered shortly before the end of the war for his fight against the Hitler regime, was absolutely certain: "Stupidity is basically not an intellectual defect, but a moral defect . . . It turns out that every strong increase of power, whether political or religious, infects a large part of humanity with stupidity. It is almost as if there were a sociological-psychological law according to which the power of one requires the stupidity of another."[23] But the process at work here, according to Bonhoeffer, is not "that human faculties such as the intellect suddenly fail. Rather, it seems to be that man, under the overwhelming influence of increasing power, is robbed of his inner independence and more or less consciously gives up his autonomous position." The abandonment of autonomy and one's own identity increases the sense of power and superiority of those in power, until they believe that there are no limits to what they can do. In this way, a vicious circle is created that is life-threatening for us, and we are already experiencing its extreme effects.

But this is also our chance! Once we recognize this vicious circle, which also makes the powerless more powerless, as an essential problem of our present situation, we can break it. This means getting rid of the false image of the mental superiority of the powerful, as well as our own supposed lack of intellect, power, and influence. Furthermore, we must correct our assumption that human beings are basically evil. This narrative is the real fundamental problem that has brought us to this precarious situation, the infamous beginning of all evil. This, then, is the crucial judgment, dear jury, that I hope you will all make about all of us: We are basically good! We only have to learn again what children are from birth, no matter where in the world they are born, what color their skin is, what faith their parents profess—they are *a priori* free of prejudice. Only when we understand that we are only victims of indoctrinated narratives can the world belong to all of us again.

Basically Good?

"Man is the most compassionate, intelligent, imaginative, and humorous animal on the planet. He has created works of art of breathtaking beauty and developed the most ingenious methods of unraveling the mysteries of the universe. Never before has there been a creature that cared so sacrificially for the sick and the weak, that fought so tirelessly for freedom and justice—despite all defeats," writes Michael Schmidt-Salomon in his book *Hope Man: A Better World Is Possible*, adding, "Much has been written about the dark side of humanity; its sunny side has usually been left under the table."[24]

I've been wondering about this for a long time: murder and manslaughter, rampages, terrorist attacks, and atrocities dominate the news, but hardly a word is spoken about the real life in which we help each other or have ideas about how to overcome challenges together. Why is that? Surely, it's all about the particular emotion, and perhaps the news is watched with the feeling that as long as it's bad elsewhere, you're fine!

Ultimately, negative news stories feed into the notion that man is evil. At least since the beginning of recorded cultural history, we have been indoctrinated with that idea, because such a narrative provides the essential justification for religious as well as state power: evil man must be controlled! This is also the basis of the concept of original sin, which is supposed to be inherent in human nature and transmitted to all humanity through reproduction. The Christian story of the Fall, however, reveals what exactly is the crucial flaw in human nature. According to biblical tradition, Adam and Eve I the first humans to transgress a prohibition of God by eating from the Tree of Knowledge. So, man is bad or evil because he is willing to disobey (nonsensical) prohibitions in order to satisfy his thirst for knowledge (nonsensical because the fruit was obviously not poisonous). The problem is only his curiosity, and that is indeed part of his hippocampal nature. But with the mantra "basically evil" a domination-legitimizing image of man was created. And since it is explained by the Biblical story of the Fall, it must not be questioned. Paradoxically, however, only through constant and thoroughly critical self-observation has this becomes anchored in our self-image and also becomes a self-fulfilling prophecy. Those who consider others to be fundamentally evil behave in a hostile manner, which causes the other side not to be very friendly either. The narrative vicious circle is complete.

Gradually, worldly rulers slipped into the thus-created role of the necessary supervisor to control evil and thereby consolidated their "God-given power" over man. The social point systems are also a manifestation of this medially cherished and cultivated image of man: the dangerous and destructive nature of the thoroughly evil human being can only be nipped in the bud by seamless surveillance and strict rules. Since this fatal idea of us being fundamentally evil is part of our cultural identity, we run the risk of also accepting, and possibly even demanding, such intensive and invasive surveillance and regimentation of the people around us, and thus also of ourselves, which is absurd, because of course hardly anyone is convinced of having a fundamentally bad character. I would also, without hesitating, exclude my friends, all my relatives, and all acquaintances so far as being basically evil, and certify them as having a fundamentally good character. And I assume and hope you have made a similar experience. Rather, the person we know outside the media is distinguished by kindness, or as Bregman calls him, a *homo puppy*.

Homo puppy

"For decades," writes science journalist Charles Q. Choi, "scientists have noted that mature humans physically resemble immature chimps—we, too, have small jaws, flat faces, and sparse body hair. The retention of juvenile features, called *neoteny* in evolutionary biology, is especially apparent in domesticated animals—thanks to human preferences, many dog breeds have puppy features such as floppy ears, short snouts and large eyes."[25] But is this true? This question was investigated by the Russian geneticist Dmitry K. Belyayev (1917–1985). His hypothesis, as Rutger Bregman reports, was radical: "He suspected these cute forms were merely *by-products* of something else, a metamorphosis that happens organically if over a sufficiently long period of time are consistently selected for one specific quality."[26]

To test his idea, his student Lyudmila Trut was asked to domesticate untamed and naturally highly aggressive silver foxes on a Siberian animal farm in the late 1950s. The selection criterion was "friendliness."[27] By the fourth generation, the first animals were wagging their tails, and with each successive generation, their appearance changed more and more: It remained childlike (puppy-like) even as they became adults. "The more amiable foxes produced fewer stress hormones, but more serotonin (the 'happy hormone') and oxytocin (the 'love hormone')."[28] That is exactly the combination of neurotransmitters that makes the hippocampus grow. Decades later, US scientist Brian Hare, now a professor of evolutionary anthropology, found that the friendly silver foxes were significantly more intelligent than their aggressive, wild ancestors. "If you want a smart fox," he revolutionarily concluded, "you don't select for smartness, you select for friendliness."[29] This conclusion makes sense, because if you want to survive on kindness, you have to be good at reading the behavior of others around you. But it runs counter to the more common thesis today that violence and aggression prevail. Even then, Belyayev, who initiated the unusual project, was certain that these findings "can also, of course, apply to human beings," Bregman reports.[30] So our "original sin," curiosity, arose because of another virtue for which we were selected in prehistoric clans: kindness. And that makes sense, too, because all unfriendly, aggressive offspring were presumably expelled from the collective, and this selection brought with it more social intelligence, empathy, and, last but not least, rational compassion.

But if we do not consider ourselves and many people in our assessable environment to be fundamentally evil, how can we believe that most people outside our immediate experience are? This is statistically implausible. Either we humans are (almost) all basically evil, or hardly anyone is (psychopaths and sociopaths would then be the exception that proves the rule). This should be clear to us, as long as we do not make the mistake of inferring the character of the ruled from the character of the rulers. However, in many cases our expectations influence our experiences, and this is especially true in the social realm. If you go into a social interaction with the idea that the other person means no good to you, your own behavior triggers a confirming reaction in the other person, according to the motto "As you shout into the forest, so it resounds out." This vicious cycle must be broken.

So, if we had the courage to reorient our expectations around the idea that human beings are basically good, that alone could "start a revolution," Bregman said.[31] After all, he said, it is "an idea that's long been known to make rulers nervous. An idea denied by religions and ideologies, ignored by the news media and erased from the annals of world history." Yet "it's an idea," Bregman continued, "that's legitimized by virtually every branch of science. One that's corroborated by evolution and confirmed by everyday life. An idea so intrinsic to human nature that it goes unnoticed and gets overlooked."

Smarter Than a Yeast?

When just one tiny, single-celled yeast fungus is added to a bottle of grape juice, the cell begins to multiply rapidly. The yeast even multiplies exponentially at first, so one cell becomes two, then four, sixteen, and so on. From the grape sugar, its energy source, carbon dioxide (it foams) and alcohol are produced as waste products—good for us, because wine is produced. But it's bad for the yeast, because even before all the sugar has been used up, the alcohol content in its limited habitat rises to such an extent that all the yeast cells eventually perish. You could say that the yeast has grown itself to death. Although a yeast cell is extremely efficient, it is not equipped with the intelligence to foresee its self-inflicted end and avert it by adjusting its behavior.

Our bottle is planet Earth, and we are like the yeast. Our economy is highly efficient, and it festers in every corner. Are we smarter than a yeast colony that, unlike us, naturally has no brain? Or will we too perish from the waste products of our constant economic growth? Unfortunately, it sure looks like the latter. Fish has become virtually inedible due to toxins like methylmercury and many others that we dump in the world's oceans. Harmful microplastics are found in fish flesh as well, but as we know, not only there.[32] It's almost everywhere. It is a major factor responsible for the decline in male fertility.[33] The largest plastic island floats in the Great Pacific Garbage Patch, located between California and Hawaii, which already extended a staggering 1.6 million square kilometers in 2018—and it's far from the only one growing rapidly and unchecked.[34] If the technocrats really want to decimate the world's population, ignoring the problems associated with plastic pollution of our habitat is very conducive.

The argument of King Charles, Schwab, and Gates that things can't go on like this is not out of the blue. Striving for constant growth only brings us closer and closer to the abyss. The fact that we are constantly increasing our speed only creates the illusion of progress. In reality, we are moving ever faster toward the destruction of our habitat. But the elitist solution of an autocratic dictatorship ruling over a destitute and totally dependent, constantly AI-monitored, pharmaceutically spiked, and birth-controlled humanity is anything but a real solution to even one of the real problems facing our generation; for in all aspects it is contrary to human nature and leads humanity into an unknown world, the very outlines of which appear to us as sheer horror and in which solution-oriented innovation through diversity of uniqueness is no longer even conceivable. What we need is cooperation instead of confrontation, intelligent collaboration instead of destructive opposition.

We are no closer to a real solution if we entrust our future to technocrats who have made themselves suspect of sociopathy. They have long since lost their credibility. No, it is up to us to find species-appropriate solutions for local and global coexistence. Our own organism shows us every day how this can work. To keep it healthy, every cell in the body must cooperate directly or indirectly with every other cell. And cells all do this without complaint, because it is in their nature to do so. We humans, too, would be able to cooperate directly or indirectly with each other in such a way that each group could keep itself healthy for itself and thus ultimately keep all of humanity alive in its only common habitat. We would be quite adept at this, because the success of our evolutionary history is based on our communal cooperation. We have selected for it because it has secured our existence.[35] The American sociobiologist Edward O. Wilson (1929–2021) therefore speaks rightly of "the social conquest of Earth." Not only cellular, but also social interaction is in our genes.

Yet this deeply human capacity for solidarity is often used against us by those in power. They sell to us what is in fact harmful as "good behavior" to show everyone that we ourselves are among the good guys. They count on the value we place on conformity. Take spiking, for example: here, because of our genetically programmed tendencies, we could be baited with arguments aimed at empathy, social cooperation, and conformity. "The evolutionarily evolved capacity for empathy," writes Schmidt-Salomon, "was the prerequisite for successful lying, cheating, cooperation, and intrigue, and created—as a side effect, so to speak—the basis for altruistic behavior motivated by empathy (and co-joy!)."[36] Unfortunately, the flawed argument of protection of others alone has made far too many people willing to have not only themselves, but even their completely safe children spiked, supposedly to contribute to the socially required protection of those in need. On one hand, this makes me angry, because the will to do good in human beings has been instrumentalized for evil, but on the other hand, it also offers every reason to look at human nature with hope. It shows that we are quite willing to help others and are even prepared to make sacrifices if necessary. But we need to ask ourselves much more often where we should show solidarity and whether the supposedly good intentions behind the things we are urged to do are not rather paving the proverbial road to hell.

I wonder if perhaps the often-fatal consequences of our good will have shaped the image of man as a fundamentally evil being, when essentially good people do terrible things. I had a frightening glimpse of this mystery of good human nature in the summer of 2021, when a doctor urged me during a routine checkup to finally get vaccinated against COVID-19. He justified this with the role-model function as a doctor, but above all with the argument of "protection of others." At that time, however, it had long been known in professional circles that spiking did not offer any external protection and was unhealthy and that there was a healthy alternative, which I pointed out to him. Among other things, I mentioned that up to 4 percent of the plasma level of the injected viral genetic material could reach the brain and make our unique nerve cells the target of immunological killer cells. In addition, I informed him that the flawed argument of protection of others is also used to justify the completely useless lockdowns, which caused massive damage, not only to our society. After all, in the context of their financing, there has been an almost complete shutdown of world hunger aid, which, according to UNICEF, has caused a great many people, especially children, to starve and die of hunger in the countries of the global South. He left my question unanswered as to whether he understood this to be protection of others. Neither my arguments about a healthy alternative nor the global impact seemed to impress him. He was just glad, he said, that we live in a country where food and good medical care are not a problem. And in those poorer countries, he said, infant deaths are normal. As he left the office, he excitedly shouted after me that if 4 percent of the vaccinated got brain cancer in a few years, it would still be better than dying horribly from COVID-19 today. The here and now was obviously more important to him than events far away, both in time (brain tumors in the future) and in space (starving children in poorer countries).

Apart from his probable misunderstanding of the 4 percent in the heat of the argument, I was deeply shocked and surprised by so much apparent callousness, as I had hitherto regarded him as a highly committed and very sensitive doctor. This contradiction raised central questions in me that would not let go: *Should I see him as a bad person because he obviously (at the moment) only cared about the people closest to him? Or should I see him as a good person because of his intention to protect the people around him by trying to persuade me to get vaccinated?* The answer to these questions, I was sure, would say a lot about the nature of human beings. After some study of the literature, much reflection, and many conversations, I came to believe that he was driven by *an excess* of empathy and was probably blocked in his rational thinking because of it. Although empathy is generally considered a good quality, the resulting kindhearted or even loving focus on one's neighbor actually obscures one's view of the bigger picture.

This is also the conclusion of Paul Bloom, a professor of psychology at Yale University in the United States. According to his studies, most of us have a completely false idea of empathy. In his book *Against Empathy*, Bloom uses clinical studies and accessible logic to argue *against* empathy and instead *for* what he calls rational compassion in decision making: "Far from helping us to improve the lives of others, empathy is a capricious and irrational emotion that appeals to our narrow prejudices. It muddles our judgment and, ironically, often leads to cruelty."[37] Empathy, however well-intentioned, is a poor guide to ethical deliberation because it makes one "less sensitive to the suffering of greater and greater numbers of people."[38] Bloom thus provides a convincing explanation for the irritating thinking and behavior I experienced during my visit to the doctor: a great deal of empathy for the acutely ill in my own professional circle, and absolutely no empathy for people outside that circle. So, my doctor's reaction to my arguments was not the result of a lack of empathy but of a rationally completely unbridled empathy. Empathy in itself is therefore not a bad thing, but it is problematic for dealing with global challenges when it is not embedded in a rational assessment of the overall situation. "Empathy has certain design features that do make it positive in certain restricted circumstances," Bloom explained in an interview, giving an example: "If you and I are the only people on earth and you're in pain and I can help you and make your pain go away, and I feel empathy toward you and so I make your life better, empathy has done something good. But the real world is nowhere near as simple. Empathy's design failings have to do with the fact that it acts like a spotlight. It zooms you in. But spotlights only illuminate where you point them at, and for that reason empathy is biased."

Such love of the close by and the fatal lack of love for the far away in our interconnected world are paradoxically caused by the hippocampal effects of oxytocin. This neurobiological dual function of oxytocin as a love-hate hormone also provides an essential and compelling explanation for why we tend to perceive people close to us as good but to more critically evaluate people far away.

The Hate/Love Hormone

Released by the pituitary gland through physical contact and also through eye contact with other people (or one's dog),[39] oxytocin stimulates hippocampal neurogenesis to promote autobiographical memory necessary for pair bonding. As a birthing hormone, it supports lifelong mother-infant bonding.

The bonding hormone is therefore also known as the cuddle hormone, but this is where the dark side of this molecule becomes apparent, because obviously you do not want to cuddle with everyone. This explains the little-known ambivalent effect of oxytocin, which promotes both in-group love and affection and outgroup hate and dislike. Hippocampal receptors for oxytocin are necessary for us to efficiently discriminate socially relevant stimuli into positive ones that convey a sense of belonging and negative ones that convey avoidance.[40] Oxytocin is thus an essential part of a genetic program that emotionally primes us for herd behavior and blind obedience—following often hidden rules of interaction harmful to us. The effects become particularly clear when blind trust in one's own group leads to unjustified distrust of foreign groups or ethnicities, even to xenophobia.[41] The demarcation line is easy to see when you walk between the fan blocks at a soccer derby. Color, especially that of skin or blood (red versus "blue"), is also often a sharp dividing line, as is religious affiliation. The emotional divide between rich and poor could also be explained in this way.

Correspondingly, too much unthinking empathy within one's group becomes a problem in an increasingly globalized world, according to Bloom: "I actually feel a lot less empathy for people who aren't in my culture, who don't share my skin color, who don't share my language. This is a terrible fact of human nature, and it operates at a subconscious level, but we know that it happens. There's dozens, probably hundreds, of laboratory experiments looking at empathy and they find that empathy is as biased as can be."[42] It divides us humans into good and evil in a moralizing way. Thinking back to my experience with my doctor, the question remains whether I should characterize his behavior more as good or more as evil under these conditions. But how far do these categories take us, especially when we consider such difficult cases? Not far, and it is better to think beyond good and evil and leave this moral abyss.

Beyond Good and Evil

This is the title of a book by the German philosopher Michael Schmidt-Salomon. In it, the evolutionary humanist explains that concepts such as *good* or *evil* have no place in science, partly because they are morally evaluative, and partly because no special power can be attributed to them: "The idea of evil, which is used not only to evaluate human actions but also to explain them, is a violation of scientific principles of knowledge because of the supernatural implication it contains ('There is a separate realm of evil that cannot be explained by natural causes!')"[43] Moreover, the good/evil dualism is a poor moral compass, since it always leads us in the direction of a double standard that is dangerous to life: "Morality [as opposed to ethics, which is strictly a scientific discipline that examines divergent systems of norms and attempts to justify them from a neutral perspective] is only understood as morality when it constructs an enemy, as it were, a life-practical antithesis to itself."[44] It is therefore no coincidence, he says, that the most vocal moralists stir up images of the enemy by preaching the struggle for the supposed good, something we have clearly witnessed in the war against COVID-19, and which will be exacerbated in the war against climate change.

How do we deal with the knowledge that our feelings can lead us astray and that we may do more harm than good in our efforts to help? Again, Bloom has a suggestion: "I want to make a case for the value of conscious, deliberative reasoning in everyday life, arguing that we should strive to use our heads rather than our hearts."[45] In the moral realm, empathy leads us astray, as studies show: "Empathy zooms me in on one but it doesn't attend to the difference between one and 100 or one and 1,000. It's because of empathy we often care more about a single person than 100 people or 1,000 people, or we care more about an attractive white girl who went missing than we do 1,000 starving children who don't look like we do or live where we don't live." In other words, we tend to automatically feel local, but we have to actively force ourselves to think global; because of the widespread misunderstanding of these states of mind, we often take pride in doing just the former. After all, we tend to be much more suspicious of cold reason than of warm feeling, because supposedly only the latter makes us truly warm-hearted people. This unnecessary dualism of favoring one over the other can have dangerous consequences. This is the thesis of Dane Rasmus Hougaard, coauthor of the groundbreaking book *Compassionate Leadership*.[46] As he writes in a *Forbes* article, "Empathy is the brain's wired tendency to identify with those who are close to us—close in proximity, close in familiarity, or close in kinship. And when we empathize with those close to us, those who are not close or are different seem threatening. When unchecked, empathy can create more division than unity."[47] Therefore, as Bloom suggested, we need to distinguish between empathy and rational compassion. But Hougaard recognized another fundamental difference: empathy is impulsive, whereas rational compassion is deliberate; indeed, the strong empathy for those in my doctor's immediate environment seems to have blocked his ability to think rationally. His sense of an imminent threat to a group worth protecting, which needed to be averted, was clearly evident in the conversation. It resembled an almost panic-like state, which is known to reduce the ability to think rationally.

Moreover, according to Hougaard's insight, rational compassion would unite, while empathy would divide. Bregman agrees: "The truth is that empathy and xenophobia go hand in hand. They are two sides of the same coin."[48] According to Bregman, perfectly healthy people (psychopaths and sociopaths are excluded) do essentially evil things only because they empathically fight for themselves at the expense of others, and he provides many studies and evidence for this in his book *Humankind*. Too much empathy without rational compassion would thus be an ultimate explanation for why people are basically good but still capable of evil (when looked from the outside). In this insight, however, lies a solution to our dilemma, one that goes directly to the root of social dysfunction. We could save ourselves from ourselves, so to speak, if we learned to use wisely in combination (and not, as Bloom suggested, to elevate one above the other) these two profoundly natural human capacities. Through empathy, we can sympathize with the problems of people close to us. But only with rational compassion can we prevent ourselves from losing sight of the bigger picture, and even being enlisted in wars of suffering because of our ability to empathize. If we have the foresight to find solutions that are good for everyone, not just for ourselves and for those in our immediate surroundings, then we can also overcome our false image of humanity.

This is what gives the powerful the legitimacy to control and tyrannize us. Almost all of us are basically good, even if we sometimes fail to channel our good intentions in the optimal way. We do not, however, need a social scoring system that ultimately treats us as if we had no ethical compass of our own.

Good and Evil Rules

Having recognized and internalized that human beings are basically good does not mean that we suddenly no longer need laws that protect us, for example, from sociopaths and psychopaths. Rules are good, as long as they benefit the human community. So, I am glad that there are rules about which side of the road to drive on. It would be a danger to the community if complete arbitrariness prevailed here—besides, the encroachment on basic rights (freedom of movement) by such a rule is minimal to nonexistent. But these rules and laws should be moderate, respect the dignity and basic rights of people in general, and be democratically legitimized; they must not come about by operating without a corrective, with flimsy arguments and scientifically unjustifiable claims under normal circumstances (free research), or even by undermining the democratic process of the legislature (as we experienced with COVID-19).

Basically, the dualism of empathy and rational compassion reflects our two ways of acting and thinking, respectively, which we know as System 1 and System 2. System 1 is the older system, which certainly existed when our direct animal ancestors lived in packs and we, as early humans, developed our social skills in small communities. Here, the ability to empathize was central to living together. However, the later developmental interaction of the frontal brain and the hippocampus of the rational-thinking system 2 enabled us to act in an inventive and planning way and also to think outside the box. It is true that we only feel charity for our neighbor, that is one side of our nature, and that has its place. But we can also very well rationalize with compassion and recognize that people are outside our field of vision who may be affected by our decisions, and that is also urgently necessary in some circumstances. Also, both the capacity for empathic action (System 1) and rational compassion (System 2) allow us to mentally play out the global consequences of our local decisions and act accordingly. And that's critical, because our planet, like the bottle of grape juice to the yeast, is of limited usability and capacity.

Excessive empathy (System 1 behavior) and a lack of rational compassion (System 2 thinking), coupled with our false view of humanity as basically evil, lead us to see only ourselves as good and others as threatening, even though they are usually no more or less so than we are. To restore the balance of the systems and to change our self-destructive view of man, we need a fully functioning hippocampus. So, it is high time to provide for a clear System 2–capable brain, particularly in the light of the acute technocratic upheavals.

Healthier Brain, Healthier Decisions

We are in the midst of a global war, not only against our freedom of thought and speech and our most basic beliefs, as Naomi Wolf has put it, but also against our ability to think and our individuality. This war is designed to indoctrinate us. But we can still win this war against this smug and arrogant elite, because we are basically good and therefore quite capable of doing the right thing in times of crisis, especially when not only our own future is at stake but also that of our children and all future generations—indeed, their future and even the question of whether they, as "climate pests," should be allowed to have an existence at all.

The battleground of this war is in our brain, so the defense must take place there. Our weapons to protect the hippocampus as the primary target of attack are therefore of a purely mental nature: our memory, our System 2 thinking (rational compassion), creativity, self-awareness, psychological resilience, willpower and stamina, and empathy and social conscience—all direct or indirect properties of productive adult hippocampal neurogenesis. To optimally sharpen these mental weapons, the Hippocampal Anti-Indoctrination Formula (see figure 7 in chapter 2) gives us an overview of the relevant areas of life where we can start. However, productive hippocampal neurogenesis offers much more than protection against long-term indoctrination. It can also help us decide this war for ourselves as quickly as possible, in order to thrive as individuals and as humanity. The reversal of human development driven by the technocrats' agenda paradoxically leads us into exactly the scenario that the yeast cell faces in the fermentation process because it does not change its behavior. If we, are allowed to pursue our urge to explore, to quench our thirst for new experiences, and to live out our joy in inventing intelligent solutions to the challenges we face, humanity will emerge stronger from this crisis. It will find a suitable answer to all the pressing questions of the present, of this I am completely confident (first examples will follow). In this sense, the goal of making the world a better place for everyone already determines the strategy for winning this war:

- We must first internalize that all human beings are products of the same evolutionary process, and therefore we all have the same basic desires and needs, precisely in those areas on which the Hippocampal Anti-Indoctrination Formula is built.
- Furthermore, one of the oldest and most culture-shaping narratives is a major cause of the predicament in which we find ourselves. If we are truly to achieve victory and progress, we must abandon the notion that human beings are essentially evil.
- We will actually have to forgive ourselves, because we cannot change the past. But we can and must use it to understand, clearly and without guilt, what went wrong in order to learn from it. Only from this understanding can we create a better future for all of us.

We are fighting not only against the technocratic indoctrination with its insane Great Narrative but also for a new image of man, because the old one has prevented us from thinking and acting in a truly cooperative way. Cooperation should strengthen and unite us. Ultimately, it is about giving our lives a higher meaning that will benefit the whole of humanity. With this in mind, let's review the essential elements of the Hippocampal Anti-Indoctrination Formula. By putting the strategy into practice, we can actually kill two birds with one stone: by making our brains more System 2 capable, we simultaneously increase our chances of creating a better cultural future for all of us.

Social Life

Since spring of 2020, there has been a clear increase in solidarity among those who have recognized the signs of the times. This circle needs to be widened. Currently, more and more communities are forming that govern themselves locally and according to economic criteria. Empathic interaction is closely interwoven with rational compassion in global thinking. This already shows that the approach of a world government cannot work—it is contrary to human nature.

A good example of a successful community that aligns with people's natural tendencies are the so-called ecovillages. Developing worldwide from existing traditional communities or as newly formed, they all share the goal of becoming socially, culturally, economically, and ecologically sustainable through the conscious design and behavior of their inhabitants. That is, they have as little negative impact on the natural environment as possible. Collective identity, or the sense of "we" that develops, helps with the sustainability transformation, according to a US study.[49] The ecovillages analyzed in this study illustrate how multiple values can be cultivated alongside behavioral change. In its 2017 annual report, the Global Ecovillage Network said about ten thousand ecological communities are in 114 countries.[50] By working together in local communities according to local needs, people are trying to create a true reset based on empathy and reason; after all, the idea goes back to the medieval commons, which was the essential communal economic form until the eighteenth century. The word comes from the Old Norse word *almenningr*, which means "what belongs to everyone." Thus, the commons was that part of the community's property that all community members could use. Even then, people were trying to combine community and ecological thinking. In his book *Humankind*, Bregman cites examples from many nations of how true democracy can succeed, especially in such smaller communities, once residents are allowed to govern themselves.[51] "It may not be breaking news," Bregman writes, "but since then the [medieval] commons has made a spectacular comeback."[52]

This development does not surprise Tine de Moor of the Netherlands, because "history teaches us," writes the professor of Social Enterprise and Institutions for Collective Action at Erasmus University Rotterdam, "that man is essentially a cooperative being, a *homo cooperans*."[53] In an academic article, she speaks of a "Silent Revolution" and offers "A New Perspective on the Emergence of Commons, Guilds, and Other Forms of Corporate Collective Action in Western Europe."[54]

The immense importance attached to this revolution is evidenced by the fact that the former US professor of political science and world leader in the field of environmental economics, Elinor Ostrom (1933–2012), was awarded the Nobel Prize in Economics in 2009 "for her analysis of economic governance, especially the commons."[55] In her Nobel Prize acceptance speech, entitled "Beyond Markets and States: Polycentric Management of Complex Economic Systems," Ostrom showed that communities (commons) function as a third economic force, not to be underestimated, alongside the state and the market.[56] This means that, in contrast to global and centrally controlled developments, we need local solutions to local challenges. Contrary to the threatening and in some cases advanced development of a worldwide uniform culture, we need more cultural diversity, not less. This ecological movement toward more local community, which began decades before the current permacrisis, has been given a tremendous boost by it, which could ultimately help it to adapt worldwide. It may be the seed of a cultural revolution.

However, for this natural grassroots movement (i.e., initiatives that come primarily from private individuals and emerge from below, so to speak, initially without any formal organizational at all) to prevail against the dictates of the technocrats and become a globally sustainable organizational model of human life, we must always cultivate our competence in rational compassion in addition to locally valuable empathy. This means always being aware that all people (no matter where they live) have the same basic human needs and interests as we do. Hence the title of de Moor's inaugural lecture at Utrecht University in 2013, *Homo Cooperans. Institutions for Collective Action and the [Rationally] Compassionate Society*—with the emphasis on *compassionate*.[57]

In such village communities live the people whom Auken, in her vision of the AI-controlled technocracy, might consider pitiful because they have to think for themselves. I don't feel sorry for them, because I think it's important that we are still allowed or obliged to think for ourselves.

We should dare to have more multigenerational families living together. The traditional extended family has its advantages: on one hand, there is no need for day-care centers and retirement homes, which of course saves money; on the other hand, both the youngest and the oldest in the family are given a place, and an important part of valuable life is made possible in the family community. As a result, all family members are less dependent on the super-father state or the technocracy.

Of course, this kind of social collaboration and extended-family coexistence can work in urban communities as well, if the will is there. Interesting in this context is an MIT report on Toronto's exit from the smart-city concept:

> "The smart city has been perhaps the dominant paradigm in urban planning over the past two decades. The term was originally coined by IBM in hopes that technology could improve the way cities functioned, but as a strategy for city-building, it's been most successfully deployed under authoritarian regimes (Putin is a fan). Critics say it tends to overlook the importance of human beings in the quest for technological solutions. Even when the architectural renderings were fabulous, the idea of the smart city has always had problems. The phrase itself suggests that existing cities are lacking in brain power, even though they have—throughout human history—been incubators for culture, ideas, and intellect.[58]

With that, the MIT article goes on to point out the real problem, which is "that with their emphasis on the optimization of everything, smart cities seem designed to eradicate the very thing that makes cities wonderful." After all, "New York, Rome, and Cairo (and Toronto) are not great cities because they're efficient: people are attracted to the messiness, to the compelling and serendipitous interactions within a wildly diverse mix of people living in close proximity." But instead, smart-city advocates have "embraced instead the idea of the city as something to be quantified and controlled." One can only hope that more cities will eschew the technocratically smart concept that robs people their smartness sense and purpose in life.

Exercise, Sleep, and Time

The areas of exercise and sleep in the Hippocampal Anti-Indoctrination Formula are also of immense importance to hippocampal neurogenesis. As mentioned in chapter 2, just one hour of walking a day is enough to stimulate the necessary hippocampal growth hormones and ultimately promote healthy sleep. Those who garden in a community project, for example, not only get enough physical exercise but also provide themselves and their families with untreated, homegrown fruits and vegetables, thus ecologically ensuring a healthy diet. It is hard to kill more birds with one stone. Such a combination of different areas of the formula also saves a lot of time, of course, and is a major reason why our Paleolithic ancestors most likely worked less and had more free time than we do. This can still be seen today in hunter-gatherer societies.[59]

Nutrition

Whole books can be written about a brain-friendly diet, as I and many others have done. However, it is necessary to make such a diet available to *all* the people who currently populate our planet and will continue to do so, if we are to stop destroying nature and simultaneously regenerate it. We know, as reported in chapter 2, that there are no longer enough fish, and therefore not enough aquatic omega-3 fatty acids, to ensure healthy physical and mental development for all people and to keep everyone healthy into old age. One solution is offered by *The Algae Oil Revolution*, one of my books in which I describe a viable way to solve this global problem.[60] In an ecologically sound way, we could use microalgae to produce the essential aquatic fatty acids for the world's needs, while ending environmentally destructive large-scale fishing.

Because there are good vegan sources for all other essential micronutrients (vitamins and trace elements) that neither the hippocampus nor our entire organism can do without, the only remaining nutritional question is how we can manage to supply all people with sufficient macronutrients in an equally environmentally friendly way. To put it bluntly, insects as an alternative protein source to factory-farmed meat is not an option, even though the European Commission (EU) has approved it for several insect species.[61] The origin of this ecologically and healthily questionable development, which is now enshrined in EU legislation and which, according to a 2022 survey, will spoil the appetite of about 80 percent of Germans, is the WEF with its climate agenda. As the *New York Post* reports, "Warnings like 'an extinction of large parts of our global population' were shared from center stage, and bugs have gradually been championed as one solution to the climate crisis"—as an alternative source of protein to factory-farmed meat.[62] However, because insects need raw materials to thrive, they are always only partially converted into animal protein. This cannot be a reasonable way to go, especially since there are many reasonable alternatives.

Of all the macronutrients that provide us with energy, among other things, proteins are the most important because our organism can synthesize both sugars and fatty acids from them. Conversely, this works only to a limited extent or not at all with the essential amino acids (EAA for short). We have to take these in with our food to be able to build up the body's own proteins. The amount of EAA in a protein source is therefore crucial. When comparing foods, it therefore makes sense to look not only at the amount of protein, but above all at the EAA content. This is also very suitable for comparatively evaluating the ecological footprint of the protein production or protein source.[63] By *footprint*, I mean not only carbon dioxide, which is the subject of particular political attention, but also water consumption, the need for agricultural land, and the length of transport routes.

An easy and vegan alternative to animal meat, fish, and insects are legumes such as lentils, peas, and beans. Many are rich in protein, which is also rich in EAA. However, unbeatable in terms of ecological value, as demonstrated in my book *The Algae Oil Revolution*, are single-celled microalgae. These could be used to supply all the people in the world without exception. An example of a very undemanding, robust, and extremely nutrient-rich microalgae is *Nannochloropsis oculata* (*Nanno* for short). This single-cell plant could be grown practically anywhere, even in places in the global South where there is hunger today. The comparison with conventional meat production is impressive: to produce one kilogram of EAA from beef requires about 148,000 liters of fresh water. *Nanno*, on the other hand, requires only 20 liters of water, a factor of 7,400.[64] Considering the increasing scarcity of fresh water worldwide, this would be an enormous savings. There is also a significant difference in land requirements: to produce one kilogram of EAA from beef, about 125 square meters of fertile land are needed, whereas *Nanno* requires only 1.5 square meters of land. Because the microalga grows in sun-flooded glass containers, it does not take up any valuable agricultural land, so its micro- and macronutrients could even be produced in desert areas. If the full potential of microalgae such as *Nanno* were realized, it would be possible to stop clearing forests to create new agricultural land and instead replant trees. They do not even leave a carbon footprint; on the contrary, microalgae feed directly on carbon dioxide and even reduce the concentration of this gas in the atmosphere, while cattle farming does exactly the opposite by releasing methane and carbon dioxide.[65] Last but not least, *Nanno* also contains many other valuable micronutrients—and what cannot be consumed provides valuable humus. For all these reasons, the future could belong to this sustainable way of vegan food production.

Purpose in Life

This war is a war over knowledge, which the technocrats are trying to win with their narratives. Hence the censorship, the vilification of alternative interpretations and their interpreters, and the insanity that man no longer needs vitamin D, even in a state of deficiency (a contradiction in itself). Therefore, the first step toward winning this war is to expose the obvious errors in the narratives. But this can only be done by accepting that an essential aspect of human life is to gain hippocampal experience and to use the experiential knowledge to protect oneself and those entrusted to one's care (see also "Evolution of the Grandmother" in chapter 2). New knowledge also holds the power to make a difference by making better choices. However, this requires us to be critical and to seek alternative perspectives and sources of information. The best source is scientific evidence. Science, however, is not a stable source of undoubted knowledge, because it is sometimes influenced by secondary interests. We even know that a large part of active research does not produce correct and reliable publications, as already explained by the Greek-American health scientist John P. A. Ioannidis (one of the world's most renowned statisticians) in 2005 in his article "Why Most Published Research Findings Are False."[66] Often, economic interests tempt researchers to do favors for their industry funders, to the detriment of us all.

After a lecture on this problem, I was once asked how a layman could still inform himself under these circumstances, if he did not want to fall for the often one-sided (and possibly erroneous) research and its interpretation by technocratic propaganda. This is indeed difficult. The only option I can see is to seek information from industry-independent researchers to get a diverse opinion on a topic. Again, this requires a certain amount of trust, since no one can be an expert in everything these days, and it also takes some time—but it is worth it, as I know from my own experience.

For example, in some of my earlier books I referred to manmade climate change. I was completely unthinkingly accepting the opinion that our mainstream media and the selected experts had been presenting to us for decades. When several readers pointed this out to me and recommended scientific studies and books by climate experts, who of course do not have a say in the public media, I recognized the error of my credulity in this regard. The COVID-19 staging made me more aware of the fact that the mainstream media is not to be trusted outright, but it was only those readers who prompted me to look for alternative interpretations in this other area (although the two issues seem closely related). Since there is no real climate debate in this sense, I was amazed to find, for the first time, information outside the public discourse that seemed quite plausible and worthy of discussion. I came to the conclusion that the little time one has to inform oneself should not be spent on the propagandistic news of the mainstream media but rather on the search for and analysis of alternative information. Granted, not all that glitters is gold, but at least you'll find more food for thought and less to be afraid of.

The News Deprived

"Imagine the news is coming and no one is watching," writes German communications expert Michael Meyen in the magazine *ViER* (meaning "four"), in reference to real journalism, the Fourths Power in the state.[67] In his article, Meyen refers to a study by the University of Zurich, which found 38 percent of the Swiss refuse to listen to the mainstream news and are therefore considered to be undersupplied with information from the leading media. According to the University of Zurich press release, this is "problematic for a democracy, because people who are underserved with news are less interested in politics, less involved in the political process, and less trusting of political institutions."[68] But that's not quite true, because they still spend about seven minutes a day looking for information, albeit from alternative sources on the internet, and in doing so they destroy the interpretive authority of the leading media.

With their alternative knowledge, they are already influencing elections in Switzerland, where they mostly vote against what the mainstream media would like them to vote for. For example, in a referendum on a ban on tobacco advertising in February 2022, where the "news deprived" tipped the scales, as Meyen reports. Seven minutes a day isn't much, but it's enough to find some useful information on the internet that didn't make it into the newspapers, at least as long as censorship still has some limits. Of course, there is no question that you can read nonsense on the internet. But as we know, this is not fundamentally better in newspapers, otherwise there would be no migration away from the mainstream news. You have to become a journalist of your own knowledge and at least look at two or three different sources, read or listen to different opinions and use your own mind to classify them, because, as Meyen says, "Journalism is dead. It died with or of COVID-19, after a long decay. Even before that, the Fourth Power was seriously ill, incapacitated and infected with politics on an industrial drip. The virus only gave the patient the final blow. In its demise, the mainstream media fights to the death anyone who might take over its work. It is banned, slandered, censored and deleted. Those who ask the wrong questions are silenced."[69]

Even *before* the beginning of the COVID-19 pandemic and the accompanying accelerated decline in journalistic quality, Bregman expressed the opinion that we should avoid the mainstream news because the media does not serve us and divides people instead of uniting them: "Watching the evening news may leave you feeling more attuned to reality, but the truth is that it skews your view of the world. The news tend to generalize people . . . Worse, the news zooms in on the bad apples."[70] And Bregman sees the same problem with social media: "What starts as a couple of bullies spewing hate speech at a distance gets pushed by algorithms on the top of our Facebook and Twitter feeds. It's by tapping into our negativity bias that these digital platforms make their money, turning higher profits the worse people behave." Not only does this create a false image of humanity, but it also gives us a one-sided picture of the danger and the possible solutions. Furthermore, it takes too much of our precious life time to process this nonsense. And what's worse, it makes us mentally ill.[71]

The purpose of the lifelong expansion of our knowledge, which a healthy hippocampus enables us to do, is to implement the newly acquired, meaningful knowledge in our own lives and also to pass it on to others. This is particularly relevant in this ongoing war against our mental freedom. Share knowledge with those who are already fighting on our side and especially with those who still need to be convinced. This is where the strength and multiple functionalities of the hippocampus are needed, but it should be worth it. According to the Vaccination Dashboard of the German Federal Ministry of Health, as of April 8, 2023, about 18.4 million people in Germany have not yet been "vaccinated" against COVID-19.[72] This corresponds to 22.1 percent of the German population who apparently withstood the indoctrination efforts and did not convert to the belief in the holy vaccination (although surely some "vaccinated" people did not actually convert, but felt compelled to be inoculated for various reasons). Surprisingly, this corresponds to the 23 percent of subjects in Solomon Asch's conformity experiment who ignored the group's false opinion rather than the truth (see "Conformity at All Costs" in chapter 4). However, the pressure to conform, which involved only a judgment about the length of a line, was much less than the pressure to "inoculate," where the stakes for nonconforming behavior, such as freedom, were much higher—making this high percentage all the more surprising!

Let us further assume that a similar percentage of people are slowly but surely realizing that they have been badly played and are falling away from the faith or have already fallen away. This assumption is supported by the fact that, according to the German Vaccination Dashboard, only 62.6 percent of those vaccinated have received the first booster shot and only 15.2 percent of those vaccinated have received the second booster shot. This means that even now, as I write this in the spring of 2023, more than half of the people may already realize that this health dictatorship was never about protecting their health. And at least a portion of that group should be receptive to the broader circumstantial evidence I have presented here, which suggests that it was more about indoctrination as part of a plan for a great upheaval. With luck, a hopefully ever-growing jury will reach the necessary critical mass (which need not be a majority of all humans) to address existing grievances and align social development with the pillars of species-appropriate living and hippocampal health for all. It is now necessary to convey that we all face the great and extremely acute danger that, after the upheaval is complete, we will live under totalitarian conditions or be governed by humans and their machine and digital minions who have stepped over corpses and will most likely continue to do so in order to gain or retain power.

Assuming that each of these critical people can inform or convince only one or two other people in their own environment, the situation will quickly change in our favor. Those who want to create a diverse culture of mutual understanding and coexistence could win any political election with a theoretically conceivable 50 to 75 percent, assuming, of course, that there is a party that has not already been infiltrated by YGLs or other emissaries of the other side and thus proves to be actually electable. The problem with representative democracy is that politicians are beholden only to their "conscience," not to the promises on which they were elected. If a new party was formed, perhaps its members could commit themselves to empathic-rational humanism and thus address all of our society's challenges through the application of healthy empathy and rational compassion. But even without a common party, millions of courageous people could march as a people's movement for the enforcement of their human ideals, and thus strike fear into the hearts of the still-ruling stooges of the technocrats. Nothing is as dangerous to the rulers as public opinion!

However, getting out of your comfort zone is essential for positive change. It requires some mental strength and also involves certain risks, which is why we need civil courage. But there is no other way than to take action if we want to escape the dystopia described. Remember, the constant dripping wears away the stone. If we stop trying to avoid uncomfortable conversations and instead clearly state the danger that threatens us, we have a good chance of success. We are not dependent on the methodology of indoctrination and manipulation but can convince with hard facts that such influences are taking place. We do not want people to believe anything in particular; rather, each person should develop his or her own perspective and subsequently realize that this is precisely what is not desired in the current system. As a result, they will understand that we can only succeed if we stand together for a profound right to individuality and the protection of the basic prerequisite for the development of strong, independent personalities. In doing so, we must also believe in success and, above all, in ourselves, in the belief that the cooperative power and social capacity of human nature will defeat the technocratic mechanisms of oppression, both spiritual and material. This faith in the strength of our own nature begins with the simple but far-reaching realization that we do not need genetic "vaccinations" to successfully protect ourselves against respiratory viruses. We can internalize that such respiratory infections are usually harmless if we are adequately supplied with micronutrients. We can rely on our natural immunity and do not need to expose ourselves to such a "vaccination" with side effects.

Our organism is a highly efficient product of billions of years of evolutionary optimization. Given for species-appropriate, meaningful life, our brains reach their maximum efficiency. And just as our immune system fends off viral attacks, our brain will deal with technocratic whispers. After all, it will not be the first mental grip that humanity has broken. It can do it again—but only if we band together!

Concluding Remarks

Man, like any other living being, is a fantastic product of evolution. However, unlike unicellular yeasts and microalgae, humans are capable of self-reflection, empathy, rational compassion, and learning. This advantage, however, can easily become a disadvantage: as we have now seen, all cultural (mis)developments are based on that the misuse by individual groups, mostly so-called elites, of these positive characteristics for the purpose of developing their power. Bregman writes, "In fact, you could look at the entire evolution of civilization as a history of rulers who continually devised new justifications [narratives] for their privileges."[73] The most fatal narrative man has been indoctrinated with is that he is a fatal aberration of nature. But that's simply not true, and it would be a shame if humans were to disappear from the earth, explains philosopher Michael Schmidt-Salomon, because "the biological and cultural development of our species shows that we have the potential to become better and better, more and more 'humane.'"[74] "More humane" is in the sense that we are returning to our still unbiased view of the world before we succumbed to cultural indoctrination.

Ultimately, we have no choice but to resist being forced into a certain worldview, and time is of the essence. If we do not address this issue, it will come to pass, as the French novelist and journalist George Bernanos (1888–1948) once envisioned, "Then it will not be cruelty that is responsible for our extinction, and of course even less the indignation that cruelty arouses, or the retaliations and acts of vengeance that will grow out of it . . . but weakness, the lack of responsibility of modern man, his false submissive acceptance of any order from above."[75] Bernanos continues: "The horrors that we have seen, the still greater horrors we shall presently see, are not signs that rebels, insubordinate, untamable men are increasing in number throughout the world, but rather that there is a constant increase in the number of obedient, docile men."

So we need to rethink if we are going to evolve as a society in a way that preserves our individuality and our environment. If we do not do this, others will realize their own visions, but diametrically opposed to our interests. This *poly-crisis*, as the WEF calls the current state in which the whole of humanity finds itself, is our great opportunity to take a cultural step that begins with a new image of human nature and, in contrast to the vision of the Great Reset, entails a genuine evolution of human coexistence. In the process, we should understand that human nature is basically good, and a society of the future should be based on this premise. This change of attitude would cost the powerful much of their power over us, and it would also make our lives much more pleasant. Our destiny and our values are in our own hands. If we follow the principle of human autonomy and implement it in our lives, we will become stronger, and together we can venture into a new culture of cooperative, altogether considerate coexistence that respects the realities of our natural needs and the environment. Therefore, there is still a chance that all will end well.

ENDNOTES

INTRODUCTION

1 Elizabeth Flock, "'Curveball,' Man Who Lied about WMDs, Comes Clean," *Washington Post*, April 3, 2012, https://www.washingtonpost.com/blogs/blogpost/post/curveball-man-who-lied-about-wmds-comes-clean/2012/04/03/gIQAUdditS_blog.html.

2 T. J. Dunning, *Trade Unions and Strikes: Their Philosophy and Intention* (London: self-pub., 1860), 36, https://archive.org/details/tradesunionsstri00dunnrich/page/n3/mode/2up?view=theater.

3 World Economic Forum, *The Global Risks Report 2023*, 18th ed. (Geneva: World Economic Forum, January 2023), 35, https://www3.weforum.org/docs/WEF_Global_Risks_Report_2023.pdf.

4 "How WHO Is Funded," World Health Organization, accessed April 28, 2023, https://www.who.int/about/funding.

5 "'The Great Reset': Wie das Wef ins Zentrum aller Verschwörungstheorien Geriet," *Handelszeitung*, November 20, 2020, https://www.handelszeitung.ch/politik/the-great-reset-wie-das-wef-ins-zentrum-aller-verschworungstheorien-geriet.

6 The Royal Family, "#The Great Reset," June 3, 2020, YouTube video, 1:56, https://www.youtube.com/watch?v=hRPQqfwwuhU.

7 Chloe Taylor, "Coronavirus Crisis Presents a 'Golden Opportunity' to Reboot the Economy, Prince Charles Says," CNBC, June 3, 2020, https://www.cnbc.com/2020/06/03/prince-charles-covid-19-a-golden-opportunity-to-reboot-the-economy.html.

8 Aaron Wherry, "The 'Great Reset' Reads Like a Globalist Plot with Some Plot Holes," CBC, November 27, 2020, https://www.cbc.ca/news/politics/great-reset-trudeau-poilievre-otoole-pandemic-covid-1.5817973; Global News, "Coronavirus: Trudeau Tells UN Conference That the Pandemic Provided 'Opportunity for a Reset,'" September 29, 2020, YouTube video, 6:11, https://www.youtube.com/watch?v=n2fp0Jeyjvw.

9 "Scholz Kündigt Grössten Umbruch Seit 100 Jahren an—und Sagt: 'Danke, Frau Doktor Merkel,'" *Stern*, December 15, 2021, https://www.stern.de/politik/deutschland/kanzler-olaf-scholz-stimmt-deutschland-auf-groessten-umbruch-seit-100-jahren-ein-31424536.html.

10 Philipp Saul, "Dieser Grosse Umbruch Wird Gut Ausgehen," *Süddeutsche Zeitung,* March 16, 2023, https://www.sueddeutsche.de/politik/scholz-eu-bundestag-1.5769999.

11 "'The Great Reset,'" *Handelszeitung.*

12 Klaus Schwab and Thierry Malleret, *COVID-19: The Great Reset* (Geneva: Forum Publishing, 2020).

13 European Commission, "Health-EU Newsletter 240—Focus," European Union, September 12, 2019, https://health.ec.europa.eu/other-pages/basic-page/health-eu-newsletter-240-focus_en.; "Johns Hopkins Center for Health Security, World Health Forum and Bill & Melinda Gates Foundation Host Live-Streamed Pandemic Preparedness Excercise," Business Wire, October 16, 2019, https://www.businesswire.com/news/home/20191016005962/de/.

14 Mattias Desmet, *The Psychology of Totalitarianism* (White River Junction, VT: Chelsea Green Publishing, 2022), cover text.

15 John Mac Ghlionn, "America Is in a State of Mass Formation Paralysis," *The Spectator,* January 8, 2022, https://spectatorworld.com/topic/america-state-mass-formation-paralysis/.

16 Francis Crick and Christof Koch, "A Framework for Consciousness," *Nature Neuroscience* 6, no. 2 (February 2003): 119–26, https://doi.org/10.1038/nn0203-119.

17 Ida Auken, "Welcome to 2030. I Own Nothing, Have No Privacy, and Life Has Never Been Better," World Economic Forum, November 11, 2016, https://web.archive.org/web/20161125135500/https://www.weforum.org/agenda/2016/11/shopping-i-can-t-really-remember-what-that-is.

18 Agnieszka Golec de Zavala, "Collective Narcissism and In-Group Satisfaction Are Associated with Different Emotional Profiles and Psychological Wellbeing," *Frontiers in Psychology* 10 (February 14, 2019): 203, https://doi.org/10.3389/fpsyg.2019.00203; Aline Vater, Steffen Moritz, and Stefan Roepke, "Does a Narcissism Epidemic Exist in Modern Western Societies? Comparing Narcissism and Self-Esteem in East and West Germany," *PLoS One* 13, no. 1 (January 2018): https://doi.org/10.1371/journal.pone.0188287.

19 "How to Ensure the Benefits of 'Creative Destruction' Are Shared by All," World Economic Forum, August 31, 2021, https://intelligence.weforum.org/monitor/latest-knowledge/5f148e06f3e14966b999ad8db09d670e.

20 Aldous Huxley, *Brave New World,* https://www.studocu.com/en-us/document/caldwell-university/intro-to-philosphy/huxley-brave-new-world/11540325 p. 51.

CHAPTER 1

1 Michael Nehls, *Das Erschöpfte Gehirn: Der Ursprung Unserer Mentalen Energie—und Warum Sie Schwindet—Willenskraft, Kreativität und Fokus Zurückgewinnen* (Munich: Heyne Verlag, 2022).

2 Klaus Schwab and Thierry Malleret, *COVID-19: Der Grosse Umbruch* (Geneva: World Economic Forum, 2021).

3 Ida Auken, "Welcome to 2030. I Own Nothing, Have No Privacy, and Life Has Never Been Better," World Economic Forum, November 11, 2016, https://web.archive.org/web/20161125135500/https://www.weforum.org/agenda/2016/11/shopping-i-can-t-really-remember-what-that-is.
4 C. E. Nyder, *Young Global Leaders: Die Saat des Klaus Schwab* (Rottenburg, Germany: Kopp Verlag, 2022), 10.
5 George Orwell, *1984* (New York: Penguin Books, 1982). First published 1949 by Secker & Warburg (London).
6 Nicoletta Lanese, "Scientists Design Algorithm That 'Reads' People's Thoughts from Brain Scans," *LiveScience* (website), October 24, 2022, https://www.livescience.com/algorithm-mind-reading-from-fmri.
7 Yu Takagi and Shinji Nishimoto, "High-Resolution Image Reconstruction with Latent Diffusion Models from Human Brain Activity," *bioRxiv* (forthcoming). https://www.biorxiv.org/content/10.1101/2022.11.18.517004v2.
8 J. D. Rucker, "Elon Musk Is a Former Klaus Schwab WEF Young Global Leader," April 16, 2022, in *America Out Loud Podcast Network, podcast*, https://www.imdb.com/title/tt20309596.
9 Tim Urban, "Neuralink and the Brain's Magical Future," *Wait but Why* (website), April 20, 2017, https://waitbutwhy.com/2017/04/neuralink.html.
10 Schwab and Malleret, *COVID-19*.
11 https://www.youtube.com/watch?v=iPJqOBSrBDU. Posted on June 28, 2022, removed from YouTube; but the audible version can be found here: https://kaisertv.de/2022/06/28/wer-vitamin-d-nimmt-braucht-keine-impfung-dr-michael-nehls-im-gesprach/ (56:27)
12 William B. Grant et al., "Evidence That Vitamin D Supplementation Could Reduce Risk of Influenza and COVID-19 Infections and Deaths," *Nutrients* 12, no. 4 (April 2020): 988, https://doi.org/10.3390.nu12040988.
13 Ashu Rastogi et al., "Short Term, High-Dose Vitamin D Supplementation for COVID-19 Disease: A Randomised, Placebo-Controlled, Study (SHADE Study)," *Postgraduate Medical Journal* 98, no. 1156 (February 2022): 87–90, https://doi.org/10.1136/postgradmedj-2020-139065.
14 Hermann Brenner and Ben Schöttker, "Vitamin D Insufficiency May Account for Almost Nine of Ten COVID-19 Deaths: Time to Act. Comment on: 'Vitamin D Deficiency and Outcome of COVID-19 Patients.'" *Nutrients* 12, no. 12 (December 2020): 3642, https://doi.org/10.3390/nu12123642.
15 Lorenz Borsche, Bernd Glauner, and Julian von Mendel, "COVID-19 Mortality Risk Correlates Inversely with Vitamin D3 Status, and a Mortality Rate Close to Zero Could Theoretically Be Achieved at 50 ng/mL 25(OH)D3: Results of a Systematic Review and Meta-Analysis," *Nutrients* 13, no. 10 (October 2021): 3596, https://doi.org/10.3390/nu13103596.
16 Marta Entrenas Castillo et al., "Effect of Calcifediol Treatment and Best Available Therapy versus Best Available Therapy on Intensive Care Unit Admission and

Mortality among Patients Hospitalized for COVID-19: A Pilot Randomized Clinical Study," *Journal of Steroid Biochemistry and Molecular Biology* 203 (October 2020): 105751, https://doi.org/10.1016/j.jsbmb.2020.105751; Irwin Jungreis and Manolis Kellis, "Mathematical Analysis of Córdoba Calcifediol Trial Suggests Strong Role for Vitamin D in Reducing ICU Admissions of Hospitalized COVID-19 Patients," *medRxiv* (forthcoming), https://www.medrxiv.org/content/10.1101/2020.11.08.20222638v1/; Juan F. Alcala-Diaz et al., "Calcifediol Treatment and Hospital Mortality Due to COVID-19: A Cohort Study," *Nutrients* 13, no. 6 (June 2021): 1760, https://doi.org/10.3390/nu13061760; Xavier Nogues et al., "Calcifediol Treatment and COVID-19-Related Outcomes," *Journal of Clinical Endocrinology and Metabolism* 106, no. 10 (September 2021): 4017–27, https://doi.org/10.1210/clinem/dgab405.

17 Dr. Nehls, "Ist Vitamin D Völlig Unnütz? Eine Analyse," September 19, 2022, YouTube video, 38:42, https://www.youtube.com/watch?v=1PvkvfJqcSQ; Akademie für Menschliche Medizin, "Corona und Vitamin D–Hilft das Sonnenhormon doch Nicht?! Prof. Dr. Jörg Spitz & Dr. Michael Nehls," August 5, 2022, YouTube video, 45:43, https://www.youtube.com/watch?v=fRQI8fXHCJE.

18 Karl Lauterbach, Twitter, September 8, 2020, https://twitter.com/karl_lauterbach/status/1303266098901643266?lang=de.

19 "Karl Lauterbach Betont Wichtigkeit Allgemeiner Impfpflicht," *Zeit Online*, January 8, 2022, https://www.zeit.de/politik/deutschland/2022-01/corona-massnahmen-karl-lauterbach-allgemeine-impfpflicht.

20 Michael Nehls et al., "New Member of the Winged-Helix Protein Family Disrupted in Mouse and Rat Nude Mutations," *Nature* 372, no. 6501 (November 3, 1994): 103–7, https://doi.org/10.1038/372103a0; Michael Nehls et al., "Two Genetically Separable Steps in the Differentiation of Thymic Epithelium," *Science* 272, no. 5263 (May 10, 1996): 886–89, https://doi.org/10.1126/science.272.5263.886.

21 "Klaus Schwab: Bis 2026 Sollen Wir Alle Gechipt Sein," *Transition News* (website), May 10, 2021, https://transition-news.org/bis-2026-sollen-wir-alle-gechipt-sein.

22 "Digitaler Impfpass Immer Dabei: Schweden Lassen Sich Mikrochip unter die Haut Implantieren," *Stern*, December 22, 2021, https://www.stern.de/gesellschaft/digitaler-impfpass--schweden-lassen-sich-mikrochip-implantieren-31446566.html.

23 United Nations, "Transforming Our World: The 2030 Agenda for Sustainable Development," accessed January 23, 2023, https://sdgs.un.org/publications/transforming-our-world-2030-agenda-sustainable-development-17981; "Ziele der Agenda 2030," Bundeskanzleramt, accessed May 6, 2023, https://www.bundeskanzleramt.gv.at/themen/nachhaltige-entwicklung-agenda-2030/entwicklungsziele-agenda-2030.html.

24 World Bank Group, "Identification for Development," accessed January 23, 2023, https://www.worldbank.org/content/dam/Worldbank/Governance/GGP%20ID4D%20flyer.pdf.

25 "Digitaler Impfpass Immer Dabei," *Stern*.

26 Kevin McHugh et al., "Biocompatible Near-Infrared Quantum Dots Delivered to the Skin by Microneedle Patches Record Vaccination, Science Translational Medicine 11, no. 523 (2019): https://doi.org/10.1126/scitranslmed.aay7162.
27 "Immunization: The Basics," Centers for Disease Control and Prevention, accessed May 6, 2023, http://web.archive.org/web/20210826113846/https://www.cdc.gov/vaccines/vac-gen/imz-basics.htm.
28 "Immunization: The Basics," Centers for Disease Control and Prevention, accessed January 16, 2023, https://www.cdc.gov/vaccines/vac-gen/imz-basics.htm.
29 "Israel Hopes Boosters Can Avert New Lockdown as COVID Vaccine Efficacy Fades," *Financial Times*, August 23, 2021, https://www.ft.com/content/23cdbf8c-b5ef-4596-bb46-f510606ab556.
30 Techno Fog [pseud.],"CDC Emails: Our Definition of Vaccine Is 'Problematic,'" *The Reactionary*, November 2, 2021, https://technofog.substack.com/p/cdc-emails-our-definition-of-vaccine?justPublished=true.
31 https://www.studocu.com/en-us/document/caldwell-university/intro-to-philosphy/huxley-brave-new-world/11540325p. 6.
32 Ibid., 13.
33 Ibid., 14.
34 Ibid., 14–15.
35 Ibid., 249.
36 Ibid., 247.
37 Ibid.
38 Ibid., 103–104.
39 Ibid., 30.
40 Ibid., 16.
41 Ibid., 42.
42 Ibid., 264.
43 Ibid., 245.
44 Ibid., 51.
45 Richard Florida, *The Great Reset: How the Post-Crash Economy Will Change the Way We Live and Work* (New York: Harper, 2011), cover text.
46 Gerry Allan, "Do We Have 'Creative Destruction,' or Just Plain 'Destruction?'" AI-eCoach (website), July 12, 2022, https://ai-ecoach.com/do-we-have-creative-destruction-or-just-plain-destruction/.
47 Michael Maier, "Scholz Sagt Ukraine in Davos Deutsche Unterstützung Zu," *Berliner Zeitung*, January 18, 2023, https://www.berliner-zeitung.de/wirtschaft-verantwortung/scholz-pandemie-ist-noch-nicht-vorbei-li.308386.
48 Cedric C. S. Tan et al., "Transmission of SARS-CoV-2 from Humans to Animals and Potential Host Adaptation," *Nature Communications* 13 (May 27, 2022): https://doi.org/10.1038/s41467-022-30698-6.
49 Wikispooks, s.v. "WEF/Global Leaders for Tomorrow," last modified March 24, 2023, 16:30, https://wikispooks.com/wiki/WEF/Global_Leaders_for_Tomorrow#Vladimir_Putin.

50 Wladimir Kaminer, "Jetzt Sitzt Sein Regime in der Falle," *t-online*, January 16, 2023, https://www.t-online.de/nachrichten/ukraine/id_100110824/militaerexperte-zu-moeglichem-kriegsende-putins-regime-sitzt-in-der-falle.html.
51 "WEF Young Global Leaders—die Liste der Deutschen Teilnehmer," *Business Leaders* (website), June 12, 2022, https://www.business-leaders.net/wef-young-global-leaders-die-liste-der-deutschen-teilnehmer/.
52 Christian Spöcker and Björn Widmann, "Kritik nach Ukraine-Äusserungen: Was Hat Baerbock Wirklich Gesagt?" *SWR3* (website), September 3, 2023, https://www.swr3.de/aktuell/nachrichten/baerbock-waehler-ukraine-100.html.
53 Florian Neuhann, "Hat Baerbock Russland den Krieg Erklärt?" *ZDF* (website), January 26, 2023, https://www.zdf.de/nachrichten/politik/annalena-baerbock-kriegserklaerung-ukraine-krieg-russland-100.html.
54 Arnaud Boehman, "The Case for Going to War against Climate Change," *Bulletin of the Atomic Scientists*, December 20, 2021, https://thebulletin.org/2021/12/the-case-for-going-to-war-against-climate-change/.
55 "UK's Prince Charles says Coronavirus Reset Is a New Chance for Sustainability," Reuters, June 3, 2020, https://www.reuters.com/article/us-health-coronavirus-britain-royals-idUSKBN23A2AC.
56 Klaus Schwab and Thierry Malleret, *Das Grosse Narrativ: Für eine Bessere Zukunft* (Geneva: Forum Publishing, 2022), 102 (translated by the author).
57 https://www.studocu.com/en-us/document/caldwell-university/intro-to-philosphy/huxley-brave-new-world/11540325 p.53
58 Ibid., 250.
59 Naomi Wolf, *The Bodies of Others: The New Authoritarians, COVID-19 and The War against the Human* (Fort Lauderdale, FL: All Seasons Press, 2022), 4.
60 European Commission, "Health-EU Newsletter 240—Focus," European Union, September 12, 2019, https://health.ec.europa.eu/other-pages/basic-page/health-eu-newsletter-240-focus_en.
61 Meta, "Keeping People Safe and Informed about the Coronavirus," Working with Industry Partners, March 16, 2020, https://about.fb.com/news/2020/12/coronavirus/#joint-statement.
62 "Mark Zuckerberg," The Forum of Young Global Leaders, n.d., https://www.younggloballeaders.org/community?utf8=%E2%9C%93&q=Zuckerberg.
63 Ernst Wolff, "Deutschlands Eliten Erhalten Ausbildung Beim WEF: Die Kaderschmiede des Klaus Schwab," *Deutsche Wirtschaftsnachrichten*, August 8, 2021, https://deutsche-wirtschafts-nachrichten.de/513721/Deutschlands-Eliten-erhalten-Ausbildung-beim-WEF-Die-Kaderschmiede-des-Klaus-Schwab.
64 Wikispooks, s.v. "WEF/Young Global Leaders," last modified March 24, 2023, 16:14, https://wikispooks.com/wiki/WEF/Young_Global_Leaders.
65 "Rajiv Pant," World Economic Forum, accessed January 17, 2023, https://www.weforum.org/people/rajiv-pant.

66 The Forum of Young Global Leaders, "Maja Kuzmanovic Has Been Designated a Young Global Leader in 2006," press release, January 9, 2006, https://libarynth.org/_media/wef-ygl_press_release.pdf.

67 "5 Million YouTube Channels Canceled, 5.6 Million Videos Deleted," *Bangla* (website), https://digibanglatech.news/english/90149/.

68 https://www.studocu.com/en-us/document/caldwell-university/intro-to-philosphy/huxley-brave-new-world/11540325 53.

69 "What We Do," Project Syndicate, accessed January 17, 2023, https://www.project-syndicate.org/about.

70 "George Soros," World Economic Forum, accessed January 17, 2023, https://www.weforum.org/agenda/authors/georgesoros.

71 Peter Singer, "Why Vaccination Should Be Compulsory," Project Syndicate, August 4, 2021, https://www.project-syndicate.org/commentary/why-covid-vaccine-should-be-compulsory-by-peter-singer-2021-08.

72 "Jim Smith," World Economic Forum, accessed May 7, 2023, https://www.weforum.org/agenda/authors/jim-smith.

73 André Jasch, "Die Weltweite Einfluss von Bill Gates auf die Medien," *Deutsche Wirtschaftsnachrichten*, June 29, 2022, https://deutsche-wirtschafts-nachrichten.de/520644/Der-weltweite-Einfluss-von-Bill-Gates-auf-die-Medien; Gerd Roettig, "Bill Gates als Heimlicher Medienmogul," Telepolis (website), November 20, 2021, https://www.telepolis.de/features/Bill-Gates-als-heimlicher-Medienmogul-6273016.html.

74 Business Wire, "Johns Hopkins Center for Health Security, World Economic Forum and Bill & Melinda Gates Foundation Host Live-Streamed Pandemic Preparedness Excercise," October 16, 2019, https://www.businesswire.com/news/home/20191016005962/de/; "Tabletop Exercise: Event 201," Johns Hopkins Bloomberg School of Public Health, accessed February 27, 2023, https://www.centerforhealthsecurity.org/our-work/exercises/event201/.

75 Alberto Mingardi, "'Der Stakeholder-Kapitalismus' Ist Nur für die Managerkaste ein Besserer Kapitalismus," January 20, 2021, https://austrian-institute.org/de/blog/der-stakeholder-kapitalismus-ist-nur-fuer-die-managerkaste-ein-besserer-kapitalismus/.

76 Marcel Fratzcher, "Milliardäre Sind die Pandemiegewinner," Zeit Online, May 20, 2021, https://www.zeit.de/wirtschaft/2021-05/vermoegenskonzentration-corona-pandemie-ungleichheit-milliardaere-zunahme-reichtum-aktienmarkt.

77 "Biden's Build Back Better Agenda," Americans for Tax Fairness, October 18, 2021, https://americansfortaxfairness.org/issue/u-s-billionaires-wealth-surged-70-2-1-trillion-pandemic-now-worth-combined-5-trillion/.

78 John Hopkins Center for Health Security, "Event 201 Pandemic Exercise: Segment Five, Hotwash and Conclusion," November 4, 2019, YouTube video, 41:06, https://www.youtube.com/watch?v=0-_FAjNSd58. Forward to around the five-minute mark.

79 "Tabletop Exercise," Johns Hopkins.

80 Center for Health Security, "Statement about nCoV and Our Pandemic Exercise," accessed January 24, 2020, https://centerforhealthsecurity.org/2020/statement-about-ncov-and-our-pandemic-exercise-0.

81 "VAERS COVID Vaccine Adverse Event Reports," OpenVAERS, https://openvaers.com/covid-data. Data was taken from December 31, 2021.

82 Agency for Healthcare Research and Quality, *Electronic Support for Public Health—Vaccine Adverse Event Reporting System (ESP:VAERS)* (Rockville, MD: US Department of Health and Human Services, n.d.), https://digital.ahrq.gov/sites/default/files/docs/publication/r18hs017045-lazarus-final-report-2011.pdf

83 Katharina Röltgen et al., "Immune Imprinting, Breadth of Variant Recognition, and Germinal Center Response in Human SARS-CoV-2 Infection and Vaccination." *Cell* 185, no. 6 (January 25, 2022): 1025–40, https://doi.org/10.1016/j.cell.2022.01.018.

84 Michael Nehls, *Herdengesundheit: Der Weg aus der Corona-Krise und die Natürliche Alternative zum Globalen Impfprogramm* (n.p.: Mental Enterprises, 2022).

85 Margaret Menge, "Indiana Life Insurance CEO Says Deaths are Up 40% among People Ages 18–64," *Santa Barbara News-Press,* January 2, 2022, https://newspress.com/indiana-life-insurance-ceo-says-deaths-are-up-40-among-people-ages-18-64/; The Alex Jones Channel, "Insurance Deaths are Up 40% People 18–64 Scott Davison OneAmerica Indiana," January 3, 2022, YouTube video, 1:09, https://www.youtube.com/watch?v=Op6kKQzAoxc.

86 Destatis, "1.06 Millionen Sterbefälle im Jahr 2022," press release, January 10, 2023, https://www.destatis.de/DE/Presse/Pressemitteilungen/2023/01/PD22_012_126.html; Stephan Sander-Faes, "19% Übersterblichkeit in Deutschland im Dez. 2022 im Vergleich zum Vorjahr (mit Nachtrag)," *Tkp* (blog), https://tkp.at/2023/01/10/19-uebersterblichkeit-in-deutschland-2022/.

87 Jakob Simmank, "Der Heimliche WHO-Chef Heisst Bill Gates," *Zeit Online*, April 4, 2017, https://www.zeit.de/wissen/gesundheit/2017-03/who-unabhaengigkeit-bill-gates-film.

88 Thomas Kruchem, "Die WHO am Bettelstab: Was Gesund Ist, Bestimmt Bill Gates," September 4, 2020, https://www.swr.de/swr2/wissen/who-am-bettelstab-was-gesund-ist-bestimmt-bill-gates-100.html.

89 "One Health," World Health Organization, September 21, 2017, https://www.who.int/news-room/questions-and-answers/item/one-health.

90 Peter F. Mayer, "Enthüllt: WHO Will Änderungen der Internationalen Gesundheitsvorschriften Diese Woche in Geheimverhandlungen Beschliessen," *Tkp* (blog), January 10, 2023, https://tkp.at/2023/01/10/enthuellt-who-will-aenderungen-der-internationalen-gesundheitsvorschriften-diese-woche-in-geheimverhandlungen-beschliessen/.

91 David M. Herszenhorn, "Leaders Join Charles Michel's Push for Pandemic Treaty," *Politico*, March 30, 2021, https://www.politico.eu/article/leaders-join-charles-michels-push-for-pandemic-treaty/.

92 Magda von Garrel, "Die WHO-Ermächtigung," *Rubikon*, June 8, 2022, https://www.rubikon.news/artikel/die-who-ermachtigung.

93 World Health Organization, "Global Leaders Unite in Urgent Call for International Pandemic Treaty," March 30, 2021, https://www.who.int/news/item/30-03-2021-global-leaders-unite-in-urgent-call-for-international-pandemic-treaty.

94 Thomas Oysmüller, "Vorschlag für Epidemiegesetz: Entwurf für Deutsche Gesundheitsdiktatur," *Tkp* (blog), March 11, 2023, https://tkp.at/2023/03/11/vorschlag-fuer-epidemiegesetz-entwurf-fuer-deutsche-gesundheitsdiktatur/.

95 "Tracking the Situation of Children during COVID-19," UNICEF, November 2021, https://data.unicef.org/resources/rapid-situation-tracking-covid-19-socioeconomic-impacts-data-viz/. The page resource is an interactive and constantly updated page on the consequences of the corona pandemic for children.

96 Timothy Roberton et al., "Early Estimates of the Indirect Effects of the COVID-19 Pandemic on Maternal and Child Mortality in Low-Income and Middle-Income Countries: A Modelling Study," *Lancet Global Health* 8, no. 7 (May 12, 2020): https://doi.org/10.1016/s2214-109x(20)30229-1.

97 Health Effects Institute, *State of Global Air 2019* (Boston: Health Effects Institute, 2019), https://www.stateofglobalair.org/report.

98 "More Than 90% of the World's Children Breathe Toxic Air Every Day," World Health Organization, news release, October 29, 2018, https://www.who.int/news/item/29-10-2018-more-than-90-of-the-worlds-children-breathe-toxic-air-every-day.

99 "Vaccines and Pregnancy: 8 Things You Need to Know," Centers for Disease Control and Prevention, last medically reviewed April 18, 2023, https://www.cdc.gov/vaccines/pregnancy/pregnant-women/need-to-know.html.

100 Angelo Maria Pezzullo et al., "Age-Stratified Infection Fatality Rate of COVID-19 in the Non-Elderly Population," *Environmental Research* (January 1, 2023): https://www.ncbi.nlm.nih.gov/pmc/articles/PMC9613797/.

101 "VAERS COVID Vaccine Reproductive Health Related Reports," OpenVAERS, last updated June 2, 2023, accessed January 24, 2023, https://openvaers.com/covid-data/reproductive-health.

102 Jenna Greene, "'Paramount Importance': Judge Orders FDA to Hasten Release of Pfizer Vaccine Docs," Reuters, January 7, 2022, https://www.reuters.com/legal/government/paramount-importance-judge-orders-fda-hasten-release-pfizer-vaccine-docs-2022-01-07/.

103 Naomi Wolf, "Foreword to the Amazon Kindle Version of the War Room/DailyClout Pfizer Documents Analysis Reports eBook," DailyClout, January 21, 2023, https://dailyclout.io/foreword-to-the-amazon-kindle-version-of-the-war-room-dailyclout-pfizer-documents-analysis-reports/.

104 Serra Utkum Ikiz, "EctoLife—the World's First Artificial Womb Facility," Parametric Architecture, December 23, 2022, https://parametric-architecture.com/ectolife-the-worlds-first-artificial-womb-facility/.

105 GBD 2019 Diseases and Injuries Collaborators, "Global Burden of 369 Diseases and Injuries in 204 Countries and Territories, 1990–2019: A Systematic Analysis for the Global Burden of Disease Study 2019," *Lancet* 396, no. 10258 (October 17, 2020): 1204–1222, https://doi.org/10.1016/s0140-6736(20)30925-9.

106 Hani Choudhry and Md Nasrullah, "Iodine Consumption and Cognitive Performance: Confirmation of Adequate Consumption. *Food Science and Nutrition* 6, no. 6 (June 1, 2018): 1341–1351, https://pubmed.ncbi.nlm.nih.gov/30258574/.

107 Petra Plaum, "Immer Noch Oft Jodmangel in der Schwangerschaft—EU-Gefördertes Projekt Nimmt Politik und Ärzte in die Pflicht," *Medscape*, June 5, 2018, https://deutsch.medscape.com/artikelansicht/4907016.

108 B. G. Biban and C. Lichiardopol, "Iodine Deficiency, Still a Global Problem?" *Current Health Sciences Journal* 43, no. 2 (April-June 2017): 103–11, https://www.ncbi.nlm.nih.gov/pmc/articles/PMC6284174/.

109 F. Delange, "The Role of Iodine in Brain Development," *Proceedings of the Nutrition Society* 59, no. 1 (February 2000): 75–79, https://pubmed.ncbi.nlm.nih.gov/10828176/.

110 Jod," Deutsche Gesellschaft für Ernährung e.V., n.d., www.dge.de/wissenschaft/referenzwerte/jod.

111 World Health Organization, *Salt Reduction and Iodine Fortification Strategies in Public Health* (Geneva: World Health Organization, 2014), https://apps.who.int/iris/bitstream/handle/10665/101509/9789241506694_eng.pdf.

112 Wubet Worku Takele et al., "Two-Thirds of Pregnant Women Attending Antenatal Care Clinic at the University of Gondar Hospital Are Found with Subclinical Iodine Deficiency, 2017," *BMC Research Notes* 11 (2018): 738, https://www.ncbi.nlm.nih.gov/pmc/articles/PMC6192361/.

113 Charles Bitamazire Businge, Benjamin Longo-Mbenza, and Andre Pascal Kengne, "Iodine Nutrition Status in Africa: Potentially High Prevalence of Iodine Deficiency in Pregnancy Even in Countries Classified as Iodine Sufficient," *Public Health Nutrition* 24, no. 12 (August 2021): 3581–86, https://www.ncbi.nlm.nih.gov/pmc/articles/PMC8369456/.

114 Jakob Pallinger, "Schluss mit dem Heldenimage! Philanthropen Werden Unsere Welt Nicht Retten," *Der Standard*, April 11, 2021, https://www.derstandard.de/story/2000125169572/schluss-mit-dem-heldenimage-philanthropen-werden-unsere-welt-nicht-retten.

115 Wolf, *Bodies of Others*, 3.

116 Bundesministerium für Umwelt, Naturschutz, Bau, und Reaktorsicherheit, *Smart City Charta* (Bonn, Germany: Bundesinstitut für Bau-, Stadt- und Raumforschung, May 2017), https://www.smart-city-dialog.de/wp-content/uploads/2020/03/Langfassung-Smart-City-Charta-2017.pdf.

117 Ibid., 4.

118 Ibd., 43.

119 Ceri Parker, "8 Predictions for the World in 2030," World Economic Forum, November 12, 2016, https://web.archive.org/web/20230122004142/https://www.weforum.org/agenda/2016/11/8-predictions-for-the-world-in-2030/.
120 Chris Skinner, "Life, Materialism and Privacy in 2030," *The Finanser* (blog), May 31, 2022, https://thefinanser.com/2022/05/life-materialism-and-privacy-in-2030 (31.05.2022, last accessed on 05.09.2023)
121 https://www.studocu.com/en-us/document/caldwell-university/intro-to-philosphy/huxley-brave-new-world/11540325 36.
122 Diego de Landa, *Bericht aus Yucatán* (Ditzingen, Germany: Reclam, 2017).
123 https://www.studocu.com/en-us/document/caldwell-university/intro-to-philosphy/huxley-brave-new-world/11540325 44–45.
124 Ibid., 195.

CHAPTER 2

1 Jacques Monod, *Chance and Necessity: An Essay on the Natural Philosophy of Modern Biology* (New York: Penguin, 1997).
2 Christie Aschwanden, "Five Reasons Why COVID Herd Immunity Is Probably Impossible,'" *Nature* 591, no. 7851 March 2021): 520–22, https://pubmed.ncbi.nlm.nih.gov/33737753/.
3 Esther Herrmann et al., "Humans Have Evolved Specialized Skills of Social Cognition: The Cultural Intelligence Hypothesis," *Science* 317, no. 5843 (September 7, 2007): 1360–66, https://pubmed.ncbi.nlm.nih.gov/17823346/; Tyler Tretsven, "The Cultural Intelligence Hypothesis," *The Cultural Niche* (blog), April 13, 2012, https://tylertretsven.wordpress.com/2012/04/13/the-cultural-intelligence-hypothesis/; Rutger Bregman, *Humankind: A Hopeful History* (London: Bloomsbury Publishing, 2021), 71.
4 Hyeonjin Jeon and Seung-Hwan Lee, "From Neurons to Social Beings: Short Review of the Mirror Neuron System Research and Its Socio-Psychological and Psychiatric Implications," *Clinical Psychopharmacology and Neuroscience* 16, no. 1 (2018): 18–31, https://www.ncbi.nlm.nih.gov/pmc/articles/PMC5810456/pdf/cpn-16-018.pdf.
5 Lois Holzman, "What's the Opposite of Play?" *Psychology Today*, April 5, 2016, https://www.psychologytoday.com/intl/blog/conceptual-revolution/201604/what-s-the-opposite-play.
6 Peter Gray, "The Decline of Play and the Rise of Psychopathology in Children and Adolescents," *American Journal of Play* 3, no. 4 (Spring 2011): 443–63, https://www.researchgate.net/publication/265449180.
7 Peter Gray, "The Play Deficit," Aeon (website), September 18, 2013, https://aeon.co/essays/children-today-are-suffering-a-severe-deficit-of-play.
8 Kyiung Hee Kim, "The Creativity Crisis: The Decrease in Creative Thinking Scores on the Torrance Tests of Creative Thinking," *Creativity Research Journal* 23, no. 4 (2011): 285–95, https://www.tandfonline.com/doi/abs/10.1080/10400419.2011.627805.

9 Lothar Wieler, "Lothar Wieler: Corona-Regeln Dürfen Nie Hinterfragt Werden," July 28, 2020, *Ruhrkultour* (blog), transcript and video, 1:32, https://ruhrkultour.de/lothar-wieler-faq/corona-regeln/; "RKI-Präsident: 'Die Entwicklung Macht Uns Grosse Sorgen," Deutschlandfunk, July 28, 2020, https://www.deutschlandfunk.de/mehr-covid-19-faelle-in-deutschland-rki-praesident-die-100.html.

10 Michael Nehls, *Das Erschöpfte Gehirn: Der Ursprung Unserer Mentalen Energie—und Warum Sie Schwindet—Willenskraft, Kreativität und Fokus Zurückgewinnen* (Munich: Heyne Verlag, 2022).

11 Figure is adapted from iStock ID 461850387, https://www.istockphoto.com/photo/brain-hippocampus-anatomy-of-female-gm461850387-32159354.

12 William Beecher Scoville and Brenda Milner, "Loss of Recent Memory after Bilateral Hippocampal Lesions," *Journal of Neurology, Neurosurgery, and Psychiatry* 20, no. 1 (February 1957): 11–21, https://www.ncbi.nlm.nih.gov/pmc/articles/PMC497229/.

13 Philip J. Hilts, *Memory's Ghost: The Nature of Memory and the Strange Tale of Mr. M.* (New York: Touchstone, 1996), 119.

14 Ibid., 111.

15 Jessica D. Payne et al., "Sleep Preferentially Enhances Memory for Emotional Components of Scenes," *Psychological Science* 19, no. 8 (August 2008): 781–88, https://www.ncbi.nlm.nih.gov/pmc/articles/PMC5846336.

16 Allan T. Scholz et al., "Imprinting to Chemical Cues: The Basis for Home Stream Selection in Salmon," *Science* 192, no. 4245 (June 18, 1976): 1247–49, https://www.science.org/doi/10.1126/science.1273590.

17 Matthew A. Wilson and Bruce L. McNaughton, "Dynamics of the Hippocampal Ensemble Code for Space," *Science* 261, no. 5124 (August 20, 1993): 1055–58, https://www.science.org/doi/10.1126/science.8351520.

18 The Nobel Prize, "Nobel Prize in Physiology or Medicine 2014," Advanced Information, n.d., https://www.nobelprize.org/prizes/medicine/2014/advanced-information.

19 L. M. Rangel et al., "Temporally Selective Contextual Encoding in the Dentate Gyrus of the Hippocampus," *Nature Communications* 5 (February 2014): https://www.nature.com/articles/ncomms4181.

20 Gray Umbach et al., "Time Cells in the Human Hippocampus and Entorhinal Cortex Support Episodic Memory," *Proceedings of National Academy of Science* 117, no. 45 (November 10, 2020): 28463–74, https://www.pnas.org/doi/epdf/10.1073/pnas.2013250117.

21 Howard Eichenbaum, "Time Cells in the Hippocampus: A New Dimension for Mapping Memories," *Nature Reviews Neuroscience* 15 (2014): 73244, https://www.nature.com/articles/nrn3827.

22 Albert K. Lee and Matthew A. Wilson, "Memory of Sequential Experience in the Hippocampus during Slow Wave Sleep," *Neuron* 36, no. 6 (December 19, 2002): 1183–94, https://pubmed.ncbi.nlm.nih.gov/12495631.

23 Penelope A. Lewis, Günter Knoblich, and Gina Poe, "How Memory Replay in Sleep Boosts Creative Problem-Solving," *Trends in Cognitive Sciences* 22, no. 6 (June 2018):

491–503, https://www.ncbi.nlm.nih.gov/pmc/articles/PMC7543772/; Robert Stickgold, "How Do I Remember? Let Me Count the Ways," *Sleep Medicine Reviews* 13, no. 5 (October 2009): 305–8, https://www.ncbi.nlm.nih.gov/pmc/articles /PMC2739268/.

24 Susan J. Sara, "Sleep to Remember," *Journal of Neuroscience* 37, no. 3 (January 18, 2017): 457–63, https://www.jneurosci.org/content/37/3/457.

25 "Memory Town System for Languages," Art of Memory, n.d., https://artofmemory .com/wiki/Memory_Town_System_for_Languages/.

26 Tom Hale, "How Sherlock Holmes's 'Mind Palace' Trick Can Boost Your Memory, as Shown by Brain Scans," IFL Science, March 8, 2021, https://www.iflscience.com /how-sherlock-holmess-mind-palace-trick-can-boost-your-memory-as-shown-by -brain-scans-58969.

27 I. C. Wagner et al., "Durable Memories and Efficient Neural Coding through Mnemonic Training Using the Method of Loci," *Science Advances* 7, no. 10 (March 2021): https://www.ncbi.nlm.nih.gov/pmc/articles/PMC7929507/.

28 Shikha Jain Goodwin, "Neurogenesis: Remembering All or Forgetting Some," *Journal of Neurophysiology* 119, no. 6 (June 1, 2018): 2003–6, https://pubmed.ncbi.nlm.nih .gov/29442554/.

29 Christian Mirescu et al., "Sleep Deprivation Inhibits Adult Neurogenesis in the Hippocampus by Elevating Glucocorticoids," *Proceedings of the National Academy of Sciences of the United States of America* 103, no. 50 (December 12, 2006): 19170–75, https://www.ncbi.nlm.nih.gov/pmc/articles/PMC1748194/; Deependra Kumar et al., "Sparse Activity of Hippocampal Adult-Born Neurons during REM Sleep Is Necessary for Memory Consolidation," *Neuron* 107, no. 3 (August 5, 2020): 552–65, https://www.cell.com/neuron/fulltext/S0896-6273(20)30354-8.

30 Kirsty L. Spalding et al., "Dynamics of Hippocampal Neurogenesis in Adult Humans," *Cell* 153, no. 6 (June 6, 2013): 1219–27, https://www.ncbi.nlm.nih.gov/pmc/articles /PMC4394608/.

31 Maura Boldrini et al., "Human Hippocampal Neurogenesis Persists throughout Aging," *Cell Stem Cell* 22, no. 4 (April 5, 2018): 589–99, https://www.ncbi.nlm.nih .gov/pmc/articles/PMC5957089.

32 L. M. Rangel et al., "Temporally Selective Contextual Encoding in the Dentate Gyrus of the Hippocampus," *Nature Communications* 5 (2014): https://doi.org/10.1038 /ncomms4181.

33 Shaoyu Ge et al., "A Critical Period for Enhanced Synaptic Plasticity in Newly Generated Neurons of the Adult Brain," *Neuron* 54, no. 4 (May 24, 2007): 559–66, https://www.ncbi.nlm.nih.gov/pmc/articles/PMC2040308/; Christoph Schmidt -Hieber, Peter Jonas, and Josef Bischofberger, "Enhanced Synaptic Plasticity in Newly Generated Granule Cells of the Adult Hippocampus," *Nature* 429, no. 6988 (May 13, 2004): 184–87, https://pubmed.ncbi.nlm.nih.gov/15107864/.

34 Goodwin, "Neurogenesis."

35 Julia Freund et al., "Emergence of Individuality in Genetically Identical Mice," *Science* 340 (May 10, 2013): 756–59, http://library.mpib-berlin.mpg.de/ft/jf/JF_Emergence_2013.pdf.

36 Jason S. Snyder, "Adult Hippocampal Neurogenesis Buffers Stress Responses and Depressive Behavior," *Nature* 476, no. 7361 (August 25, 2011): 458–61, https://www.ncbi.nlm.nih.gov/pmc/articles/PMC3162077/; Djoher Nora Abrous, Muriel Koehl, and Maël Lemoine, "A Baldwin Interpretation of Adult Hippocampal Neurogenesis: From Functional Relevance to Physiopathology," *Molecular Psychiatry* 27, no. 1 (2022): 383–402, https://www.ncbi.nlm.nih.gov/pmc/articles/PMC8960398/.

37 Lindsay Tannenholz, Jessica C. Jimenez, and Mazen A. Kheirbek, "Local and Regional Heterogeneity Underlying Hippocampal Modulation of Cognition and Mood," *Frontiers in Behavioral Neuroscience* 8 (2014): https://www.ncbi.nlm.nih.gov/pmc/articles/PMC4018538/; Barry L. Jacobs, Henriette van Praag, and Fred H. Gage, "Depression and the Birth and Death of Brain Cells," *American Scientist* 88 no. 4 (July-August 2000): 340–45, https://www.jstor.org/stable/27858057.

38 Antoine Besnard and Amar Sahay, "Adult Hippocampal Neurogenesis, Fear Generalization, and Stress," *Neuropsychopharmacology* 41, no. 1 (January 2016): 24–44, https://www.ncbi.nlm.nih.gov/pmc/articles/PMC4677119/.

39 Michael Nehls, Unified Theory of Alzheimer's Disease (UTAD): Implications for Prevention and Curative Therapy," *Journal of Molecular Psychiatry* 4 (2016): https://www.ncbi.nlm.nih.gov/pmc/articles/PMC4947325/.

40 James S. Snyder and Michael R. Drew, "Functional Neurogenesis over the Years," *Behavioural Brain Research* 382 (March 16, 2020): https://www.ncbi.nlm.nih.gov/pmc/articles/PMC7769695/.

41 A. Surget et al., "Antidepressants Recruit New Neurons to Improve Stress Response Regulation," *Molecular Psychiatry* 16, no. 12 (December 2011): 1177–88, https://www.ncbi.nlm.nih.gov/pmc/articles/PMC3223314/; Tarique D. Perera et al., "Necessity of Hippocampal Neurogenesis for the Therapeutic Action of Antidepressants in Adult Nonhuman Primates, *PLoS One* 6, no. 4 (April 15, 2011): https://www.ncbi.nlm.nih.gov/pmc/articles/PMC3078107/.

42 Thomas Frodl et al., "Effect of Hippocampal and Amygdala Volumes on Clinical Outcomes in Major Depression: A 3-Year Prospective Magnetic Resonance Imaging Study," *Journal of Psychiatry & Neuroscience* 33, no. 5 (September 2008): 423–30, https://www.ncbi.nlm.nih.gov/pmc/articles/PMC2527720/.

43 Alexis S. Hill, Amar Sahay, and René Hen, "Increasing Adult Hippocampal Neurogenesis Is Sufficient to Reduce Anxiety and Depression-Like Behaviors," *Neuropsychopharmacology* 40, no. 10 (September 2015): 2368–78, https://www.ncbi.nlm.nih.gov/pmc/articles/PMC4538351/.

44 "The Sveriges Riksbank Prize in Economic Sciences in Memory of Alfred Nobel 2002," The Nobel Prize, https://www.nobelprize.org/prizes/economic-sciences/2002/summary/.

45 Francis Crick and Christof Koch, "A Framework for Consciousness," *Nature Neuroscience* 6 (2003): 119–26, https://doi.org/10.1038/nn0203-119.

46 Daniel Kahneman, *Thinking, Fast and Slow* (New York: Penguin, 2012).

47 Michael Nehls, *Das Erschöpfte Gehirn: Der Ursprung Unserer Mentalen Energie—und Warum Sie Schwindet—Willenskraft, Kreativität und Fokus zurückgewinnen* (Munich: Heyne Verlag, 2022).

48 Robert Biegler et al., "A Larger Hippocampus Is Associated with Longer-Lasting Spatial Memory," Proceedings of the National Academy of Sciences of the United States of America 98, no. 12 (June 5, 2001): 6941–44, https://www.ncbi.nlm.nih.gov/pmc/articles/PMC34457/.

49 Hamid Taher Neshat-Doost, Tim Dalgleish, and Ann-Marie J. Golden, "Reduced Specificity of Emotional Autobiographical Memories Following Self-Regulation Depletion," *Emotion* 8, no. 5 (October 2008): 731–36, https://pubmed.ncbi.nlm.nih.gov/18837625/.

50 Carlos Arturo González-Acosta et al., "Von Economo Neurons in the Human Medial Frontopolar Cortex," *Frontiers in Neuroanatomy* 12 (2018): 64, www.ncbi.nlm.nih.gov/pmc/articles/PMC6087737/.

51 Lazaros C. Triarhou, "The Signalling Contributions of Constantin von Economo to Basic, Clinical and Evolutionary Neuroscience," *Brain Research Bulletin* 69, no. 3 (April 2006): 223–43, https://pubmed.ncbi.nlm.nih.gov/16564418/.

52 Joseph M. Allman, et al., "The von Economo Neurons in Frontoinsular and Anterior Cingulate Cortex in Great Apes and Humans," *Brain Structure & Function* 214, no. 5-6 (June 2010): 495–517, https://pubmed.ncbi.nlm.nih.gov/20512377/.

53 Carina R. Oehrn et al., "Human Hippocampal Dynamics during Response Conflict," *Current Biology* 25, no. 17 (August 31, 2015): 2307–13, https://pubmed.ncbi.nlm.nih.gov/26299515/; Franco Cauda, Giuliano Carlo Geminiani, and Alessandro Vercelli, "Evolutionary Appearance of von Economo's Neurons in the Mammalian Cerebral Cortex," *Frontiers in Human Neuroscience* 8 (March 14, 2014): 104, https://www.ncbi.nlm.nih.gov/pmc/articles/PMC3953677/.

54 A. F. Santillo, C. Nilsson, and E. Englund, "Von Economo Neurones Are Selectively Targeted in Frontotemporal Dementia," *Neuropathology and Applied Neurobiology* 39, no. 5 (August 2013): 572–79, https://www.ncbi.nlm.nih.gov/pmc/articles/PMC3749467/.

55 Simon N. Chapman et al., "Limits to Fitness Benefits of Prolonged Post-Reproductive Lifespan in Women," *Current Biology* 29, no. 4 (February 18, 2019): 645–50, https://pubmed.ncbi.nlm.nih.gov/30744967/.

56 Hillard Kaplan, et al., "A Theory of Human Life History Evolution: Diet, Intelligence, and Longevity," *Evolutionary Anthropology* (2000): https://www.unm.edu/~hkaplan/KaplanHillLancasterHurtado_2000_LHEvolution.pdf.

57 Michael Nehls, "Unified Theory of Alzheimer's Disease (UTAD): Implications for Prevention and Curative Therapy," *Journal of Molecular Psychiatry* 4 (2016): 3, https://www.ncbi.nlm.nih.gov/pmc/articles/PMC4947325/.

58 Michael Gurven and Hillard Kaplan H, "Longevity among Hunter-Gatherers: A Cross-Cultural Examination," *Population and Development Review* 33, no. 2 (June 2007): 321–65, https://onlinelibrary.wiley.com/doi/abs/10.1111/j.1728-4457.2007.00171.x.

59 Michael Nehls, *Die Methusalem-Strategie: Vermeiden, Was Uns Daran Hindert, Gesund Älter und Weiser zu Werden* (n.p., Mental Enterprises 2011), 87.

60 Michael Nehls, *Die Formel Gegen Alzheimer: Die Gebrauchsanweisung für ein Gesundes Leben—Ganz Einfach Vorbeugen und Rechtzeitig Heilen* (Munich: Heyne Verlag, 2018), 36.

61 Nehls, *Erschöpfte Gehirn*, 132.

62 Samuel Pavard, C. Jessica E. Metcalf, and Evelyne Heyer, "Senescence of Reproduction May Explain Adaptive Menopause in Humans: A Test of the "'Mother' Hypothesis," *American Journal of Physical Anthropology* 136, no. 2 (June 2008): 194–203, https://pubmed.ncbi.nlm.nih.gov/18322919/.

63 Patricia A. Boyle et al., "Effect of Purpose in Life on the Relation between Alzheimer Disease Pathologic Changes on Cognitive Function in Advanced Age," *Archives of General Psychiatry* 69, no. 5 (May 2012): 499–505, https://www.ncbi.nlm.nih.gov/pmc/articles/PMC3389510/; Angelina R. Sutin, Martina Luchetti, and Antonio Terracciano, "Sense of Purpose in Life and Healthier Cognitive Aging," *Trends in Cognitive Sciences* 25, no. 11 (November 2021): 917–19, https://www.ncbi.nlm.nih.gov/pmc/articles/PMC8987293/.

64 Michael Lehmann et al., "Glucocorticoids Orchestrate Divergent Effects on Mood through Adult Neurogenesis," *Journal of Neuroscience* 33, no. 7 (February 13, 2013): 2961–72, https://www.ncbi.nlm.nih.gov/pmc/articles/PMC3711562/.

65 Helene Sisti, Arnold L. Glass, and Tracey J. Shors, "Neurogenesis and the Spacing Effect: Learning over Time Enhances Memory and the Survival of New Neurons," *Learning & Memory* 14, no. 5 (May 2007): 368–75, https://www.ncbi.nlm.nih.gov/pmc/articles/PMC1876761/.

66 Nehls, "Unified Theory."

67 Kirk I. Erickson et al., "Exercise Training Increases Size of Hippocampus and Improves Memory," *Proceedings of the National Academy of Sciences of the United States of America* 108, no. 7 (February 15, 2011): 3017–22, https://www.ncbi.nlm.nih.gov/pmc/articles/PMC3041121/.

68 Darshana Kapri, Sashina E. Fanibunda, and Vidita A. Vaidya, "Thyroid Hormone Regulation of Adult Hippocampal Neurogenesis: Putative Molecular and Cellular Mechanisms," in *Vitamins and Hormones*, ed. Gerald Litwack (Cambridge, MA: Academic Press, 2022), 1–33, https://www.sciencedirect.com/science/article/abs/pii/S0083672921000686.

69 Philip C. Calder, "Docosahexaenoic Acid," Supplement, *Annals of Nutrition and Metabolism* 69, no. S1 (2016): 8–21, https://karger.com/anm/article-abstract/69/Suppl.%201/8/42341/Docosahexaenoic-Acid?redirectedFrom=fulltext.

70 James V. Pottala et al., "Higher RBC EPA + DHA Corresponds with Larger Total Brain and Hippocampal Volumes," *Neurology* 82, no. 5 (February 4, 2014): 435–42, https://www.ncbi.nlm.nih.gov/pmc/articles/PMC3917688/.

71 Ken D. Stark et al., "Global Survey of the Omega-3 Fatty Acids, Docosahexaenoic Acid and Eicosapentaenoic Acid in the Blood Stream of Healthy Adults," *Progress in Lipid Research* (July 2016): 132–52, https://pubmed.ncbi.nlm.nih.gov/27216485/.

72 "Omega-3 Index of 8 to 11 Is Optimal," Vitamindwiki.com, October 7, 2019, https://vitamindwiki.com/Omega-3+index+of+8+to+11+is+optimal+%28German%29+-+Oct+2019.

73 Joanne Bradbury, "Docosahexaenoic Acid (DHA): An Ancient Nutrient for the Modern Human Brain," *Nutrients* 3, no. 5 (May 2011): 529–54, https://www.ncbi.nlm.nih.gov/pmc/articles/PMC3257695/; Curtis W. Marean, "The Origins and Significance of Coastal Resource Use in Africa and Western Eurasia," *Journal of Human Evolution* 77 (December 2014): 17–40, https://www.sciencedirect.com/science/article/abs/pii/S0047248414002292.

74 Michael A. Crawford and C. Leigh Broadhurst, "The Role of Docosahexaenoic and the Marine Food Web as Determinants of Evolution and Hominid Brain Development: The Challenge for Human Sustainability," *Nutrition and Health* 21, no. 1 (January 2012): 17–39, https://pubmed.ncbi.nlm.nih.gov/22544773/.

75 Michael Nehls, *Die Algenöl-Revolution: Lebenswichtiges Omega-3—das Pflanzliche Lebenselixier aus dem Meer* (Munich: Heyne Verlag, 2022).

76 Arie Steinvil et al., "Vitamin D Deficiency Prevalence and Cardiovascular Risk in Israel," *European Journal of Clinical Investigation* 41, no. 3 (March 2011): 263–68, https://pubmed.ncbi.nlm.nih.gov/20955219/; Ritu G. and Ajay Gupta, "Vitamin D Deficiency in India: Prevalence, Causalities and Interventions," *Nutrients* 6, no. 2 (February 2014): 729–75, https://www.ncbi.nlm.nih.gov/pmc/articles/PMC3942730/; Carlos H. Orces, "Vitamin D Status among Older Adults Residing in the Littoral and Andes Mountains in Ecuador," *Scientific World Journal* (2015):, https://www.ncbi.nlm.nih.gov/pmc/articles/PMC4537767/; Felipe Rezende Giacomelli et al.,"Vitamin D Deficiency in Brazil: Questions about Potential Causes and Clinical Characteristics," *International Journal of Nutrology* 14, no. 1 (2021): 26–32, https://www.researchgate.net/publication/351287551.

77 Lorenz Borsche, Bernd Glauner, and Julian von Mendel,"COVID-19 Mortality Risk Correlates Inversely with Vitamin D3 Status, and a Mortality Rate Close to Zero Could Theoretically Be Achieved at 50 ng/mL 25(OH)D3: Results of a Systematic Review and Meta-Analysis," *Nutrients* 13, no. 10 (October 2021): https://www.ncbi.nlm.nih.gov/pmc/articles/PMC8541492/.

78 Michael Nehls, *Alzheimer Ist Heilbar: Rechtzeitig Zurück in ein Gesundes Leben* (Munich: Heyne Verlag, 2017), 220ff; Carolina Di Somma et al., "Vitamin D and Neurological Diseases: An Endocrine View," *International Journal of Molecular Science* 18, no. 11 (November 2017): https://www.ncbi.nlm.nih.gov/pmc/articles/PMC5713448/; Ibrar Anjum et al., "The Role of Vitamin D in Brain Health: A Mini

Literature Review," *Cureus* 10, no. 7 (July 10, 2018): https://www.ncbi.nlm.nih.gov/pmc/articles/PMC6132681/.

79 Sonia Melgar-Locatelli et al., "Nutrition and Adult Neurogenesis in the Hippocampus: Does What You Eat Help You Remember?" *Frontiers in Neuroscience* 17 (February 23, 2023): https://www.ncbi.nlm.nih.gov/pmc/articles/PMC9995971/.

80 Yound-Min Han, Tharmarajan Ramprasath, and Ming-Hui Zou, "β-Hydroxybutyrate and Its Metabolic Effects on Age-Associated Pathology, *Experimental & Molecular Medicine* 52 (2020): 548–55, https://doi.org/10.1038/s12276-020-0415-z; Lian Wang, Peijie Chen, and Weihua Xiao, "β-Hydroxybutyrate as an Anti-Aging Metabolite," *Nutrients* 13, no. 10 (October 2021): https://www.ncbi.nlm.nih.gov/pmc/articles/PMC8540704/; Krisztina Marosi et al., "3-Hydroxybutyrate Regulates Energy Metabolism and Induces BDNF Expression in Cerebral Cortical Neurons," *Journal of Neurochemistry* 139, no. 5 (December 2016): 769–81, https://www.ncbi.nlm.nih.gov/pmc/articles/PMC5123937/.

81 Christine T. Ekdahl et al., "Inflammation Is Detrimental for Neurogenesis in Adult Brain," *Proceedings of the National Academy of Sciences of the United States of America* 100, no. 23 (Novemver 11, 2003): 13632–37, https://www.ncbi.nlm.nih.gov/pmc/articles/PMC263865/.

82 K. Yaffe et al., "Advanced Glycation End Product Level, Diabetes, and Accelerated Cognitive Aging," *Neurology* 77, no. 14 (October 4, 2011): 1351–56, https://www.ncbi.nlm.nih.gov/pmc/articles/PMC3182758/.

83 Nehls, Erschöpfte Gehirn, 112ff.

84 Jaime Uribarri et al., "Advanced Glycation End Products in Foods and a Practical Guide to Their Reduction in the Diet," *Journal of the American Dietetic Association* 110, no. 6 (June 2010): 911–16, https://www.ncbi.nlm.nih.gov/pmc/articles/PMC3704564/.

85 Yu-Ting Lin et al., "Oxytocin Stimulates Hippocampal Neurogenesis via Oxytocin Receptor Expressed in CA3 Pyramidal Neurons," *Nature Communications* 8 (September 14, 2017): https://www.ncbi.nlm.nih.gov/pmc/articles/PMC5599651/; Benedetta Leuner, Julia M. Caponiti, and Elizabeth Gould, "Oxytocin Stimulates Adult Neurogenesis Even under Conditions of Stress and Elevated Glucocorticoids," *Hippocampus* 22, no. 4 (April 2012): 861–68, https://www.ncbi.nlm.nih.gov/pmc/articles/PMC4756590/.

86 C. M. Larsen and D. R. Grattan, "Prolactin, Neurogenesis, and Maternal Behaviors," *Brain, Behavior, and Immunity* 26, no. 2 (February 2012): 201–9, https://pubmed.ncbi.nlm.nih.gov/21820505/.

87 Cristina Cachán-Vega et al., "Chronic Treatment with Melatonin Improves Hippocampal Neurogenesis in the Aged Brain and under Neurodegeneration," *Molecules* 27, no. 17 (September 2022): https://www.ncbi.nlm.nih.gov/pmc/articles/PMC9457692/.

88 Christian Mirescu et al., "Sleep Deprivation Inhibits Adult Neurogenesis in the Hippocampus by Elevating Glucocorticoids," *Proceedings of the National Academy of*

Sciences of the United States of America 103, no. 50 (December 12, 2006): 19170–75, https://www.ncbi.nlm.nih.gov/pmc/articles/PMC1748194/.

89 Josephine Barnes et al., "A Meta-Analysis of Hippocampal Atrophy Rates in Alzheimer's Disease," *Neurobiology of Aging* 30, no. 11 (November 2009): 1711–23, https://www.ncbi.nlm.nih.gov/pmc/articles/PMC2773132/.

90 Lisa Nobis et al., "Hippocampal Volume across Age: Nomograms Derived from over 19,700 People in UK Biobank," *Neuroimage: Clinical* 23 (2019): https://www.ncbi.nlm.nih.gov/pmc/articles/PMC6603440/.

91 Ibid.

92 Scott Small et al., "Imaging Hippocampal Function across the Human Life Span: Is Memory Decline Normal or Not?" *Annals of Neurology* 51, no. 3 (March 2002): 290–95, https://pubmed.ncbi.nlm.nih.gov/11891823/; Naftali Raz et al., "Regional Brain Changes in Aging Healthy Adults: General Trends, Individual Differences and Modifiers," *Cerebral Cortex* 15 (November 2005): 1676–89, https://pure.mpg.de/rest/items/item_2101154/component/file_2101153/content.

93 M. J. Friedrich, "Depression Is the Leading Cause of Disability Around the World," *JAMA* 317, no. 15 (April 18, 2017): 1517, https://pubmed.ncbi.nlm.nih.gov/28418490/.

94 "Depressive Disorder (Depression)," World Health Organization, March 31, 2023, https://www.who.int/news-room/fact-sheets/detail/depression.

95 "WHO Reveals Leading Causes of Death and Disability Worldwide: 2000–2019," World Health Organization, news release, December 9, 2020, https://www.who.int/news/item/09-12-2020-who-reveals-leading-causes-of-death-and-disability-worldwide-2000-2019.

96 Regina Guthold et al., "Worldwide Trends in Insufficient Physical Activity from 2001 to 2016: A Pooled Analysis of 358 Population-Based Surveys with 1.9 Million Participants," *Lancet Global Health* 6, no. 10 (October 2018): 1077–86, https://www.thelancet.com/journals/langlo/article/PIIS2214-109X(18)30357-7/fulltext.

97 Martina Rabenberg et al., "Vitamin D Status among Adults in Germany—Results from the German Health Interview and Examination Survey for Adults (DEGS1)," *BMC Public Health* 15 (2015): https://www.ncbi.nlm.nih.gov/pmc/articles/PMC4499202/.

98 Ezra Klein, "Bill Gates's Vision for Life beyond the Coronavirus," *Vox* (website), April 27, 2020, https://www.vox.com/coronavirus-covid19/2020/4/27/21236270/bill-gates-coronavirus-covid-19-plan-vaccines-conspiracies-podcast.

99 R. E. Hope-Simpson, "The Role of Season in the Epidemiology of Influenza," *Journal of Hygiene* 86 no. 1 (February 1981): 35–47, https://www.ncbi.nlm.nih.gov/pmc/articles/PMC2134066/.

100 J. J. Cannell et al., "Epidemic Influenza and Vitamin D," *Epidemiology and Infection* 134, no. 6 (December 2006): 1129–40, https://www.ncbi.nlm.nih.gov/pmc/articles/PMC2870528/.

CHAPTER 3

1 J. K. Rowling, *Harry Potter and the Prisoner of Azkaban* (London, Great Britain: Bloomsbury, 1999), 183.

2 M. Di Paola et al., "Hippocampal Atrophy Is the Critical Brain Change in Patients with Hypoxic Amnesia," *Hippocampus* 18, no. 7 (2008): 719–28, https://pubmed.ncbi.nlm.nih.gov/18446831/.

3 Rodgrigo G. Mira et al., "Effect of Alcohol on Hippocampal-Dependent Plasticity and Behavior: Role of Glutamatergic Synaptic Transmission," *Frontiers in Behavioral Neuroscience* 13 (2020): https://www.ncbi.nlm.nih.gov/pmc/articles/PMC6993074/.

4 "Fear vs. Anxiety: Understanding the Difference," Baton Rouge Behavioral Hospital, accessed May 13, 2023, https://batonrougebehavioral.com/fear-vs-anxiety-understanding-the-difference/.

5 Glenn Beck and Justin Haskins, *The Great Reset: Joe Biden and the Rise of the 21st Century Fascism* (New York: Mercury Ink, 2022), 73.

CHAPTER 4

1 "Angst Essen Seele Auf," *Caritas für Köln* (blog), March 31, 2017, https://blog-caritas-koeln.de/2017/03/31/angst-essen-seele-auf/.

2 Graphic was adapted from Eun Joo Kim, Blake Pellman, and Jeansok J. Kim, "Stress Effects on the Hippocampus: A Critical Review," *Learning & Memory* 22, no. 9 (September 2015): 411–16, https://www.ncbi.nlm.nih.gov/pmc/articles/PMC4561403/.

3 Ibid.

4 Mark W. Logue et al., "Smaller Hippocampal Volume in Posttraumatic Stress Disorder: A Multisite ENIGMA-PGC Study: Subcortical Volumetry Results from Posttraumatic Stress Disorder Consortia," *Biological Psychiatry* 83, no. 3 (February 1, 2018): 244–53; https://www.ncbi.nlm.nih.gov/pmc/articles/PMC5951719/.

5 Georgina L. Moreno, Joel Bruss, and Natalie L. Denburg, "Increased Perceived Stress Is Related to Decreased Prefrontal Cortex Volumes among Older Adults," *Journal of Clinical and Experimental Neuropsychology* 39, no. 4 (May 2017): 313–25, https://pubmed.ncbi.nlm.nih.gov/27615373/.

6 Risë B. Goldstein et al., "The Epidemiology of DSM-5 Posttraumatic Stress Disorder in the United States: Results from the National Epidemiologic Survey on Alcohol and Related Conditions-III," *Social Psychiatry and Psychiatric Epidemiology* 51, no. 8 (August 2016): 1137–48, https://www.ncbi.nlm.nih.gov/pmc/articles/PMC4980174/.

7 Bruce P. Dohrenwend et al., "The Psychological Risks of Vietnam for U.S. Veterans: A Revisit with New Data and Methods," *Science* 313, no. 5789 (August 18, 2006): 979–82, https://www.ncbi.nlm.nih.gov/pmc/articles/PMC1584215/.

8 Dorthe Berntsen and David C. Rubin, "Pretraumatic Stress Reactions in Soldiers Deployed to Afghanistan," *Clinical Psychological Science* 3, no. 5 (September 2015): 663–74, https://www.ncbi.nlm.nih.gov/pmc/articles/PMC4564108.

9 "What Is Pre-Traumatic Stress Disorder?," Alta Loma Transformational Services, accessed May 14, 2023, https://www.altaloma.com/what-is-pre-traumatic-stress-disorder/.

10 Victoria M. E. Bridgland et al., "Why the COVID-19 Pandemic Is a Traumatic Stressor," *PLoS One* 16, no. 1 (January 2021): https://www.ncbi.nlm.nih.gov/pmc/articles/PMC7799777/.

11 "What Is Pre-Traumatic Stress Disorder?," Alta Loma.

12 Helen Catt, "Matt Hancock: Leaked Messages Suggest Plan to Frighten Public," BBC, March 5, 2023, https://www.bbc.com/news/uk-64848106.

13 Martin Knobbe, "Vertrauliche Regierungsstudie Beschreibt Corona-Szenarien für Deutschland," *Der Spiegel*, March 27, 2020, www.spiegel.de/politik/deutschland/corona-in-deutschland-vertrauliche-regierungsstudie-beschreibt-verschiedene-szenarien-a-1cafaac1-3932-434d-b4de-2f63bce0315d.

14 "Wie Wir COVID-19 unter Kontrolle Bekommen," FragDenStaat, accessed May 14, 2023, https://fragdenstaat.de/dokumente/4123-wie-wir-covid-19-unter-kontrolle-bekommen/.

15 "Klinische Kinder und Jugendpsychologie und Psychotherapie," Deutsche Gesellschaft für Psychologie, accessed February 28, 2023, http://ig-kjpt.de/covid-19-pandemie-auswirkungen-auf-die-psychische-gesundheit-von-kindern-und-jugendlichen.

16 World Economic Forum, *The Global Risks Report 2020* (Geneva: World Economic Forum, 2020), https://www3.weforum.org/docs/WEF_Global_Risk_Report_2020 .pdf.

17 Lise Van Susteren, "Our Children Face 'Pretraumatic Stress' from Worries about Climate Change," *The BMJ* (blog), November 19, 2020, https://blogs.bmj.com/bmj/2020/11/19/our-children-face-pretraumatic-stress-from-worries-about-climate-change/.

18 Susan Clayton et al., *Mental Health and Our Changing Climate: Impacts, Implications, and Guidance* (Washington, DC: American Psychological Association and ecoAmerica, 2017), https://www.apa.org/news/press/releases/2017/03/mental-health-climate.pdf.

19 Anthony Leiserowitz et al., *Climate Change in the American Mind, April 2022* (New Haven, CT: Yale Program on Climate Change Communication, 2022), https://climatecommunication.yale.edu/wp-content/uploads/2022/07/climate-change-american-mind-april-2022.pdf.

20 Solomon E. Asch, "Studies of Independence and Conformity: I. A Minority of One against a Unanimous Majority," *Psychological Monographs: General and Applied* 70, no. 9 (1956): 1–70, https://psycnet.apa.org/record/2011-16966-001.

21 Reitschuster.de, "Lauterbach: 'Der Ausnahmezustand Wird die Normalität Sein, Klimawandel Bringt Neue Pandemien,'" March 15, 2022, YouTube video, 1:09, https://www.youtube.com/watch?v=0lMfh8tSkB4.

22 Christopher M. Worsham et al., "Association between UFO Sightings and Emergency Department Visits," *American Journal of Emerging Medicine* 66 (April 2023): 164–66, https://pubmed.ncbi.nlm.nih.gov/36681598/.

23 "Gesundheitsforscher: UFO-Sichtungen Sind Weitgehend Harmlos," *Ärzte Zeitung,* February 22, 2023, https://www.aerztezeitung.de/Medizin/Gesundheitsforscher-UFO-Sichtungen-sind-weitgehend-harmlos-436651.html.

24 Hendrik Streeck et al., "Infection Fatality Rate of SARS-CoV2 in a Super-Spreading Event in Germany," *Nature Communications* 11 (2020): https://www.ncbi.nlm.nih.gov/pmc/articles/PMC7672059.

25 Angelo Maria Pezzullo et al., "Age-Stratified Infection Fatality Rate of COVID-19 in the Non-Elderly Population," *Environmental Research* 216 (January 1, 2023): https://www.ncbi.nlm.nih.gov/pmc/articles/PMC9613797/.

26 Robert F. Kennedy Jr., *The Real Anthony Fauci: Bill Gates, Big Pharma, and the Global War on Democracy and Public Health* (New York, Skyhorse Publishing, 2021).

27 David M. Morens, Jeffery K. Taubenberger, and Anthony S. Fauci, "Rethinking Next-Generation Vaccines for Coronaviruses, Influenzaviruses, and Other Respiratory Viruses," *Cell Host Microbe* 31, no. 1 (January 11, 2023): 146–57, https://www.ncbi.nlm.nih.gov/pmc/articles/PMC9832587/.

28 Emily A. Voigt et al., "A Self-Amplifying RNA Vaccine against COVID-19 with Long-Term Room-Temperature Stability,' *Nature Partner Journals Vaccines* 7 (2022): https://www.ncbi.nlm.nih.gov/pmc/articles/PMC9628444/.

29 https://www.aerztezeitung.de/Medizin/Mit-neuen-Techniken-schneller-zu-wirksamen-Impfstoffen-439746.html (June 6, 2023).

30 Luc Vallières et al., "Reduced Hippocampal Neurogenesis in Adult Transgenic Mice with Chronic Astrocytic Production of Interleukin-6," *Journal of Neuroscience* 22, no. 2 (January 15, 2002): 486–92, https://www.ncbi.nlm.nih.gov/pmc/articles/PMC6758670/.

31 Wei Wang et al., "Up-Regulation of IL-6 and TNF-Alpha Induced by SARS-Coronavirus Spike Protein in Murine Macrophages via NF-KappaB Pathway," *Virus Research* 128, no. 1 (September 2007): 1–8, https://www.ncbi.nlm.nih.gov/pmc/articles/PMC7114322/

32 Anne-Maj Samuelsson et al., "Prenatal Exposure to Interleukin-6 Results in Inflammatory Neurodegeneration in Hippocampus with NMDA/GABA(A) Dysregulation and Impaired Spatial Learning," *American Journal of Physiology Regulatory Integrative and Comparative Physiology* 290, no. 5 (May 2006): 1345–56, https://pubmed.ncbi.nlm.nih.gov/16357100/.

33 Abdeslam Mouihate and Samah Kalakh, "Maternal Interleukin-6 Hampers Hippocampal Neurogenesis in Adult Rat Offspring in a Sex-Dependent Manner," *Developmental Neuroscience* 43, no. 2 (2021): 106–15, https://pubmed.ncbi.nlm.nih.gov/34023825/.

34 Anna L. Marsland et al., "Interleukin-6 Covaries Inversely with Hippocampal Grey Matter Volume in Middle-Aged Adults," *Biological Psychiatry* 64, no. 6 (September 2008): 484–90, https://doi.org/10.1016/j.biopsych.2008.04.016.

35 Shohei Takahashi et al., "Tumor Necrosis Factor α Negatively Regulates the Retrieval and Reconsolidation of Hippocampus-Dependent Memory," *Brain, Behavior, and Immunity* 94 (May 2021): 79–88, https://pubmed.ncbi.nlm.nih.gov/33677026/.

36 Michael D. Wu et al., "Sustained IL-1β Expression Impairs Adult Hippocampal Neurogenesis Independent of IL-1 Signaling in Nestin+ Neural Precursor Cells," *Brain, Behavior, and Immunity* 32 (August 2013): 9–18, https://www.ncbi.nlm.nih.gov/pmc/articles/PMC3686979/; Sebastian J. Theobald et al., "Long-Lived Macrophage Reprogramming Drives Spike Protein-Mediated Inflammasome Activation in COVID-19," *EMBO Molecular Medicine* 13, no. 8 (August 2021): https://www.ncbi.nlm.nih.gov/pmc/articles/PMC8350892/.

37 Anupriya Anand, Abimanyu Sugumaran, and Damodharan Narayanasamy, "Brain Targeted Delivery of Anticancer Drugs: Prospective Approach Using Solid Lipid Nanoparticles," *IET Nanobiotechnology* 13, no. 4 (June 2019): 353–62; https://www.ncbi.nlm.nih.gov/pmc/articles/PMC8676006/.

38 Itziar Gómez-Aguado et al., "Nucleic Acid Delivery by Solid Lipid Nanoparticles Containing Switchable Lipids: Plasmid DNA vs. Messenger RNA," *Molecules* 25, no. 24 (December 2020): https://www.ncbi.nlm.nih.gov/pmc/articles/PMC7766580/.

39 European Medicines Agency, *Assessment Report: COVID-19 Vaccine Moderna* (Amsterdam: European Medicines Agency, March 11, 2021), https://www.ema.europa.eu/en/documents/assessment-report/spikevax-previously-covid-19-vaccine-moderna-epar-public-assessment-report_en.pdf.

40 "IL-1-Mediated Inflammation Induced by Different RNA Vaccines Is Context-Specific," *Nature Immunology* 23, no. 4 (April 2022): 485–86, https://pubmed.ncbi.nlm.nih.gov/35354959/.

41 Ahmad A. Ballout et al., "A Single-Health System Case Series of New-Onset CNS Inflammatory Disorders Temporally Associated with mRNA-Based SARS-CoV-2 Vaccines," *Frontiers in Neurology* 13 (2022): https://www.ncbi.nlm.nih.gov/pmc/articles/PMC8908032/; Mahsa Khayat-Khoei et al., "COVID-19 mRNA Vaccination Leading to CNS Inflammation: A Case Series," *Journal of Neurology* no. 3 (2022): https://www.springermedizin.de/covid-19/covid-19-mrna-vaccination-leading-to-cns-inflammation-a-case-ser/19632772; Sydney Lee et al., "Acute Central Nervous System Inflammation Following COVID-19 Vaccination: An Observational Cohort Study," *Multiple Sclerosis Journal* 29, no. 4-5 (April 2023): 595–605, https://journals.sagepub.com/doi/10.1177/13524585231154780.

42 World Health Organization, "Pandemic Preparedness," accessed May 14, 2023, http://web.archive.org/web/20030427193056/http://www.who.int/csr/disease/influenza/pandemic/en/print.html.

43 Peter Doshi, "The Elusive Definition of Pandemic Influenza," *Bulletin of the World Health Organization* 89, no. 7 (July 1, 2011): 532–38, https://www.ncbi.nlm.nih.gov/pmc/articles/PMC3127275/.

44 Elizabeth Cohen, "When a Pandemic Isn't a Pandemic," CNN, May 4, 2009, http://edition.cnn.com/2009/HEALTH/05/04/swine.flu.pandemic/index.html.

45 Ahmed Yaqinuddin, "Cross-Immunity between Respiratory Coronaviruses May Limit COVID-19 Fatalities," *Medical Hypotheses* 144 (November 2020): https://www.ncbi.nlm.nih.gov/pmc/articles/PMC7326438/; Claudia Giesecke-Thiel and Andreas Thiel, "Prior Exposure to Common Cold Coronaviruses Enhances Immune Response to SARS-CoV-2," Max Planck Gesellschaft, August 31, 2021, https://www.mpg.de/17434954/0907-moge-prior-exposure-to-common-cold-coronaviruses-enhances-immune-response-to-sars-cov-2-151795-x.

46 Heng Weili, "Questions Raised over Code in Moderna Patent," *China Daily*, last modified March 21, 2022, https://global.chinadaily.com.cn/a/202203/21/WS6237da55a310fd2b29e52288.html.

47 Joseph Mercola, "COVID-19 Spike Protein Sequence '100% Match' to Sequence Patented in 2016 by Moderna, Study Shows," *The Defender* (website), March 7, 2022, https://childrenshealthdefense.org/defender/covid-spike-protein-sequence-match-moderna-patent/.

48 Balamurali K. Ambati et al., "MSH3 Homology and Potential Recombination Link to SARS-CoV-2 Furin Cleavage Site," *Frontiers in Virology* 2 (February 2022): https://www.frontiersin.org/articles/10.3389/fviro.2022.834808/full.

49 Peter Daszak, "Proposal: Volume I," DARPA, March 24, 2018, 11, https://s3.documentcloud.org/documents/21066966/defuse-proposal.pdf; Sharon Lerner and Maia Hibbett, "Leaked Grant Proposal Details High-Risk Coronavirus Research," *The Intercept* (website), September 23, 2021, https://theintercept.com/2021/09/23/coronavirus-research-grant-darpa/; Yujia Alina Chan and Shing Hei Zhan, "The Emergence of the Spike Furin Cleavage Site in SARS-CoV-2," *Molecular Biology and Evolution* 39, no. 1 (January 2022): https://www.ncbi.nlm.nih.gov/pmc/articles/PMC8689951/.

50 EcoHealth Alliance, "Annual Report & Financials," accessed May 14, 2023, https://www.ecohealthalliance.org/financials-strategy.

51 Lizhou Zhang et al., "The D614G Mutation in the SARS-CoV-2 Spike Protein Reduces S1 Shedding and Increases Infectivity," *bioRxiv* (forthcoming). https://www.ncbi.nlm.nih.gov/pmc/articles/PMC7310631/.

52 Elizabeth M. Rhea et al., "The S1 Protein of SARS-CoV-2 Crosses the Blood-Brain Barrier in Mice," *Nature Neuroscience* 24, no. 3 (March 2021): 368–78, https://www.ncbi.nlm.nih.gov/pmc/articles/PMC8793077/.

53 Amy Maxmen and Smriti Mallapaty, "The COVID Lab-Leak Hypothesis: What Scientists Do and Don't Know," *Nature* 594 (June 2021): 313–15, https://www.nature.com/articles/d41586-021-01529-3; Jonathan Latham and Allison K. Wilson, "The Hunt for the Origins of COVID—Where It Led and Why It Matters," *The Defender* (website), August 20, 2021, https://childrenshealthdefense.org/defender/chinese-international-searches-origins-covid-zoonotic-lab-leak/.

54 Valentin Bruttel, Alex Washburne, and Antonius VanDongen, "Endonuclease Fingerprint Indicates a Synthetic Origin of SARS-CoV-2," *bioRxiv* (forthcoming), https://www.biorxiv.org/content/10.1101/2022.10.18.512756v1.

55 Michael R. Gordon, "Lab Leak Most Likely Origin of COVID-19 Pandemic, Energy Department Now Says," last modified February 26, 2023, https://www.wsj.com/articles/covid-origin-china-lab-leak-807b7b0a.

56 "China Scoffs at FBI Claim That Wuhan Lab Leak Likely Caused COVID Pandemic," Reuters, March 1, 2023, https://www.reuters.com/business/healthcare-pharmaceuticals/fbi-director-says-china-lab-leak-likely-caused-covid-pandemic-2023-03-01/.

57 BionTech, *Konzernlagebericht für das Geschäftsjahr 2019*, May 2020, https://investors.biontech.de/static-files/9db3ce1d-ef4e-48fd-9a6e-c885dc034f78.

58 Ruth Young et al., "Developing New Health Technologies for Neglected Diseases: A Pipeline Portfolio Review and Cost Model," *Gates Open Research* 2 (2018): 23, https://www.ncbi.nlm.nih.gov/pmc/articles/PMC6139384/.

59 Stephanie Seneff and Greg Nigh, "Worse Than the Disease? Reviewing Some Possible Unintended Consequences of the mRNA Vaccines against COVID-19," *International Journal of Vaccine Theory, Practice, and Research,* May 10, 2021, https://dpbh.nv.gov/uploadedFiles/dpbhnvgov/content/Boards/BOH/Meetings/2021/SENEFF~1.PDF.

60 Martin Weiss, "Bill Gates: Auf Diese 4 Corona-Impfstoff-Aktien Setzt der Multimilliardär," *Der Aktionär,* September 15, 2020, https://www.deraktionaer.de/artikel/aktien/bill-gates-auf-diese-4-corona-impfstoff-aktien-setzt-der-multimilliardaer-20207054.html; Zach Anchors, "Gates Foundation Bets Big on Moderna's mRNA Technology," *Drug Discovery News,* March 9, 2020, https://www.drugdiscoverynews.com/gates-foundation-bets-big-on-moderna-s-mrna-technology-10450.

61 S. Seneff and G. Nigh, "Worse Than the Disease? Reviewing Some Possible Unintended Consequences of the mRNA Vaccines Against COVID-19," *International Journal of Vaccine Theory, Practice, and Research* 2 (2021): 38–79, https://ijvtpr.com/index.php/IJVTPR/article/view/23.

62 World Health Organization, *Novel Coronavirus (201`9-nCoV) Situation Report-1,* January 21, 2020, https://www.who.int/docs/default-source/coronaviruse/situation-reports/20200121-sitrep-1-2019-ncov.pdf?sfvrsn=20a99c10_4.

63 "Berliner Biotech-Firma Ist Vorreiter bei Coronavirus-Tests," *Cash* (website), March 13, 2020, https://www.cash.ch/news/politik/berliner-biotech-firma-ist-vorreiter-bei-coronavirus-tests-431941.

64 Christian Drosten, "'Der Körper Wird Ständig von Viren Angegriffen," interview by Susan Kutter, *Wirtschafts Woche,* May 16, 2014, https://www.wiwo.de/technologie/forschung/virologe-drosten-im-gespraech-2014-der-koerper-wirdstaendig-von-viren-angegriffen/9903228.html.

65 Leibnitz-Institut für Wirtschaftsforschung, *Analysen zum Leistungsgeschehen der Krankenhäuser und zur Ausgleichspauschale in der Corona-Krise* (Essen, Germany: Leibnitz-Institut für Wirtschaftsforschung, April 30, 2021), 20, https://www.bundesgesundheitsministerium.de/fileadmin/Dateien/3_Downloads/C/Coronavirus/Analyse_Leistungen_Ausgleichszahlungen_2020_Corona-Krise.pdf.

66 "Vaccine Procurement during an Influenza Pandemic and the Role of Advance Purchase Agreements: Lessons from 2009-H1N1," https://eprints.keele.ac.uk/id/eprint/2837/1/Vaccine%20procurement%20during%20an%20influenza%20pandemic%20and%20the%20role%20of%20Advance%20Purchase%20Agreements-%20lessons%20from%202009-H1N1.pdf; "New HHS Contracts Enhance Pandemic Preparedness. BARDA Takes Historic Steps with Master Vaccine Seed Lots, Vaccines for Pre-Pandemic Stockpile," US Department of Health and Human Services, news release, September 6, 2012, https://www.phe.gov/Preparedness/news/Pages/pandemic-120906.aspx.

67 Magdalena Robert, "Global Health Leaders Launch Decade of Vaccines Collaboration," Bill & Melinda Gates Foundation, news release, accessed May 15, 2023, https://www.gatesfoundation.org/ideas/media-center/press-releases/2010/12/global-health-leaders-launch-decade-of-vaccines-collaboration.

68 Andrej Hunko, "H1N1: Weltsgesundheitsorganisation vom Druck der Profitinteressen der Pharmaindustrie Befreien," Andrej-Hunko.de, June 24, 2010, https://www.andrej-hunko.de/en/europarat/reden/171-rede-h1n1-pharmaindustrie.

69 World Health Organization, *Global Vaccine Action Plan: 2011–2020* (Geneva: World Health Organization, 2013), www.who.int/iris/bitstream/10665/78141/1/9789241504980_eng.pdf.

70 Ibid.

71 Keith Speights, "4 Coronavirus Vaccine Stocks the Bill & Melinda Gates Foundation Is Betting On," The Motley Fool, September 24, 2020, https://www.fool.com/investing/2020/09/24/4-coronavirus-vaccine-stocks-the-bill-melinda-gate/.

72 Bill Gates, "Bill Gates: The Next Outbreak? We're Not Ready," TED talk, YouTube video, 8:36, www.youtube.com/watch?v=6Af6b_wyiwI; "Not Missiles, Microbes: Bill Gates Had Warned the World of an Epidemic 5 Yrs Ago," *Economic Times,* last modified March 18, 2020, https://economictimes.indiatimes.com/magazines/panache/not-missiles-microbes-bill-gates-had-warned-the-world-of-an-epidemic-5-yrs-ago/articleshow/74690072.cms?from=mdr.

73 Bill Gates, "Bill Gates and the Return of Investment in Vaccinations," interview by Becky Quick, CNBC, video, 10:26, https://www.cnbc.com/video/2019/01/23/bill-gates-and-the-return-on-investment-in-vaccinations-davos.html.

74 "EU Puts Faith in Pfizer Jab with Plan for 1.8 Billion Doses," Deutsche Welle, April 14, 2021, https://www.dw.com/en/eu-puts-faith-in-pfizer-jab-with-plan-for-18-billion-doses/a-57201551.

75 European Parliament, "Special Committee on COVID-19 Pandemic," August 30, 2022, video, 2:13:52, https://multimedia.europarl.europa.eu/en/webstreaming/special-committee-on-covid-19-pandemic_20220830-0900-COMMITTEE-COVI. Gallina responded at 9:48 a.m., according to the video recording.

76 Michael Bergmann, "Wer Sind die Ungeimpften?," Max Planck Gesellschaft, October 7, 2021, https://www.mpg.de/17668113/impfbereitschaft-in-europa.

77 *Manufacturing and Supply Agreement by and among Pfizer Export B.V., Albania Ministry of Health and Social Protection, Minister of State for Reconstruction, and Institute of Public Health*, Pfizer draft, January 6, 2021, http://ti-health.org/wp-content/uploads/2021/05/Albania-Pfizer.pdf.

78 Risna K. Radhakrishnan and Mahesh Kandasamy, "SARS-CoV-2-Mediated Neuropathogenesis, Deterioration of Hippocampal Neurogenesis and Dementia," *American Journal of Alzheimer's Disease & Other Dementias* 37 (2022): https://journals.sagepub.com/doi/full/10.1177/15333175221078418.

79 Ashutosh Kumar et al., "COVID-19 Vaccination May Enhance Hippocampal Neurogenesis in Adults," *Brain Behavior, and Immunity* 107 (January 2023): 87–89, https://www.ncbi.nlm.nih.gov/pmc/articles/PMC9527215/.

80 Karl Lauterbach, "Faktenbooster—Was Wir Tun Können," *Badische Zeitung*, August 27, 2022.

81 Gerard J. Nuovo et al., "Endothelial Cell Damage Is the Central Part of COVID-19 and a Mouse Model Induced by Injection of the S1 Subunit of the Spike Protein," *Annals of Diagnostic Pathology* 51 (April 2021): https://www.ncbi.nlm.nih.gov/pmc/articles/PMC7758180/.

82 Giovanni C. Actis Davide G. Ribaldone, and Rinaldo Pellicano, "COVID Vaccine's Hot Problems: Erratic Serious Blood Clotting, Ill-Defined Prion-Like Reactogenicity of the Spike, Unclear Roles of Other Factors," *Minerva Medica* 112, no. 6 (December 2021): 695–97, https://pubmed.ncbi.nlm.nih.gov/35168305/; Yuhai Zhao, Vivian R. Jaber, and Walter J. Lukiw, "SARS-CoV-2, Long COVID, Prion Disease and Neurodegeneration," *Frontiers in Neuroscience* 16 (2022): https://www.ncbi.nlm.nih.gov/pmc/articles/PMC9551214/.

83 Michael Nehls, Unified Theory of Alzheimer's Disease (UTAD): Implications for Prevention and Curative Therapy," *Journal of Molecular Psychiatry* 4 (2016): https://www.ncbi.nlm.nih.gov/pmc/articles/PMC4947325/; Cameron Wells et al., "The Role of Amyloid Oligomers in Neurodegenerative Pathologies," *International Journal of Biological Macromolecules* 181 (June 2021): 582–604, https://pubmed.ncbi.nlm.nih.gov/33766600/.

84 John Tsu-An Hsu et al., "The Effects of Aβ1-42 Binding to the SARS-CoV-2 Spike Protein S1 Subunit and Angiotensin-Converting Enzyme 2," *International Journal of Molecular Science* 22, no. 15 (August 2021): https://www.ncbi.nlm.nih.gov/pmc/articles/PMC8347908/; Sofie Nyström and Per Hammarström, "Amyloidogenesis of SARS-CoV-2 Spike Protein," *Journal of the American Chemical Society* 144, no. 20 (May 25, 2022): 8945–50, https://www.ncbi.nlm.nih.gov/pmc/articles/PMC9136918/.

85 Hyeryung Kwon and Taewon Kim, "Autoimmune Encephalitis Following ChAdOx1-S SARS-CoV-2 Vaccination," *Neurological Sciences* 43, no. 3 (2022): 1487–89, https://www.ncbi.nlm.nih.gov/pmc/articles/PMC8630512/; Sankha Shubhra Chakrabarti et al., "Rapidly Progressive Dementia with Asymmetric Rigidity Following ChAdOx1

nCoV-19 Vaccination," *Aging and Disease* 13, no. 3 (June 2022): 633–36, https://www.ncbi.nlm.nih.gov/pmc/articles/PMC9116920/.

86 Marco Cosentino and Franca Marino, "The Spike Hypothesis in Vaccine-Induced Adverse Effects: Questions and Answers," *Trends in Molecular Medicine* 28, no. 10 (October 2022): 797–99, https://www.ncbi.nlm.nih.gov/pmc/articles/PMC9494717/.

87 "Honorar für COVID-19-Impfungen Soll bis April Unverändert Bleiben," *Ärzte Zeitung,* December 11, 2022, https://www.aerztezeitung.de/Politik/Honorar-fuer-COVID-19-Impfungen-soll-bis-April-unveraendert-bleiben-435000.html.

88 "STIKO Empfiehlt Aspiration bei COVID-19-Impfung als Vorsichtsmassnahme," *Ärzte Zeitung,* February 18, 2022, https://www.aerzteblatt.de/nachrichten/131915/STIKO-empfiehlt-Aspiration-bei-COVID-19-Impfung-als-Vorsichtsmassnahme. Compare with "Mit Impfungen Richtig Geld Verdienen," *Ärzte Zeitung,* March 9, 2015, https://www.aerztezeitung.de/Wirtschaft/Mit-Impfungen-richtig-Geld-verdienen-250037.html.

89 Chaogeng Zhu et al., "Molecular Biology of the SARs-CoV-2 Spike Protein: A Review of Current Knowledge," *Journal of Medical Virology* 93, no. 10 (October 2021): 5729–41, https://doi.org/10.1002/jmv.27132.

90 Fabio Angeli et al., "SARS-CoV-2 Vaccines: Lights and Shadows," *European Journal of Internal Medicine* 88 (June 2021): 1–8, https://doi.org/10.1016/j.ejim.2021.04.019.

91 Yuyang Lei et al., "SARS-CoV-2 Spike Protein Impairs Endothelial Function via Downregulation of ACE2," *bioRxiv* (forthcoming), https://www.ncbi.nlm.nih.gov/pmc/articles/PMC7724674.

92 "Vaccine Administration," Centers for Disease Control and Prevention, last medically reviewed January 20, 2023, accessed May 16, 2023, https://www.cdc.gov/vaccines/hcp/acip-recs/general-recs/administration.html.

93 Anding Liu et al., "Seropositive Prevalence of Antibodies against SARS-CoV-2 in Wuhan, China," *JAMA Network Open* 3, no. 10 (October 2020), https://www.ncbi.nlm.nih.gov/pmc/articles/PMC7584925/.

94 "COVID-19: Fallzahlen in Deutschland und Weltweit," Robert Koch Institut, accessed April 12, 2023, https://www.rki.de/DE/Content/InfAZ/N/Neuartiges_Coronavirus/Fallzahlen.html.

95 Katharina Röltgen et al., "Immune Imprinting, Breadth of Variant Recognition, and Germinal Center Response in Human SARS-CoV-2 Infection and Vaccination," *Cell* 185, no. 6 (March 17, 2022): 1025–40, https://www.ncbi.nlm.nih.gov/pmc/articles/PMC8786601/.

96 Simone Cristoni et al., "Detection of Recombinant Spike Protein in Plasma from Vaccinated against SARS-CoV-2 Individuals," *medRxiv* (forthcoming), https://doi.org/10.5281/zenodo.5831816.

97 Pedro Morais, Hironori Adachi, and Yi-Tao Yu, "The Critical Contribution of Pseudouridine to mRNA COVID-19 Vaccines," *Frontiers in Cell and Developmental Biology* 9 (2021): https://www.ncbi.nlm.nih.gov/pmc/articles/PMC8600071

/; Callum J. C. Parr et al., "N 1-Methylpseudouridine Substitution Enhances the Performance of Synthetic mRNA Switches in Cells," *Nucleic Acids Research* 48, no. 6 (April 6, 2020): https://www.ncbi.nlm.nih.gov/pmc/articles/PMC7102939/.

98 "Chefarzt über Wachsende 'Impf'-Nebenwirkungen: Achlimmste je Erlebte Erkrankungen," Fassandenkratzer (website), February 17, 2023, https://fassadenkratzer.wordpress.com/2023/02/17/chefarzt-uber-wachsende-impf-nebenwirkungen-schlimmste-je-erlebte-erkrankungen/.

99 "STIKO will Zweite COVID-19-Booster-Impfung für Etliche Personengruppen Empfehlen," *Ärzte Zeitung*, August 15, 2022, https://www.aerztezeitung.de/Medizin/STIKO-will-zweite-COVID-19-Booster-Impfung-ab-60-empfehlen-und-fuer-alle-mit-Grunderkrankungen-431520.html.

100 Peter Nordström, Marcel Ballin, and Anna Nordström, "Risk of Infection, Hospitalisation, and Death up to 9 Months after a Second Dose of COVID-19 Vaccine: A Retrospective, Total Population Cohort Study in Sweden," *Lancet* 399, no. 10327 (February 26–March 4, 2022): 814–23, https://www.ncbi.nlm.nih.gov/pmc/articles/PMC8816388/.

101 Ibid., figure adapted.

102 Chaolin Huang et al., "Clinical Features of Patients Infected with 2019 Novel Coronavirus in Wuhan, China," *Lancet* 395, no. 10223 (February 15, 2020): 497–506, https://www.thelancet.com/article/S0140-6736(20)30183-5/fulltext.

103 Pierre Miossec, "Understanding the Cytokine Storm during COVID-19: Contribution of Preexisting Chronic Inflammation," Supplement, *European Journal of Rheumatology* 7, no. S2 (August 2020): 97–98, https://www.ncbi.nlm.nih.gov/pmc/articles/PMC7431332/.

104 Shintaro Hojyo et al., "How COVID-19 Induces Cytokine Storm with High Mortality," *Inflammation and Regeneration* 40 (2020): https://www.ncbi.nlm.nih.gov/pmc/articles/PMC7527296/.

105 Oliver Klein, "Wie Oft die Impfung Auffrischen? EMA Warnt vor zu Häufigem Boostern," *ZDF* (website), January 13, 2022, https://www.zdf.de/nachrichten/politik/corona-booster-impfungen-warnung-ema-100.html.

106 Søren Wengel Mogensen et al., "The Introduction of Diphtheria-Tetanus-Pertussis and Oral Polio Vaccine Among Young Infants in an Urban African Community: A Natural Experiment," *EBioMedicine* 17 (2017): 192–98, https://www.ncbi.nlm.nih.gov/pmc/articles/PMC5360569/pdf/main.pdf.

107 "Study: Bill Gates DTP Vaccine Killed 10 Times More African Girls Than the Disease Itself," *Great Game India* (website), January 6, 2021, https://greatgameindia.com/bill-gates-dtp-vaccine-africa/.

108 Nicola P. Klein, "Licensed Pertussis Vaccines in the United States: History and Current State," *Human Vaccines & Immunotherapeutics* 10, no. 9 (September 2014): 2684–90, https://www.ncbi.nlm.nih.gov/pmc/articles/PMC4975064/.

109 "Performance Based Funding for Health System Strengthening Cash Support," GAVI Alliance, February 2014, https://www.gavi.org/sites/default/files/document/performance-based-funding-information-sheetpdf.pdf.

110 Dan Shan et al., "Post-COVID-19 Human Memory Impairment: A PRISMA-Based Systematic Review of Evidence from Brain Imaging Studies," *Frontiers in Aging Neuroscience* 14 (2022): https://www.ncbi.nlm.nih.gov/pmc/articles/PMC9780393/.

111 Ioannis P. Trougakos et al., "Adverse Effects of COVID-19 mRNA Vaccines: The Spike Hypothesis," *Trends in Molecular Medicine* 28, no. 7 (July 2022): 542–54, https://www.ncbi.nlm.nih.gov/pmc/articles/PMC9021367/.

112 Brian Oronsky et al., "Nucleocapsid as a Next-Generation COVID-19 Vaccine Candidate," *International Journal of Infectious Diseases* 122 (September 2022): 529–30, https://www.ncbi.nlm.nih.gov/pmc/articles/PMC9250828/.

113 Sara Diani et al., "SARS-CoV-2—the Role of Natural Immunity: A Narrative Review," *Journal of Clinical Medicine* 11, no. 21 (November 2022): https://www.ncbi.nlm.nih.gov/pmc/articles/PMC9655392/.

114 Stefan Oelrich, speech, World Health Summit, Twitter video, 0:27, posted by Henning Rosenbusch, November 4, 2021, https://twitter.com/rosenbusch_/status/1456319266245038089.

115 "COVID-19 Vaccines While Pregnant or Breastfeeding" Centers for Disease Control and Prevention, last modified October 20, 2022, https://www.cdc.gov/coronavirus/2019-ncov/vaccines/recommendations/pregnancy.html.

116 "Impfung bei Schwangeren, Stillenden und bei Kinderwunsch," Robert Koch Institut, last modified May 25, 2023, https://www.rki.de/SharedDocs/FAQ/COVID-Impfen/FAQ_Liste_Impfung_Schwangere_Stillende.html.

117 Nazeeh Hanna et al., "Detection of Messenger RNA COVID-19 Vaccines in Human Breast Milk," *JAMA Pediatrics* 176, no. 12 (2022): 1268–70, https://jamanetwork.com/journals/jamapediatrics/fullarticle/2796427.

118 OLG Frankfurt 6. Senat für Familiensachen (August 17, 2021), ECLI: DE:OLGHE:2021:0817.6UF120.21.00, Bürgerservice Hessenrecht, https://www.rv.hessenrecht.hessen.de/bshe/document/LARE210001496.

119 Magdalena Pötsch, "Werden Wir Uns Künftig Jedes Jahr Gegen Corona Impfen," *Der Standard,* March 7, 2023, https://www.derstandard.de/story/2000144188357/werden-wir-uns-kuenftig-jedes-jahr-gegen-corona-impfen.

120 "US-Arzneimittelbehörde Wohl für Jährliches Impfschema bei Corona," *Der Standard,* January 23, 2023, https://www.derstandard.de/story/2000142900427/amerikanische-fda-wohl-fuer-jaehrliches-impfschema-bei-corona; "FDA Proposes Once-a-Year COVID Vaccine Shots for Most Americans," CBS News, January 23, 2023, https://www.cbsnews.com/news/fda-covid-shots-yearly-for-most-americans/.

121 Karen Gilchrist, "Bill Gates Says Covid Risks Have 'Dramatically Reduced' but Another Pandemic Is Coming," CNBC, February 18, 2022, https://www.cnbc.com/2022/02/18/bill-gates-covid-risks-have-reduced-but-another-pandemic-will-come.html.

122 Camille Bello, "Bill Gates Says the Next Big Threat Facing Humanity Is Bioterrorism. Interpol Agrees," Euronews (website), last modified February 14, 2023, https://www.euronews.com/next/2023/02/14/bill-gates-says-the-next-big-threat-facing-humanity-is-bioterrorism-interpol-agrees.

123 Sergio Imparato and Sarosh Nagar, "The WHO's New Pandemic Treaty Is Good for the World—and the US," *Stat* (website), January 20, 2023, https://www.statnews.com/2023/01/20/new-pandemic-treaty-good-for-world-and-america/.

124 Sprouts Deutschland, "Bonhoeffer's Theorie der Dummheit," January 23, 2022, YouTube video, 6:32, https://www.youtube.com/watch?v=wnhL1W9dj1w.

125 Sophie Eicher et al., "Quality of Life during the COVID-19 Pandemic—Results of the CORONA HEALTH App Study," Supplement, *Journal of Health Monitoring* 6, no. S6 (October 2021), 2–21, https://www.ncbi.nlm.nih.gov/pmc/articles/PMC8832366/.

126 Michiel A. J. Luijten et al., "The Impact of Lockdown during the COVID-19 Pandemic on Mental and Social Health of Children and Adolescents," *Quality of Life Research* 30, no. 10 (2021): 2795–804, https://www.ncbi.nlm.nih.gov/pmc/articles/PMC8122188/.

127 Sandra Düzel et al., "Structural Brain Correlates of Loneliness among Older Adults," *Scientific Reports* 9 (2019): https://www.ncbi.nlm.nih.gov/pmc/articles/PMC6753249/.

128 Risna K. Radhakrishnan and Mahesh Kandasamy, "SARS-CoV-2-Mediated Neuropathogenesis, Deterioration of Hippocampal Neurogenesis and Dementia," *American Journal of Alzheimer's Disease & Other Dementias* 37 (2022): https://journals.sagepub.com/doi/10.1177/15333175221078418.

129 Jiaqi Xiong et al., "Impact of COVID-19 Pandemic on Mental Health in the General Population: A Systematic Review," *Journal of Affective Disorders* 277 (December 1, 2020): 55–64, https://www.ncbi.nlm.nih.gov/pmc/articles/PMC7413844/.

130 Carlo Lazzari and Marco Rabottini, "COVID-19, Loneliness, Social Isolation and Risk of Dementia in Older People: A Systematic Review and Meta-Analysis of the Relevant Literature," *International Journal of Psychiatry in Clinical Practice* 26, no. 2 (June 2022): 196–207, https://pubmed.ncbi.nlm.nih.gov/34369248/.

131 Xiaohuan Xia, Yi Wang, and Jialin Zheng "COVID-19 and Alzheimer's Disease: How One Crisis Worsens the Other," *Translational Neurodegeneration* 10 (2021): 15, https://www.ncbi.nlm.nih.gov/pmc/articles/PMC8090526/.

132 Narayanaperumal Mugunthan et al., "Effects of Long Term Exposure of 900-1800 MHz Radiation Emitted from 2G Mobile Phone on Mice Hippocampus—a Histomorphometric Study," *Journal of Clinical & Diagnostic Research* 10, no. 8 (August 2016): 1–6, https://www.ncbi.nlm.nih.gov/pmc/articles/PMC5028475/.

133 Mahsa Eghlidospour et al., "Effects of Radiofrequency Exposure Emitted from a GSM Mobile Phone on Proliferation, Differentiation, and Apoptosis of Neural Stem Cells," *Anatomy & Cell Biology* 50, no. 2 (June 2017): 115–23, https://www.ncbi.nlm.nih.gov/pmc/articles/PMC5509895/.

134 Shearwood McClelland III and Jerry J. Jaboin, "The Radiation Safety of 5G Wi-Fi: Reassuring or Russian Roulette?," *International Journal of Radiation Oncology, Biology, Physics* 101, no. 5 (August 1, 2018): 1274–75, https://pubmed.ncbi.nlm.nih.gov/30012534/.

135 Jin-Hwa Moon, "Health Effects of Electromagnetic Fields on Children," *Clinical and Experimental Pediatrics* 63, no. 11 (November 2020): 422–28, https://www.ncbi.nlm.nih.gov/pmc/articles/PMC7642138/.

136 "EHT Wins in Historic Decision, Federal Court Orders FCC to Explain Why It Ignored Scientific Evidence Showing Harm from Wireless Radiation." Environmental Health Trust, August 16, 2021, https://ehtrust.org/in-historic-decision-federal-court-finds-fcc-failed-to-explain-why-it-ignored-scientific-evidence-showing-harm-from-wireless-radiation/.

137 Alexander C. Stahn et al., "Brain Changes in Response to Long Antarctic Expeditions," *New England Journal of Medicine* 381, no. 23 (December 5, 2019): 2273–75, https://www.nejm.org/doi/pdf/10.1056/NEJMc1904905.

138 "Isolation und Monotonie Lassen das Hirn Schrumfen," *SWR* (website), December 13, 2019, https://www.swr.de/wissen/artikel-hirn-schrumpft-bei-isolation-100.html.

139 Helmut Traindl, "Zusammenfassendes Gutachten zur Unwirksamkeit von Masken als Virenschutz und Gesundheitsschädigende Auswirkungen," *Fortschrittinfreiheit* (website), December 9, 2022, https://fortschrittinfreiheit.de/gutachten-unwirksamkeit-von-masken/; Helmut Trendl, *Argumentationschilfe zur Maskenproblematik für Eltern von Schulkindern* (self-pub., October 20, 2022), https://www.afa-zone.at/allgemein/auswirkungen-von-masken-neues-gutachten-ueber-medizinische-psychologische-und-soziologische-vor-und-nachteile/.

140 Sunah Hyun et al., "Psychological Correlates of Poor Sleep Quality among U.S. Young Adults during the COVID-19 Pandemic," *Sleep Medicine* 78 (February 2021): 51–56, https://www.ncbi.nlm.nih.gov/pmc/articles/PMC7887075/.

141 Prerna Varma et al., "Younger People Are More Vulnerable to Stress, Anxiety and Depression during COVID-19 Pandemic: A Global Cross-Sectional Survey," *Progress in Neuro-Psychopharmacology & Biological Psychiatry* (July 13, 2021): https://www.ncbi.nlm.nih.gov/pmc/articles/PMC7834119/.

142 Stephanie Stockwell et al., "Changes in Physical Activity and Sedentary Behaviours from before to during the COVID-19 Pandemic Lockdown: A Systematic Review," *BMJ Open Sport & Exercise Medicine* 7, no. 1 (2021): https://www.ncbi.nlm.nih.gov/pmc/articles/PMC7852071/.

143 Paulo José Puccinelli et al., "Reduced Level of Physical Activity during COVID-19 Pandemic Is Associated with Depression and Anxiety Levels: An Internet-Based Survey," *BMC Public Health* 21 (2021): 425, https://www.ncbi.nlm.nih.gov/pmc/articles/PMC7919983/.

144 Steffen C. E. Schmidt et al., "Physical Activity and Screen Time of Children and Adolescents before and during the COVID-19 Lockdown in Germany: A Natural

Experiment," *Scientific Reports* 10 (2020): https://www.nature.com/articles/s41598-020-78438-4.

145 "Oberärztin: 'Gewichtszunahme bei Kindern in Bischer Nie Gesehenem Ausmass," *Ärzte Zeitung*, May 31, 2022, https://www.aerztezeitung.de/Medizin/Oberaerztin-Gewichtszunahme-bei-Kindern-in-bisher-nie-gesehenem-Ausmass-429557.html.

146 Susan E. Wozniak et al., "Adipose Tissue: The New Endocrine Organ? A Review Article," *Digestive Diseases and Sciences* 54, no. 9 (September 2009): 847–56, https://pubmed.ncbi.nlm.nih.gov/19052866/; Luigi Fontana et al., "Visceral Fat Adipokine Secretion Is Associated with Systemic Inflammation in Obese Humans," *Diabetes* 56, no. 4 (April 2007): 1010–13, https://diabetesjournals.org/diabetes/article/56/4/1010/12937/.

147 Nehls, "Unified Theory."

148 Stéphanie Debette et al., "Visceral Fat Is Associated with Lower Brain Volume in Healthy Middle-Aged Adults," *Annals of Neurology* 68, no. 2 (August 2010): 136–44, https://www.ncbi.nlm.nih.gov/pmc/articles/PMC2933649/; April J. Ho et al., "Obesity Is Linked with Lower Brain Volume in 700 AD and MCI Patients," *Neurobiological Aging* 31, no. 8 (August 2010): 1326–39, https://www.ncbi.nlm.nih.gov/pmc/articles/PMC3197833/.

149 April J. Ho et al., "The Effects of Physical Activity, Education, and Body Mass Index on the Aging Brain," *Human Brain Mapping* 32, no. 9 (September 2011): 1371–82, https://www.ncbi.nlm.nih.gov/pmc/articles/PMC3184838/.

150 Natalia Gomes Gonçalves et al., "Association Between Consumption of Ultraprocessed Foods and Cognitive Decline," *JAMA Neurology* 80, no. 2 (February 2023): 142–50, https://pubmed.ncbi.nlm.nih.gov/36469335/; Barbara R. Cardoso et al., "Association between Ultra-Processed Food Consumption and Cognitive Performance in US Older Adults: A Cross-Sectional Analysis of the NHANES 2011–2014," *European Journal of Nutrition* 61, no. 8 (December 2022): 3975–85, https://pubmed.ncbi.nlm.nih.gov/35778619/.

151 Darryl Walter Eyles, "Vitamin D: Brain and Behavior," *Journal of Bone and Mineral Research Plus* 5, no. 1 (January 2020): https://www.ncbi.nlm.nih.gov/pmc/articles/PMC7839822/.

152 Jan Terock et al., "Vitamin D Deficit Is Associated with Accelerated Brain Aging in the General Population," *Psychiatry Research: Neuroimaging* 327 (December 2022): https://www.sciencedirect.com/science/article/abs/pii/S0925492722001172.

153 Hanze Chen et al., "25-Hydroxyvitamin D Levels and the Risk of Dementia and Alzheimer's Disease: A Dose-Response Meta-Analysis," *Frontiers in Aging Neuroscience* 10 (2018): 368, https://www.ncbi.nlm.nih.gov/pmc/articles/PMC6237859/.

154 J. Bart Classen, "US COVID-19 Vaccines Proven to Cause More Harm Than Good Based on Pivotal Clinical Trial Data Analyzed Using the Proper Scientific Endpoint, 'All Cause Severe Morbidity,'" *Trends Internal Medicine* 1, no. 1 (2021): 1–6, https://www.scivisionpub.com/pdfs/us-covid19-vaccines-proven-to-cause-more-harm

-than-good-based-on-pivotal-clinical-trial-data-analyzed-using-the-proper-scientific--1811.pdf.

155 J. J. Cannell et al., "Epidemic Influenza and Vitamin D," *Epidemiology & Infection* 134, no. 6 (December 2006): 1129–40, https://www.ncbi.nlm.nih.gov/pmc/articles/PMC2870528/.

156 Andrea Giustina, "Rapid Response to: Preventing a Covid-19 Pandemic," *British Medical Journal* 368 (February 2020): https://www.bmj.com/content/368/bmj.m810/rr-36.

157 William B. Grant et al., "Evidence That Vitamin D Supplementation Could Reduce Risk of Influenza and COVID-19 Infections and Deaths," *Nutrients* 12, no. 4 (April 2020): https://www.ncbi.nlm.nih.gov/pmc/articles/PMC7231123/.

158 Marta Entrenas-Castillo et al., "Calcifediol for Use in Treatment of Respiratory Disease," *Nutrients* 14, no. 12 (June 2022): https://www.ncbi.nlm.nih.gov/pmc/articles/PMC9231174/; Indra Ramasamy, "Vitamin D Metabolism and Guidelines for Vitamin D Supplementation," *Clinical Biochemist Reviews* 41, no. 3 (December 2020): 103–26, https://www.ncbi.nlm.nih.gov/pmc/articles/PMC7731935/.

159 Dieter De Smet et al., "Serum 25(OH)D Level on Hospital Admission Associated with COVID-19 Stage and Mortality," *American Journal of Clinical Pathology* 155, no. 3 (February 11, 2021): 381–88, https://www.ncbi.nlm.nih.gov/pmc/articles/PMC7717135/.

160 Ariel Israel et al., "Vitamin D Deficiency Is Associated with Higher Risks for SARS-CoV-2 Infection and COVID-19 Severity: A Retrospective Case-Control Study," *Internal and Emergency Medicine* 17, no. 4 (June 2022):1053–63, https://pubmed.ncbi.nlm.nih.gov/35000118/.

161 Martina Rabenberg et al., "Vitamin D Status among Adults in Germany—Results from the German Health Interview and Examination Survey for Adults (DEGS1)," *BMC Public Health* 15 (2015): 641, https://www.ncbi.nlm.nih.gov/pmc/articles/PMC4499202/.

162 Aleksandar Radujkovic et al., "Vitamin D Deficiency and Outcome of COVID-19 Patients," *Nutrients* 12, no. 9 (September 2020): https://www.mdpi.com/2072-6643/12/9/2757.

163 Marta Entrenas Castillo et al., "Effect of Calcifediol Treatment and Best Available Therapy versus Best Available Therapy on Intensive Care Unit Admission and Mortality among Patients Hospitalized for COVID-19: A Pilot Randomized Clinical Study," *Journal of Steroid Biochemistry and Molecular Biology* 203 (October 2020): https://www.ncbi.nlm.nih.gov/pmc/articles/PMC7456194.

164 Igor H. Murai et al., "Effect of a Single High Dose of Vitamin D3 on Hospital Length of Stay in Patients with Moderate to Severe COVID-19: A Randomized Clinical Trial," *JAMA* 325, no. 11 (March 16, 2021): 1053–60, https://www.ncbi.nlm.nih.gov/pmc/articles/PMC7890452/.

165 Maria Weiss, "Nahrungsergänzung als Schutz for Schwerem COVID-19-Verlauf: Hochdosiertes Vitamin D3 Versagt in Brasilianischer Studie," Medscape, March 2, 2021, https://deutsch.medscape.com/artikelansicht/4909769.

166 Irwin Jungreis and Manolis Kellis, "Mathematical Analysis of Córdoba Calcifediol Trial Suggests Strong Role for Vitamin D in Reducing ICU Admissions of Hospitalized COVID-19 Patients, *medRxiv* (forthcoming), https://www.medrxiv.org/content/10.1101/2020.11.08.20222638v2.

167 Jorge B. Cannata-Andía et al., "A Single-Oral Bolus of 100,000 IU of Cholecalciferol at Hospital Admission Did Not Improve Outcomes in the COVID-19 Disease: The COVID-VIT-D—a Randomised Multicentre International Clinical Trial," *BMC Medicine* 20 (2022): 83, https://www.ncbi.nlm.nih.gov/pmc/articles/PMC8853840/; Javier Mariani et al., "High-Dose Vitamin D versus Placebo to Prevent Complications in COVID-19 Patients: Multicentre Randomized Controlled Clinical Trial," *PLoS One* 17, no. 5 (2022): https://www.ncbi.nlm.nih.gov/pmc/articles/PMC9140264/.

168 Juan F. Alcala-Diaz et al., "Calcifediol Treatment and Hospital Mortality Due to COVID-19: A Cohort Study," *Nutrients* 13, no. 6 (June 2021): https://www.ncbi.nlm.nih.gov/pmc/articles/PMC8224356/; Xavier Nogues et al., "Calcifediol Treatment and COVID-19-Related Outcomes," *Journal of Clinical Endocrinology and Metabolism* (June 7, 2021): 4017–27, https://www.ncbi.nlm.nih.gov/pmc/articles/PMC8344647/.

169 Yasmine M. Elamir et al., "A Randomized Pilot Study Using Calcitriol in Hospitalized COVID-19 Patients," *Bone* 154 (2022); https://www.ncbi.nlm.nih.gov/pmc/articles/PMC8425676/pdf/main.pdf.

170 Meryl S. LeBoff et al., "Supplemental Vitamin D and Incident Fractures in Midlife and Older Adults," *New England Journal of Medicine* 387, no. 4 (July 28, 2022): 299–309, https://www.ncbi.nlm.nih.gov/pmc/articles/PMC9716639/.

171 Lorenz Borsche, Bernd Glauner, and Julian von Mendel, "COVID-19 Mortality Risk Correlates Inversely with Vitamin D3 Status, and a Mortality Rate Close to Zero Could Theoretically Be Achieved at 50 ng/mL 25(OH)D3: Results of a Systematic Review and Meta-Analysis," *Nutrients* 13, no. 10 (October 2021): https://www.ncbi.nlm.nih.gov/pmc/articles/PMC8541492/.

172 Jill Hahn et al., "Vitamin D and Marine Omega 3 Fatty Acid Supplementation and Incident Autoimmune Disease: VITAL Randomized Controlled Trial," *British Medical Journal* 376 (2022): https://www.ncbi.nlm.nih.gov/pmc/articles/PMC8791065/.

173 Tobias Niedermaier et al., "Potential of Vitamin D Food Fortification in Prevention of Cancer Deaths—A Modeling Study," *Nutrients* 13, no. 11 (November 2021): https://www.ncbi.nlm.nih.gov/pmc/articles/PMC8621821/.

174 Koh [pseud.], "Vitamin D Supplementation: Possible Gain in Life Years plus Cost Savings," news release, Deutsches Krebsforschungszentrum, November 2, 2021, https://www.dkfz.de/en/presse/pressemitteilungen/2021/dkfz-pm-21-07-Vitamin-D-supplementation-possible-gain-in-life-years-plus-cost-savings.php.

175 Hermann Brenner, Ben Schöttker, and Tobias Niedermaier, "Vitamin D3 for Reducing Mortality from Cancer and Other Outcomes before, during and beyond the COVID-19 Pandemic: A Plea for Harvesting Low-Hanging Fruit, *Cancer Communications* 42, no. 8 (August 2022): 679–82, https://www.ncbi.nlm.nih.gov/pmc/articles/PMC9395316/.

176 Steven R. Cummings and Clifford Rosen, "VITAL Findings—a Decisive Verdict on Vitamin D Supplementation," *New England Journal of Medicine* 387 (July 28, 2022): 368–70, https://www.nejm.org/doi/full/10.1056/NEJMe2205993.

177 Stephan Martin, "Kein Mangel—Kein Nutzen: Woher Kommt der Vitamin-Hype und War die Fischöl-Studie 'Eigentlich ein Pharma-Skandal'?" Medscape, August 29, 2022, https://deutsch.medscape.com/artikelansicht/4911508?src=WNL_mdplsfeat_220829_mscpedit_de&uac=163807MK&impID=4583728&faf=1#vp_2.

178 Mirjam E. Belderbos et al., "Cord Blood Vitamin D Deficiency Is Associated with Respiratory Syncytial Virus Bronchiolitis," *Pediatrics* 127, no. 6 (June 2011): 1513–20, https://pubmed.ncbi.nlm.nih.gov/21555499/.

179 F. Martin Ferolla et al., "Serum Vitamin D Levels and Life-Threatening Respiratory Syncytial Virus Infection in Previously Healthy Infants," *Journal of Infectious Diseases* 226, no. 6 (September 2022): 958–66, https://pubmed.ncbi.nlm.nih.gov/35106574/.

180 Xirui Qiu et al., "Development of mRNA Vaccines against Respiratory Syncytial Virus (RSV)," *Cytokine Growth Factor Reviews* 68 (December 2022): 37–53, https://pubmed.ncbi.nlm.nih.gov/36280532/.

181 Cuizhen Zhu et al., "Vitamin D Supplementation Improves Anxiety but Not Depression Symptoms in Patients with Vitamin D Deficiency," *Brain and Behavior* 10, no. 11 (November 2020): https://www.ncbi.nlm.nih.gov/pmc/articles/PMC7667301/; Fatme Al Anouti et al., "Associations between Dietary Intake of Vitamin D, Sun Exposure, and Generalized Anxiety among College Women," *Nutrients* 14, no. 24 (December 2022): https://www.ncbi.nlm.nih.gov/pmc/articles/PMC9780868/.

182 Moritz Breit, et al., "Students' Intelligence Test Results after Six and Sixteen Months of Irregular Schooling Due to the COVID-19 Pandemic," *PLoS One* 18, no. 3 (2023): https://www.ncbi.nlm.nih.gov/pmc/articles/PMC9994686/.

183 "Depressive Disorder (Depression)," World Health Organization, March 31, 2023, https://www.who.int/news-room/fact-sheets/detail/depression.

184 Lisa Nobis et al., "Hippocampal Volume across Age: Nomograms Derived from over 19,700 People in UK Biobank," *Neuroimage Clinical* 23 (2019): https://www.ncbi.nlm.nih.gov/pmc/articles/PMC6603440/.

185 Elizabet Alzueta et al., "Risk for Depression Tripled during the COVID-19 Pandemic in Emerging Adults Followed for the Last 8 Years," *Psychological Medicine* 53, no. 5 (April 2021): 2156–63, https://pubmed.ncbi.nlm.nih.gov/34726149/.

186 Catherine K. Ettman et al., "Prevalence of Depression Symptoms in US Adults before and during the COVID-19 Pandemic," *JAMA Network Open* 3, no. 9 (September 2020): https://www.ncbi.nlm.nih.gov/pmc/articles/PMC7489837/. Figure adapted.

187 Andie MacNeil et al., "Incident and Recurrent Depression among Adults Aged 50 Years and Older during the COVID-19 Pandemic: A Longitudinal Analysis of the Canadian Longitudinal Study on Aging," *International Journal of Environmental Research and Public Health* 19, no. 22 (November 2022): https://www.ncbi.nlm.nih.gov/pmc/articles/PMC9690838/. Figure adapted.

188 Asim Handy et al., "Prevalence and Impact of Diagnosed and Undiagnosed Depression in the United States," *Cureus* 14, no. 8 (August 2022): https://www.ncbi.nlm.nih.gov/pmc/articles/PMC9470500/.

189 J. S. Saczynski et al., "Depressive Symptoms and Risk of Dementia: The Framingham Heart Study," *Neurology* 75, no. 1 (July 6, 2010): 35–41, https://www.ncbi.nlm.nih.gov/pmc/articles/PMC2906404/.

190 Laura Zahodne, Yaakov Stern, and Jennifer J. Manly, "Depressive Symptoms Precede Memory Decline, but Not Vice Versa, in Non-Demented Older Adults," *Journal of the American Geriatrics Society* 62, no. 1 (January 2014): 130–34, https://doi.org/10.1111/jgs.12600.

191 Deutsche Alzheimer Gesellschaft e.V. Selbsthilfe Demenz, *Die Häufigkeit von Demenzerkrankungen* (Berlin: Deutsche Alzheimer Gesellschaft e.V. Selbsthilfe Demenz, n.d.), https://www.deutsche-alzheimer.de/fileadmin/Alz/pdf/factsheets/infoblatt1_haeufigkeit_demenzerkrankungen_dalzg.pdf.

192 Ibid.

193 Deutsche Alzheimer Gesellschaft e.V. Selbsthilfe Demenz, *Das Wichtigste die Epidemiologie der Demenz* (Berlin: Deutsche Alzheimer Gesellschaft e.V. Selbsthilfe Demenz, n.d.), https://alzheimer-mv.de/wp-content/uploads/2018/11/die-epidemiologie-der-demenz.pdf.

194 Alzheimer's Association, *2023 Alzheimer's Disease Facts and Figures* (Chicago: Alzheimer's Association, 2023), 31, https://www.alz.org/media/documents/alzheimers-facts-and-figures.pdf.

195 Ibid. p. 30

196 Deutsche Alzheimer Gesellschaft, *Die Häufigkeit.*

197 "GBD 2019 Dementia Forecasting Collaborators: Estimation of the Global Prevalence of Dementia in 2019 and Forecasted Prevalence in 2050: An Analysis for the Global Burden of Disease Study 2019," *Lancet Public Health* 7, no. 2 (February 2022): 105–25, https://www.ncbi.nlm.nih.gov/pmc/articles/PMC8810394/.

198 Martin Prince et al., "The Global Prevalence of Dementia: A Systematic Review and Metaanalysis," *Alzheimer's & Dementia* 9, no. 1 (January 2013):: 63–75, https://pubmed.ncbi.nlm.nih.gov/23305823/.

199 Bundesärztekammer, *Post-COVID-Syndrom (PCS)* (Berlin: Bundesärztekammer, 2022), https://doi.org/10.3238/arztebl.2022.Stellungnahme_PCS.

200 Felicia Ceban et al., "Fatigue and Cognitive Impairment in Post-COVID-19 Syndrome: A Systematic Review and Meta-Analysis," *Brain, Behavior, and Immunity* 101 (March 2022): 93–135, https://www.ncbi.nlm.nih.gov/pmc/articles/PMC8715665/.

201 Robyn Klein et al., "COVID-19 Induces Neuroinflammation and Loss of Hippocampal Neurogenesis," *Research Square* (forthcoming), https://www.ncbi.nlm.nih.gov/pmc/articles/PMC8562542/pdf/nihpp-rs1031824v1.pdf; Alessandra Borsini et al., "Neurogenesis Is Disrupted in Human Hippocampal Progenitor Cells upon Exposure to Serum Samples from Hospitalized COVID-19 Patients with Neurological Symptoms," *Molecular Psychiatry* 27 (2022): 5049–61, https://doi.org/10.1038/s41380-022-01741-1.

202 Siwen Wang et al., "Associations of Depression, Anxiety, Worry, Perceived Stress, and Loneliness Prior to Infection with Risk of Post-COVID-19 Conditions," *JAMA Psychiatry* 79, no. 11 (November 2022): 1081–91, https://www.ncbi.nlm.nih.gov/pmc/articles/PMC9453634/.

CHAPTER 5

1 Rutger Bregman, *Humankind: A Hopeful History* (London: Bloomsbury Publishing 2021). First published 2019 by De Correspondent BV (Amsterdam).

2 George Orwell, review of *Power: A New Social Analysis,* by Bertrand Russell, *Adelphi,* January 1939, https://www.lehman.edu/faculty/rcarey/BRSQ/06may.orwell.htm.

3 George Orwell, *1984* (New York: Penguin Books, 1982), 68. First published 1949 by Secker & Warburg (London).

4 Ibid.

5 C. E. Nyder, *Young Global Leaders: Die Saat des Klaus Schwab* (Rottenburg, Germany: Kopp Verlag, 2022), 30.

6 Ibid., 132–33.

7 World Health Organization, *Zero Draft of the WHO CA+ for the Consideration of the Intergovernmental Negotiating Body at Its Fourth Meeting* (Geneva: World Health Organization, February 1, 2023), https://apps.who.int/gb/inb/pdf_files/inb4/A_INB4_3-en.pdf.

8 Deutscher Bundestag, "Bundestag Fordert Reform der Weltgesundheitsorganisation," May 12, 2023, text and video, 47:26, https://www.bundestag.de/dokumente/textarchiv/2023/kw19-de-weltgesundheitsorganisation-947084.

9 World Economic Forum, "The Great Narrative," November 10–13, 2021, https://www.weforum.org/events/the-great-narrative-2021.

10 Tim Hinchliffe, "WEF's 'Great Narrative' Blends Tech, Society, Economy, Politics & Nature into Story for Humankind," *The Sociable* (blog), November 16, 2021, https://sociable.co/government-and-policy/wef-great-narrative-tech-society-economy-politics-nature/.

11 Ibid.

12 Klaus Schwab and Thierry Malleret, *The Great Narrative: For a Better Future* (Geneva: Forum Publishing, 2022), 102 in the German version, translated by the author.

13 Jess Hill, "'It's Like You Go to Abuse School': How Domestic Violence Always Follows the Same Script," *The Guardian,* June 23, 2019, https://www.theguardian.com/society/2019/jun/24/its-like-you-go-to-abuse-school-how-domestic-violence-always-follows-the-same-script.

14 Lawrence E. Hinkle and Harold G. Wolff, "The Methods of Interrogation and Indoctrination Used by the Communist State Police," *Bulletin of the New York Academy of Medicine* 33, no. 9 (September 1957): 600–15, https://www.ncbi.nlm.nih.gov/pmc/articles/PMC1806200/.

15 Hill, "'It's Like You Go to Abuse School.'"

16 Hinkle and Wolff, "The Methods."

17 Albert D. Biderman, "Communist Attempts to Elicit False Confessions from Air Force Prisoners of War," *Bulletin of the New York Academy of Medicine* 33, no. 9 (September 1957): 616–25, https://www.ncbi.nlm.nih.gov/pmc/articles/PMC1806204/.

18 Ibid.

19 William Beecher Scoville and Brenda Milner, "Loss of Recent Memory after Bilateral Hippocampal Lesions," *Journal of Neurology, Neurosurgery, and Psychiatry* 20, no. 1 (February 1957): 11–21, https://www.ncbi.nlm.nih.gov/pmc/articles/PMC497229/.

20 J. Altman and G. D. Das, "Autoradiographic and Histological Evidence of Postnatal Hippocampal Neurogenesis in Rats," *Journal of Comparative Neurology* 124, no. 3 (June 1965): 319–35, https://pubmed.ncbi.nlm.nih.gov/5861717/.

21 H. George Kuhn, Tomohisa Toda, and Fred H. Gage, "Adult Hippocampal Neurogenesis: A Coming-of-Age Story," *Journal of Neuroscience* 38, no. 49 (December 5, 2018): 10401–10, https://www.ncbi.nlm.nih.gov/pmc/articles/PMC6284110/.

22 Michael Nehls,: *Das Erschöpfte Gehirn: Der Ursprung Unserer Mentalen Energie—und Warum Sie Schwindet—Willenskraft, Kreativität und Fokus zurückgewinnen* (Munich: Heyne Verlag, 2022).

23 "COVID-19-Impfempfehlung (Stand 5.6.2023)," Robert Koch Institut, June 5, 2023, https://www.rki.de/SharedDocs/FAQ/COVID-Impfen/FAQ_Liste_STIKO_Empfehlungen.html.

24 Scott Shane, "China Inspired Interrogations at Guantánamo," *New York Times,* July 2, 2008, https://www.nytimes.com/2008/07/02/world/americas/02iht-02detain.14154569.html.

25 Hill, "'It's Like You Go to Abuse School.'"

26 "Fahrlässige Tötung? Ungeimpfte Ex-Pflegeheim-Mitarbeiterin vor Gericht," *Donaukurier,* February 22, 2023, https://www.donaukurier.de/nachrichten/panorama/ungeimpfte-ex-pflegeheim-mitarbeiterin-vor-gericht-10589188.

27 "Covid: Australian Anti-Lockdown Suspect's Arrest Draws Controversy," BBC News, September 3, 2020, https://www.bbc.com/news/world-australia-54007824.

28 Hinkle and Wolff, "The Methods."

29 Nyder Dr CE: *Great Reset: Der Angriff auf Demokratie, Nationalstaat und bürgerliche Gesellschaft.* Kopp 2021, p. 200 (translated by the author)

30 Bettina Gruber, *Leben unterm Regenbogen: Das Neue Geschlechterregime und Seine Folgen* (Warsaw: Manuscriptum Publishing House, 2020) https://www.manuscriptum.de/leben-unterm-regenbogen.html (zum Buch).

31 "Stockholm Syndrome," Cleveland Clinic, last medically reviewed February 14, 2022, https://my.clevelandclinic.org/health/diseases/22387-stockholm-syndrome.

32 Somya Singh, "Stockholm Syndrome: A Psychiatric Diagnosis or Just a Myth?" *International Journal of Trend in Scientific Research and Development* 6, no. 2 (January-February 2008): 354–61, https://www.ijtsrd.com/papers/ijtsrd49242.pdf.

33 "WEF Young Global Leaders—die Liste der Deutschen Teilnehmer," *Business Leaders* (website), n.d., https://www.business-leaders.net/wef-young-global-leaders-die-liste-der-deutschen-teilnehmer/.

34 "Beliebtester Politiker Deutschlands Jens Spahn Zieht an Angela Merkel Vorbei," *Tagesspiegel*, December 27, 2020, https://www.tagesspiegel.de/politik/jens-spahn-zieht-an-angela-merkel-vorbei-7709026.html.

35 "Wir Impfen Deutschland Zurück in die Freiheit," *Welt* (website), August 24, 2021, https://www.welt.de/politik/deutschland/article233333163/Jens-Spahn-zu-Corona-Wir-impfen-Deutschland-zurueck-in-die-Freiheit.html.

36 Luisa Weckesser, "Umfrage zu Deutschlands Beliebtesten Politikern: Karl Lauterbach an der Spitze," *HNA* (website), January 27, 2022, https://www.hna.de/politik/umfrage-deutschlands-beliebteste-politiker-karl-lauterbach-platz-eins-hna-news-91264436.html.

37 Laurel Wamsley, "Vaccinated People with Breakthrough Infections Can Spread the Delta Variant, CDC Says," NPR, July 30, 2021, www.npr.org/sections/coronavirus-live-updates/2021/07/30/1022867219/cdc-study-provincetown-delta-vaccinated-breakthrough-mask-guidance.

38 Catherine M. Brown et al., "Outbreak of SARS-CoV-2 Infections, Including COVID-19 Vaccine Breakthrough Infections, Associated with Large Public Gatherings—Barnstable County, Massachusetts, July 2021," *Morbidity and Mortality Weekly Report* 70, no. 31 (August 6, 2021): 1059–62, https://www.ncbi.nlm.nih.gov/pmc/articles/PMC8367314/.

39 https://www.mass.gov/doc/daily-covid-19-vaccine-report-july-30-2021/download.

40 Berkeley Lovelace Jr., "CDC Study Shows 74% of People Infected in Massachusetts Covid Outbreak Were Fully Vaccinated," CNBC, July 30, 2021, https://www.cnbc.com/2021/07/30/cdc-study-shows-74percent-of-people-infected-in-massachusetts-covid-outbreak-were-fully-vaccinated.html; Catherine M. Brown et al., "Outbreak of SARS-CoV-2 Infections, Including COVID-19 Vaccine Breakthrough Infections, Associated with Large Public Gatherings—Barnstable County, Massachusetts, July 2021," *Morbidity and Mortality Weekly Report* 70, no. 31 (August 6, 2021): 1059–62, https://www.cdc.gov/mmwr/volumes/70/wr/mm7031e2.htm.

41 "Viel Bessere Situation als im Letzten Herbst," *Süddeutsche Zeitung*, August 3, 2022, https://www.sueddeutsche.de/politik/infektionsschutzgesetz-corona-herbst-1.5633304.

42 Jens Spahn, *Wir Werden Einander Viel Verzeihen Müssen: Wie die Pandemie Uns Verändert Hat—und Was Sie Uns für die Zukunft Lehrt. Innenansichten einer Krise* (Munich: Heyne Verlag, 2022).

43 Charles W. Simon and William H. Emmons, "EEG, Consciousness, and Sleep," *Science* 124 (1956): 1066–69, https://www.rand.org/content/dam/rand/pubs/papers/2015/P655.pdf.

44 Hinkle and Wolff, "The Methods."

45 Paul D. Thacker, "Covid-19: Researcher Blows the Whistle on Data Integrity Issues in Pfizer's Vaccine Trial," *British Medical Journal* 375 (2021): https://www.bmj.com/content/375/bmj.n2635.

46 Karina Acevedo-Whitehouse et al., "SARS-CoV-2 Mass Vaccination: Urgent Questions on Vaccine Safety That Demand Answers from International Health Agencies, Regulatory Authorities, Governments and Vaccine Developers," *ScienceOpen* (forthcoming), https://www.scienceopen.com/document?vid=2e541e0b-64fd-4a3f-bf5b-735425cfd39d.

47 "Die Geschichte des Impfens und Seiner Gegner," *NDR* (website), February 11, 2022, https://www.ndr.de/geschichte/chronologie/Pocken-Polio-Covid-Geschichte-des-Impfens-und-seiner-Gegner,impfen446.html; W. U. Eckart and H. Vondra, "Malaria and World War II: German Malaria Experiments 1939–45," *Parassitologia* 42, no. 1-2 (June 2000): 53–58, https://pubmed.ncbi.nlm.nih.gov/11234332/.

48 "Great Barrington Declaration," accessed April 1, 2023, https://gbdeclaration.org/.

49 "How Fauci and Collins Shut Down Covid Debate," *Wall Street Journal*, December 21, 2021, https://www.wsj.com/articles/fauci-collins-emails-great-barrington-declaration-covid-pandemic-lockdown-11640129116.

50 Yaffa Shir-Raz et al., "Censorship and Suppression of Covid-19 Heterodoxy: Tactics and Counter-Tactics," *Minerva* (November 1, 2022): 1–27, https://www.ncbi.nlm.nih.gov/pmc/articles/PMC9628345/.

51 Nandita Bose, "Exclusive: White House Working with Facebook and Twitter to Tackle Anti-Vaxxers," Reuters, February 19, 2021, https://www.reuters.com/article/us-health-coronavirus-white-house-exclus-idUSKBN2AJ1SW.

52 "Schwere Verlaufsformen bei Infektion mit dem Coronavirus SARS-CoV-2 Reduzieren—Vitamin D-Mangel in der Bevölkerung Beseitigen, Immunabwehr Stärken," Deutscher Bundestag, 19th legislative period, https://dip.bundestag.de/vorgang/.../263715; Drucksache 19/20118, 19th legislative period, June 17, 2020, https://dserver.bundestag.de/btd/19/201/1920118.pdf.

53 "Schwere Verlaufsformen bei Infektion," Deutscher Bundestag; "Beschlussempfehlung und Bericht des Ausschusses für Gesundheit, case 19/20709, January 7, 2020, https://dserver.bundestag.de/btd/19/207/1920709.pdf.

54 Hellin Jankowski, "Kickl und die '3B' zur Bekämpfung der Pandemie," *Die Presse*, December 1, 2021, https://www.diepresse.com/6056027/kickl-und-die-3b-zur-bekaempfung-der-pandemie.

55 Eva Wolfangel, "Nein, Bayern Bereitet Keine Überwachung Chinesischer Art Vor," *Zeit Online*, July 27, 2022, https://www.zeit.de/digital/datenschutz/2022-07/oeko-token-bayern-belohnungssystem-social-scoring.
56 "AfD Verlangt Stopp des Digital-Euro," 321/2022, Deutscher Bundestag, June 22, 2022, https://www.bundestag.de/presse/hib/kurzmeldungen-900260.
57 Jessica C. Jimenez et al., "Anxiety Cells in a Hippocampal-Hypothalamic Circuit," *Neuron* 97, no. 3 (February 7, 2018): 670–83, https://www.ncbi.nlm.nih.gov/pmc/articles/PMC5877404/.
58 Helmut Laschet, "'Tyrannei der Ungeimpften': Der Zorn der Vernünftigen," *Ärzte Zeitung*, November 8, 2021, https://www.aerztezeitung.de/Politik/Tyrannei-der-Ungeimpften-Der-Zorn-der-Vernuenftigen-424260.html.
59 "Ursula von der Leyen, World Economic Forum, n.d., https://www.weforum.org/agenda/authors/ursula-von-der-leyen.
60 Laura Wolf, Anna Kröning, and Jörg Rössner, "Spahn Offen für Dauer-2G- 'Nur noch Supermarkt oder Rathaus für Ungeimpfte," *Welt* (website), November 27, 20212, https://www.welt.de/wissenschaft/article235318154/Corona-Spahn-will-Einschraenkungen-fuer-Ungeimpfte-und-2G-auf-lange-Zeit.html)
61 Viola Ulrich and Sandra Will, "In Deutschland Reicht es Nicht, den Ungeimpften auf die Nerven zu Gehen, Da Muss Man Mehr Tun," *Welt* (website), February 9, 2022, https://www.welt.de/vermischtes/article236773399/Lauterbach-Es-reicht-nicht-den-Ungeimpften-nur-auf-die-Nerven-zu-gehen.html.
62 Metin Gülmen, "Tafel in NRW: Deutliche 2G-Ansage! 'Jeder Hatte die Chance, Sich Impfen zu Lassen,'" *Der Westen* (website), November 25, 2021, https://www.derwesten.de/region/tafel-in-nrw-corona-impfung-news-3g-2g-unna-id233932473.html; Leslie Brook, "Tafel Nur für Geimpfte und Genesene," *Rheinische Post,* April 26, 2022, https://rp-online.de/nrw/staedte/moenchengladbach/moenchengladbach-tafel-gibt-lebensmittel-nur-noch-an-geimpfte-und-genesene-aus_aid-68319147.
63 "Zeitlese," *Zeit Online*, January 6, 1984, https://www.zeit.de/1984/02/zeitlese.
64 Biderman, "Communist Attempts."
65 "Infektionsgeschehen Rührt von den Ungeimpften Her," *Welt* (website), December 7, 2021, https://www.welt.de/politik/deutschland/article235509824/Designierter-Kanzler-Scholz-Infektionsgeschehen-ruehrt-von-den-Ungeimpften-her.html.
66 Marco Blanco-Ucles, "Corona-Impfung Umsonst? Obwohl Gibraltar Fast Durchgeimpft Ist, Liegt die Inzidenz bei 600," *Merkur.de*, July 30, 2021, http://www.merkur.de/welt/corona-impfung-wirkung-umsonst-inzidenz-infektionszahlen-gibraltar-entwicklung-zr-90887550.html.
67 "Stille Nacht, der Nachbar Gafft," *Blick*, December 6, 2012, https://www.blick.ch/schweiz/denunzianten-sind-durch-corona-im-aufschwung-stille-nacht-der-nachbar-gafft-id16231318.html.
68 "Ausgangssperre Wegen Corona Bundesweit Einheitlich Geregelt," Bussgeldkatalog 2023, May 14, 2023, https://www.bussgeldkatalog.org/ausgangssperre-corona/.

69 Christina Berndt, "Komm, Guter Tod!," *Süddeutsche Zeitung*, April 15, 2022, https://www.sueddeutsche.de/gesundheit/tod-sterben-pandemie-corona-covid-19-1.5566773.

70 Hilmar Klute, "November des Zorns," *Süddeutsche Zeitung,* November 21, 2021, https://www.sueddeutsche.de/meinung/freiheit-ungeimpfte-zorn-verantwortung-solidaritaet-1.5468187?reduced=true.

71 "Ethikrat-Mitglied fordert Impfgegner sollen auf Beatmung verzichten," ntv, December 19, 2020, https://www.n-tv.de/panorama/Impfgegner-sollen-auf-Beatmung-verzichten-article22246339.html.

72 Michael Bang Petersen, "'Ungeimpfte Wurden als Weniger Intelligent Wahrgenommen. Die Vorturteile Gegen Sie Waren Verbreiteter als Vorurteile Gegen Migranten," interview by Pauline Voss, *Neue Zürcher Zeitung,* February 25, 2023, https://www.nzz.ch/international/corona-pandemie-ungeimpfte-galten-als-weniger-intelligent-ld.1725006.

73 Alexander Bor, Frederik Jørgensen, and Michael Bang Petersen, "Discriminatory Attitudes against Unvaccinated People during the Pandemic," *Nature* 613 (2023): 704–11, https://www.nature.com/articles/s41586-022-05607-y.

74 Klaus Wilhelm, "Vom Segen und Fluch des Hoffens," *Psychologie Heute*, September 9, 2020, https://www.psychologie-heute.de/leben/artikel-detailansicht/40779-vom-segen-und-fluch-des-hoffens.html.

75 Biderman, "Communist Attempts."

76 "Piks auf Kassenkosten Soll Möglich Bleiben," *Tagesschau,* March 22, 2023, https://www.tagesschau.de/inland/corona-impfungen-201.html.

77 "Weisswurst-Impfen am Nockherberg—Samstag 15.1.2022," *Nachrichten München*, January 11, 2022, https://www.nachrichten-muenchen.com/weisswurst-impfen-am-nockherberg-samstag-15-1-2022/163431/.

78 Tobias Becker, "Sonderurlaub: Impfung, Umzug, Kinder—Wann Gibt's Extra Freie Tage?," *Heidelberg 24*, September 29, 2021, https://www.heidelberg24.de/verbraucher/sonderurlaub-antrag-kinder-job-hochzeit-impfung-umzug-zr-91018154.html.

79 Jens Thurau, "Kommentar: Politik der Kleinen Schritte Verspricht Grosses," Deutsche Welle, November 30, 2005, https://www.dw.com/de/kommentar-politik-der-kleinen-schritte-verspricht-gro%C3%9Fes/a-1797355.

80 "The Tale of the Boiling Frog," *Canadian Medical Association Journal* 172, no. 12 (December 7, 2004): https://www.ncbi.nlm.nih.gov/pmc/articles/PMC534568/

81 Raul G. Nogueira et al., "Global Impact of COVID-19 on Stroke Care," *International Journal of Stroke* 16, no. 5 (July 2021): 573–84, https://www.ncbi.nlm.nih.gov/pmc/articles/PMC8010375/.

82 Olivier Aubert et al., "COVID-19 Pandemic and Worldwide Organ Transplantation: A Population-Based Study," *Lancet Public Health* 6, no. 10 (October 2021): 709–19, https://www.thelancet.com/journals/lanpub/article/PIIS2468-2667(21)00200-0/fulltext.

83 "Weniger Vorsorge: AOK Warnt vor Krebs-Zunahme," *ZDF Heute*, February 2, 2023, https://www.zdf.de/nachrichten/panorama/aok-krebserkrankungen-corona-100.html.
84 "Mehrheit der Bevölkerung Gegen Ende der Corona-Massnahmen," *Süddeutsche Zeitung,* December 29, 2022, https://www.sueddeutsche.de/panorama/jahreswechsel-mehrheit-der-bevoelkerung-gegen-ende-der-corona-massnahmen-dpa.urn-newsml-dpa-com-20090101-221229-99-40412.
85 Helmut Traindl, "Zusammenfassendes Gutachten zur Unwirksamkeit von Masken als Virenschutz und Gesundheitsschädigende Auswirkungen," *Fortschrittinfreiheit* (website), December 9, 2022, https://fortschrittinfreiheit.de/gutachten-unwirksamkeit-von-masken/.
86 "Cochrane Review zum Nutzen von Masken Gegen Atemwegsinfektionen," Cochrane Deutschland, February 2, 2023, https://www.cochrane.de/news/cochrane-review-zum-nutzen-von-masken-gegen-atemwegsinfektionen.
87 World Economic Forum, *The Global Risks Report 2023*, 18th ed. (Geneva: World Economic Forum, January 2023), 35, https://www3.weforum.org/docs/WEF_Global_Risks_Report_2023.pdf.
88 Theresa Hitchens, "A Musk Monopoly? For Now, Ukraine Has Few Options outside Starlink for Battlefield Satcoms," *Breaking Defense* (website), October 19, 2022, https://breakingdefense.com/2022/10/a-musk-monopoly-for-now-ukraine-has-few-options-outside-starlink-for-battlefield-satcoms/.
89 Jesse Hirsh, "COVID-19 as a Case for Social Scoring Systems," Centre for International Governance Innovation, September 15, 2020, https://www.cigionline.org/articles/covid-19-case-social-scoring-systems/
90 Anna Hornik et al., *Zukunft von Wertvorstellungen der Menschen in Unserem Land* (Berlin: Prognos AG, August 2020), https://www.vorausschau.de/SharedDocs/Downloads/vorausschau/de/BMBF_Foresight_Wertestudie_Kurzfassung.pdf?__blob=publicationFile&v=3 (August 2020,, last accessed on 05.21.2023), p. 34

CHAPTER 6

1 Stephen McDermott, "Debunked: A Quote by Yuval Noah Harari That Technology Will 'Replace People' Is Missing Context," *The Journal,* September 2, 2022, https://www.thejournal.ie/factcheck-yuval-noah-harari-quote-we-dont-need-vast-majority-population-debunked-5849188-Sep2022/.
2 Yuval Noah Harari, "The Rise of the Useless Class," *Ideas.TED.com*, February 24, 2017, https://ideas.ted.com/the-rise-of-the-useless-class/.
3 "What Do We Need So Many Humans For—Yuval Noah, Advisor to Klaus Schwab," Bit Chute, video, 1:13, https://www.bitchute.com/video/fQqONRrwkXiM/.
4 Aldous Huxley, preface to *Brave New World*, 2nd ed. (1947), http://www.wealthandwant.com/auth/Huxley.html.
5 "Elon Musk and Others Call for Pause on AI, Citing 'Profound Risks to Society,'" *New York Times,* March 29, 2023, https://www.nytimes.com/2023/03/29/technology/ai-artificial-intelligence-musk-risks.html.

6 Harari, “Rise of the Useless Class.”
7 Marcus du Sautoy, *Creativity Code: Art and Innovation in the Age of AI* (Cambridge, MA: Belknap Press, 2020), 13.
8 Eva Wolfangel, “Das Richtige Gefühl,” *Spektrum*, May 23, 2018, https://www.spektrum.de/news/emotionen-perfektionieren-kuenstliche-intelligenz/1566366; Patrick Krauss and Andreas Maier, “Der Geist in der Maschine,” *Spektrum*, June 16, 2021, https://www.spektrum.de/magazin/bewusste-ki-der-geist-in-der-maschine/1875787.
9 Stephen Hawking et al., “Stephen Hawking: ‘Transcendence Looks at the Implications of Artificial Intelligence—But Are We Taking AI Seriously Enough?,’” *Independent*, May 1, 2014, https://www.independent.co.uk/news/science/stephen-hawking-transcendence-looks-implications-artificial-intelligence-are-we-taking-ai-seriously-enough-9313474.html.
10 Bill Gates, “Innovating to Zero!,” TED video, 27:33, https://www.ted.com/talks/bill_gates_innovating_to_zero/transcript. Referenced quote is at about the 3:42 mark.
11 Magdalena Robert, “Global Health Leaders Launch Decade of Vaccines Collaboration,” Bill & Melinda Gates Foundation, news release, accessed May 15, 2023, https://www.gatesfoundation.org/ideas/media-center/press-releases/2010/12/global-health-leaders-launch-decade-of-vaccines-collaboration.
12 World Health Organization, *Fertility Regulating Vaccines* (Geneva: World Health Organization, August 17–18, 1992), https://apps.who.int/iris/bitstream/handle/10665/61301/WHO_HRP_WHO_93.1.pdf.
13 John Oller et al., “HCG Found in WHO Tetanus Vaccine in Kenya Raises Concern in the Developing World,” *Open Access Library Journal* 4, no. 10 (October 2017): 1–30, https://www.researchgate.net/publication/320641479_HCG_Found_in_WHO_Tetanus_Vaccine_in_Kenya_Raises_Concern_in_the_Developing_World.
14 “Tetanus Vaccine May Be Laced with Anti-Fertility Drug. International/Developing Countries,” *Vaccine Weekly* (May 29–June 5, 1995): 9–10, https://pubmed.ncbi.nlm.nih.gov/12346214/.
15 James A. Miller, “Baby-Killing Vaccine: Is It Being Stealth Tested?,” EWTN Global Catholic Network, accessed April 15, 2023, https://www.ewtn.com/catholicism/library/babykilling-vaccine-is-it-being-stealth-tested-11055.
16 Robert Sinden and Julian Crampton, US Patent20020124274A1, filed November 11, 1994, abandoned, https://patents.google.com/patent/US20020124274A1/en.
17 D. S. Yamamoto, H. Nagumo, and S. Yoshida, “Flying Vaccinator; a Transgenic Mosquito Delivers a Leishmania Vaccine Via Blood Feeding,” *Insect Molecular Biology* 19, no. 3 (June 2010): 391–98, https://doi.org/10.1111/j.1365-2583.2010.01000.x.
18 Martin Enserink, “Researchers Turn Mosquitoes into Flying Vaccinators,” *Science*, March 18, 2010, https://www.science.org/content/article/researchers-turn-mosquitoes-flying-vaccinators.
19 Damian Carrington, “Want to Fight Climate Change? Have Fewer Children,” *The Guardian*, July 12, 2017, https://www.theguardian.com/environment/2017/jul/12/want-to-fight-climate-change-have-fewer-children.

20 Seth Wynes and Kimberly A. Nicholas, "The Climate Mitigation Gap: Education and Government Recommendations Miss the Most Effective Individual Actions," *Environmental Research Letters* 12 (2017): https://iopscience.iop.org/article/10.1088/1748-9326/aa7541/pdf.

21 Norbert Schäfer, "No Babies for the Climate," Christian Network Europe, July 30, 2022, https://cne.news/article/1510-no-babies-for-the-climate.

22 "Mitverantwortung," *Ärzte Zeitung*, October, 18, 2022, https://www.aerztezeitung.de/Wirtschaft/Mitverantwortung-433378.html.

23 "Künstliche Intelligenz Überholt Menschen bis 2030," Computerwoche Tec Workshop, accessed May 22, 2023, https://www.tecchannel.de/a/kuenstliche-intelligenz-ueberholt-menschen-bis-2030,1747252.

CHAPTER 7

1 Pierre Azoulay, Christian Fons-Rosen, and Joshua S. Graff Ziven, "Does Science Advance One Funeral at a Time?," *American Economic Review* 109, no. 8 (2019): 2889–920, https://pubs.aeaweb.org/doi/pdfplus/10.1257/aer.20161574.

2 Enzyklo.de, s.v. "Lastenausgleichsgesetz Bedeutung," https://www.enzyklo.de/Begriff/Lastenausgleichsgesetz.

3 "Gesetz zur Regelung des Sozialen Entschädungsrechts," *Bundesgesetzblatt*, December 12, 2019, https://www.bgbl.de/xaver/bgbl/start.xav#__bgbl__%2F%2F*[%40attr_id%3D'bgbl119s2652.pdf']__1641283293927.

4 Karl Lauterbach, "Lauterbach Verspricht Hilfe nach Impfschäden," interview by Christian Sievers, *ZDF* (website), transcript and audio, 7:00, https://www.zdf.de/nachrichten/politik/corona-hilfe-impfschaeden-long-covid-lauterbach-100.html.

5 Max Müller, "Corona-Impfschäden 'Totgeschwiegen': Was Sagt das Gesundheitsministerium zu Brisantem Arzt-Interview?," *TZ* (website), April 24, 2023, https://www.tz.de/politik/corona-impfschaeden-impfen-gesundheitsministerium-karl-lauterbach-long-covid-biontech-zr-92231329.html.

6 "Jean-Claude Juncker's Most Outrageous Political Quotations," *The Telegraph*, July 15, 2014, https://www.telegraph.co.uk/news/worldnews/europe/eu/10967168/Jean-Claude-Junckers-most-outrageous-political-quotations.html.

7 Naomi Wolf, *The Bodies of Others: The New Authoritarians, COVID-19 and The War against the Human* (Fort Lauderdale, FL: All Seasons Press, 2022), 4.

8 "Ford: Symbol Analysis," LitCharts, review of *Brave New World* by Aldous Huxley, n.d., https://www.litcharts.com/lit/brave-new-world/symbols/ford.

9 Bill Gates, "Bill Gates's Vision for Life beyond the Coronavirus," interview by Ezra Klein, *Vox*, April 27, 2020, https://www.vox.com/coronavirus-covid19/2020/4/27/21236270/bill-gates-coronavirus-covid-19-plan-vaccines-conspiracies-podcast.

10 "Superreiche Sorgen für die Zerstörung Tropischer Waldgebiete," *Der Standard*, February 26, 2020, https://www.derstandard.de/story/2000115038226/superreiche-sorgen-zunehmend-fuer-die-zerstoerung-von-tropischen-waldgebieten.

11 M. Graziano Ceddia, "The Super-Rich and Cropland Expansion via Direct Investments in Agriculture," *Nature Sustainability* 3 (2020): 312–18, https://doi.org/10.1038/s41893-020-0480-2.

12 Evelyn Bahn, "Biosprit Macht Hunger," *INKOTA* (website), July 21, 2021, https://www.inkota.de/news/biosprit-macht-hunger.

13 Marc Keuschnigg, Arnouit van de Rijt, and Thijs Bol, "The Plateauing of Cognitive Ability among Top Earners," *European Sociological Review* (2023): https://doi.org/10.1093/esr/jcac076.

14 Martin Farrer, "Historian Berates Billionaires at Davos over Tax Avoidance," *The Guardian*, January 30, 2019, https://www.theguardian.com/business/2019/jan/30/historian-berates-billionaires-at-davos-over-tax-avoidance.

15 Rutger Bregman, *Humankind: A Hopeful History* (London: Bloomsbury Publishing 2021). First published 2019 by De Correspondent BV (Amsterdam), 228.

16 Jeremy Hogeveen, Michael Inzlicht, and Sukhvinder S. Obhi, "Power Changes How the Brain Responds to Others," *Journal of Experimental Psychology: General* 143, no. 2 (2014): 755–62, https://www.oveo.org/fichiers/power-changes-how-the-brain-responds-to-others.pdf.

17 Jerry Useem, "Power Causes Brain Damage," *The Atlantic*, July-August 2017, https://www.theatlantic.com/magazine/archive/2017/07/power-causes-brain-damage/528711/.

18 Ibid.

19 Bregman, *Humankind*, 229.

20 M. Ena Inesi, Deborah H. Gruenfeld, and Adam D. Galinsky, "How Power Corrupts Relationships: Cynical Attributions for Others' Generous Acts," *Journal of Experimental Social Psychology* 48, no. 4 (July 2012): 795–803, https://www.sciencedirect.com/science/article/abs/pii/S002210311200011X.

21 Bregman, *Humankind*, 229.

22 Rutger Bregman, *De Meeste Mensen Deugen: Een Nieuwe Geschiedenis van de Mens* (Amsterdam: De Correspondent BV, 2019).

23 Sprouts Deutschland, "Bonhoeffer's Theorie der Dummheit," January 23, 2022, YouTube video, 6:32, https://www.youtube.com/watch?v=wnhL1W9dj1w.

24 Michael Schmidt-Salomon, *Hoffnung Mensch: Eine Bessere Welt Ist Möglich* (Munich: Piper Verlag, 2015).

25 Charles Q. Choi, "Being More Infantile May Have Led to Bigger Brains," *Scientific American*, July 1, 2009, https://www.scientificamerican.com/article/being-more-infantile/.

26 Bregman, *Humankind*, 63.

27 Lee Alan Dugatkin and Lyudmila Trut, "How to Tame a Fox and Build a Dog," *American Scientist* 105, no. 4 (July-August 2017): 240, https://www.americanscientist.org/article/how-to-tame-a-fox-and-build-a-dog.

28 Bregman, *Humankind*, 65.

29 Ibid., 70.

30 Ibid., 65.

31 Ibid., 2.

32 Zhihao Yuan, Rajat Nag, and Enda Cummins, "Human Health Concerns Regarding Microplastics in the Aquatic Environment—From Marine to Food Systems," *Science of the Total Environment* 823 (June 1, 2022): https://pubmed.ncbi.nlm.nih.gov/35143789/.

33 Stefania D'Angelo and Rosaria Meccariello, "Microplastics: A Threat for Male Fertility," *International Journal of Environmental Research and Public Health* 18, no. 5 (March 2021): https://www.ncbi.nlm.nih.gov/pmc/articles/PMC7967748/; Chenming Zhang et al. "Microplastics May Be a Significant Cause of Male Infertility," *American Journal of Men's Health* 16, no. 3 (May-June 2022): https://www.ncbi.nlm.nih.gov/pmc/articles/PMC9134445/.

34 "The Great Pacific Garbage Patch," *The Ocean Cleanup* (website), n.d., https://theoceancleanup.com/great-pacific-garbage-patch/; L. Lebreton et al., "Evidence That the Great Pacific Garbage Patch Is Rapidly Accumulating Plastic," *Scientific Reports* 8 (2018): https://www.ncbi.nlm.nih.gov/pmc/articles/PMC5864935/.

35 Edward O. Wilson, *The Social Conquest of Earth* (New York: Liveright Publishing, 2012).

36 Michael Schmidt-Salomon, *Jenseits von Gut und Böse: Warum Wir Ohne Moral die Besseren Menschen Sind* (Munich: Pendo Verlag, 2009), 66–67.

37 Paul Bloom, *Against Empathy: The Case for Rational Compassion* (New York: Vintage Books, 2018), back-cover text.

38 Paul Bloom, "The Case against Empathy," interview by Sean Illing, *Vox*, last modified January 16, 2019, https://www.vox.com/conversations/2017/1/19/14266230/empathy-morality-ethics-psychology-compassion-paul-bloom.

39 Miho Nagasawa et al., "Oxytocin-Gaze Positive Loop and the Coevolution of Human-Dog Bonds," *Science* 348 (2015): 333–36, https://www.science.org/doi/10.1126/science.1261022.

40 Tara Raam et al., "Hippocampal Oxytocin Receptors Are Necessary for Discrimination of Social Stimuli," *Nature Communications* 8 (2017): https://doi.org/10.1038/s41467-017-02173-0.

41 Carsten K. W. De Dreu, "Oxytocin Modulates Cooperation within and Competition Between Groups: An Integrative Review and Research Agenda," *Hormones and Behavior* 61, no. 3 (March 2012): 419–28, https://pubmed.ncbi.nlm.nih.gov/22227278/.

42 Bloom, "Case against Empathy."

43 Schmidt-Salomon, *Jenseits von Gut und Böse*, 37 (translated by the author).

44 Ibid., 75 (translated by the author).

45 Bloom, "Case against Empathy."

46 Rasmus Hougaard and Jacqueline Carter, *Compassionate Leadership: How to Do Hard Things in a Human Way* (Boston: Harvard Business Review Press, 2022).

47 Rasmus Hougaard, "Four Reasons Why Compassion Is Better for Humanity than Empathy," *Forbes,* July 8, 2020, https://www.forbes.com/sites

/rasmushougaard/2020/07/08/four-reasons-why-compassion-is-better-for-humanity-than-empathy/.

48 Bregman, *Humankind*, 219.

49 Cisca Ulug, Lummina Horlings, and Elen-Maarja Trell, "Collective Identity Supporting Sustainability Transformations in Ecovillage Communities," *Sustainability* 13, no. 15 (2021): https://doi.org/10.3390/su13158148.

50 "Ecovillages as an Ecological Alternative," *Iberdrola* (website), accessed May 4, 2023, https://www.iberdrola.com/sustainability/ecovillages-alternative-ecological-communities.

51 Bregman, *Humankind*, 299–319.

52 Ibid., 315.

53 Ibid., 316.

54 Tine De Moor, "The Silent Revolution: A New Perspective on the Emergence of Commons, Guilds, and Other Forms of Corporate Collective Action in Western Europe," Supplement, *International Review of Social History* 53, no. S16 (2008): S179–212, https://doi.org/10.1017/s0020859008003660.

55 "The Sveriges Riksbank Prize in Economic Sciences in Memory of Alfred Nobel 2009," The Nobel Prize, https://www.nobelprize.org/prizes/economic-sciences/2009/summary/.

56 Elinor Ostrom, "Beyond Markets and States: Polycentric Governance of Complex Economic Systems," December 8, 2009, https://www.nobelprize.org/uploads/2018/06/ostrom_lecture.pdf.

57 Tine De Moor, "*Homo Cooperans. Institutions for Collective Action and the Compassionate Society.* (Utrecht, Netherlands: Utrecht University, 2013), https://www.researchgate.net/publication/336220852.

58 Karrie Jacobs, "Toronto Wants to Kill the Smart City Forever," *MIT Technology Review,* June 29, 2022, https://www.technologyreview.com/2022/06/29/1054005/toronto-kill-the-smart-city.

59 James Suzman, *Work: A History of How We Spend Our Time* (London: Bloomsbury Publishing, 2021).

60 Michael Nehls, *Die Algenöl-Revolution: Lebenswichtiges Omega-3—das Pflanzliche Lebenselixier aus dem Meer* (Munich: Heyne Verlag, 2022).

61 Ajit Niranjan, "Insects on the Menu as EU Approves Two for Human Comsumption," *Deutsche Welle*, January 24, 2023, https://www.dw.com/en/eu-insects-climate-change/a-64503440.

62 Fox News, "Activist Warns Global Push to Add Bugs to the Menu Is Part of Alarming Trend," *New York Post,* April 15, 2023, https://nypost.com/2023/04/15/activist-warns-of-global-push-adding-bugs-to-the-menu/.

63 Paolo Tessari, Anna Lante, and Giuliano Mosca, "Essential Amino Acids: Master Regulators of Nutrition and Environmental Footprint?," *Science Reports* 6 (2016): https://www.ncbi.nlm.nih.gov/pmc/articles/PMC4897092.

64 William Moomaw, Isaac Berzin, and Asaf Tzachor, "Cutting Out the Middle Fish: Marine Microalgae as the Next Sustainable Omega-3 Fatty Acids and Protein Source," *Industrial Biotechnology* 13, no. 5 (October 2017): 234–43, https://www.researchgate.net/publication/320439837.

65 Gowri Koneswaran and Danielle Nierenberg, "Global Farm Animal Production and Global Warming: Impacting and Mitigating Climate Change," *Environmental Health Perspectives* 116, no. 5 (May 2008): 578–82, https://www.ncbi.nlm.nih.gov/pmc/articles/PMC2367646/.

66 John P. A. Ioannidis, "Why Most Published Research Findings Are False," *PLoS Medicine* 2, no. 8 (August 2005): https://www.ncbi.nlm.nih.gov/pmc/articles/PMC1182327/.

67 M. Meyen, "Stell Dir vor, es Kommen Nachrichten und Keiner Schaut Hin," *ViER*, June 6, 2022, S. 66.

68 "Zunehmende News-Deprivation Hat Negative Folgen für die Demokratie," Universität Zürich, October 24, 2022, https://www.news.uzh.ch/de/articles/media/2022/Jahrbuch_foeg.html.

69 Michael Meyen, *Die Propaganda-Matrix: Der Kampf für Freie Medien Entscheidet über unsere Zukunft* (Munich: Rubikon, 2021), back cover.

70 Bregman, *Humankind*, 393–94.

71 Charlotte Huff, "Media Overload Is Hurting Our Mental Health. Here Are Ways to Manage Headline Stress," *Monitor on Psychology* 53, no. 8 (November 1, 2022): https://www.apa.org/monitor/2022/11/strain-media-overload.

72 "Übersicht zum Impfstatus," Impfdashboard.de, April 8, 2023, https://impfdashboard.de/.

73 Bregman, *Humankind*, 393–94.

74 Schmidt-Salomon, *Hoffnung Mensch*, cover text (translated by the author).

75 M. B. Rosenberg, *Gewaltfreie Kommunikation: Eine Sprache des Lebens* (Paderborn, Germany: Junfermann, 2010), 40 (translated by the author).

ACKNOWLEDGMENTS

I would like to thank all the doctors and scientists who, despite the threat of reprisals, have dared to continue asking questions and publishing their professional assessments and uncensored research results. In doing so, they provided concrete evidence of how and to what end the orchestrated actions of the Great Reset's creators and profiteers are specifically damaging the human brain. Without them, this book could never have been written. The same goes for the few remaining investigative journalists who earn the attributes of courage, determination, and drive every day. In this new age of global censorship, they are the last rays of hope for a chance at open discourse.

In particular, I would like to thank some special people. I would like to thank Bettina Simonis, a graduate biologist, and my son Sebastian, both of whom have given me many hints, comments, and suggestions, as they did with my previous books on this subject. I would also like to thank Holger Brueck, an IT consultant, who gave me the crucial idea that led to this book during one of our many conversations. My special thanks go to the literary advisor of the original German edition, Corvin P. Rabenstein, for his support and expert editing of my English translation as well. My thanks are also due to the graphic designer Malin Singh, whose creative design suggestions more than shaped the look of the book, both in the German and in the English version. Of course, I would also like to thank all the many unnamed supporters who have encouraged me along the way.

I would also like to thank Tony Lyons of Skyhorse Publishing for having the courage to publish outside the narrow confines of the increasingly censored mainstream press. Thanks also to Joseph Webb for his expert polishing of my translation, and to Hector Carosso for his copyediting throughout the publishing process. A special word of thanks goes to Naomi Wolf. Her meticulous study of the Pfizer contracts, as well as her unparalleled documentation of the role of fear in the deterioration of our formerly free societies, made her the ideal person to write the foreword to this book. It is a truly unique work that will undoubtedly appeal to many readers.

Last but not least, I would like to thank my wife, Sabine: Not only did she take the time to critically review each and every version of the book, but she also did not let fear of reprisal stop her from walking this path with me.